Wordsmith

A Guide to Paragraphs and Short Essays

Wordsmith

A Guide to Paragraphs and Short Essays

Second Edition

Pamela Arlov
Macon State College

PEARSON
Prentice
Hall

Upper Saddle River, New Jersey 07458

Library of Congress Cataloging-in-Publication Data

Arlov, Pamela.
 Wordsmith : a guide to paragraphs and short essays / Pamela Arlov.—2nd ed.
  p. cm.
Includes index.
 ISBN 0-13-048895-X
 1. English language—Paragraphs. 2. English language—Rhetoric. 3.
Report writing. I. Title.
 PE1439.A74 2004
 808'.042—dc21

                                                            2003011542

Senior Acquisitions Editor: Craig Campanella
Editor-in-Chief: Leah Jewell
Editorial Assistant: Joan Polk
Senior Marketing Manager: Rachel Falk
Director of Marketing: Beth Gillette Mejia
Production Liaison: Fran Russello
Prepress and Manufacturing Buyer: Brian Mackey
Cover Designer: Bruce Kenselaar
Cover Photo: © Getty Images
Composition/Full-Service Project Management: Pine Tree Composition, Inc./
 Karen Berry
Printer/Binder: RR Donnelley & Sons
Cover Printer: Phoenix Color Corp.

Credits and acknowledgments borrowed from other sources and reproduced,
with permission, in this textbook appear on pages 545–546.

Pearson Education LTD., London
Pearson Education Singapore, Pte. Ltd
Pearson Education Canada, Ltd
Pearson Education-Japan
Pearson Education Australia PTY,
 Limited

Pearson Education North Asia Ltd.
Pearson Educación de Mexico, S.A.
 de C.V.
Pearson Education Malaysia, Pte. Ltd
Pearson Education, Upper Saddle
 River, New Jersey

10 9 8 7 6 5 4 3 2 1
ISBN: 0-13-048895-X
AIE ISBN: 0-13-049250-7

In loving memory of my mother, Virginia S. Roberts

Contents

Chapter 10   Writing an Essay   157

Chapter 11   Writing Summary Reports   179

Part 2 Grammar   199

Part 3 Readings   437

List of Readings by Rhetorical Mode

Description

Narration

Example

Definition

Classification

Process

Comparison-Contrast

Cause-Effect

Argument

List of Readings by Subject

Self-Examination

Inspiration and Celebration

Society and Civilization

Language and Education

Preface
Updates to the Second Edition

For the convenience of instructors, the new Instructor's Edition provides answers to exercises as an integral part of the text. The back pages of the Instructor's Edition contain icebreaker activities, suggestions on using the chapters and readings, an examination of grading issues, and model syllabi for ten-week and fifteen-week courses.

Updates to Part 1 Composition

- **The section on writing paragraphs has been expanded.** The number of exercises has doubled, and there are now three chapters on paragraph writing instead of one. Separate chapters on writing a topic sentence, supporting the essay, and providing unity and coherence allow students to focus separately on each aspect of the paragraph.

- **A chapter on writing a summary report has been added to help students make the transition from personal writing to academic writing.** The chapter includes a discussion of the differences between academic and personal writing, a section on paraphrasing and summarizing, and a model summary report.

- **The chapter "Revising and Proofreading" is now titled "Revising, Proofreading, and Formatting."** It discusses various methods of formatting a paper and provides general instructions on formatting handwritten and word-processed documents.

- **A new Progressive Writing Assignment allows students to choose a topic and develop it as they move from prewriting in Chapter 2 to revised draft in Chapter 6.** Each chapter's assignment guides students through one step of the paragraph. In Chapter 2, students focus on prewriting. In Chapter 3, students complete a topic sentence and outline, and in Chapter 4, they provide support for the topic sentence. The Chapter 5 Progressive Writing Assignment guides students through the process of checking for unity and coherence, and in Chapter 6, students revise and proofread. By the time they finish the chapters they have a completed the entire paragraph, step by step.

   I have used some form of the Progressive Writing Assignment in my own classes for years. Here are some of the advantages I have found in using a Progressive Writing Assignment:

  - It guides students through each step of the writing process and each part of the paragraph.

  - It promotes understanding of how each part of the paragraph relates to the other parts.

  - It provides the opportunity for instructor or peer feedback at each stage, resulting in a strong, carefully written composition.

  - It emphasizes process and careful crafting.

  - It allows instructors, if they wish, to assign some form of credit to each portion of the assignment, thus placing emphasis on the process as well as the product.

- **Boxes in the methods of development chapters (Chapters 7, 8, and 9) specifically point out connections among the methods of development.** In addition, these chapters now end with assignments headed "Mixed Methods." These assignments deliberately direct students to mix the methods in the chapters. For example, an assignment in Chapter 7, "Showing and Telling: Description, Narration, and Example," asks students to use techniques of narration and example in a single paragraph.

Updates to Part 2   Grammar

- Practices in the grammar chapters now have titles to remind students exactly which principles are being discussed and practiced.

- Minor changes have been made throughout the text. For example, a chart summarizing five methods for correcting run-on sentences has been added to Chapter 16, "Run-on Sentences."

- Eight Editing Exercises have been added at the end of the Part 2, Grammar.

Updates to Part 3   Readings

- Three carefully chosen readings have been added and three old ones removed. The additions include Cara DiMarco's "Setting Boundaries," which discusses the process of setting personal boundaries and models the techniques of process and example. Shoba Narayan's essay, "I Wonder—Was It Me or Was It My Sari?" is a delightful narrative that shows how the author's decision to wear the clothing of her native India for a month affected people's perception of her. Finally, in the haunting narrative "What If My Friends Hadn't Run?" Bill Pippin re-examines a long-ago impulse to pick up a gun in anger.

Preface
To the Instructor

Thank you for choosing *Wordsmith: A Guide to Paragraphs and Short Essays, Second Edition,* as your textbook.

Like you, I am a teacher of writing. Like you, I struggle to find the best way to teach a subject that, on its surface, seems as simple as touching pen to paper. Yet writing is remarkably complex, incorporating the personality and experience of each writer and each reader. It requires adherence to agreed-upon rules of grammar, punctuation, and form. It is, in fact, a craft that might be best taught to a small group of students in a series of unhurried sessions and individual conferences over an extended period of time. But our reality is the fifty-minute hour, the class of twenty or more, the term that is measured in weeks. How best to handle that reality?

Most of us constantly refine our teaching methods, striving to make difficult concepts clear and tedious details interesting. Most of all, we try to ignite the spark that will help our students see writing as a meaningful, life-enriching activity. A good textbook should reinforce our efforts. I have spent considerable time trying to analyze what a good textbook should do, above and beyond presenting information in a given field. Here is what I have come up with: The book should be orderly and user-friendly, with a flexible format. Explanations should be clear and supported by numerous exercises and examples. The book should contain much more than is strictly necessary: it should be a smorgasbord, not just a meal. Finally, if it includes a little bit of fun, so much the better—for us and for our students. I have written *Wordsmith* with those principles in mind.

Features of *Wordsmith: A Guide to Paragraphs and Short Essays*

- A three-part layout allows the freedom to mix and match writing chapters, grammar chapters, and readings.
- A structured yet flexible approach to writing encourages clarity and creativity.
- A direct, conversational, student-friendly approach is used throughout.
- Lighthearted chapter openings promote a positive and playful approach to learning.

Although each of you will use the book in a different way and adapt it to your own students' needs, the following overview of each section may give you some ideas. For more ideas and for sample ten- and fifteen-week syllabi, check the Instructor's Guide in the back of the book.

Part 1   Composition

Part 1, Composition, takes the paragraph as its primary focus but provides an extensive chapter (Chapter 10) on the five-paragraph essay and a chapter (Chapter 11) on the summary report. Include or omit these chapters, as you prefer. The book begins with an overview of the writing process (Chapter 1), followed by a chapter on prewriting (Chapter 2). Planning and drafting, the next two steps in the writing process, are addressed in Chapters 3, 4, and 5. Chapter 6 addresses revising and proofreading.

Chapters 7, 8, and 9 address methods of development. I have sacrificed some flexibility by grouping the methods, so let me explain why. The first reason is philosophical. I believe it is more realistic to group the modes, since they are seldom used in isolation in "real-world" writing. Modes with a similar purpose are grouped together, and the optional "Mixed Methods" assignments at the end of the chapter show how the modes can be used together in a single piece of writing. The second reason for grouping modes is more practical. No matter how hard I try, I can never cover nine rhetorical modes in one term. Grouping them allows me to assign a chapter containing three modes and address only one or two in depth. If all three rhetorical modes chapters are assigned, students are exposed to all nine modes even if they practice only a few.

Special Features of Part 1   Composition

- A student paragraph is presented in all drafts and stages along with a transcript of a student writing group's discussion of the work in progress. (Chapter 1)
- A section "For Right-Brained Writers" gives tips for students who tend to think in terms of "the whole" rather than in terms of a step-by-step process. (Chapter 1)
- The five steps in the writing process are presented in the order in which most writers address them: prewriting, planning, drafting, revising, and proofreading. (Chapters 1–6)
- Methods of development are grouped into three chapters to highlight their relationship to one another and to allow students to read about all methods even if they use only a few. (Chapters 7, 8, and 9)
- Two paragraphs provide models for each method of development. (Chapters 7, 8, and 9)
- Throughout Part 1, topics for paragraph, essay, and journal writing provide a basis for assignments and encourage further practice.
- Students are introduced to academic writing in Chapter 11, "Writing a Summary Report."

Part 2   Grammar

Part 2, Grammar, can be used in a variety of ways: with direct, in-class instruction, in a lab setting, as a supplement, or for independent study. Part 2, Grammar, also works well for instructors who want to address more difficult grammar topics in class while assigning easier material or review material for independent study.

In the grammar chapters, explanations are clear and each topic is taken one skill at a time, with numerous practice exercises for each skill. At the end of each chapter are review exercises in increasing order of difficulty, ending with a paragraph-length editing exercise.

Special Features of Part 2   Grammar

- Explanations are clear, logical, and user-friendly.
- Step-by-step, easy-to-understand presentation is suitable for classroom discussion or independent study.

- An abundance of practice exercises allows instructors to assign as much or as little as they wish, without the need for supplemental exercises.
- Text boxes—Real-World Writing, Building Connections, Grammar Alert, and Punctuation Pointers—add liveliness and interest.
- Practice exercises allow immediate review of each skill, while review exercises at the end of each chapter allow practice on increasing levels of difficulty.

Part 3   Readings

Part 3, Readings, offers essays by professional writers. In any craft, the works of accomplished artisans can inspire the apprentice. These essays model writing at its best: entertaining, challenging, and thought-provoking. Each reading is followed by a comprehension exercise that includes questions about content, questions about the writer's techniques, and related topics for discussion and writing. Diversity in authorship, subject matter, and rhetorical method is emphasized.

Special Features of Part 3   Readings

- High-interest readings provide professional models, reinforce reading skills, and serve as springboards for discussion and assignments.
- Questions help students understand both the content of the essays and the writer's techniques.
- Suggested topics for journal, paragraph, and essay writing connect students' writing to ideas they have explored in the readings.

Supplements

Instructor's Edition. For the first time *Wordsmith* has an Instructor's Edition. The IE contains in-text answers to help instructors best prepare for class and a 26-page built-in instructor's guide bound directly into the back. Written by Pam Arlov, the Instructor's Guide provides sample syllabi, teaching tips, and additional chapter-specific assignments. Free to adoptors. ISBN: 0-13-049250-7.

Instructor's Resource Manual. The Instructor's Resource Manual contains additional sample syllabi and two chapter tests for each of the 27 chapters in the text. For each chapter there is one short answer and one multiple-choice test for instructors to choose from. There is also a grammar pretest and posttest. All are ready for easy duplication. Free to adoptors. ISBN: 0-13-049261-2.

Companion Website™ (www.prenhall.com/arlov). Free to students, the companion website for *Wordsmith: A Guide to Paragraphs and Short Essays 2E* provides chapter learning objectives that help students organize key concepts, online quizzes, which include instant scoring and coaching, dynamic web links that provide a valuable source of supplemental information, and built-in routing that gives students the ability to forward essay responses and graded quizzes to their instructors.

PH WORDS. An internet-based, course management program, PH WORDS gives English instructors the ability to measure and track students' mastery of the elements of writing from the writing process, to patterns of development, to grammar. Covering over 100 topics, PH WORDS allows students to work on their specific areas of weakness, freeing up class time for instructors. Sold at a discount when packaged with *Wordsmith: A Guide to Paragraphs and Short Essays 2E*. Visit www.prenhall.com/phwords for more information. Package ISBN: 0-13-104622-5.

The Prentice Hall Writing Skills Test Bank. Written as a source of extra tests for instructors, this printed test bank includes over 50 additional quizzes for instructors to give students. Covering the writing process, patterns of development and grammar, the Prentice Hall Writing Skills Test Bank offers two quizzes for each skill—one multiple choice and one short answer. It can be used with any Prentice Hall writing text. Free to adoptors. ISBN: 0-13-111628-2.

The New American Webster Handy College Dictionary. Available free to students when packaged with *Wordsmith*, this dictionary has over 1.5 million Signet copies in print and over 115,000 definitions, including current phrases, slang, and scientific terms. It offers more than 1,500 new words, with over 200 not found in any other competing dictionary and features boxed inserts on etymologies and language. Package ISBN: 0-13-104567-9.

The Prentice Hall ESL Workbook. Available free to students when packaged with *Wordsmith*, this 138-page workbook is divided into seven major units, providing explanations and exercises in the most challenging grammar topics for non-native speakers. With over 80 exercise sets, this guide provides ample instruction and practice in nouns, articles, verbs, modifiers, pronouns, prepositions, and sentence structure. ISBN: 0-13-092323-0.

The Prentice Hall Grammar Workbook. Available free when packaged with *Wordsmith*, this 21-chapter workbook is a comprehensive source of instruction and practice for students who need additional grammar, punctuation, and mechanics instruction. Each chapter provides ample explanation, examples, and exercise sets. ISBN: 0-13-092321-4.

The Prentice Hall TASP Writing Study Guide. Available free to students when packaged with *Wordsmith*, this guide prepares students for the writing portion of the Texas Academic Skills Program test. In addition, it familiarizes the reader with the elements of the test and provides strategies for success. There are exercises for each part of the exam, and then a full-length practice test with answer key so students can gauge their own progress. ISBN: 0-13-041585-5.

The Prentice Hall Florida Exit Test Study Guide for Writing. Free when packaged with *Wordsmith*, this guide is designed to prepare students for the writing section of the Florida Exit test. It also acquaints readers with the parts of the test and provides strategies for success. ISBN: 0-13-111652-5.

Research Navigator™. Research Navigator™ is the one-stop research solution—complete with extensive help on the research process and three exclusive databases including EBSCO's ContentSelect Academic Journal Database, The New York Times Search by Subject Archive, and Best of the Web Link Library. Take a tour on the web at http://www.researchnavigator. com. Your students get FREE ACCESS to Research Navigator™ when you package Along These Lines with our exclusive Evaluating Online Resources: English 2003 guide. Contact your local Prentice Hall sales representative for ordering details.

To order any of these supplements, please contact your local Prentice Hall sales representative, or contact customer service at 1-800-526-0485.

Acknowledgments

I could not have written this book without the help, support, and collaboration of a great many people. First, I would like to thank the people who worked directly with me on the book: Craig Campanella, Senior Editor, English, who has vision and a knack for seeing the big picture; Joan Polk, Editorial Assistant, who is knowledgeable, helpful, and truly a class act;

Christy D. Schaack, Media Editor, who worked tirelessly on the *Wordsmith* Web sites; and Rachel Falk, Senior Marketing Manager, who always has just the right words. I also thank the incomparable Karen Berry of Pine Tree Composition, Project Coordinator; Jeanne Tibbetts of Pine Tree Composition, Pager; Elizabeth Morgan, Development Editor; Michael Farmer, Permissions Specialist, and Erica Orloff, Copyeditor.

Also, I thank the reviewer, whose candid, generous, and detailed comments helped to shape this book: Wendy Jean Frandsen, Vance-Grenville Community College.

I also thank Larry Fennelly, Chair of the Division of Learning Support at Macon State College, for his support as a department chair and as a friend; Deb Brennan, my declutter buddy and friend, for her encouraging words and for setting a disgustingly good example; and especially Nick Arlov, my husband, for his love and support, and for making sacrifices so many years ago so that I could attend college. Thanks, honey! I will always be grateful.

Pamela Arlov

Preface
To the Student

A Look at the Future

Outside the classroom window, two students pass by, laughing and clutching graduation robes packaged in plastic bags. But inside, the atmosphere is tense as the professor passes out term papers. These papers count as one-third of the course grade.

The professor sweeps by and drops a paper on the desk of Carl, who sits next to you. Carl opens his paper, then rubs his temples as if he has a sudden headache. You shoot him a questioning look. He unfolds his paper, and you see the large red F and the scrawled words. "Your writing skills are unacceptable!" You think of graduation, and realize that Carl will probably not march.

The professor sweeps by again, this time dropping a paper on your desk. Holding your breath, you open it and look at your grade.

No Time Like the Present

Writing is not the only skill you need in college, but it's one of the more important ones. In the classroom and beyond, the people who do well are most often those who think logically, who consider all the possibilities, and who communicate clearly. Writing can help you develop those skills.

In the college classroom, those who stand out also tend to be good writers. They write clearly, they state their ideas completely, and they don't embarrass themselves with poor grammar or misspelled words.

Perhaps, like most people, you feel like there's room for improvement in your writing skills. Maybe you feel that your grammar is not up to par, or you're just never sure where to put commas. Or perhaps you go blank when you see an empty page in front of you, waiting to be filled.

But there's good news. Whether your writing needs a little help or a lot, you can be a better writer. Writing is not a talent bestowed by fate, it is a skill, like driving a car, playing a guitar, or designing a Web page on the computer. It is built through your own hard work and improved by practice.

How can you become a better writer? You're in the right place, enrolled in a writing course, and you are holding the right object in your hand—this textbook. But the real key is not the course, the textbook, or even your instructor. The key is you. If you take guitar lessons but never practice, how well will you play? Or think of weight training—if you buy a book about it but never exercise your muscles, how much change will occur? You have a book on writing and a "personal trainer"—your instructor—ready to help you, so exercise your writing muscles as much as possible. If you work at it, you will amaze yourself.

There's no time like the present to shape your future.

How This Textbook Can Help

Wordsmith: A Guide to Paragraphs and Short Essays, Second Edition, is designed to help you on your journey to becoming the writer you want to be, the writer your future demands. Read on to find out how each section can help you develop your writing skills.

Part 1   Composition

Part 1, Composition, gives you an overview of the writing process and provides step-by-step instructions for writing a paragraph, the basic building block for any longer piece of writing. Part 1 also presents nine methods of paragraph development: description, narration, example, definition, classification, process, comparison-contrast, cause-effect, and argument. Finally, it introduces the essay, perhaps the most flexible and adaptable form of writing that you will ever learn. Shrunk down a bit, it can be used to answer a question on an essay test. Expanded a bit, it can be used to write a research paper, a term paper, or even a master's thesis.

Part 2   Grammar

Part 2, Grammar, provides wide coverage of grammar and punctuation. Some of the concepts covered are probably review for you while others are new. The chapters are user-friendly and take a step-by-step approach, so that you can work with them in class or on your own.

Feel free to use the chapters in this section as a reference. If you aren't sure of a comma rule, look it up. If you aren't sure of your subject-verb agreement, check it out in the chapter entitled "Subject-Verb Agreement." You will gain knowledge as you improve your writing.

You can also use the chapters as a way to improve your grammar. If your instructor marks several sentence fragments on your paper, don't wait until the topic is covered in class. Work through the chapter on sentence fragments on your own so that you can correct the problem now.

Part 3   Readings

Part 3, Readings, contains readings from professional writers. You will notice differences between the journalistic writing of these professionals and the academic form you are encouraged to use. Topic sentences are not always placed at the beginning of each paragraph. The language is often informal. But these are merely differences of audience—writing in the academic world is expected to be more formal than journalistic essays written for a general audience. You will see similarities, too. The essays have the same qualities you are encouraged to incorporate in your paragraphs: direction, unity, coherence, and support.

Good readers make good writers. The more you read, the better your writing will become.

Just the Beginning

Writing is hard work. But it is also worthwhile. The more you write, the more skilled you become. Whatever your major, whatever your vocation, writing will serve you well. May this book mark just the beginning of your journey as a writer.

Pamela Arlov

Wordsmith

A Guide to Paragraphs and Short Essays

Part 1
Composition

1

The Writing Process

prewrite PLAN draft PLAN REVISE proofread DRAFT plan PREWRITE plan DRAFT revise PROOFREAD prewrite DRAFT revise REVISE plan PREWRITE proofread PLAN REVISE plan REVISE plan PROOFREAD plan PROOFREAD

Writing is not a single act, but a process composed of several steps. As with most processes—swinging a baseball bat, playing the clarinet, or surfing the Internet—it is sometimes easier to do than to analyze. When people try to analyze how they write, their descriptions of the process are uniquely their own. Yet from a sea of individual accounts, the same steps emerge.

One writer, Antonio, describes the process this way:

> Well, first, I need time to think. If I have a while before the paper is due, I never start right away. Some people might call it procrastination, but it works for me. After the ideas have had time to percolate, I sit at the computer and just start writing. I just let my ideas flow, good or bad. If that doesn't work, sometimes I try a more organized approach, jotting down an outline. It's all a part of finding my focus. Then, once I know what I want to say, I just write. I am a slow writer because I try to get it right the first time. But I never do. If I look at it the next day, I see where the holes are—where I've left out details. I'm bad about that. So my second draft is always better than my first. When I'm finished, I check to make sure my commas are in the right place and my grammar is okay. Then I'm ready to turn it in.

3

The Writing Process

Though everyone approaches writing a little differently, most people follow a process similar to the one just described. The writer in the example above may not be aware of it, but he is following all of the steps in the **writing process:** prewriting, planning, drafting, revising, and proofreading.

Prewriting

| "... first, I need time to think."

Prewriting covers a range of activity from casually thinking about your topic to going through a prewriting exercise to get your thoughts on paper. You will probably find yourself doing some form of prewriting throughout the writing process. When you are sitting at a traffic light and the perfect example to illustrate your point pops into your head, you are prewriting. When you realize that your paragraph isn't working the way you wanted and you stop to list ideas or figure out another approach, you are returning to the prewriting stage. Prewriting *is* thinking, and the more thought you put into your paper, the stronger it will be.

Planning

| "It's all a part of finding my focus."

Careful and thoughtful **planning** makes a paragraph easier for you to write and easier for your readers to read. Your plan may include a topic sentence, your statement of the main idea. Because it states the main idea, the topic sentence forms the cornerstone of your paragraph. Besides a topic sentence, your planning will probably include an informal outline. An outline can be as simple as a list of the points you will develop in a paragraph. Don't be afraid that planning will waste your time. Careful planning—or lack of it—always shows in the final draft.

Drafting

| "I just write."

Sometimes **drafting** is a quick process, with ideas flowing faster than you can get them down on paper. At other times, the process is slow and difficult. Your thoughts grind to a standstill and you become frustrated, thinking you have nothing to say. If you get stuck during the drafting process, don't quit in frustration. The creative process is still at work. What is happening to you happens to all writers. *Write through* the problem, or, if necessary, return to the planning or prewriting stage.

As you draft your paper, you should not worry about grammar, spelling, or punctuation. Stopping to look up a comma rule will only distract you. Concentrate on ideas and save the proofreading for later.

Revising

| "I see where the holes are."

In its Latin roots, the word *revising* means "seeing again." **Revising** is difficult because it is hard to see your work with the eyes of a reader. Writers often see what they *meant* to say rather than what they really said. Sometimes they take for granted background knowledge that the reader may not have. Because of these difficulties, it helps to put your draft aside for a day or so before trying to revise it. With twenty-four hours between writing and revising, you will see your paper more clearly. It is also helpful to ask someone else to look at your work—a friend, classmate, or relative. Ask the person to focus on the *content* of your paper rather than on grammar, spelling, or punctuation. Ask which ideas are clear and which ones need more explanation. Ask how well your examples illustrate your points. A reader's comments can help you see your paper in a new light.

One word of advice—if you don't know how to use a computer, learn. Writing multiple drafts is much easier on a computer. Once you learn to write on a computer, the paragraphs, essays, term papers, and reports you will write in college will look much less intimidating.

Proofreading

| "I check to make sure my commas are in the right place and my grammar is okay."

Proofreading is the final polish that you put on your paragraph. When you proofread, consider such things as grammar, spelling, and word choice. Replace vague words with specific words. Take out words that are not carrying their weight. Look at connections, making sure ideas flow smoothly from one sentence to the next. Because the stages of the writing process overlap, you have probably done some minor proofreading along the way. Before the final proofreading, set your paragraph aside for a while. Then proofread it once more to give it the luster of a finished piece.

An Important Point

If you go through the writing process expecting the steps to fall in order, like the steps involved in changing the oil in your car, you may think the process is not working. However, writing a paragraph is not a sequential process. It is a repetitive process, more like driving a car than changing its oil.

If you take a two-hundred-mile trip, the steps you follow might be described as "Turn on the ignition. Put the car in drive. Accelerate. Brake. Put the car in park. Turn off the ignition." Yet it is not that simple. During a two-hundred-mile drive, you repeat each step not once but several times, and you may even stop for rest or fuel.

Writing a paragraph works in the same way. You may list the steps as "prewrite, plan, draft, revise, proofread," but it is not that simple. You may change the order of the sentences as you write the first draft or correct a spelling mistake as you revise. Sometimes you repeat a step several times. You may even stop for rest or fuel, just as you do when you drive. Eventually, both processes will get you where you want to go.

EXERCISE 1   THE WRITING PROCESS

Answer the questions below to review your knowledge of the writing process.

1. The five steps in the writing process are _____, _____, _____, _____, and _____.

2. The "thinking step" in the writing process is called _____.

3. The part of the writing process that involves correcting grammar and punctuation is called _____.

4. Major changes would most likely be made during the _____ step in the writing process.

5. True or false? The steps in the writing process often overlap. _____

The Writing Process: Stephanie's Paragraph

The next section follows the development of one writer's paragraph from start to finish. In writing her paragraph, Stephanie went through several forms of prewriting, made two different outlines, conferred with members of her writing group and her instructor, and wrote two rough drafts. (Only the first of the two drafts is shown here because the final draft reflects all of the changes Stephanie made.) Before turning in her final draft, Stephanie also proofread the paragraph once from top to bottom and twice from bottom to top. Then she asked a member of her writing group to look over the final draft for any mistakes she had overlooked.

The steps that Stephanie goes through are steps that you will take as you learn the writing process. You will also share some of her frustrations. But like Stephanie, you will find that what seems difficult at first is attainable, one step at a time.

Stephanie's Assignment

Stephanie's instructor handed out a list of three paragraph topics. Stephanie chose to write on this one: "Write about a piece of music or art that has a message for you. Don't just describe the piece of music or art; tell your reader how it affected you."

Stephanie's instructor suggested that the students prewrite, then make an outline. Earlier, the class had been divided into writing groups of four or five people who would help one another during the term. The instructor suggested that the writing groups meet to discuss each student's outline. Then, students would write a rough draft to bring to individual writing conferences with the instructor.

Stephanie's Prewriting

In class, Stephanie did a form of prewriting called *freewriting.* (For more information on freewriting and other forms of prewriting, see Chapter 2.) In this prewriting, Stephanie did not worry about grammar or spelling, but focused on gathering ideas. Stephanie's prewriting is reproduced here without correction.

> I remember the day my art class went to an exhibit at the museum and I saw a piece of art — I don't know what to call it. Not a painting or a drawing, but something the artist had put together. Built. I was trailing behind the class and something just pulled me over into the corner where it was. It was just me and that piece of art, and when I lifted the curtain — Wow! I was so knocked out. I remember my art teacher used to talk about what art meant, and I never understood until that day. I felt all sorts of emotion. I think I'll go over to the Tubman this weekend and see if it's still there.

Later, Stephanie visited the museum and took the following notes:

"Beauty Standard" by Ce Scott

Black frame, masks placed at top & bottom. Each side has female figure tied at ankles, wrist, and eyes with golden cord. They have bodies like models — thin & beautiful. Masks are just blank — no real features. Frame has tiny words repeated over

and over "dark brown eyes big full lips flat wide nose." Velvet curtain — very myste-
rious hangs there. Golden tassels hang down. "Mirror" embroidered on. Card says
"Lift the curtain to see the image by which each of us should be judged."

Stephanie's Rough Draft

Ce Scott's artwork <u>Beauty Standard</u> is a piece of
art with a message. It hangs in the Tubman African
American Museum. It has a black frame decorated with
female figures bound at the wrists, ankles, and eyes
with golden cord. They have bodies like models, thin
and beautiful. At the center of the frame is a black
velvet curtain embroidered with the word "Mirror."
On the frame, in small writing are the words "dark
brown eyes big full lips flat wide nose." A card
beside the work invites the viewer to lift the cloth
and see "the image by which each of us should be
judged." Underneath is a mirror—not the one held
up by society, but one that reflects the image of
whoever looked into it. The message is that the
only beauty standard you need to meet is your own.

Stephanie's Writing Group Meets

Next, Stephanie met with her writing group. A transcript of the portion of
the session dealing with Stephanie's outline appears below.

Transcript: Writing Group Session,
Monday, September 7

Eddie: Okay, who's the first victim? Tran?

Tran: I don't want to go first. Stephanie?

Stephanie: I may as well. I think I need major help.
(Stephanie passes out copies of her
prewriting and rough draft, and the group
reads silently.)

Tran: I like it. You have good grammar and
spelling.

Stephanie: You're just saying that because I got you
off the hook. You didn't have to go first.
(Laughter.)

Kelly:	I like it, too. But your prewriting is really different from the rough draft.
Stephanie:	Yeah, the prewriting doesn't have much detail. I had to go back to the museum to look at the piece again because I had forgotten a lot.
Eddie:	Yes, but I like the prewriting. I can tell you were really excited about the painting.
Stephanie:	It's not a painting. I'm not sure what you'd call it.
Eddie:	Whatever. But in the prewriting, I can tell it really had an effect on you. In the rough draft, the excitement disappears. It's just a description.
Kelly:	Eddie is right. I mean, it's a good description, but it needs more of you in it.
Stephanie:	Yeah, I see what you mean.
Tran:	I chose the same topic, except I'm doing my paragraph on music. Anyway, I remember that the assignment said to tell how the music or art affected you.
Stephanie:	That's right! I do need to put more of my reaction in there somehow. But won't that make it too long?
Kelly:	Well, you heard what Dr. Pettis said. Plenty of support.
Stephanie:	Okay, guys. Thanks. You've been a big help. Anything else?
Tran:	Yeah. Will you help me with my grammar?
	(Laughter.)

Stephanie's Final Draft

Stephanie wrote a second rough draft. Then, she met with her instructor for a conference before writing her final draft. Stephanie's final draft appears below.

Beauty Standard

I always thought of art as something to hang on a wall, never as something that had a message for me. Then last fall, at the Tubman African American

Museum, I saw a piece of art called <u>Beauty Standard</u> by Ce Scott. It had a black frame decorated with female figures bound at the wrists, ankles, and eyes with golden cord. At the center of the frame hung a black velvet curtain embroidered with the word "Mirror." A card beside the work invited the viewer to lift the cloth and see "the image by which each of us should be judged." On the frame, in small writing were the words "dark brown eyes big full lips flat wide nose." The words made me think of the sixties slogan, "Black is beautiful." It was a statement of pride and at the same time a demand to be included. At the time, society's beauty standard was a white one. And even though ideas of beauty now include different races, so many people are still left out—the old, those who are overweight, and even those who are just average. Suddenly, I felt angry and a little afraid to lift the velvet curtain. I looked at the bound female figures and understood that society binds me, too. Hesitantly, I lifted the curtain. My own face, skeptical and a bit defiant, looked back at me. It <u>was</u> a mirror—not the one held up by society, but one that reflected the image of whoever looked into it. As clearly as if she were in the room, the artist was telling me, "The only beauty standard you need to meet is your own."

Stephanie's Approach to Writing—and Yours

Stephanie's final draft is the product of many hours' thought and work, and it is at least partly a result of her willingness to listen to the advice and comments of others.

Writing is a process of trial and error, and sometimes it feels like mostly error. Even experienced writers often find writing difficult, often wonder if they have anything worthwhile to say or the ability to say it. If you fear writing, even if you dislike it, you are not alone. But writing is a skill that improves with practice, and if you give it serious effort, you will amaze yourself. The following list, "Five Quick Takes on Writing," may help you put the task of writing in perspective.

---

* *Five Quick Takes on Writing*

1. Take it a step at a time. Writing is often a slow process, and it always requires thought.
2. Take it seriously. The ability to write clearly and well will benefit you academically, professionally, and personally throughout your life.
3. Take it easy. Don't expect yourself to be perfect.
4. Take it to the limit. Stretch the limits of your imagination. Refuse to limit yourself by labeling yourself a poor writer.
5. Take it with you. Writing is a vital part of the real world. Make it a part of your life.

Group Exercise 1   The Ideal Conditions for Writing

In a group of three or four, discuss the ideal conditions for writing. Think about questions such as these: What tools do you enjoy working with? Do you write best with music or in absolute silence? Do you like having others around or do you prefer to be alone? Do you need coffee or snacks when you write? Do you need room to pace or do you think best seated in front of a desk or computer? After each group member has contributed, see what differences and similarities exist among members of your group. Have a spokesperson report your group's findings to the rest of the class.

Writing for Right-Brained Writers

This section is for those of you who rebel at the idea of a step-by-step approach like the one described in this chapter and outlined in the writing assignment at the chapter's end. Although prewriting, planning, drafting, revising, and proofreading are identifiable steps in the writing process, there's no law that says everyone has to approach them in exactly the same way.

For some people, a step-by-step approach does not come naturally. These people have a thinking style that is most often called "right-brained" or "holistic." The human brain is divided into two halves, or hemispheres, and most people are wired to rely heavily on the left hemisphere—the half responsible for logical, sequential, step-by-step thinking. Some people, however, rely more heavily on the right half of the brain, the part responsible for seeing the whole, for thinking in images, and for flashes of insight.

The following questions may help you decide if you are a right-brained thinker.

1. If you were asked to analyze how you write, would your answer be "I don't know. I just do it"?

2. When you are required to turn in an outline, do you usually complete it *after* you have written the paper?

3. If you were asked to describe your usual prewriting technique, would you say, "I never prewrite"?

4. Do you often arrive at the right answer to math problems without following the steps?

5. Do you have a hard time getting detail into your writing?

6. Are you a "big-picture person" rather than a "detail person"?

If you answered "yes" to three or more of the questions above, you may have been seen as a rebel because you don't always follow a step-by step, conventional approach to your work. But the chances are that whatever other characteristics you possess, you are also a right-brained writer.

Right-brained people are often intuitive, seeing the big picture before others do. They have a strong creative streak. They sometimes grasp ideas easily without knowing why or understanding how. But unlike their persistent, list-making, left-brained brothers and sisters, right-brained people often have trouble with the details. Planning isn't in their natures, and they tend not to have systems or specific steps to rely on. Whatever the task is, they "just do it."

If you are right-brained, does that mean that the methods in this text won't work for you? No. They *will* work. But you may have to work at them a bit harder. Give them a chance. Don't count them out until you have had enough experience with them to determine whether they work for you or not.

There are other strategies you can use, too. Unlike more conventional methods, the following tips were crafted with you in mind. These ideas may give you the extra boost you need to harness your creativity and let your right-brained way of thinking work for you, not against you. If your thinking style is left-brained, read on anyway. There may be something here that you can use along with the logical, step-by-step approach that works so well for you.

Tips for Right-Brained Writers

Find your most creative time and use it for writing. Some people find that they are at their best in the mornings. Others find that their creative juices begin to flow around 9:00 or 10:00 P.M. Writing will be easier if you schedule it during your natural period of creativity.

Use your rough draft as your prewriting. Since you think in terms of the whole, you may find it easier to do a rough draft than to prewrite. Consider your rough draft a form of prewriting, to be extensively revised before you turn it in.

Give your brain an assignment. When you have writing to do, let your right brain work on it while you are doing other things. At the beginning of the day, for instance, look over the assignment for a few minutes. Then come back to it in the evening and reap the benefits of having worked on the topic subconsciously. Or think about your topic before you go to sleep at night, then write in the morning. This technique can work not only in prewriting but also in revising.

Realize that doing the grunt work is a necessary evil. Right-brained people are less likely to put in the time it takes to master the basics because doing so may be tedious and boring to them. They are also less likely to plan. But even the most brilliantly creative people need self-discipline. It's a hard lesson to learn, but mastering the basics is essential to creative work. Singers spend endless time on breath control and scales. Artists learn anatomy and basic drawing. It is those efforts that set them free to do their best work. The payoff in mastering the basics is that once you learn them, you can forget about them. They will be second nature. The same goes for planning. Once you have made a plan, you are free to do the creative work. Doing the grunt work now always pays off in more freedom later.

Make a commitment to writing. Many professional writers are right-brained and face the same resistance that you do. Invariably, they say that the only way they can maintain the extended effort it takes to write books, plays, or novels is to have a routine and to write every day.

Writing Assignment 1   Writing and You

Write a paragraph describing your attitudes toward writing. Use the following steps.

Step 1: Prewrite. Jot down a few of the words that come to mind when you think of writing. Think of any significant experiences you have had that have shaped your attitude toward writing. Consider your writing habits. Are you organized? Do you procrastinate?

Step 2: Plan. Look over your prewriting. Try to sum up your attitude toward writing in a single word or phrase, and then construct an opening sentence for your paragraph using that word or phrase. Use one of the sentences below, filling in the blank with your word or phrase, or construct your own sentence.

My attitude toward writing is _____

_____.

When I think about writing, I feel _____

_____.

My feelings about writing have always been _____

_____.

Once you have constructed an opening sentence, decide how to organize your paragraph. A couple of possibilities are listed below.

1.   Take a historical approach, describing the influences that have shaped your writing. Use chronological (time) order.

2.   Try a step-by-step approach, describing what you do and how you feel as you go through a writing assignment.

Complete the planning stage by making an outline that briefly lists the points you plan to make in support of your opening sentence.

Step 3: Draft. Write out a rough draft of your paragraph. Focus on expressing your ideas rather than on grammar and punctuation.

Step 4: Revise. Read over your rough draft. Have you left out anything important? Is each idea clearly expressed? Does the paragraph flow smoothly? Is the sequence of ideas logical and effective? If possible, ask a classmate to look over your rough draft with the same questions in mind. Then revise your paragraph, incorporating any necessary changes.

Step 5: Proofread. Check your paragraph for mistakes in spelling, grammar, or punctuation. Look at each sentence individually. Then proofread once more. You have now completed all the steps in the writing process.

2

Preparing to Write

Q: What do spiders, heights, and enclosed spaces have in common with the ordinary item pictured below?

A blank sheet of paper

A: They sometimes inspire fear. Many people suffer from arachnophobia (fear of spiders), acrophobia (fear of heights), or claustrophobia (fear of enclosed spaces). Some people also develop a fear called "writer's block" when they are confronted with a blank sheet of paper or a blank computer screen. They fear that they will not be able to think of anything to say, or that if they do find something to say, it will be wrong. Writer's block happens to almost everyone at one time or another. It is not an indication of poor writing ability. In fact, writers who get writer's block are usually those who care about how they present themselves.

One of the best defenses against this kind of fear is prewriting. Prewriting is a playful "safety zone" that you can enter without fear. In prewriting, your purpose is to generate ideas, not to judge them, so you can't go wrong. Even if you don't have writer's block, prewriting can give your writing a jump-start.

Prewriting

Prewriting is the first step in the writing process. It is the act of sorting out your thoughts on a topic and finding out what you have to say about it. Depending on the assignment you are given, prewriting may also include narrowing your topic to a manageable size. Prewriting begins the moment you receive an assignment. Quietly, in the background, part of your mind begins to gather information. However, it usually takes a bit of effort to bring that information to the surface. The prewriting methods in this chapter can jump-start the writing process by helping you collect your thoughts on a topic and get them on paper.

Prewriting Methods

The aim of all **prewriting methods** is the same: to help you get ideas on paper. At this point in the writing process, it is not the quality of ideas that counts, but the quantity.

When you are ready to prewrite, sit at the computer or in a comfortable spot with pen and paper. Relax your mind and body, and remind yourself that prewriting is a playful exercise of the imagination and that it is okay to write down anything that comes to mind. As for the part of your mind that automatically jumps in to criticize what you think and say, give it some time off. Your purpose in prewriting is to put down every thought on your topic, no matter how ridiculous it seems. Later, you can discard what is not usable.

Some of the methods may feel awkward at first. But try them all. One will be right for you.

Brainstorming

Brainstorming, a listing technique, is one of the easiest prewriting techniques. To brainstorm, take a few minutes to list whatever comes to mind on your topic. Your purpose is not to censor or come up with the "right" items for your list, but to generate ideas.

Example

Here's how one writer, James, approached a brainstorming exercise on the topic "Describe a favorite holiday memory."

Last 4th of July — family reunion
Lake Sinclair
plenty of food
Aunt Mil's fried chicken
baked beans
over 100 relatives
Mo's girlfriend!
saw Grandaddy Bennett for the last time
paper checkered tablecloths
ants
kids running and screaming
fireworks over lake — color and noise
Jim stretched out in back seat asleep on the way home

When James looked at his prewriting, he was not sure he could use it all, but he knew he had captured some of the vivid images and important memories from his Fourth of July family reunion.

EXERCISE 1   **BRAINSTORMING**

Brainstorm on one of the following topics; then see if you have an idea for a possible paragraph.

1. the importance of money
2. a holiday memory
3. an unexpected kindness
4. being an outsider
5. a bad habit

Freewriting

Freewriting is nonstop writing on a topic for a set time. The point of freewriting is that your flow of words never ceases; your pen never stops moving. If you have nothing to say, repeat your last thought again and again until a new thought replaces it. Do not worry about spelling, about clarity, or about whether your thoughts are logically connected. Just write.

Example

Emily did the following freewriting when her instructor asked the class to write on the topic "Discuss one of your pet peeves and why it annoys you."

Let's see. Right now I am peeved about having to write about a pet peeve. Ha, ha! Seriously, I am an easy going person and do not get too upset over anything. I don't like telephone salespeople. I don't like loud commercials. I don't like my ex-boyfriend. I don't like people who are late. I don't like it when a class or meeting is held up because some people are late. Yesterday, in Freshman Orientation, we had a quiz and when it was time for class to start, the instructor said, "we'll just wait a minute or two in case someone else comes in." Excuse ME, but I made it to class on time. Why should I wait for someone who is late? I can think of plenty of other examples. Is my ten minutes up yet? No. The minister at our church always starts services on time and it doesn't matter how many people come in late but when my cousin got married the ceremony was supposed to be at 7 PM and it did not start until 7:30. People just keep coming in, right up until about 7:25. I think spending a lot of money on a wedding is a waste — they should just buy furniture or something.

EXERCISE 2   FREEWRITING

Freewrite on one of the following topics; then see if you have a focus for a possible paragraph.

1. What is your pet peeve?
2. What is your favorite time of day?
3. Is honesty always the best policy?
4. What is your biggest complaint about college professors?
5. What can you tell about a person from the way he or she dresses?

Invisible Writing: A Computer Technique

Invisible writing is a freewriting technique especially for writing on a computer. Turn on your computer, and once you have a blank screen in front of you, type the words "Invisible Writing" at the top of the page. Then turn your monitor off or adjust the contrast button at the bottom of your screen until the words are no longer visible and your screen is completely dark.

Freewrite for five to ten minutes. It is especially important not to worry about spelling errors. With this method, you can hardly avoid them. At first, you may feel strange, even anxious, pouring your words into the dark computer screen. Soon, though, your fingers and your thoughts will fly.

EXERCISE 3   INVISIBLE WRITING

Do an invisible writing on one of the following topics.

1. taking chances
2. superstitions

3. television or radio commercials
4. driving habits
5. ending a friendship

Clustering

Clustering is a technique designed to boost your creativity by stimulating both hemispheres of the brain. The left hemisphere, or "left brain," is used in logical tasks that move in 1-2-3 order. When you count to ten, write a sentence, or make an outline, you use your left brain. Your right brain, on the other hand, specializes in tasks involving visual images and intuition. Since clustering involves both listing (a left-brain task) and drawing (a right-brain task), it allows you to tap both your logical side and your creative side.

To cluster, begin with a circled word—your topic. From there, map out associations. Some people branch ideas from the central word like quills on a porcupine. Others group ideas when they cluster, with smaller clusters branching out from larger ones. When this type of cluster is finished, it resembles a biology textbook's diagram of a molecule.

What your diagram looks like does not matter. In clustering, what matters is that you get your thoughts on paper using both images and words.

Look at the following examples of clustering.

Example

Brandon did his "porcupine" cluster on the topic "your chosen career."

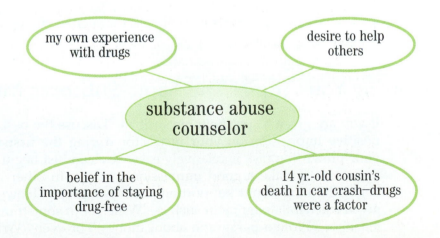

Example

Here is Kara's "molecule" cluster on the topic "Internet shopping."

Exercise 4   Clustering

Draw a cluster diagram using one of the following topics.

1. credit cards
2. your favorite sport
3. your best or worst date
4. advantages or disadvantages of public transportation
5. your eating habits

Narrowing Your Topic: The Topic-Subtopic Method

If you are given a specific topic such as "Discuss the best way to make a positive impression on your instructor during the first week of class," your prewriting task is relatively easy. You can just begin thinking about the ways to make a good impression in class. In other words, you can begin thinking about supporting your paragraph. However, if you are given a general assignment such as "Write about something related to college," or "Write a paragraph about money," or even "Write a paragraph about a topic of your own choosing," then your task is a much larger one. Entire books have been written about college, and the books and magazines about money take up considerable shelf space in any bookstore. Therefore, you need to narrow and focus the topic so that it is manageable in a single paragraph.

For some writers, narrowing a topic becomes a natural part of the prewriting process. Other prefer to narrow their topic in a separate step or series of steps.

One way to narrow a topic is with a simple method called the **topic-subtopic method.**

Steps in the Topic-Subtopic Method

Step 1: Write down the topic.

Step 2: List possible subtopics.

Step 3: Look over the list of subtopics and pick the one you are most interested in. This subtopic now becomes your topic.

Step 4: Repeat the process until you have narrowed your topic to an appropriate size for a paragraph.

In the example below, the writer has taken a general topic, "animals," through three narrowings. In the first narrowing, she has made a list of subtopics. From that list, she has chosen the subtopic "pets." From there, she will repeat the process until she has narrowed the topic to the right size for the paragraph she wants to write.

General topic	Subtopics
animals	wild animals
	endangered species
	pets ← (new topic)
	farm animals
	animals raised for food
	working animals (seeing-eye dogs, police dogs)

"Pets" is narrower than "animals," but it is still a very broad topic. The writer does a second narrowing, this time with "pets" as the general topic.

General topic	Subtopics
pets	dogs ← (new topic)
	cats
	how to bathe a pet

Subtopics, continued

pampered pets

mistreated pets

exotic pets (snakes, hedgehogs, etc.)

Once the writer has decided on the topic "dogs," she decides to do a third narrowing of the topic:

Topic	*Subtopic*	
dogs	training	← (new topic)
	breeds	
	working dogs (drug-sniffing dogs, assistance dogs for blind)	
	feeding	

The writer decides to take the subtopic "training" and make it the subject of a paragraph. She is through with the narrowing process. Now, to flesh out the details of her paragraph, she does a brainstorming exercise. Her brainstorming follows.

Basic Training for Dogs

based on kindness and reward

no yelling or hitting

use food rewards

one trick or skill at a time

the basics — "down," "sit," "stay"

persistence and repetition

be consistent — don't say "down" one time and "get down" the next

EXERCISE 5   NARROWING A TOPIC

Take one of the following broad topics and narrow it to paragraph size, following the topic-subtopic method shown above. Take your topic through as many narrowings as are needed to bring it down to paragraph size.

1. the environment
2. alcohol
3. education
4. money
5. transportation

Outlining

Outlining is often the last step in the prewriting process. Once you have used one of the other prewriting methods, making an outline will take you one step further in the writing process. Forget about the formal outline with its Roman numerals, ABCs, and 123s. A short paragraph calls for a short outline. Your outline may be just a few words jotted on a page, or it may include a topic sentence and a brief listing of support. Below is Emily's outline of her paragraph describing her pet peeve.

```
Topic Sentence: I am an easygoing person, but it
annoys me when a meeting, class, or other event
does not begin on time because some people are
late.
    Freshman orientation class—quiz delayed because
      of people who were late
    Meeting with friends in restaurant—waited fifteen
      minutes to order until Kylie came.
    Cousin's wedding—delayed a half hour because of
      late arrivals.
    Summary sentence: Classes, meetings, and other
gatherings should not be arranged for the con-
venience of latecomers, but for those who care
enough to arrive on time.
```

EXERCISE 6   OUTLINING

Take one of the topics you have done a practice prewriting on and make an outline for a paragraph.

Journal Writing

Journals are "daily writings"—the word *journal* comes from *jour*, the French word for *day*. Journals are usually composed of informal writings on a variety of subjects. **Journal writing** allows you to experiment with the techniques you are learning in your writing class. In a journal, the only form of writing you should avoid is "diary mode." An "I-got-up-I-fed-the-dog-I-went-to-school" format makes for dull writing and even duller reading. Write about issues that matter to you. Tell your dreams.

Describe your grandfather's tool shed. Work toward detailed writing that follows a logical pattern.

Whether or not you receive credit for it in class, make journal writing a habit. Practice is the only thing that is guaranteed to make you a better writer. Courses and texts are of limited value without time spent alone with a word processor or pen and paper. If you think, "It won't matter. I'll never be a good writer," ask yourself this: How good a driver would you be if the only driving you had done was in a driver education course? You can be a better writer. Journal writing will start you on your way.

Journal Topics

1. What are some reasons for keeping a journal or diary?

2. If you had one day of your life to live over, which one would it be?

3. If you were cleaning out your mental closet, what would you most want to throw away?

4. Who is your role model? Why?

5. Is it better to have an assertive, in-your-face personality or to be laid-back and slow to show anger?

6. Other than food, water, and sleep, what *must* you have every day? Why?

7. If every job or career paid the exact same salary, what kind of work would you choose?

8. Discuss one item that fits this description: "It plugs into the wall, and I couldn't live without it."

9. If people had fur, what changes would take place in society?

10. If you had to live without television, how would you spend your extra time?

11. If you could have one talent that you do not now possess, what would it be?

12. If you could bring one fictional character to life (for whatever reason— to be your friend, to benefit humanity, or to solve a problem), who would it be?

13. If you could travel to any place in the world, where would you go?

14. Describe one effective method you use to reduce stress.

15. Describe the one place that, for you, is "heaven on earth."

16. What can you tell about people from the way they carry themselves— that is, the way they stand, sit, or move?

17. Is it better to have a wide circle of friends or just a few close friends?

18. Describe your general style of dealing with problems. Do you meet problems head-on, or do you hide your head in the sand and hope they will go away? Do you enlist the help of others, or try to solve your problems alone? Illustrate your journal entry with at least one example.

19. Which is more important, independence or security?

20. By the end of the twenty-first century, what change, development, or discovery would you most like to see? Why?

The Progressive Writing Assignment

How It Works

Begin by choosing one of the topics below; it will serve as the basis your first paragraph. In this chapter, you will complete prewriting for the paragraph. Throughout the next four chapters, each Progressive Writing Assignment will take you a step further toward a paragraph. By the time you have finished the final assignment, you will have completed all the steps in the writing process and will have a complete paragraph.

Progressive Writing Assignment: Prewriting

In this chapter, your Progressive Writing Assignment is a prewriting assignment. Choose one of the topics below—one you would like to write a paragraph about—and follow the instructions.

Topic 1: Discuss the results of taking a specific piece of advice from a friend or family member.

Tips for Prewriting

Prewrite on the topic, using one or several of the methods outlined in this chapter. As you prewrite, consider the different types of advice you have been offered: bad advice, good advice, advice that got you in trouble, or advice that cost you money. Consider the different people who have offered you advice. Taking a broad approach allows you to consider many different possibilities.

What Now?

After you have completed your prewriting, you should have more material than you will be able to use. To prepare for the next step in the Progressive Writing Assignment, choose piece of advice that you want to focus on in your paragraph.

Topic 2: Discuss your decision to attend college.

Tips for Prewriting

Prewrite on the topic, using one or several of the methods outlined in this chapter. As you prewrite, consider all factors that surround your decision. What are they? Some people are motivated to attend college by the expectations of family or friends. Some are trying to put the past behind them, while others are trying to fulfill lifelong ambitions. Some people arrive certain of success; other fear failure. Consider everything surrounding your decision to attend college: your reasons, your expectations, the reaction of friends and family, and your own hopes and fears.

What Now?

After you have completed your prewriting, you should have more material than you will be able to use. To prepare for the next step in the Progressive Writing Assignment, decide which ideas you want to focus on.

Topic 3: Discuss your greatest fear.

Tips for Prewriting

Prewrite on the topic, using one or several of the methods outlined in this chapter. Consider that fears sometimes have a strong basis in reality: A person whose parents and grandparents died young may have a fear of not living long enough to see her children grow up. Just as often, though, fears seem irrational. A person with a steady job and a comfortable home may fear being homeless. Write down your fears, rational and irrational, and try to decide what lies behind them. Consider also how you deal with your fears. Do you have a specific method for coping with them, or do you just live with them?

What Now?

After you have completed your prewriting, you should have more material than you will be able to use. To prepare for the next step in the Progressive Writing Assignment, decide which ideas you want to focus on in your paragraph.

Topic 4: Discuss types of stress experienced by college students.

Tips for Prewriting

Prewrite on the topic, using one or several of the methods outlined in this chapter. Everyone experiences stress from many sources, such as overwork, family problems, or even boredom. However, there are some kinds of stress that may be specifically associated with college. In this paragraph, you will write about some of the types of stress experienced by college students. Thinking about your own stress is a good starting point, but imagine the kinds of stress experienced by students who may not be like you: older students, working students, students who have children. What kinds of stress are common to all college students, and which are particular to certain groups?

What Now?

After you have completed your prewriting, you should have more material than you will be able to use. To prepare for the next step in the Progressive Writing Assignment, decide which types of stress you want to focus on in your paragraph.

3

Writing Paragraphs: Topic Sentences

> **A Silly Riddle**
> How is a topic sentence like a compass?
> a. It always points to magnetic north.
> b. It's useful on a hiking expedition.
> c. It shows exactly where you are headed.

The riddle in the box above may be silly, but the comparison it makes is valid. A topic sentence *is* like a compass. It shows your reader exactly where your paragraph is headed, and it also helps to keep you on track as you write your paragraph. It gives **direction** to your paragraph.

Direction is one of four characteristics of effective writing that you will read about in this text and learn to develop in your own writing. Before exploring the topic sentence further, look at the four characteristics of effective writing introduced below.

Characteristics of an Effective Paragraph

1. **Direction** means that the paragraph has a strong topic sentence that states the main idea and sets the course that the paragraph will follow.
2. **Unity** means that the paragraph makes one main point and sticks to that point.

3. **Coherence** means that the ideas in the paragraph are logically connected and easy to follow.

4. **Support** means that the paragraph contains specific and detailed discussion of the idea stated in the topic sentence.

Direction: Shaping the Topic Sentence of a Paragraph

A topic sentence provides direction by stating the main idea of a paragraph and answering the reader's unspoken question, "What is your point?"

Functions of a Topic Sentence

A topic sentence does two things. First of all, it tells the *general topic* of the paragraph. Second, it makes a *specific point about the topic.*

Example

                    topic   specific point about the topic

✔ Carrying a homemade lunch instead of eating out has had unexpected benefits.

                  topic   specific point about the topic

✔ Knowing how to research using a computer is an essential skill in college.

            specific point   topic

✔ There are many creative ways to hide thinning hair.

EXERCISE 1   ANALYZING TOPIC SENTENCES

In each of the topic sentences below, underline the topic and double-underline the specific point the writer is making about the topic.

1. Praise can be a powerful motivator.
2. Saying "no" is a skill that my brother Brian has never developed.
3. Talk shows on television are often offensive.
4. My willpower unravels at the sight of chocolate.

5. Some of my coworkers have little patience with machines.

6. Stromboli's Italian Grill is my favorite restaurant.

7. A successful letter of complaint has three essential elements.

8. My brother's fondness for loud music irritates the rest of the family.

9. The woman who lives next door is incurably nosy.

10. Poor organization can make studying difficult.

EXERCISE 2   ANALYZING TOPIC SENTENCES

In each of the topic sentences below, underline the topic and double-underline the specific point the writer is making about the topic.

1. Gossip can be hurtful.

2. Listening is difficult for some people.

3. Watching television is often a waste of time.

4. Finding time to exercise is difficult for me.

5. Peer pressure can weaken even the strongest will.

6. My experience working at the Burger Basket convinced me to avoid fast-food places.

7. Trying to find information on the Internet can be frustrating.

8. During the past year, my cola habit has gotten out of hand.

9. Gas prices vary in different parts of town.

10. My vacation will give me a chance to do some work around the house.

EXERCISE 3   COMPLETING TOPIC SENTENCES

Complete the topic sentences below. Underline the topic once. Then double-underline the point about the topic.

1. Taking an aerobics class _____.

2. _____ is something no home should be without.

3. In the morning, _____ helps me prepare to face the day.

4. _____ is my favorite piece of furniture.

5. To avoid last-minute cramming for tests, _____.

EXERCISE 4   WRITING TOPIC SENTENCES

Write five topic sentences. Underline the topic once. Then double-underline your point about the topic.

1. _____
   _____

2. _____
   _____

3. _____
   _____

4. _____
   _____

5. _____
   _____

Writing Topic Sentences That Fit

A topic sentence also provides direction by precisely outlining the territory the paragraph will cover. A topic sentence that is *too broad* outlines more territory than a paragraph can comfortably cover. A topic sentence that is *too narrow* draws the boundaries of the paragraph uncomfortably small, usually by focusing on some fact that would make a good supporting detail but that does not lend itself to development.

Look at the following sample topic sentences on the subject "computers."

✗   Computers have changed modern society.

This topic sentence is too broad. It promises more than one paragraph can deliver. Think of all the ways computers have changed modern life: they have changed the way stores keep track of inventories, the way banks work, and the way groceries are checked out. They have created new jobs and made others obsolete. They have altered our ideas about what skills are essential and have raised new concerns about privacy and access to information. The topic "how computers have changed society" could easily be the subject of a book.

✘ My computer has a floppy drive and a CD drive.

This topic is too narrow. It tells the reader that the writer will discuss a specific computer, her own, and that the focus will be the computer's CD and floppy drives. While the sentence might work as a supporting point in a paragraph, it is too narrow to be a topic sentence. A topic sentence that is too narrow is a dead-end statement, a fact that does not invite exploration. A good topic sentence opens a door to discussion.

✔ A computer can link a person who is disabled or homebound to the outside world.

This topic sentence is neither too broad nor too narrow. Within this paragraph, the writer can discuss how a computer helps a disabled person to bank or shop online. She can tell how a computer links a homebound person to people and information sources around the world. The sentence opens a door to an area of discussion and exploration that is neither too narrow nor too broad to develop in one paragraph.

EXERCISE 5 ANALYZING TOPIC SENTENCES

Each set of sentences below contains one topic sentence that is too broad, one that is too narrow, and one that would make a good topic sentence for a paragraph. In the blank to the left of each sentence, label it TB (too broad), TN (too narrow), or TS (topic sentence).

Set 1

_____ a. The functions of a bank are many and varied.

_____ b. Fees that banks charge seem to target lower-income customers.

_____ c. My checking account is with First National Bank.

Set 2

_____ a. My brother Simon often stays awake until 2:00 or 3:00 A.M.

_____ b. My brother Simon is a night owl.

_____ c. My brother Simon has different levels of energy at different times of the day, week, month, and year.

Set 3

_____ a. Ordering merchandise by mail has several advantages.

_____ b. I received a Land's End catalog in today's mail.

_____ c. Mail-order firms have been a vital part of American business for many decades.

Set 4

_____ a. Coping with my father's illness has been difficult for my family.

_____ b. Life has its ups and downs.

_____ c. Last year, my father had major surgery.

Set 5

_____ a. The commercials for Mercedes project a classy image.

_____ b. CNN and MSNBC are news channels.

_____ c. Television exerts a positive influence on American society.

EXERCISE 6   ANALYZING TOPIC SENTENCES

Each set of sentences below contains one topic sentence that is too broad, one that is too narrow, and one that would make a good topic sentence for a paragraph. In the blank to the left of each sentence, label it TB (too broad), TN (too narrow), or TS (topic sentence).

Set 1

_____ a. My cat has a marking on her back that looks like the number three.

_____ b. Training a dog to sit on command is a simple process.

_____ c. Pets are wonderful.

Set 2

_____ a. Housing costs vary widely across the United States.

_____ b. A one-bedroom apartment in the Aspen Forest apartment complex costs $570 per month.

_____ c. A first time homebuyer should consider several factors when searching for a home.

Set 3

_____ **a.** Gasoline stations have been a part of the American landscape for almost a century.

_____ **b.** In my grandfather's time, gasoline cost fifty cents per gallon.

_____ **c.** The gasoline station of my grandfather's time offered services that are unheard of today.

Set 4

_____ **a.** Requiring fingerprints of citizens who obtain drivers' licenses is a bad idea.

_____ **b.** Many laws are unjust and should be repealed.

_____ **c.** In some states, a driver's license must bear the driver's fingerprint.

Set 5

_____ **a.** Fish are fascinating creatures.

_____ **b.** My sister's angelfish is named Gabriel.

_____ **c.** An aquarium is like a small entertainment center for the home.

Group Exercise 1   Writing a Topic Sentence Exercise   Confident? Go solo!

Have you had enough test *taking*? Form a test *making* team with two or three of your classmates and write an exercise similar to the one above. Choose three to five of the topics below, and for each topic, write a topic sentence that is too broad, one that is too narrow, and one that would fit a paragraph. Then trade tests with another group and see how your group's performance—as test makers and as test takers—stacks up to theirs.

Topics

1. books
2. garbage
3. beverages
4. music
5. schools
6. furniture
7. nature
8. people
9. food
10. television

Where Should a Topic Sentence Go?

If you look carefully at the paragraphs in textbooks, essays, and news stories, you will see that a topic sentence may appear anywhere in a paragraph. However, the most common position for a topic sentence is at or near the beginning of a paragraph. Placing the topic sentence at the beginning of a paragraph lets your reader know exactly where the paragraph is going and gives the impression that you have thought about the organization of your paragraph. And you *will* have thought about it. The very act of constructing a topic sentence places your focus on the main idea of your paragraph and helps keep you on track in supporting that idea.

Topic Sentence First

Placing the topic sentence first is often your best choice. A topic sentence conveys your main idea and provides a strong, clear opening for your paragraph.

Example

Since I began carrying a homemade lunch to my part-time job at the mall, I have discovered the benefits of brown-bagging. The most obvious benefit is that bringing a lunch from home saves money. At the mall's food court, the price of a sandwich and chips or a slice of pizza and a soft drink can easily approach five dollars. But for less than ten dollars, I can buy a six-pack of soft drinks, a loaf of bread, and enough pimento cheese and peanut butter to make lunches for a week or more. Another benefit of brown-bagging—an unexpected one—is that I feel less rushed. Before I started bringing a lunch, my thirty-minute lunch break was consumed by a mad dash to the food court to stand in line, find a table, gulp down my food, and rush back to work. Now, I take a leisurely lunch in the employee break room, reading a magazine as I eat. Usually, I have an extra fifteen minutes to read and relax or take a stroll around the mall's upper level. I also benefit from the improved nutrition of my homemade lunches. Turkey on whole wheat or even peanut butter and jelly from home is lower in fat and calories than a hamburger or slice of pizza from the food court. For me, brown-bagging means that a healthier wallet, a more relaxed lunch break, and improved nutrition are "in the bag."

Topic Sentence after an Introductory Sentence

Sometimes, you may wish to include background material before you state the main point of your paragraph. In these instances, condense the background material to one introductory sentence. After your introductory sentence, state the topic sentence.

Example

Baldness runs in my family, and at thirty-five, I have come to accept my hair loss. **But as my hairline receded over the years, I discovered several creative ways to hide thinning hair.** My first solution to baldness was to wear a hat. Baseball caps in summer and knit caps in winter were only the beginning. During an "arty" phase in my mid-twenties, I wore a beret, and in the back of a closet somewhere, I still have a dashing Indiana-Jones-style hat. Another method I used to hide my thinning hair was the "comb-over"—combing hair over a bald spot. In the earliest stages of baldness, the method worked well for me. But as my hairline receded further, I stopped using the comb-over. I had seen too many men who looked ridiculous with just a few strands of foot-long hair covering a completely bald dome. The best method I have found to hide thinning hair is the one I use now. I have shaved my head completely. Now, no one can tell whether I am bald by nature or by choice. Shaving my head has helped me to get over my embarrassment at being bald. I have finally come to realize that bald is beautiful.

EXERCISE 7   FINDING TOPIC SENTENCES

One of the following paragraphs begins with an introductory sentence, while the other starts with the topic sentence. Underline the topic sentence in each paragraph.

Paragraph A

The glamour of Tyra Banks, Cindy Crawford, or Kate Moss may appeal to some, but my favorite models are not the ones who strut the runways for six figures a year. I like the real people who model the clothes in the Wal-Mart ads. In this week's Wal-Mart flyer, "Nellie, Associate" is modeling a red sweatshirt and matching sweatpants. She is not as thin or regal-looking as Tyra Banks, but I can tell her smile is real. She is looking up at Tequila, her daughter, who is modeling a powder-blue sweat outfit and reaching for her mother as she perches on the shoulders of "Calvin, Brother in Law of Nellie, Associate." On another page is "Brent, Tire and Lube Manager Trainee," a young man with a goatee and a shaved head. He wears a corduroy vest and a plaid shirt that looks ready to have its sleeves rolled up for some real work. In another section of the flyer, "Wendy, Customer Service Manager" models a cranberry-colored mock turtleneck. With her flying red hair, scrubbed, natural-looking skin, and ample frame, she doesn't look like a model. But a size-eighteen woman could look at the picture and have no doubt that she, like Wendy, would look really good in that top. The models in the Wal-Mart ads, real people who look good in real clothes, are much more appealing to me than the highly paid models whose only business is beauty.

Paragraph B

My brothers, Brad and Roy, are very different in their attitudes about money. Brad and his wife Lexie believe in living for today. They have a new house on the north side of town, a new sport utility vehicle, and a two-year-old Volvo. Their clothes are always designer labels in the latest fashions, and their home is a showplace of fine furniture. But they seldom have time to enjoy these things because they both work two jobs to pay off the massive debt they have accumulated. It is as though their possessions own them. My brother Roy goes a bit too far in the opposite direction. He puts every spare penny away for the future. Though he has a good job, he drives a thirteen-year-old car that rattles as if only habit is holding it together. He argues constantly with his wife, who simply wants decent clothes for herself and their children. Worse yet, he insists on buying nothing but practical gifts. I thought Andrea would divorce him when he gave her a hand-held vacuum for her birthday so that she could vacuum the inside of her car at home instead of taking it to the car wash. My two brothers agree on politics, football, and religion, but they will never agree about money.

Progressive Writing Assignment

Progressive Writing Assignment: Topic Sentence

If your instructor has assigned the Progressive Writing Assignment, you have already completed your prewriting for one of the topics below. In this chapter, you will complete your topic sentence.

Topics and Tips for Writing a Topic Sentence

The Topics

> Topic 1: Discuss the results of taking a specific piece of advice from a friend or family member.
>
> Topic 2: Discuss your decision to attend college.
>
> Topic 3: Discuss your greatest fear.
>
> Topic 4: Discuss types of stress experienced by college students.

Tips for Writing a Topic Sentence

- Decide on the points you will cover in your paragraph and the order in which you will present them. Then write a tentative topic sentence.
- Make sure that the topic sentence presents a specific topic and makes a point about that topic.
- Check to make sure that your topic sentence is not too broad. For example, for Topic 4, "Discuss types of stress experienced by college students," the following topic sentence would be too broad:

  ✗ Everybody experiences stress at one time or another.

  The sentence is too broad because the paragraph is not about "everybody"; it is about college students. Two better topic sentences are shown below:

  ✔ College students are prone to certain kinds of stress.

  ✔ College students most often experience stress related to academic performance and lack of time.

- Check to make sure that your topic sentence is not too narrow. For example, for Topic 2, "Discuss your decision to attend college," the following topic sentence would be too narrow:

  ✗ I began college just two months ago.

  The sentence is too narrow because it does not address the idea of a decision to attend college. While the sentence might be appropriate as a supporting detail, it is too narrow to be a topics sentence. Two better topics sentences are shown below:

  ✔ Stuck in a dead-end job, I decided to attend college so that I could do something that will make a difference.

  ✔ Attending college will help me realize my lifelong dream of being a nurse.

4

Writing Paragraphs:
Support

Which party sounds more appealing?

You are invited to hang out with Andrew on the third or fourth Saturday of this month. We will get the party started whenever everyone gets there, and we will all have a great time. Call me and I'll let you know where the party will be held.

You are invited to an end-of-summer bash at Michael's place on Saturday, August 24. We will start at 7:30 P.M. with party games and volleyball. Then we will have grilled chicken, seafood and drinks. Later, we'll dance to some great music. Dress is casual—shorts or jeans are fine.

In the box above, the second invitation would be the clear winner for most people. It's not just the appeal of games, food, and music that make the invitation interesting. The invitation's appeal lies at least partly in its specific detail. On the other hand, the first invitation gives no time, no place, and no idea of what activities to expect or how to dress. In planning a party or in writing a paragraph, the key is in the details. Specific support is one of the keys to good writing. Before looking at paragraph support, review the four principles of effective writing below. The highlighted principle, support, is the focus of this chapter.

Characteristics of an Effective Paragraph

1. **Direction** means that the paragraph has a strong topic sentence that states the main idea and sets the course that the paragraph will follow.

2. **Unity** means that the paragraph makes one main point and sticks to that point.

3. **Coherence** means that the ideas in the paragraph are logically connected and easy to follow.

4. **Support** means that the paragraph contains specific and detailed discussion of the idea stated in the topic sentence.

Support: Using Specific Detail

A strong topic sentence, unity, and smooth transitions give a paragraph structure and style. Only **support** can give it life. Without specific details, a paragraph remains on a broad, general level. What is it like to read a paragraph without specific details? Imagine watching a movie, television show, or video that never shows a closeup but instead maintains a camera distance of ten feet from every character. You would probably feel detached and uninvolved. Readers feel the same way when a writer never gets close enough to the subject to describe it in detail.

The Difference Between Topic Sentences and Supporting Sentences

A topic sentence provides direction—the road map for a paragraph—but supporting sentences supply the scenery. While topic sentences are broad and general, large enough to encompass the entire paragraph, supporting sentences are specific, giving details and examples. The following exercise provides practice in distinguishing topic sentences from supporting details.

EXERCISE 1   DISTINGUISHING TOPIC SENTENCES FROM SUPPORTING DETAILS

Each numbered item contains three supporting details and one topic sentence. Write *SD* beside each of the three details and *TS* beside the topic sentence.

1. **a.** _____ Finally, he began throwing a tennis ball for his dog, who barked loudly in appreciation.

   b. _____ Then he put on a CD by a group called the Funk Brigade and turned the volume up.

c. _____ First, he turned on the television to provide background noise.

d. _____ It was too quiet in the room, so Marcus decided to make some noise.

2. a. _____ In the second book, Harry meets Dobby, a house-elf who nearly kills Harry in an effort to help him.

   b. _____ J. K. Rowling's popular *Harry Potter* books follow the adventures of a young wizard as he learns his craft.

   c. _____ In the first book, Harry, who has always felt like the odd one out, finds out that he is a wizard and begins to discover his powers.

   d. _____ The third book introduces Harry to a mysterious character named Sirius Black and to the soul-sucking guardians of Azkaban Prison.

3. a. _____ Being late is a harmful habit to acquire.

   b. _____ People who are late to classes or meetings often miss important information.

   c. _____ People who arrive late for appointments or meetings often anger those who have to wait.

   d. _____ Although the impression may be inaccurate, people who are late are often perceived as rude or selfish.

4. a. _____ Tires that are not properly inflated can pose a danger to both driver and passengers.

   b. _____ Windshield wipers that are excessively worn can pose a danger in rainy weather.

   c. _____ Bald tires, worn tires, and tread that is unevenly worn can cause a car to lose traction on the road.

   d. _____ Failure to take care of small details of car maintenance can make driving dangerous.

5. a. _____ The close companionship that arises between the adopted animal and its owner can benefit both animal and human.

   b. _____ Shelter animals are euthanized if they are not adopted, so adopting a pet from the pound saves a life.

   c. _____ Adopting a pet from the animal shelter can benefit both animal and owner.

   d. _____ Pound puppies and kittens are usually spayed or neutered before adoption, saving the owner veterinary fees.

Recognizing Specific Detail

One of the most difficult tasks a writer faces is providing strong, specific supporting details. If a writer provides only vague, sketchy details, the picture presented to the reader will be fuzzy and out of focus. As details become sharper and more specific, the picture becomes clear. The following exercise will give you practice in recognizing sharp, clear detail.

EXERCISE 2   RECOGNIZING SPECIFIC DETAILS

Each of the following topic sentences is supported by three details. Place a check (✔) beside the two details that are sharp and specific. Place an ✗ beside the detail that needs to be more specific. Then, in the space provided, rewrite the vague sentence to make the supporting detail more specific.

1. All day long, Nicole was haunted by the number 8.

_____ a.   At the driver's license bureau, she pulled the number 8 out of a machine marked "Take a number."

_____ b.   At lunchtime, the first potato chip she pulled out of her bag was shaped like the number 8.

_____ c.   On her way home, yet another incident occurred involving the number 8.

_____

_____

2. Rodrigo's search for an apartment was long and difficult.

_____ a.   He looked at several apartments that were not suitable in terms of his financial situation.

_____ b.   Many of the apartments he could afford were too far away from work and school.

_____ c.   Finally, he found a small, affordable attic apartment close to his work and within walking distance of the college.

_____

_____

3. For several reasons, majoring in the health sciences is a good idea.

_____ a.   An aging population ensures that health-care professionals will be in demand for decades to come.

_____ b.   A variety of fields from respiratory therapy to x-ray technology gives a student a wide range of choice.

_____ c.   A nursing shortage means that anyone with a nursing degree has it made.

_____

_____

4. The small, crowded office was messy.

_____ a.   In the corner, a trash can overflowed with paper and discarded soft-drink cans.

_____ b.   The desk was also in disarray.

_____ **c.** Papers were spread in piles across the floor and around the desk, leaving little room for walking.

_____

_____

5. Elena worried that her memory was getting worse.

_____ **a.** She forgot an important appointment last week.

_____ **b.** She was constantly losing her glasses, her keys, and her wallet.

_____ **c.** She could no longer remember the items she needed at the grocery store without making a list, and she often forgot to bring the list.

_____

_____

Using Specific Words

Sometimes, a simple change in word choice makes all the difference. You paint a clearer picture for your reader when you use specific words and phrases: *four hours of research in the library* instead of *a lot of work, Ella's Soul Food Café* instead of *a restaurant, glared* instead of *looked,* or *a map of Florida, deck of cards, and two dollars in change* instead of *things.*

Making Nouns Specific

Consider the following sentence.

✗ Richard put *a heavy item* in his trunk, then drove away from the *building.*

Different readers will put different interpretations on this sentence. What did Richard put in his trunk? What kind of building did he leave? Specific detail would serve a twofold purpose: it would clearly convey the writer's meaning, and it would capture the reader's interest. Consider the revisions below.

✔ Richard put *a bulging briefcase* in his trunk, then drove away from *the law office.*

✔ Richard put *his ex-wife's body* in his trunk, then drove away from the *small white house where they had spent so many years together.*

✔ Richard put *a case of hymnals* in his trunk, then drove away from the *Harvest Religious Bookstore.*

Notice how the detail not only provides more specific information but also helps to characterize Richard. How does your impression of him change with each example?

EXERCISE 3   USING SPECIFIC WORDS

Create a new impression of Richard by varying what he puts in the trunk and the location described in the sentence.

1. Richard put _____ in his trunk, then drove away from the

   _____.

2. Richard put _____ in his trunk, then drove away from the

   _____.

3. Richard put _____ in his trunk, then drove away from the

   _____.

4. Richard put _____ in his trunk, then drove away from the

   _____.

5. Richard put _____ in his trunk, then drove away from the

   _____.

Practice in Making Vague Nouns Specific

Look at the following list. The nouns in the left-hand column provide little information, while those in the right-hand column are specific. Notice, too, that the more specific term is often not simply a noun, but a phrase.

Vague Term	Specific Term
✗ course	✔ Introduction to Social Problems
✗ clothing	✔ man's herringbone jacket, size 42
✗ student	✔ Gloria Hollinger, first-year nursing student
✗ car	✔ 1965 Ford Mustang
✗ sandwich	✔ turkey on five-grain bread with mayonnaise

EXERCISE 4   CHOOSING SPECIFIC TERMS

From the three choices for each of the sentences below, circle the most specific choice to fill in the blank.

1. Carlos ate _____ at noon.
    a. a nutritious meal
    b. a tomato sandwich
    c. delicious food

2. When Larry took _____, he felt better.
    a. a pill
    b. two Excedrin tablets
    c. the advice of a respected physician

3. Ana said the _____ was breathtaking.
    a. spectacular view of the surrounding scenery
    b. works of some nineteenth-century poets
    c. ride on the Scream Machine

4. The vendor sold _____ from the back of a pickup truck.
    a. ripe peaches and black velvet art
    b. various wares in a wide range of colors
    c. electronic devices that may have been stolen

5. Melanie's mother said, "Would you help me _____?"
    a. complete a few simple household chores
    b. chop these onions
    c. do some errands

6. The little girl sat beside her mother in the veterinarian's waiting room, carefully holding _____.
    a. her animal companion
    b. a scrawny black kitten
    c. a cute, cuddly pet

7. On the refrigerator were _____.
    a. a child's drawing of a house, a grocery list, and a dentist's appointment card, held in place by colorful magnets
    b. photographs, papers, children's art, and reminders
    c. twelve magnets, along with the usual odds and ends that tend to accumulate under refrigerator magnets

8. Gerald's parents thought Kim was weird because _____.
    a. her appearance was unusual
    b. she had a pierced tongue and two-tone hair
    c. she did not look the way they thought a normal teenager should look
9. Because Harold did not believe in banks, he kept his money _____.
    a. in a place he thought was safe
    b. hidden away where no one who might want to steal it could find it
    c. in a waterproof plastic pouch buried under a rock
10. Pat believes she was straightforward and open, but other people saw her as

    _____.

    a. rude and tactless
    b. something else
    c. a person with an attitude that was often perceived negatively by those who had to be around her

EXERCISE 5   CHOOSING SPECIFIC TERMS

Three possible replacements follow each general term. One of the possible replacements is vague, while the other two are specific and thus would be acceptable substitutes. Circle the two specific terms in each of the following items.

1. tool
    a. hammer
    b. instrument
    c. spatula
2. test
    a. examination
    b. SAT
    c. math final
3. restaurant
    a. Vernon's Veggie Bar
    b. a hot dog stand on the corner
    c. an eatery
4. shoes
    a. sandals
    b. loafers
    c. footwear

5. noise
   a. sound
   b. earsplitting rock music
   c. click
6. pet
   a. animal companion
   b. Fluffy
   c. white hamster
7. home
   a. doublewide mobile home
   b. living space
   c. mansion
8. book
   a. telephone directory
   b. *War and Peace*
   c. published volume
9. ice cream
   a. delicious dessert
   b. pint of Rocky Road
   c. Ben and Jerry's Cherry Garcia
10. illness
    a. mumps
    b. disease
    c. food poisoning

Making Pronouns Specific

"I wanted to register today, but they wouldn't let me."

"Everybody says Ms. Torres is a tough teacher."

"The candidate says he will not increase taxes, but nobody believes him."

Sentences like this are common in conversation and usually go unchallenged. In writing, though, precision is necessary. Readers usually do not have access to the writers of the books, stories, and essays they read, and so they cannot ask questions like "Who are *they?*" or "What do you mean by *everybody?*" Look at the revised versions of the statements you just read:

I wanted to register today, but the clerks in the Registrar's Office wouldn't let me.

Two of the students in my sociology class say Ms. Torres is a tough teacher.

The candidate says he will not increase taxes, but few voters believe him.

Forcing yourself to be more specific may also force you to be more accurate. The "everybody" who tells you to enroll in a certain teacher's class may turn out to be two fellow students. And if you truly wanted to prove that "nobody" believes what a candidate says, you'd have to ask every voter—an impossible task.

EXERCISE 6   REPLACING VAGUE PRONOUNS

Replace the italicized pronouns with more specific expressions.

1. *Things* were only getting worse, so Curtis decided to move out of his parents' house.

    _____

2. Sheila followed several leads from the help wanted ads and attended an interview arranged by her school's career counselor, hoping to find *something* before graduation.

    _____

3. Dr. Madison did a brain scan on the patient but didn't find *anything*.

    _____

4. My trash container sat by the curb all day, but *they* didn't pick it up.

    _____

5. The family walked into the dining room where the table was set for Thanksgiving. *Everything* looked delicious.

    _____

Making Verbs Specific

Verbs bring life and movement to writing. Vague, poorly chosen verbs add nothing to your writing, or worse yet, drag it down. Well-chosen verbs leap off the page, adding power and energy to your writing.

Choosing effective verbs means rejecting the easy choice and looking for powerful verbs that express your meaning exactly.

A *thesaurus,* or dictionary of synonyms, helps you choose the best word for the situation. But shades of meaning vary, so don't just choose a synonym at random. If you are not sure of a word's exact meaning, check your dictionary.

Examples

✗   Exhausted after studying for the exam, I *went* to bed at midnight.

✔   Exhausted after studying for the exam, I *stumbled* to bed at midnight.

✗   At 3:00 P.M. on the last day of school, the doors *were opened* and students *came* from the building, yelling and shouting.

✔   At 3:00 P.M. on the last day of school, the doors *burst* open and students *streamed* from the building, yelling and shouting.

EXERCISE 7   USING SPECIFIC VERBS

Cross out the italicized verb in each sentence and replace it with a verb that more effectively conveys the sense of the sentence.

1.   Angrily, Beatrice *retrieved* the envelope from the table.

_____

2.   Smoothly, the sailboat *moved* across the water.

_____

3.   When the cable snapped, the elevator *descended* fifteen stories.

_____

4.   Albright's glove *contacted* his opponent's jaw, sending the man reeling toward the edge of the ring.

_____

5.   A small bird *was* on the highest branch of the cherry tree.

_____

6.   The garbage truck *moved* down the street, spewing noxious fumes.

_____

7.   The crowd *reacted* as fireworks appeared in the inky night sky.

_____

8. When asked if he wanted to speak before he was sentenced, the defendant *commented*, "Please believe me! I do not know who committed this horrible crime, but I swear that I am innocent."

    _____

9. Five thousand fans *filled* the small concert hall, screaming and shouting their approval.

    _____

10. The angry customer said that a loose shopping cart had *harmed* her new car.

    _____

EXERCISE 8   MAKING VERBS SPECIFIC

Cross out the italicized verb in each sentence and replace it with a verb that more effectively conveys the sense of the sentence.

1. The ball seemed to take flight, *going* over the outfield and into the stands.

    _____

2. The squirrel grabbed the acorn and quickly *went* up the tree trunk.

    _____

3. The roller coaster made a slow ascent, then *moved* toward the ground as its passengers screamed delightedly.

    _____

4. Suddenly, Tom *came* into the room, yelling, "Quick! Somebody call an ambulance!"

    _____

5. As Andrea flipped the light switch, dozens of cockroaches *moved* across the wall and into the cracks near the baseboard.

    _____

6. Lightning *was seen* and thunder rolled.

    _____

7. The basketball *went* into the street just as a garbage truck rattled around the corner.

    _____

8. As he stormed out of his boss's office, Phil *commented*, "And you know what you can do with your lousy job!"

    _____

9. Annoyed at the interruption from a young fan, the athlete hastily *signed* his name on the program and abruptly turned away.

    _____

10. When the phone rang at 3:00 A.M., Channing sleepily *reached* for the receiver.

    _____

Making Sentences Specific

Sentences with specific language are sentences with power. As you write, strive for forceful verbs and vivid phrases. As you revise, look for opportunities to make vague language more specific. Look at the following examples to see how much stronger a sentence becomes when specific words replace vague words.

Examples

Vague Word Choice

✗ Eager shoppers *entered the toy store* when the *popular toy* came in.

Specific Word Choice

✔ Eager shoppers *mobbed Toy World* when the *Avengers of Doom action figures* came in.

Vague Word Choice

✗ When my mother comes to visit, she brings *all kinds of stuff* with her.

Specific Word Choice

✔ When my mother comes to visit, she brings *four suitcases, a shopping bag filled with homemade goodies, and her miniature poodle, Pierre.*

Vague Word Choice

✗ When Martin looked in his refrigerator, he found *there was not much to eat.*

Specific Word Choice

✔ When Martin looked in his refrigerator, he found *only a half-empty jar of pickles and the two-week-old remains of a takeout dinner from Junior's Barbecue.*

Vague Word Choice

✗ Sylvester could not concentrate on the test. *The noise around him* grated on his nerves.

Specific Word Choice

✔ Sylvester could not concentrate on the test. *The popping of gum in the back of the room, a burst of laughter from outside the building, and even the breathing of the student beside him* grated on his nerves.

EXERCISE 9   MAKING SENTENCES SPECIFIC

Rewrite the sentences so that they contain more specific detail. Feel free to use more than one sentence if you wish.

1. The newscaster reported that *a terrible thing* had happened in *a large city.*

    _____

2. The clock was shaped like *an animal* and painted *in bright colors.*

    _____

3. Lynn put a package from *a store* in the back seat because her trunk had *something* in it.

    _____

4. On their way to *their destination,* Asha and her husband stopped at *a little place by the roadside.*

    _____

5. *Bad weather* kept Mark from *doing what he had planned.*

    _____

6. When Percy saw *what had happened to his car* he *reacted strongly.*

    _____

7. *A noise* startled the *animal.*

    _____

8. The mailbox held *several unimportant pieces of mail* and *one important piece of mail.*

    _____

9. On our street, *they* have organized a neighborhood watch because of *various crimes that have taken place.*

    _____

10. *In certain situations,* Jack gets *a bad feeling.*

    _____

EXERCISE 10   MAKING SENTENCES SPECIFC

Rewrite the following paragraph, replacing the underlined vague terms with specific details.

When I decided to clean out the small storage closet in our garage, I was amazed at how much junk it contained. First, I cleared and sorted items I had meant to recycle later. Then, I tackled a pile of various garden tools that were dirty. After dealing with the gardening tools, I worked on the shelves. The top shelf was filled with items I had used when I painted the interior of the house last spring. I threw some stuff into a trash bag and kept the rest. Beneath the assorted junk I was clearing away, the middle shelf contained a surprise. A sizeable insect suddenly came out, startling me into dropping and breaking something fragile. When I had swept away what had broken, I rearranged the tools and things on the bottom shelf. Then I threw away one broken item and three empty containers. When I was finally through, I wondered how one small storage closet could have contained so much junk.

_____

_____

_____

_____

_____

_____

_____

_____

_____

_____

_____

_____

_____

_____

_____

EXERCISE 11   ANALYZING PARAGRAPHS FOR SUPPORT

One of the following paragraphs is well supported with specific details and examples, while the other is poorly supported with vague, general sentences. Read each paragraph, then answer the questions at the end of the exercise.

Paragraph A

In my experience, college professors are the worst-dressed people in the world. If there were an award for "worst-dressed professor," my history professor, Dr. Bloom, would be a leading candidate. He is the ultimate fashion victim. When I saw him walk into the classroom on the first day, I could not believe the clothes he was wearing. I thought that maybe he had just been in a hurry that morning, but on the second day of class, his clothing was just as bad. I cannot imagine where he finds that awful clothing. Then there is Professor Hunter, who teaches art. She wears the strangest clothes, even for an art teacher, who might be expected to have unusual taste. It is as if she is living in a different decade. It's a sure thing she hasn't looked at a fashion magazine lately. But I think my personal choice for the worst-dressed professor award is Mr. Nelson, my English teacher. Like clockwork, the same loud pants, jackets, and shirts appear in strict rotation, each for a different day of the week. When I go into his classroom, I make sure I sit in the back. I am not sure I could stand all those bright colors if I were sitting in the front row. I have great respect for my professors' knowledge, but most of them deserve an "F" in fashion.

Paragraph B

In my experience, college professors are the worst-dressed people in the world. If there were an award for "worst-dressed professor," my history professor, Dr. Bloom, would be a leading candidate. When I saw him walk into the classroom on the first day in a green checked shirt, red bow tie and shapeless brown sweater vest, I thought perhaps he was just having a bad day. But each day in Dr. Bloom's class is a parade of mismatched rag-bag fashions: rumpled jackets, baggy pants, and shirts in checks, plaids, and polka dots. Professor Hunter, who teaches art, looks like a folk singer from the seventies with her straight hair and ankle-length dresses. She likes delicate rainbow colors and long strands of beads, an odd combination with her heavy white athletic shoes. But I think my personal choice for the worst-dressed professor award is Mr. Nelson, my English teacher, whose taste is not just bad, but annoyingly predictable. On Mondays, he wears a yellow and green checked polyester jacket with lime-green pants. On Tuesday, it's a polyester jacket in robin's-egg blue with a pair of mustard-colored pants. The polyester parade continues through Friday, when he wakes the class up with a pair of bright red pants worn with a pink shirt. I have great respect for my professors' knowledge, but most of them deserve an "F" in fashion.

■ Questions

Fill in the blanks of each question below.

1. Paragraph _____ is less specific.
2. Paragraph _____ is more specific. Three specific details from the paragraph are _____, _____
   _____, and _____.

Progressive Writing Assignment

Progressive Writing Assignment: Providing Supporting Details and Examples

If your instructor has assigned the Progressive Writing Assignment, you have already completed your prewriting and your topic sentence. In this chapter, you will provide support for your paragraph.

Topics and Tips for Providing Supporting Details and Examples

The Topics

Topic 1: Discuss the results of taking a specific piece of advice from a friend or family member.

Topic 2: Discuss your decision to attend college.

Topic 3: Discuss your greatest fear.

Topic 4: Discuss types of stress experienced by college students.

Tips for Providing Supporting Details and Examples

- Make sure that your language is specific. Have you used words that create pictures by appealing to the reader's sense of sight, hearing, touch, taste and smell? The following sentences illustrate how specific language might be used to support Topic 3, "Discuss your greatest fear."

  ✔ If I were homeless, I would have no shelter from the hot sun or the cold rain. On chilly nights, I would lie awake, listening to my stomach growl and feeling the damp chill creep into my bones.

- Check to see that you have supported your paragraphs with specific examples. If you are writing on Topic 1, "Discuss the results of taking a specific piece of advice from a friend or family member," an example might be a *specific example* that describes what happened on a particular occasion.

  ✔ Thinking of my father's advice, I walked right into my boss's office and said, "Ms. Carmichael, the mix-up with the order yesterday was my fault." She looked at me and said, "Yes, I know that, but I really appreciate hearing it from you."

5

Writing Paragraphs:
Unity and Coherence

Not the Real Thing

Modern color copiers have made the counterfeiting of money more widespread. Experts say there are ways to tell if the bill you are holding is counterfeit. Most people say they have too many of the kind of bill they have to pay and not enough of the kind they can spend. Many things can be faked--art, for instance. Just putting a few splashes of paint on a canvas doesn't make it a Picasso. Paint is not just a way to make a house look good; it also protects the surface against weather. It's always a good idea to make sure that you have the real thing--not an imitation.

When you look at the sentences in the box above, you may notice that although they are written in paragraph form, they do not seem to connect with one another. They have no unity because each sentence discusses a different idea. They have no coherence because the sentences do not flow logically into one another. You may suspect, in fact, that the "paragraph" you are reading is not the real thing. A genuine, effective paragraph has four characteristics: direction, unity, coherence, and support.

Characteristics of an Effective Paragraph

Review the characteristics of an effective paragraph below. You have already learned how to give your paragraph direction with an effective topic sentence and how to support that topic sentence with details and examples. This chapter looks at the two final characteristics of an effective paragraph, unity and coherence.

1. **Direction** means that the paragraph has a strong topic sentence that states the main idea and sets the course that the paragraph will follow.
2. **Support** means that the paragraph contains specific and detailed discussion of the idea stated in the topic sentence.
3. **Unity** means that the paragraph makes one main point and sticks to that point.
4. **Coherence** means that the ideas in the paragraph are logically connected and easy to follow.

Unity: Sticking to the Point

Every topic sentence offers a promise of **unity** to the reader, a promise that you will discuss the point advanced in that sentence and no other. If your topic sentence is "My friend Ellen is the messiest person I have ever known," then you will discuss the specific ways in which she is messy. You will not mention the few times you have known her to be neat; you will not discuss the other qualities that make her so good to have as a friend. You will discuss only the piles of clothes stacked on every piece of furniture in her bedroom, the assortment of books, bills, and banana peels on her desk, and the mounds of fast-food wrappers in the back seat of her car. Your paragraph will have unity because it sticks to its topic and to the specific point you make about that topic.

EXERCISE 1   FINDING PROBLEMS IN UNITY

A list of possible supporting points follows each of the topic sentences in the exercise. In each group, circle the letter of the point that interferes with the unity of the paragraph.

1. Topic sentence: Some restaurant customers make trivial complaints in the hope of getting a free meal.

a. Some customers gripe when service is a bit slow.

b. Many complain if they have to make a trip to the emergency room because of food poisoning.

c. Other customers grumble if the coffee is not piping hot or the iced tea is not cold enough.

2. Topic sentence: Fear of serious injury makes many parents hesitate to encourage their children to play football.

a. Many parents fear that the child may break a bone in a football game.

b. They fear their child might sustain head injuries during a game.

c. Some parents fear their child will start to do poorly in academics.

3. Topic sentence: One way that I try to keep in shape is through a proper diet.

a. I get plenty of exercise.

b. I eat very few sweets or sugary treats.

c. I stay away from too many fats.

4. Topic sentence: If I had to give up one modern convenience, I would get rid of my telephone.

a. Getting rid of my phone would eliminate interruptions from salespeople.

b. My telephone is a vital link to emergency services.

c. Without a phone, I would waste less time chatting.

5. Topic sentence: My neighbor's yard is an eyesore.

a. In his front yard, he has an old Chevrolet up on blocks.

b. At the side of his house is a beautiful old oak tree.

c. Because he never mows his lawn, tall grass and weeds surround his house.

EXERCISE 2   FINDING PROBLEMS IN UNITY

A list of possible supporting points follows each of the topic sentences below. In each group, circle the letter of the point that interferes with the unity of the paragraph.

1. Topic sentence: Some crimes go unreported because crime victims believe they are not worth reporting.

a. petty theft

b. kidnapping

c. graffiti

2. Topic sentence: Fear that they will do poorly in the classroom makes many adults hesitant to return to school.

a. anxiety about taking tests

b. fear of not understanding the ideas presented

c. fear that their families will not accept their decision to return to school

3. Topic sentence: One way that I try to keep in shape is through exercise.
   a. lift weights
   b. eat nutritious foods
   c. attend aerobics classes

4. Topic sentence: Writing on a computer has helped me improve my papers.
   a. modern computer lab
   b. ease of revising on computer
   c. spelling check

5. Topic sentence: My neighbor's dog is an annoyance.
   a. "Heinz 57" mutt
   b. barks at night
   c. jumps fence and digs up my flowers

Reinforcing Unity: The Summary Sentence

One way to reinforce paragraph unity is to end the paragraph with a **summary sentence** that echoes the topic sentence. The summary sentence does not repeat the topic sentence; rather, it reinforces it. If the function of a topic sentence is to tell the reader where the paragraph is going, the function of a summary sentence is to tell where the paragraph has been, thus reinforcing the unity of the paragraph. A summary sentence also signals the end of the paragraph and provides a sense of closure.

Example

Topic Sentence

✔ The most valuable lesson I have learned from my parents is to be independent.

Summary Sentence

✔ I will always be grateful that my parents taught me to rely on myself and not on others.

Example

Topic Sentence

✔ A few minor changes could make our campus more welcoming to students with disabilities.

Summary Sentence

✔ These easy and inexpensive changes would ensure that all students feel safe and welcome on our campus.

EXERCISE 3   ANALYZING PARAGRAPH UNITY

In each of the following paragraphs, underline the topic and double-underline the specific point that is made about that topic. Then find the two sentences that interfere with the unity of the paragraph. If you have trouble, go back and look at the topic sentence to see the specific point that is made about the topic. Then read again to see which sentences do not support that specific point. Finally, underline the summary sentence of each paragraph.

Paragraph 1

^{1}I enjoy spring because it is a season when nature comes alive. ^{2}Each tree sports a halo of tiny, delicate leaf buds of the palest green. ^{3}Soon the leaves mature and unfurl, trumpeting a brilliant green message to the world. ^{4}Flowers nudge their way through a new growth of grass, pushing up to find the sun. ^{5}Then they open into a rainbow of springtime colors. ^{6}Each evening, a symphony of sound serenades the listener from shallow ponds where frogs call solemn invitations to prospective mates. ^{7}Toward morning, as the frogs subside, birds begin their racket, their chatter reverberating from tree to tree. ^{8}In the ballparks, the crack of the bat and the umpire's cry of "Yer out!" echo again as baseball season opens. ^{9}Lights blaze, the stands fill, and the odors of hotdogs, popcorn, and beer blend on the evening breeze. ^{10}It is spring, and nature awakens the world to new possibilities.

Numbers of the sentences that interfere with the unity of the paragraph:___, ___

Paragraph 2

^{1}The graduation ceremony at our college is dignified but dull. ^{2}In a large hall filled with well-dressed parents, relatives, and friends of the graduates, faculty and students file in, dressed in hot, heavy academic robes. ^{3}The ceremony follows a prescribed routine. ^{4}First, prospective graduates sing the alma mater, desperately searching their programs for the unfamiliar words. ^{5}The dean of the college, clad in a flowing robe, welcomes the assembled crowd with appropriate decorum. ^{6}The graduation speaker, usually a state legislator or

a distinguished graduate, delivers a lengthy
discourse as members of the audience yawn, read
their programs, or pretend to listen. [7]Then, the
anticipated moment arrives and the graduates begin
to stir excitedly, waving at parents, who quickly
ready cameras and video equipment. [8]In spite of the
dean's plea to hold applause until all diplomas
have been distributed, whoops and cheers ring out
from the audience as eager graduates file across
the stage. [9]Finally, the majestic notes of "Pomp and
Circumstance" rise in the air and the graduates
march out, heads high with the dignity of their
newly conferred degrees. [10]The ceremony, with its
air of dull formality, is over for another year.

Numbers of the sentences that interfere with the unity of the paragraph: ___ , ___

EXERCISE 4   ANALYZING PARAGRAPH UNITY

In each of the following paragraphs, underline the topic and double-underline
the specific point that is made about that topic. Then find the two sentences that
hurt the unity of the paragraph. If you have trouble, go back and look at the topic
sentence to see the specific point that is made about the topic. Then read again to
see which sentences do not support that specific point. Finally, underline the
summary sentence of each paragraph.

Paragraph 1

[1]I enjoy autumn because it is nature's season of
color and movement. [2]The temperature falls and the
wind picks up, sweeping across country roads and
city streets and serving notice that nature's show
is about to begin. [3]The summer green of the trees
gives way to a fall tapestry of red, orange, gold,
and brown. [4]People flock to the mountains to see
the autumn splendor before the winter comes.
[5]Many people, however, have already taken a summer
vacation at the beach before the children head back
to school. [6]Finally, as the grasses turn yellow and
fields shade into brown, the leaves begin to fall.
[7]They float to the ground, where the wind tosses
them, forming a multicolored carpet that crunches
underfoot as the leaves turn brown. [8]Almost as fast
as parents can rake the leaves into big piles,

children are ready to leap into the middle of them and scatter them into a colorful carpet once again. ^{9}Fall is also a season for Halloween, when children go door to door in scary costumes to collect treats. ^{10}In fall, nature puts on a spectacular show before the bleakness of winter comes on.

Numbers of the sentences that hurt the unity of the paragraph: _____, _____

Paragraph 2

^{1}Last night, the women's softball game at our college was attended by a small but enthusiastic group of supporters. ^{2}Below me, in the first row of the bleachers, two small boys yelled loudly and waved signs saying "Go, Mom!" whenever their mother came up to bat. ^{3}Four young men sitting together to my left shouted encouraging comments to the players and stood and clapped whenever the team scored. ^{4}More interested in gossip than in softball, three women sitting to the far left in the stands ignored the game completely. ^{5}When Number 34 came up to bat, a woman sitting in a wheelchair beside the bleachers turned to bystanders and said proudly, "That's my daughter." ^{6}A cluster of students seated near the field clapped rhythmically and cheered, "Go, team, go!" ^{7}It is a shame that our men's athletic teams have cheerleaders, but our women's teams do not. ^{8}Entering the ninth inning, our team was winning by five runs, but the fans stayed and cheered as enthusiastically as if the score were tied. ^{9}As the team left the field, the enthusiastic cheers of the small crowd told the players that their winning efforts had been appreciated.

Numbers of the sentences that hurt the unity of the paragraph: _____, _____

Coherence: Holding the Paragraph Together

If your writing does not have **coherence**, then the sentences in your paragraph are like a pile of loose bricks: there is little connection between them. Coherence is the mortar you use to make your paragraph a brick wall, with solid and strong connections between ideas. To achieve coherence, first make sure your ideas are logically related and well thought out. Then use **coherence tools** to cement the connections between those ideas in the most effective way possible. Two common and easy-to-use coherence tools are *transitional expressions* and *repetition*.

Transitional Expressions

As a writer, you must not only express an idea clearly, you must keep your reader oriented in time and space and aware of relationships between ideas. *Transitional expressions* help you juggle these multiple tasks without detracting from the ideas you express. Ideally, these words and phrases do their job in the background, as guideposts that show the path of your logic and the movement of your ideas through time and space. Below is a list of transitional words and expressions, organized by their function within the sentence.

Some Common Transitional Words and Expressions

---

* Transitions of Time

after	during	later	now	suddenly	when
as	first	meanwhile	often	temporarily	while
before	immediately	next	previously	then	yet

---

* Transitions of Space

above	beside	down	next to	toward
around	between	in	on	under
behind	by	near	over	

---

* Transitions of Addition

also	finally	furthermore	in addition	next
another	first			

---

* *Transitions of Importance*

as important	essential	major	primary
equally important	just as important	most important	significant

---

* *Transitions of Contrast*

although	even though	in contrast	instead	on the other hand
but	however	in spite of	nevertheless	yet

---

* *Transitions of Cause and Effect*

a consequence of	because	since	therefore	for
as a result	consequently	so	thus	

---

* *Transitions of Illustration or Example*

for example	for instance	including	such as

EXERCISE 5   USING TRANSITIONAL EXPRESSIONS

In the following paragraph, provide the indicated type of transition in each blank.

¹Nothing had gone right lately, so _____ (time signal) the doorbell rang, Sam had a feeling it was not the Prize Patrol with a million-dollar check. ²_____ (contrast signal), he did not expect quite as much trouble as he got. ³Two police officers were standing _____ (space signal) his porch. ⁴"Mr. Williams, we have information that your dog may have bitten a child who lives _____ (space signal) the street," said the tall officer. "It couldn't

have been Killer," said Sam, [5]"_____ (cause-effect signal) he never goes outside except on a leash." [6]"Please bring the dog out _____ (time signal)," said the officer. "I'm afraid we'll have to take him to the pound." Sam knew that his dog had not bitten anyone, [7]_____ (contrast signal) he saw no alternative but to hand over his dog. Would he ever see Killer again? [8]_____ (time signal) he brought Killer out on a leash, the officers had their hands near their guns, as if fearful of being attacked. [9]_____ (contrast signal), when they saw Killer, the officers began to laugh. "That's not the dog we're looking for," said the tall officer, bending to pet the tiny, trembling Chihuahua on the head. "We are looking for a large, fierce dog." [10]_____ (time signal), to Sam's relief, the two officers apologized for bothering him and left.

1. _____   6. _____

2. _____   7. _____

3. _____   8. _____

4. _____   9. _____

5. _____   10. _____

EXERCISE 6 USING TRANSITIONAL EXPRESSIONS

In the following paragraph, provide the indicated type of transition in each blank.

[1]_____ (time) the Fresh-Food Supermart was robbed, Shawna had the bad luck to be the only cashier on duty. The robber came in about 7:00 A.M., [2]_____ (time) the store opened. She noticed him right away [3]_____ (cause-effect) his ball cap was pulled low over his eyes and he wore a jacket [4]_____ (contrast) the morning was warm. He loitered for a while [5]_____ (space) the door; [6]_____ (time) he walked up to her register. She must have suspected him [7]_____ (cause-effect) she suddenly remembered

Mr. Monroe, the store manager, saying: "If you are ever robbed, remember that your life is worth more than whatever is in that cash drawer. Stay cool and hand over the money." [8]_____ (time) the robber leaned [9]_____ (space) her and mumbled, "I have a gun. Put the money in a bag." Remembering Mr. Monroe's words, Shawna quickly withdrew the money from the register. [10]_____ (time) she reached for a bag, she was surprised at the words that automatically fell from her lips: "Paper or plastic?" Much [11]_____ (time) Mr. Monroe teased that not only had she remembered his instructions, she had [12]_____ (addition) remembered to offer her unwelcome "customer" a choice.

1. _____   7. _____

2. _____   8. _____

3. _____   9. _____

4. _____   10. _____

5. _____   11. _____

6. _____   12. _____

Using Transitions Effectively

Used skillfully, transitional expressions bring coherence to your writing, but moderation is the key. Using these words unnecessarily or artificially is worse than not using them at all.

Hints for Using Transitional Expressions

- Less is more. Skillfully weaving a few transitional expressions into a paragraph is better than forcing in as many as possible.

- For variety, place transitions somewhere other than the beginning of a sentence. Instead of "However, Arturo refused to place the pink plastic flamingo on his lawn," try "Arturo, however, refused to place the pink plastic flamingo on his lawn."

- Examples are sometimes more effective when they are not preceded by *for example* or *for instance*. If you feel uncomfortable putting an example in without announcement, try using *for example* in your rough draft and editing it out later.

* When you feel that a particular example needs to be announced, try placing the announcement somewhere other than at the beginning of a sentence. Instead of, "For instance, pasta is filling and low in calories," try "Pasta, for instance, is filling and low in calories."

EXERCISE 7   ANALYZING USE OF TRANSITIONS

Look at the two paragraphs that follow. Underline the transitional expressions in each. In which paragraph are transitional expressions used more skillfully? Can you pinpoint some of the reasons?

Paragraph 1

The third week of a student's first year in college is often a dangerous one. Like the "seven-year itch" that supposedly makes people give up on romantic relationships, the "three-week shock syndrome" sometimes signals the end of a student's academic career. After the excitement of the first week or two of classes begins to wear off, reality starts to set in. There is more than just the excitement of meeting new people and buying textbooks in a well-stocked bookstore. Those books, with their crisp pages and new smell, must be opened and read, marked and highlighted. The smiling professors who leaned on their lecterns and cracked jokes on the first day of class have turned into serious-faced people who talk faster than their students can write and whose lectures are sometimes boring. Worst of all is the work. Reading assignments, writing assignments, library assignments, and computer lab assignments pile up, waiting to be completed. Who has time to remember it all, much less do it all? Students who make it past the third week of classes usually find that they can adjust, that they can keep up. But some, faced with the shock that college means work, never stay long enough to find out whether they can succeed or not.

Paragraph 2

First of all, the third week of a student's first
year in college is often a dangerous one. For
example, the "seven-year itch" supposedly makes
people give up on romantic relationships, and the
"three-week shock syndrome" often signals the end
of a student's academic career. In addition, the
excitement of the first week or two of classes
begins to wear off, and reality starts to set in.
More importantly, there is more than just the
excitement of meeting new people and buying
textbooks in a well-stocked bookstore. In contrast,
those books, with their crisp pages and new smell,
must be opened and read, marked and highlighted.
Furthermore, the smiling professors who leaned on
their lecterns and cracked jokes on the first day
of class have turned into serious-faced people who
talk faster than their students can write and whose
lectures are sometimes boring. Just as important,
worst of all is the work. To enumerate, there are
reading assignments, writing assignments, library
assignments, and computer lab assignments. Further,
who has time to remember it all, much less do it
all? Nevertheless, students who make it past the
third week of classes usually find that they can
adjust, that they can keep up. In conclusion, some,
faced with the shock that college means work, never
stay long enough to find out whether they can
succeed or not.

The paragraph in which transitions are used more successfully is paragraph ____.

Some reasons are _____

_____

_____

EXERCISE 8   ANALYZING USE OF TRANSITIONS

Look at the two paragraphs that follow. Underline the transitional expressions in
each. In which paragraph are transitional expressions used more skillfully? Can
you pinpoint some of the reasons?

Paragraph 1

One characteristic of successful students is that they know how to study. They know, for instance, that the time to begin studying is not the night before the test but much earlier. The first time they read a section of the textbook, successful students begin their study. They highlight or underline important sections and jot down key terms. When taking notes in class, they use a similar technique, jotting down the most important ideas and later transcribing their notes into a format that will be easy to study. Unsuccessful students, on the other hand, often postpone highlighting the text and organizing their notes until the night before the test, when time is short. Successful study, then, partly depends on beginning well before the date of the test.

Paragraph 2

First, successful students know how to study. First of all, they know that the time to begin studying is not the night before the test but much earlier. For example, successful students usually begin their study the first time they read a section of the textbook. In addition, they highlight or underline important sections and jot down key terms. Next, when taking notes in class, they jot down the most important ideas. Furthermore, they transcribe their notes into a format that will be easy to study from later. However, unsuccessful students postpone highlighting the text and organizing their notes until the night before the test. Therefore, successful study partly depends on beginning well before the date of the test.

The paragraph in which transitions are used more successfully is paragraph ____.

Some reasons are _____

_____

_____

Repetition

Repetition of Key Words and Phrases

Often, repetition is seen as a negative quality in writing. However, *repetition of key words and phrases* is a method of tying your ideas together and achieving coherence. While no one would advise endless hammering of unimportant words or ideas, repetition of key words and ideas helps to bring your point home strongly.

EXERCISE 9   EXAMINING REPETITION OF IMPORTANT TERMS

The following paragraph is about business telephone manners. Underline the repetitions of the key words *business, telephone* (or *phone*), and *manners.*

At a time when voice mail, answering machines, and computerized telephone answering systems have all but replaced the business telephone call, good telephone manners remain essential. Because the caller on the other end of the phone cannot read lips or minds, it is important for anyone who answers a business telephone to speak clearly, giving his name and the name of the department or company. If it is necessary to ask the caller to hold, it is never good manners to say "Hold, please" and leave the person wondering when, if ever, the phone will be picked up again. Good telephone manners require an explanation, such as "Ms. Smith, our manager, will be happy to help you with that. Would you mind holding for a minute while I get her?" Above all, business telephone manners require giving the caller the idea that her business is appreciated and that the phone call has been a pleasure, not a chore. For example, if the caller says, "Thank you," then the proper reply is not "Yeah, right, no problem." A reply such as "Thank you, Ms. Crabtree. We appreciate your business," demonstrates good telephone manners and excellent business sense. In an impersonal age, adding a personal touch to business telephone calls is not just good manners. It's good business.

Repetition through Pronouns

Pronouns aid coherence by allowing you to refer to someone or something without tedious repetition. Below is a partial list of pronouns often used to substitute for nouns. (For more information about using pronouns, see Chapters 18 and 19.)

Common Pronouns

Subject pronouns:	I, we, you, he, she, it, they, who
Object pronouns:	me, us, you, him, her, it, them, whom
Possessive pronouns:	my, mine, our, ours, your, yours, his, her, hers, its, their, theirs, whose
Indefinite pronouns:	one, anyone, everyone, nobody, some, somebody

In the following sentences, it's easy to see how much more smoothly the words seem to flow when pronouns link sentences and ideas together.

Example

✗ *The dog* woke up, stretched out *the dog's* legs and yawned hugely. Then, as if realizing that *the dog* was supposed to be guarding *the dog's* yard, *the dog* shambled over to the gate and gave a halfhearted bark.

Revision

✔ *The dog* woke up, stretched out *his* legs and yawned hugely. Then, as if realizing that *he* was supposed to be guarding *his* yard, *he* shambled over to the gate and gave a halfhearted bark.

EXERCISE 10   USING PRONOUNS TO AID COHERENCE

Use pronouns to replace the underlined words. Choose from the list of common pronouns above or use any appropriate pronoun.

1. Whenever Lindsay left Lindsay's new bicycle in the driveway, her mother worried that Lindsay's new bicycle would be stolen.

   _____   _____

2. When Michael tried to hand the toll booth attendant a dollar, the wind whipped the dollar out of his hand and sent the dollar sailing into the oncoming lanes of traffic.

   _____   _____

3. When personal computers first came out, Mr. Willett said that personal computers were just another fad, but now he has decided that he needs a personal computer.

   _____   _____

4. Because the pizza arrived cold and late, the delivery person did not charge us for the pizza. We decided that a cold, free pizza tasted even better than a hot, fifteen-dollar pizza.

   _____   _____

5. Timothy looked at the huge parking lot and wondered how he would ever find Timothy's car. He walked down aisle after aisle before he found Timothy's car.

   _____   _____

Progressive Writing Assignment

Progressive Writing Assignment: Unity and Coherence

If your instructor has assigned the Progressive Writing Assignment, you have already completed your prewriting, a topic sentence, and supporting details. In this chapter, you will make sure your paragraph has unity and coherence.

Topics and Tips

The Topics

Topic 1: Discuss the results of taking a specific piece of advice from a friend or family member.

Topic 2: Discuss your decision to attend college.

Topic 3: Discuss your greatest fear.

Topic 4: Discuss types of stress experienced by college students.

Tips for Unity and Coherence

Staying on Track: Tips for Unity

- Check each paragraph to make sure that every sentence supports the topic sentence.
- Include a summary sentence at the end of the paragraph to reinforce the topic sentence.
  - ✔ No matter what else they learn on campus, most college students also learn to live with stress.
  - ✔ Becoming a nurse will be the fulfillment of a lifelong dream and the beginning of a long and rewarding career.

Transitions: Tips for Coherence

- Read your paragraph aloud to make sure it flows logically.
- Check to make sure transitions between supporting ideas are smooth and that transitional expressions are used where needed.
  - ✔ Academic stress *also* affects most college students.
  - ✔ *However,* I have found ways of coping with my fear of public speaking.

6

Revising, Proofreading, and Formatting

~~making changes~~	*revising*
~~proffreading~~	*proofreading*
~~fORmatTing~~	*formatting*

To many writers, revising, proofreading, and formatting are the Rodney Dangerfield of the writing process: they get no respect. But these final steps in the writing process help you present your ideas in the best possible way. Revising helps you capture your ideas more clearly and accurately, and proofreading and formatting help give them the polish they need before they are ready for an audience.

Revising

If you have ever watched your golden ideas clatter onto the page like a load of rough gravel, you understand the need for revision. **Revising** helps you do justice to your ideas, to give them some of their original polish.

There are also more practical reasons for revision, reasons that have their roots in the difference between writing and conversation. Conversation is constantly under revision. When your listener says, "What do you mean?" and you explain, you are revising. When your listener disagrees and you reinforce your argument or concede a point, you are revising. In a conversation, revision is a response to the listener. But writing does not offer the same opportunity for response. Your reader cannot ask questions. So you have to *anticipate* a reader's objections and meet them before they arise. That means that you need to spot possible misunderstandings and clarify them before the reader sees the finished work. Revising is a process of stepping back and looking at your work with the eyes of a reader.

The word *revise* combines the Latin root meaning *to see* with the prefix meaning *again*. In its most literal sense, *to revise* means *to see again*. "Seeing again" is the essence of good revision. The difficult part is distancing yourself far enough from the work to see it with new eyes. When the work is fresh from your pen or word processor, you often see what you *meant* to say rather than what is actually on the page.

To see your work again, you need to create a space, a mental distance, between yourself and the work. Time is your best ally. Lay the writing aside for at least a twenty-four-hour period. When you return to it, words that aren't precise, sentences that aren't clear, and explanations that don't explain enough are easier to spot.

If you do not have twenty-four hours to lay the work aside, it may help to have someone else look at it. Ask your reader to focus on content and to ask questions about any point that does not seem clear. The written word carries no facial expression, no gesture, and no tone of voice, so it is more open to misinterpretation than is face-to-face communication. Discussing work with a reader can help close the gap between what you *think* you said and what your reader actually sees.

In addition to letting a work "cool" before revising and enlisting the help of a reader, you can also check your paragraph point by point to make sure that it fulfills the purpose you had in mind. There is nothing mysterious about this procedure. It works like the diagnostic test a mechanic might perform to evaluate a car, checking all major systems to make sure they are working as they should. The following revision checklist helps you to go through a paragraph, part by part, to make sure each part is doing the job you intend it to do.

Checklist for Revision

The Topic Sentence

✔ Does the paragraph have a topic sentence that clearly states the main idea of the entire paragraph?

✔ Is the topic sentence the first or second sentence in the paragraph?

The Supporting Sentences

✔ Does each sentence of the paragraph support the topic sentence?

✔ Do your examples and explanations provide specific detail to support the topic sentence?

✔ Is each point you raise adequately explained and supported?

The Ending

✔ Is the last sentence satisfying and final-sounding?

✔ Does the last sentence serve as a summary or closing sentence for the entire paragraph?

Checking Coherence

✔ Is the order of ideas clear and logical?

✔ Are transitional words used effectively?

EXERCISE 1   ANALYZING TWO VERSIONS OF AN ESSAY

Read the two versions of the paragraph, "Some Purposes of Urban Legends." Using the above Checklist for Revision as your guide, decide which version is the revision and which is the rough draft.

Version 1

Some Purposes of Urban Legends

[1]Some urban legends, such as the story of a man caught speeding by a high-tech surveillance system, are meant to amuse. [2]The man was mailed a photo of his car's license plate, a radar reading of his speed, and a ticket for $120. [3]He mailed back a photo of a check. [4]The police responded with a photo of a pair of handcuffs. [5]The motorist quickly relented and sent a check. [6]Urban legends are meant to sound a warning. [7]Urban legends that tell of escaped murderers haunting lovers' lane, of babies left alone for "just a moment" with tragic consequences, or of predators stalking women down lonely roads fit this category. [8]I myself cannot imagine a parent being careless with his or her child. [9]There is so

much that can happen to a defenseless baby in seconds. [10]These legends remind us, as we go about our lives, to be careful. [11]A final type of urban legend, the "David and Goliath" story, shows how an average person can fight big business or government and win. [12]One example is the story of a woman who asked a waitress in a department store's tearoom for the store's chocolate chip cookie recipe. [13]She was told she would be charged "two-fifty," and she agreed to what she thought was a $2.50 charge on her credit card. [14]Later, she received a charge card bill for $250. [15]This legend, which still haunts the Internet, reminds its readers that even ordinary people have some measure of power. [16]Urban legends, although mostly untrue, serve a purpose as they tell of funny incidents, tragedy, or an ordinary person's revenge.

Version 2

Some Purposes of Urban Legends

[1]Urban legends, the modern equivalent of ancient folktales, serve a variety of purposes. [2]Some urban legends, such as the story of a man caught speeding by a high-tech surveillance system, are meant to amuse. [3]The man was mailed a photo of his car's license plate, a radar reading of his speed, and a ticket for $120. [4]He mailed back a photo of a check. [5]When the police responded with a photo of a pair of handcuffs, the motorist quickly relented and sent a check. [6]Another type of urban legend is meant to sound a warning. [7]In one story of warning, a couple goes to lover's lane in spite of a news broadcast telling of an escaped murderer called "Hook Hand." [8]When they hear a noise outside the car, they become frightened and start to leave. [9]The car seems to be stuck, but finally they pull away and drive home. [10]As they get out of the car in the young woman's driveway they notice something caught on the bumper: a hook hand. [11]A final type of urban legend, the "David and Goliath" story, shows how an average person can fight big business or government and

win. ¹²An example is the story of a woman who asked a waitress in a department store's tearoom for the store's chocolate chip cookie recipe. ¹³She was told she would be charged "two-fifty" and she agreed to what she thought was a $2.50 charge on her credit card. ¹²Later, she received a charge card bill for $250. ¹⁴When the department store refused to remove the charge, the woman's revenge was swift. ¹⁵She posted the recipe on the Internet for the world to enjoy, along with a letter of explanation. ¹⁶This legend, which still haunts the Internet, reminds its readers that even ordinary people have some measure of power. ¹⁷Urban legends, although mostly untrue, serve a purpose as they tell of funny incidents, tragedy, or an ordinary person's revenge.

The revised version of the paragraph is version _____.

EXERCISE 2   ANALYZING AN UNREVISED ESSAY

Go back to the unrevised version of "Some Purposes of Urban Legends" and fill in the blanks to answer the following questions.

1. A topic sentence should appear before sentence _____ in the unrevised version.

2. A transitional word or expression is needed as the writer moves to a new point in sentence _____.

3. Two sentences that do not support the topic sentences are sentence _____ and sentence _____.

4. More support is needed to fully make the writer's point after sentence _____.

Proofreading

Think about the last time you saw a misspelling in a newspaper. The minute you saw it, your thoughts moved away from the story itself and focused on the error. Similarly, errors in your writing take a reader's focus away from your ideas and put emphasis on grammar, spelling, or punctuation. Naturally, you want the ideas to stand in the foreground while grammar, spelling, and punctuation remain in the background. Proofreading, then, is an essential last step in your writing. Though proofreading is usually a chore, it is a necessary chore.

After you have completed the final revision of your work, proofread it at least twice, once from the top down and once from the bottom up. If you have a special problem area, such as comma splices or subject-verb agreement, you should do at least one extra proofreading focusing on those skills.

Proofreading is the job that is never done. No matter how thorough you are, some little error always escapes your notice. Then, just as you are turning in your beautifully written or word-processed manuscript, the error pops out at you as if it were written in neon. Therefore, the more thorough your approach to proofreading, the better.

The Top-Down Technique

On the first proofreading, scan from the top of the page down. Check to make sure the connections between ideas are smooth and solid and that sentences and paragraphs flow smoothly into one another. Check for parallel structure, clear pronoun reference, and appropriate transitional expressions. After correcting any problems you find in the top-down proofreading, move to the second type of proofreading, the bottom-up proofreading.

The Bottom-Up Technique

The bottom-up proofreading technique is more labor-intensive and more focused than top-down proofreading. When you read from the bottom up, you are no longer reading your essay as a single piece of writing but as disconnected sentences that do *not* flow into one another. Since your focus is on a single sentence, you can look at it closely, as if it is a sentence in a grammar exercise. Read it carefully, correct any errors you find, and then move back to the next sentence.

The Targeting Technique

If you have a "favorite error"—one that seems to plague you more than any other—try an additional proofreading to target that error. Below are some common errors and shortcuts to finding those errors. As you become more experienced, you will find yourself devising your own strategies to target your problem areas.

Subject-verb agreement. Check each subject-verb sequence. Look for present-tense verb forms and make sure they agree with their subjects.

Comma splices and run-ons. Target long sentences; they are more likely to be run-ons. Target commas and see if there is a sentence on both sides of the comma; if so, you have a comma splice.

Other comma errors. Target each comma and question its reason for being there. If you aren't sure why it is there, maybe it doesn't belong.

Pronoun agreement. Look for the plural pronouns *they* and *their*, and make sure that they have a plural, not a singular, antecedent.

Sentence fragments. Using the bottom-up technique, read each sentence to see if it could stand on its own.

Proofreading the Word-Processed Paragraph

Spelling and grammar checkers can be helpful in proofreading, but they are no substitute for knowledge and judgment. A spelling or grammar checker can find possible errors and suggest possible solutions. However, it is up to you to decide what, if anything, is wrong and how to fix it.

Even when you use spelling and grammar checkers, you should do at least two separate proofreadings. The following sentence, in which all words are spelled correctly, may illustrate the need:

Weather or knot ewe use a spelling checker, you knead too proofread.

Whether to proofread onscreen or print out a hard copy to proofread is a personal choice. Some writers find it easier to scroll up and down on the computer screen, viewing the paragraph in small segments. Others swear that they cannot see their errors until they hold the printed copy in their hands. Find out what works best for you and proceed accordingly.

Group Exercise 1 Proofreading a Paragraph	Confident? Go solo!

Each of the twenty sentences in the paragraph below contains an error. Form a small proofreading team with two or three of your classmates. Pooling your knowledge, see how many errors you can identify and correct.

An Urban Legend

[1]Urban legends are stories that are often told but is seldom true. [2]One urban legend involves a young college woman traveling home for the Thanksgiving holiday's. [3]As she leaves, the dorm's custodian warned her to take precautions against the Road Killer, who is known to prey on women driving alone. [4]On the road, she stops before dark to get gas, however; she can't get the pump to work. [5]She drives off, planing to stop somewhere else. [6]But as she drive's, she begins to feel more and more apprehensive. [7]It is now fully dark, so she decide to stop at a full-service station. [8]So that she won't have to get out of the car again. [9]It seems like hrs. before she finds a station with a sign that says, "We Pump." [10]She hands the attendant her credit card, she notices he is looking at her and at her car with a strange expression. [11]As he walks toward his booth to check her credit, she feels majorly creeped out. [12]The attendant comes back and said a representative of the credit card company wants to talk to her on the phone. [13]She fears a trick but, the attendant is insistent. [14]she gets out of the car. [15]And walks toward the attendant's booth. [16]He follows closely, goes in behind her slams the door, and locks it. [17]Just as she is about to scream, he says, "I've called the police, and they're on there way. There is a man crouched in the back seat of your car." [18]Urban legends like this one are all most never true. [19]People, find them interesting. [20]Because they represent events that could happen.

Corrections

1. _____   6. _____

2. _____   7. _____

3. _____   8. _____

4. _____   9. _____

5. _____   10. _____

11. _____ 16. _____

12. _____ 17. _____

13. _____ 18. _____

14. _____ 19. _____

15. _____ 20. _____

Formatting

You have heard it all your life: first impressions count. The document you hand to your instructor, the resumé you hand to a prospective employer, or the letter you send to the editor of a newspaper has the ability to present a positive first impression or a negative one. When an instructor sees a carefully formatted paper with no smudges, crossovers, or dog-eared edges, the instructor expects that paper to be a good one, written as carefully as it was prepared. On the other hand, a hastily scrawled document smudged with eraser marks or heavily laden with White-Out suggests that the writer did not take the time to create a good impression—or to write a good paper.

Manuscript format is so important that entire books have been written about it. An instructor who asks you to use MLA style, APA style, or Chicago style is referring to styles outlined in books published by the Modern Language Association, the American Psychological Association, and the University of Chicago.

If you are given instructions for formatting a document, follow those instructions carefully. If you have no specific instructions, use the guidelines in the following section. They will help you to format a document effectively, whether that document is written in class or out of class, by hand or on a word processor.

Handwritten Documents

Paragraphs and Essays

For handwritten paragraphs and essays, use lined white 8½ × 11-inch paper and blue or black ink. Write on one side of the paper only, and leave wide margins.

In the upper right-hand corner of the page, put your name and the date. If you wish, include your instructor's name and the name of the class for which you are preparing the assignment. Center your title, if any, on the first line of the paper, but do not underline the title or put it in quotation marks. Indent each paragraph five spaces, or about three-quarters of an inch. In a handwritten document, do not skip lines unless your instructor specifically requests it. If you make an error, draw a single line through the error and rewrite your correction above the crossed-out error. Put a single paper clip, not a staple, in the upper left corner to join the pages.

Essay Tests

When you take an essay test, you may be required to use a "blue book" or to write on the test itself. If you are allowed to use your own paper, use lined paper and write on one side only.

Answers to questions on essay tests should be written in blue or black ink. Since time is too limited for a rough draft, take a moment to organize your thoughts, and then answer the question. Indent each paragraph five spaces (three-quarters of an inch to one inch). State your main idea first; then add specific supporting details and examples.

If you misspell a word or make a mistake, cross through it with a single line. Be sure to write clearly and legibly, and if your handwriting is difficult to read, try printing instead.

Word-Processed Documents

Setting up the Word-Processing Software

Choose a font and a font size that are easily readable, such as Times New Roman in a 12-point size. Do not use a bold or italic font.

Margins should be one inch all around. One-inch margins are the default on most word processors, so you probably will not have to set margins. Set the word processor to double-space the text. Leave the right edge ragged rather than justifying it. (To justify means to line up in a straight edge, like a newspaper column. Most word processors have settings that allow you to justify, but these settings are not commonly used for academic work.)

Formatting the Document

Put your name and the date in the upper right corner of the page. Other information, such as the name of your instructor or the class for which you are preparing the assignment, is optional. Center the title and indent each paragraph as shown in the sample that follows. A title page is not necessary unless your instructor asks for one.

> Derek Smith
>
> April 1, 2004
>
> Format Reform
>
> I am ashamed to say that I used to be a format abuser. I used strange fonts such as Adolescence and Space Toaster. I tried to make my papers look longer by using two-inch margins with 14-point font. At my lowest point, I turned in a report on lime-green paper printed in 15-point Star Trek font. A caring instructor saw that I had a problem, and helped me to turn my formatting around. Now, I know how to format a document perfectly.
>
> The first step in formatting a document is setting up the word processor. Margins should be set at one inch all around—left, right, top, and

Printing and Presenting Your Document

When the document has been revised and proofread, print it on good quality 8½ × 11 white paper. To hold the pages together, place a single paper clip in the upper left corner. Do not staple your document or put it in a report cover.

Progressive Writing Assignment

Progressive Writing Assignment: Revising, Proofreading, and Formatting

If your instructor has assigned the Progressive Writing Assignment, you are almost finished. All that remains is to revise the paragraph, proofread it carefully, and put it in the proper format.

Topics and Tips

The Topics

Topic 1: Discuss the results of taking a specific piece of advice from a friend or family member.

Topic 2: Discuss your decision to attend college.

Topic 3: Discuss your greatest fear.

Topic 4: Discuss types of stress experienced by college students.

Tips for Revising, Proofreading, and Formatting

- Ask someone else to look at your paragraph and tell you if any point is not clear or if any idea needs further explanation.

- Evaluate your paragraph using the "Checklist for Revision" in this chapter.

- Use your word processor's spelling and grammar checkers, but don't forget to proofread the document at least three times yourself.

- Check the formatting of your paragraph against your instructor's instructions or against the guidelines in this chapter. Improper formatting can be distracting to a reader, but proper formatting allows your paragraph to shine.

7

Showing and Telling:

Description, Narration, and Example

> Sir, could you describe the thief who stole your car?
> —She was kind of average. You know, medium.
>
> What happened when you went for your job interview?
> —It went okay.
>
> What kinds of tests does Professor Madden give?
> —Oh, you know, the usual.

The answers to the questions above would be more vivid—and more satisfactory—if the people answering had used description, narration, and example. You will find these techniques useful when you need to provide specific details. With description, you can show your reader what you see, hear, smell, touch, or taste. With narration, you can tell a reader a story that makes a point. With example, you can provide specific illustrations. Your writing comes alive when you describe, tell a story, or give a specific example.

Description

Effective descriptive writing paints a picture for the reader. Just as an artist uses canvas, brush, and paints, the successful painter of word pictures also employs tools of the trade to create a more effective picture.

Your tools as a writer of descriptive paragraphs and essays include sense impressions, spatial order, and use of a dominant impression.

Sense Impressions

Every scrap of information you collect about the world around you comes through your five senses: sight, hearing, smell, taste, and touch. It is logical, then, that descriptions using **sense impressions** present a more real and vivid picture to your reader.

Sight

Visual impressions are strong and lasting. People are not fooled by a clerk's "Thank you" if his facial expression says, "I hate my job." In fact, psychological studies confirm that people are more likely to rely on facial expressions and gestures than spoken words. If it really is true that "seeing is believing," then creating a visual picture for the reader is particularly important in descriptive writing.

Hearing

Our sense of hearing also gives us information about the world around us. We are warned by the blast of a horn, energized by the beat of rock music, or soothed by the thunder of the ocean. Imagery that appeals to a reader's sense of hearing is an essential dimension of descriptive writing.

Smell

The sense of smell has a powerful connection to memory. The smell of freshly popped popcorn may summon the claustrophobic feel of a dark, crowded movie theater. A whiff of furniture polish can bring back an elderly aunt's stately dining room. Using imagery related to smell helps to complete the picture you are creating for your reader.

Taste

Taste imagery will probably play a small role in your writing, unless you are writing about food. However, used sparingly, references to taste can add a touch of spice to your descriptive writing.

Touch

The sense of touch is a backdrop for all experience. As you sit reading this, you may feel beneath you the hard surface of a wooden chair or the softness of sofa cushions. You may be aware of the chill of air conditioning or the warmth of sunlight, the scratch of a wool sweater or the cottony caress of an old pair of jeans. Imagery that brings out textures and temperatures adds the stamp of reality to the picture you are drawing for your reader.

EXERCISE 1   RECOGNIZING WORDS OF THE SENSES

In the following paragraph, underline words and phrases that convey sense impressions.

Water Aerobics

Although I am not athletic, I enjoy my water
aerobics class. I feel comfortable around the other
women in my class because, like me, they are not
athletes. They are not picture perfect models with
smoothly muscled arms and concave stomachs, but
real women with pudgy stomachs, wide hips, or
skinny, toothpick calves. Around them, I feel less
self-conscious about the extra twenty pounds I am
carrying. I also enjoy the music that accompanies
our exercise. The music system is just a small
portable CD player, but if it is turned up loudly
enough the energizing beat of disco music echoes
throughout the pool area. It is impossible to hear
"Shake Your Groove Thing" or "Ring My Bell" without
wanting to dance. Once the music starts, we move
from the hot concrete at the side of the pool into
the shock of the cool blue water. The exercise
itself may be my favorite part of the experience.
The water buoys me up so that the laws of gravity
no longer fully apply. Each bounce sends me a foot
into the air, and I land lightly and easily. When
the class is over, the crisp smell of chlorine
stays with me, reminding me of the laughter of
classmates, the blare of music, and the temporary
freedom from gravity that I experience in my water
aerobics class.

EXERCISE 2   **WRITING SENSORY DESCRIPTIONS**

Write a phrase that describes each of the following words in sensory terms. Then note whether you describe the word through sight, hearing, smell, taste, or touch. The first one is done for you.

1. cup

    a smooth, heavy ceramic cup (touch)
    _____

2. chair

    _____

3. grass

    _____

4. hat

    _____

5. moonlight

    _____

6. air freshener

    _____

7. french fries

    _____

8. tire

    _____

9. cloud

    _____

10. dirt

    _____

Spatial Order

Spatial order shows the layout of anything that takes up space. Use spatial order to present physical objects in a way that makes sense: bottom to top, left to right, background to foreground, outside to inside—in short, in any organized fashion. Below is a partial list of words commonly used when referring to space.

above	beyond	near	right
ahead	by	next to	south
around	down	north	toward
behind	east	on	under
beside	in	over	underfoot
between	left	overhead	west

EXERCISE 3   RECOGNIZING EFFECTIVE USE OF SPATIAL ORDER

Look at the following short paragraphs. In which paragraph is spatial order used in a more organized and coherent way?

Paragraph 1

The top drawer of my desk was a mess. The tape I was looking for was all the way in the back. A deck of playing cards secured with a rubber band sat beside a flashlight that had no batteries. The first thing I saw when I opened the drawer was a jumble of papers. Near the front of the drawer were a crumpled yellow sheet with an e-mail address written on it, several grocery store and gas receipts, and an envelope that had once contained a bank statement. Pencils without points, paper clips, and assorted change were scattered in the tray at the front of the drawer. It was difficult to explain why some of the items near the back of the drawer had been saved at all: a catnip mouse without a tail, an empty tape dispenser, and an unfolded gum wrapper on which someone had written "23cd" seemed to have no use. I took the roll of tape, then closed the drawer, resolving to clean it out the moment I had time.

Paragraph 2

The top drawer of my desk was a mess. The first thing I saw when I opened the drawer was a jumble of papers. Near the front of the drawer were a crumpled yellow sheet with an e-mail address written on it, several grocery store and gas receipts, and an envelope that had once contained a bank statement. Pencils without points, paper

```
clips, and assorted change were scattered in the
tray at the front of the drawer. A deck of playing
cards secured with a rubber band sat beside a
flashlight that had no batteries. It was difficult
to explain why some of the items near the back of
the drawer had been saved at all: a catnip mouse
without a tail, an empty tape dispenser, and an
unfolded gum wrapper on which someone had written
"23cd" seemed to have no use. The tape I was
looking for was all the way in the back. I took
the roll of tape, then closed the drawer, resolving
to clean it out the moment I had time.
```

The paragraph that uses spatial order more effectively is paragraph _____.

Establishing a Dominant Impression

Description is more than a tangle of unrelated details. In descriptive writing, every detail should join in conveying a single **dominant impression.** Imagine that your job is to describe a house that you pass every day. If your description is to stick in your reader's memory, it must be more than simply a jumble of shutters, bricks, and roofing tiles. A dominant impression not only makes your description more memorable, but it also adds to the unity of the description. What is your overall impression of that house? Is it cheerful? Eerie? Prim? Dignified? The word that you choose to describe the house conveys your dominant impression. As you describe the house, each detail should contribute to the dominant impression.

If you are describing a house that is eerie, include details designed to send chills up the reader's spine: the loose, creaking shutters and the blankly staring windows. If cheerful dandelions bloom in the yard, let them bloom unseen. Details that do not reinforce the dominant impression do not belong in your description.

EXERCISE 4   SUPPORTING THE DOMINANT IMPRESSION

In each list below, circle the letter of the detail that would *not* support the dominant impression of the topic sentence.

1. The bank building looks *dignified.*
    a. Black marble covers the front of the building.
    b. The tinted glass doors look heavy and substantial.

     c. Graffiti is spray-painted on the sidewalk that leads up to the door.

     d. Gold letters spell out the bank's name.

2. The bathroom is *messy.*

     a. Toothpaste is spattered on the sink and mirror.

     b. Damp towels have been thrown on the floor.

     c. Children's tub toys are scattered on the sink and in the tub.

     d. Clean towels are folded and stored on a shelf.

3. My brother is *studious.*

     a. He finishes his homework as soon as he comes home from school.

     b. He likes to play video games.

     c. He researches subjects like astronomy and geology in the Internet.

     d. He hates to see school let out for the summer.

4. The basement is *a fire hazard.*

     a. Newspapers dating back to 1972 are stacked beside the furnace.

     b. Boxes of firecrackers sit near an open can of charcoal starter.

     c. A black widow spider has made her nest on a box of broken glass and rusty nails.

     d. A rusty chainsaw with a frayed cord is plugged into the wall.

5. The man seemed *prosperous.*

     a. He drove a new Mercedes.

     b. He lived in a large, expensive brick house on the north side of town.

     c. His battered wallet held two dollars and a picture of his family.

     d. His designer suit was tailored to perfection.

Wordsmith's Corner: Sample Descriptive Paragraphs

Below are two examples of descriptive writing. Read each paragraph and answer the questions that follow.

Descriptive Paragraph 1

In this paragraph, the writer draws a portrait of a homeless man.

Interstate Sam

    Interstate Sam is a figure of weary dignity. His tired face is an ebony mask, ancient and unreadable. His shoulders bend as if under a heavy

load. Sometimes he stands slumped onto his shopping
cart as if he has fallen asleep. In winter, a
battered green coat shrouds the many layers of
clothing that sag from his thin frame like tattered
robes. In rain, his cape is a yellow plastic
banner, positioned so that the word SALE stretches
from shoulder to shoulder across his stooped back.
He leans on his rusty cart, shifting the weight
from his overburdened feet, but he carries no sign
reading "Stranded" or "Will Work for Food." He
asks for nothing, and people say he accepts nothing
that is offered. He scrounges through dumpsters for
food or, less likely, buys it with the thick sheaf
of bills he is rumored to carry. Interstate Sam
lives his life in the street, yet holds the world
at arm's length with his stoic solitude.

■ **Questions**

1. Underline the topic sentence of the paragraph. Does it state the dominant impression?

   _____

2. What is the dominant impression in this paragraph? List three details
   that reinforce it.

   _____

   _____

   _____

   _____

3. Is the sensory imagery in the paragraph mainly sight, hearing, smell,
   taste, or touch? List three details expressed in sensory terms.

   _____

   _____

   _____

   _____

Descriptive Paragraph 2

Luis writes about a subway station as seen through a child's eyes.

The Subway Station

When I was a child, the subway station seemed like a strange and frightening place. Going down the steep steps into the dark subway, with its smell of dirt, shoes, and sweat, I felt like I was descending into a sinister underground world. In the station, standing with my father on a cement floor that was lumpy with ingrained chewing gum, I looked around at the people. They leaned against pillars, read newspapers, or sat on benches, appearing ordinary enough. But I had been warned against strangers, and here they were, loitering in close proximity. The woman in the striped dress could be a kidnapper, or the thin man's briefcase might hold a gun. I watched the strangers warily, occasionally getting an annoyed glare in return. Then my attention would turn to the steep drop at the edge of the platform. There was always one daredevil standing right at the edge, peering into the dark tunnel as if to make the train arrive faster. I hung well back. If I approached the edge, some unseen force might propel me over the steep drop and onto the third rail. Even if I survived the fall, contact with the third rail would mean instant electrocution. As I watched the person at the edge of the platform, wondering when he would fall, my ears caught the distant rumble of an approaching train. As the strangers folded their papers and rose from their benches, I covered my ears in dread. The rumble became a huge, echoing roar, and the roar became a piercing screech of brakes as the subway came to a stop. On board the train, my fears subsided as clacking, noisy wheels carried us through the dark tunnel and toward the light.

■ **Questions**

1. Underline the topic sentence of the paragraph. Does it state the dominant impression?

   _____

2. What is the dominant impression in this paragraph? List three details that reinforce it.

   _____

   _____

   _____

   _____

   _____

   _____

3. Give examples from the paragraph of imagery expressed in terms of smell, touch, and hearing.

   _____

   _____

   _____

TOPICS FOR PRACTICING DESCRIPTIVE WRITING

Descriptive Assignment 1: Fish Story

Paragraph or Journal Entry

You are a striped bass, living in the depths of a cool blue lake. Your days are peaceful and food is plentiful. You spend most of your time half hidden among the rocks and weeds, but sometimes you swim quickly, darting through the cool water. At other times, you are so filled with the joy of life that you leap high out of the water, your iridescent scales shining in the sun. Today, as you venture from among the weeds, you see a quick flash near the surface of the lake. Maybe it's food.

Describe what happens, focusing on your five senses.

Descriptive Assignment 2: A Beautiful Place

Paragraph

In a single-paragraph composition, describe the most beautiful place you have ever visited. Your dominant impression will be one of beauty, so focus on those details that contributed most to the beauty of the place you are describing.

Descriptive Assignment 3: A Place

Paragraph

In one paragraph, describe a place. It can be a store, an office, a nightclub, a park, a church sanctuary, or any place of your choosing. In your topic sentence, state the dominant impression in one word, choosing a word from the list below or thinking up your own word. Make sure all details of your description reinforce that dominant impression. *Hint:* Your topic sentence will follow this pattern:

The __(place)__ was/is __(dominant impression)__.

bleak	crowded	filthy	noisy
chaotic	depressing	gloomy	orderly
cheerful	dull	impersonal	serene
colorful	eerie	lonely	shabby
cozy	elegant	messy	spotless

Descriptive Assignment 4: A Person

Paragraph or Essay

Write a paragraph or essay describing a person. You may describe someone you know well, such as a friend or relative, or someone you see often but don't really know, such as a library worker or a fellow student. Be sure that you state a dominant impression in your topic sentence. A few possibilities are listed below. Make sure that all the details in your paragraph support the dominant impression. Focus on details that can be expressed through sight, hearing, smell, taste, and touch.

arrogant	easygoing	graceful	neat
dignified	elegant	gruff	unhappy
disorganized	forbidding	messy	upbeat

Narration

Narration is the art of storytelling. A good story pulls your readers in, captures their imaginations and keeps them wondering what will happen next. What is the difference between a narrative that succeeds and one that fails? To make your narrative a success, try some of the techniques outlined below.

Steps to Writing a Successful Narrative

Select Detail Carefully

A good narrative is not burdened by endless details. Provide details that move the story forward, but leave out anything that might slow its progress. In a successful narrative, every detail is significant. Suppose you are telling about the time you locked yourself out of your house and had to convince a passing police officer that you were not a burglar. Details about what you ate for breakfast, the decor of your house, or how you spent the hours or days leading up to the event do not matter. Focus instead on the incident itself.

Use Chronological Order

Most stories are best told in the order in which they happen, with background details near the beginning of the narrative.

Keep the Timespan Short

In a short, paragraph- or essay-length narrative, you can't tell your whole life's story. Your narrative packs more punch if you keep the timespan short—preferably less than an hour and certainly less than twenty-four hours.

Center on Conflict

Most successful narratives center around conflict. It may be inner conflict, conflict with another person, or conflict with an outside force—a tornado, an economic recession, or something else beyond the individual's control. When the conflict ends, the story ends, too.

Use Dialogue

Use dialogue for dramatic moments when you want to show your reader exactly what was said and done or when you want readers to draw their own conclusions about the events that took place. For the strongest effect, use dialogue sparingly.

Know Your Purpose

The purpose of the story is its reason for existence, the reason that you find it worth telling. If no change takes place, if no lesson is learned, if nothing happens, your reader will ask impatiently, "What is the *point?*" Before you tell a story, know your reasons for telling it.

■ Building Connections ■

Descriptive writing skills can also be incorporated into narrative writing. Your narrative becomes even stronger when you present it in terms of sight, sound, touch, taste, and smell.

EXERCISE 5   CHOOSING RELEVANT DETAILS

Imagine that you are writing a narrative about being stranded on a lonely highway. You have brainstormed to gather every available detail about the incident without trying to judge the importance of each detail. Now it is time to choose the details you will include in your paragraph. Place a checkmark beside those details that you would include in the finished paragraph and an X beside those that you would leave out. If there are details you are unsure about, mark them with an "M" for "maybe." Then compare your answers with those of your classmates and discuss the items on which you do not agree.

Topic Sentence: A few months ago, I had a frightening experience on a lonely highway.

_____ a.   It was dark.

_____ b.   There were few other cars on the road.

_____ c.   The temperature outside was a comfortable 72 degrees.

_____ d.   The radio was turned up loud, and I was singing with it.

_____ e.   I heard a loud pop.

_____ f.   Suddenly, my car became hard to steer.

_____ g.   I get an oil change every 3,000 miles.

_____ h.   My car is red.

_____ i.   I realized my tire was going flat.

_____ j.   I pulled over on the shoulder of the road.

_____ k.   I found a flashlight in the glove compartment.

_____ l.   I found a pack of spearmint gum in the glove compartment.

_____ m.   I really prefer cinnamon gum.

_____ n.   My dentist has told me that I should chew only sugarless gum.

_____ o.   The batteries in the flashlight were dead.

_____ p.   I wished I had a cell phone.

_____ q.   Not a single car had driven by.

_____ r.   I found the jack and the spare tire in the trunk.

_____ s.   I saw a single headlight in the distance.

_____ t.   I remembered a story on last night's news about the world economy.

_____ u.   I remembered a story on last night's news about the "Motorcycle Murderer" who preys on stranded motorists.

_____ v.   I have never had dandruff.

_____ w.   My heart was pounding.

_____ x.   A motorcycle pulled up and a tall, helmeted figure got off.

_____ y.   When he said "Hello," I recognized his voice and realized that it was my friend Jack.

_____ z.   He helped me change the tire, and I drove safely home.

Wordsmith's Corner: Sample Narrative Paragraphs

In the paragraphs below, look at the way two writers approach narrative writing. Then answer the questions that follow each narrative.

Narrative Paragraph 1

Melanie, the writer of this narrative paragraph, tells how a crab supper became less than appetizing.

A Painful Meal

A few years ago, I was invited for a "catch your own" crab supper at my uncle's rented beach house.

It was not the pleasant experience I expected. It started enjoyably enough as we lowered baited traps from the dock and pulled them up, sometimes with two or three crabs in each of them. Then we went back to the beach house and Uncle Ed began preparations, using tongs to place the twitching crabs in a large pot, then adding vinegar and water. "Wait a minute," I said. "You aren't going to boil them alive, are you?" Uncle Ed looked at me in surprise, but patiently explained, "That's the way they're cooked. They can't feel anything—crabs are just one step above insects." I watched as he turned on the heat. As the water became warmer, I could hear the crabs scrabbling against the sides of the metal pot. Uncle Ed looked at me and laughed at my horrified expression. "It's just a reflex," he said. But as the water became warmer, the noise from the pot grew more desperate. Finally, there was silence. Uncle Ed took the crabs from the pot and dumped them on newspapers spread on the kitchen table. Uncle Ed looked at me and said, "Mel, you're not still worried about these crabs, are you?" My mother was giving me a warning glance, so I said, "No, it's fine." I felt my stomach do a flip as my uncle put three large crabs in front of me. The crabs' white flesh was tender, but for me, it might as well have been Styrofoam. Since that day, I have not eaten crab. No one can tell me they don't suffer.

■ Questions

1. Underline the topic sentence of the paragraph.
2. About how much time does the narrative cover?

   _____

3. What is the main point of the narrative, the writer's reason for writing it?

   _____

   _____

Narrative Paragraph 2

In this paragraph, André writes about the night that changed his life.

My Last Night at the Kwik-Stop #7

Just a few months ago, as I worked the night shift at the Kwik-Stop #7, my entire life changed direction. It was about 11:00 P.M., and the store was deserted. A man came in, a baseball cap pulled low over his eyes and his jacket collar turned up to cover his face. In a flash, he was standing in front of me, pointing the metallic nose of a revolver at my head. "Give me all the money in that register. Don't pull any tricks or I'll kill you," he said. I could hear his voice trembling, and I realized he was scared. All I could think of was that a scared robber was more likely to pull the trigger. Time seemed to slow down. I could hear the robber yelling at me to hurry, but the words barely registered. Beneath the counter, I saw the red "panic button" that would silently summon the police if only I would press it. I could not. I opened the drawer and placed each stack of bills on the counter, twenties, tens, fives, and ones. The robber scooped them off the counter, jabbed the gun at me, and said "Don't call the police for at least an hour." I don't know how many minutes passed before I grabbed the keys with trembling hands, locked the door, walked back behind the counter and pushed the red button. The next day, when I took stock of the life I had almost lost, I realized I had lived twenty-three years and had done absolutely nothing I could be proud of. That day, I quit my job at the Kwik-Stop and filled out a college application. I had always said I would go to college someday, but I never thought someone would have to hold a gun to my head to make me do it.

■ **Questions**

1. Underline the topic sentence of the paragraph.

2. About how much time does the narrative cover?

_____

_____

3. What is the main point of the narrative, the writer's reason for writing it?

_____

_____

TOPICS FOR PRACTICING NARRATIVE WRITING

Narrative Assignment 1: Wake-Up Call

Journal Entry

You wake with the sun in your eyes, wondering why your bed seems to be rocking underneath you. Then you realize that you are not in your bed, but in a small boat on a vast ocean. In the distance, you see what looks like a small island.

Tell the story in a journal entry.

Narrative Assignment 2: Treat or Mistreat?

Paragraph

Write about a time when someone treated you in one of the following ways. Make sure your one-paragraph story has a purpose by focusing on the way the incident made you feel. Were you sad? Surprised? Angry?

Someone misjudged you.

Someone gave you praise or credit you did not deserve.

Someone encouraged you.

Someone ridiculed you.

Someone treated you with unexpected kindness.

Someone treated you unfairly.

Narrative Assignment 3: Transformation

Paragraph

Write a narrative paragraph describing a life-changing event that took place in less than an hour.

Narrative Assignment 4: A Significant Goodbye

Paragraph or Essay

Write a narrative paragraph or essay about a significant ending in your life. Some possibilities include your last day of high school or high school graduation, a time when you said goodbye to a person who was important in your life, or your last day on the job. Alternatively, you might focus on a symbolic ending when you realized that the end of something was at hand: the end of your childhood, the end of a relationship, or the end of a grudge or other feeling that you had held for some time. Make sure that the incident you choose is one that will fit into a paragraph or essay. It would be hard, for instance, to write a narrative that fully discussed your first marriage or first job—unless it lasted only an hour or two.

Examples

Examples are one of the best ways to get a point across because they provide a concrete illustration of your point. If you say your father is sentimental, your reader gets the general idea. If you say he gets teary-eyed over Hallmark commercials, you give specific support to the general idea. Examples are specific illustrations, exact instances. They may range in length from a single word to a single sentence to an entire paragraph.

The Short Example

A **short example** may be a word or a phrase, but it must be a specific, concrete example. It cannot simply be a synonym. The word *canine*, for instance, is a synonym for *dog*, not an example of a dog. An example illustrating the word *dog* might be *Dalmatian, Chihuahua, Raffles, my two-year-old terrier,* or *that mangy mutt across the street.*

EXERCISE 6   ADDING YOUR OWN EXAMPLES

For each of the words or phrases below, an example is given. Add your own example in a word or phrase.

1. song
   a. "Take Me Out to the Ball Game"
   b. _____
2. sport
   a. soccer
   b. _____

3. a proverb or familiar saying

   a. "A stitch in time saves nine."

   b. _____

4. an uncomfortable sensation

   a. walking barefoot across hot sand

   b. _____

5. an uncomfortable social situation

   a. Going on a date for the first time since your breakup and running into your ex's parents.

   b. _____

The Sentence-Length Example

Sometimes you need more than just a word or phrase to illustrate an idea. In such cases, try using a **sentence-length example.** Again, the example needs to be a specific, detailed illustration of the general idea you are discussing. It should not simply be a vague restatement. Look at the following examples to see the difference between a vague restatement and a specific example.

Examples

✗ *Idea + vague restatement:* The new disk jockey on the morning show is really obnoxious. He has an unpleasant attitude that makes listening to his show a bad experience.

✔ *Idea + specific example:* The new disk jockey on the morning show is really obnoxious. He tries to humiliate listeners who call in, and his jokes border on the offensive.

✗ *Idea + vague restatement:* The new grocery store has added whimsical touches to some of its departments. It's enjoyable to shop in a store that is entertaining.

✔ *Idea + specific example:* The new grocery store had added whimsical touches to some of its departments. In the produce department, "thunder" rolls and "lightning" flashes above the vegetable bins before the automatic sprinkler turns on. On the dairy aisle, recordings of mooing cows and clucking hens amuse passing shoppers.

EXERCISE 7   ELIMINATING VAGUE EXAMPLES

Circle the letter of the sentence that is not a specific example.

1. The car was dirty.
   a. The entire vehicle had a filthy appearance.
   b. Brown streaks of mud covered the bumpers and doors.
   c. The windows were specked with the tiny, squashed bodies of dead insects.
2. The man seemed angry.
   a. He spoke loudly and used vulgar language.
   b. He seemed to be in a state of fury.
   c. As he left, he slammed the door behind him.
3. I have spent money carelessly this weekend.
   a. At the mall, I bought two CDs that I could not afford.
   b. Money seemed to run through my fingers like water.
   c. I spent twenty dollars on dinner at the Steak-Out, an expenditure I had not planned.
4. Alfred spent an hour cleaning his apartment.
   a. He picked up magazines, clothes, and papers that cluttered his bedroom.
   b. He vacuumed the carpet and mopped the kitchen floor.
   c. He took the time to get the place looking good.
5. The plant had obviously been neglected.
   a. Someone had ignored the poor philodendron.
   b. Its leaves were dusty and limp.
   c. Its soil was dry.

EXERCISE 8   PROVIDING SPECIFIC EXAMPLES

For each of the following general ideas, provide a specific example in a sentence or two.

1. The garage was a mess.

   _____

   _____

2. After two cups of coffee, I started to come awake.

   _____

   _____

3. In the hallway, Leon complained about his professor.

_____

_____

4. The evidence indicated that the accused burglar was guilty.

_____

_____

5. The mailbox contained nothing but junk mail.

_____

_____

The Extended Example

Sometimes you may wish to develop an idea with an **extended, paragraph-length** example. In this case, your topic sentence states the general idea and the rest of the paragraph provides a detailed example. This sort of paragraph usually ends with a summary sentence that connects the specific example back to the general idea, as in the following short paragraph.

Example

topic sentence

Not long ago, I found myself caught in an uncomfortable social situation. I was out on my first date since the breakup of my three-year marriage. As my date and I entered the restaurant where we were going to eat, we met my ex-wife's parents. When I saw them, I half hoped that they would not speak to me, but they called out, "Andy! Hello!" I had to introduce them to my date, and, to make matters worse, they insisted on filling me in about how well my ex-wife is

summary sentence

doing without me. I tried to handle the situation gracefully, but I felt uncomfortable, and I am sure my date did, too.

Extended example

EXERCISE 9   WRITING AN EXTENDEND EXAMPLE

Write an extended example (four sentences or more) to support one of the following topic sentences. Then write a summary sentence to end the paragraph.

1. Not long ago, I found myself caught in an uncomfortable social situation.
2. I can remember how nervous I was on my first day at college.
3. Some of my classmates can be annoying.
4. Some professors can be a real pain.
5. I remember one of the proudest moments of my life.

Wordsmith's Corner: Paragraphs Developed by Example

In the paragraphs below, the writers develop their topics by using examples. Read each paragraph and answer the questions that follow.

Example Paragraph 1

In this paragraph, Justin gives examples of the excuses his friend Leo is constantly making.

No More Excuses

My friend Leo makes up lame excuses whenever there is something he doesn't want to do. Just two weeks ago, he was at my house when he decided he did not want to go in to work. He called his boss and said he had to get a new set of tires put on his truck. Then he sat down and watched TV with me. Not only had he lied, but his excuse was not a very convincing one. Another time, he canceled a date with his girlfriend at the last minute, telling her he had to get a new battery for his truck. She was angry and refused to go out with him again until he apologized. Last weekend, Leo offered the lamest excuse yet. He had promised he would help me move my furniture from my parents' house to my new apartment. He was supposed to bring his truck over

about eight o'clock Saturday morning. I waited,
then called and left a message on his machine.
About 11:30 he called and said he was sorry, but he
had been getting a new set of tires put on his
truck. I guess he had forgotten he used the same
excuse when he called his boss from my house. I
think I need a new set of friends—I am beginning to
tire of Leo's excuses.

■ Questions

1. Underline the topic sentence of the paragraph.
2. List three examples given in the paragraph.

_____

_____

_____

_____

3. Underline the paragraph's summary sentence.

Example Paragraph 2

Olivia's paragraph shows the ways her college's wellness center benefits
students.

Athletics for Everyone

Many students at the college I attend complain
about paying an athletic fee along with tuition.
However, I don't complain because I know that the
athletic fee supports a wellness program that
benefits all students. The athletic fee funds
a health club equipped with weight machines,
treadmills, stationary bikes, and free weights.
The fee also helps pay the salary of a director who
runs the club and teaches classes like stretch and
tone, step aerobics, and water aerobics. Fees at
private health clubs run hundreds of dollars per
year, but the college's athletic fee is only thirty
dollars per term. Another benefit of the wellness

program is its medical services. A nurse-practitioner offers advice on diet and nutrition, dispenses remedies for colds and allergies, and schedules private consultations on health-related matters. The athletic fee also subsidizes tetanus immunizations and flu shots. For commuter students, many of whom are not covered by health insurance, the service is essential. At some colleges, only athletic teams benefit from student athletic fees, but at our college, the athletic program benefits everyone.

■ Questions

1. Underline the topic sentence of the paragraph.
2. List three examples given in the paragraph.

   _____

   _____

   _____

   _____

   _____

3. Underline the paragraph's summary sentence.

TOPICS FOR PRACTICING WRITING WITH EXAMPLES

Example Assignment 1: No Accounting for Taste

Paragraph or Journal Entry

Modify the following topic sentence to your liking and write a paragraph or journal entry. Provide specific and detailed examples.

When I go to _____, I notice some people with _____ taste in clothing.

Example Assignment 2: Quotations and Illustrations

Paragraph

Choose one of the following quotations and write a paragraph agreeing or disagreeing with it. Your support should take the form of specific examples that help to prove or disprove the quotation. Your topic sentence will look something like this: "I agree/disagree with Juvenal's statement, 'Luxury is more deadly than any foe.'"

Quotations

Luxury is more deadly than any foe.
> —Juvenal

The impossible is often the untried.
> —James Goodwin

It is impossible for a man to be cheated by anyone but himself.
> —Ralph Waldo Emerson

Success is never final.
> —Winston Churchill

How glorious it is—and also how painful—to be an exception.
> —Alfred de Musset

In poverty and other misfortunes of life, true friends are a sure refuge.
> —Aristotle

There is nothing so easy but that it becomes difficult when you do it reluctantly.
> —Terence

Example Assignment 3: Saving and Spending

Paragraph

Are you a person who likes to save money or a person who likes to spend it? In one paragraph, support your answer with specific examples.

Example Assignment 4: People

Paragraph or Essay

Choose one topic from the following list and write a paragraph or essay that illustrates the topic with examples.

a loyal friend	an inefficient person
a jealous person	a productive person
a good or bad boss	an optimist
a good or bad teacher	a pessimist
a giving person	a self-sufficient person
a thrifty person	a bad influence

TOPICS FOR COMBINING METHODS OF DEVELOPMENT

Description, narration, and example are methods of showing or telling a reader exactly what you mean. Combining the methods adds even more power to your writing. The assignments that follow ask you to combine two or more of the methods of development in this chapter.

■ Building Connections ■

Methods of development are tools of a writer's trade. Like a carpenter's hammer, saw, and sander, they each do a specific job. Which one should you use? It depends on the job you have to do. Some pieces of writing will require just one method, but most will require you use more than one of your tools of the trade.

Mixed Methods Assignment 1: Brief Encounter

Narration and Description

Narrate a brief encounter that you have had with someone. That person may be a stranger, a relative, a coworker, or a friend. The meeting you describe may be your first meeting with that person or your last, it may be a friendly encounter or an unfriendly one, but it should be significant in some way. As you narrate the encounter, weave in a description of the other person—his appearance, her voice. Try to narrate and describe the encounter so vividly that your reader feels as though he is there with you.

Mixed Methods Assignment 2: The Joy of Life

Description and Example

Runners sometimes experience a rush of endorphins that has been described as a "runner's high." An old song by John Denver describes the feeling of being in the mountains as a "Colorado Rocky Mountain high." Both terms describe special and rare feeling of self-awareness and joy that some might call a "high" and others might simply call the joy of life. What places or activities bring you joy? Describe those place or activities and give specific examples.

Mixed Methods Assignment 3: Childhood Unhappiness

Narration and Description

Write a paragraph narrating an event that upset you when you were a child but that does not seem so serious now. It could be an argument with a childhood friend, trouble with a teacher at school, or a lost game or competition. Make sure that you narrate an even that takes place in a very short span of time—fifteen minutes or less is suggested. As you narrate the event, make sure to weave in relevant details so that your reader sees the fall leaves or the dust that you kick up as you walk across the playground; hears the musical sounds of the ice cream truck or the angry tone in your teacher's voice; or feels the cold rain that soaked you to the skin.

8

Limiting and Ordering:
Definition, Classification, and Process

With each *well* uttered by the hypothetical professor above, students sink deeper into a well of confusion. The professor needs the techniques of definition, classification, and process to clarify his lecture. You can use these techniques in your writing to limit information—that is, to outline its boundaries. You can use the techniques to put information in order by categorizing or showing steps in a process. These techniques help you answer the questions, *What is it? How many different types exist?* and *How does it work?*

Definition

Most people think of a definition as a "dictionary definition"—a brief explanation of the meaning of a word and little else. But your **definition** paragraph goes beyond a bare-bones statement of a word's meaning because you give your reader your own personal definition of a term.

115

In a personal definition, the way you define a term reflects your own feelings about it. Two dictionaries might have very similar definitions for the word *love*. Two people probably will not. A new parent might define love as a feeling that is tender but protective, while someone who has recently been disappointed in romance might define it as the quickest route to a broken heart.

Setting Up Your Definition Paragraph

The key element in a definition paragraph is the topic sentence, which presents your personal definition of the term you are defining. Look at the following examples, all defining the word *vacation*. Notice that some of the topic sentences employ personal terms like "for me" or "I can define." Although phrases such as these are not always a part of a personal definition, they often help mark the definition as the writer's personal definition rather than a dictionary definition.

Examples

To me, a vacation is a brief escape from my everyday responsibilities.

A vacation is the fastest way to waste a large amount of money in a short time.

For most people, vacations are a time of rest, but for me, they are a time of stress.

When I think of the boring family vacations I was forced to go on as a teenager, I can only define a vacation as a living nightmare.

EXERCISE 1   RECOGNIZING PERSONAL DEFINITIONS

For each term below, circle the definition that is a personal definition rather than a dictionary-type definition.

1. **music**
   a. Music is a rhythmic sound made by various instruments or with the human voice. In all cultures, it is a way of collectively expressing emotion.
   b. Music, for me, is a way of expressing or even changing my moods. I choose quiet music for quiet moods and peppy music when I am feeling energetic. If I am in a bad mood, music with a strong beat picks me up immediately.

2. **test**

   a. A test may be a teacher's way of measuring knowledge, but for me, it is an hour of anxiety. No matter how well I know the material, anxiety grips me as the test papers are passed out and does not let go until I have turned in my paper and left the room.

   b. A test is a way for a teacher to assess how well students know the material that has been taught. Tests come in a variety of formats. *Subjective tests* are oral or written tests that allow students to respond to a question in their own words. *Objective tests* may feature question formats such as multiple choice, true-false, or matching that require a student to choose a single correct answer.

3. **computer**

   a. A computer is a machine as addictive and alluring as any slot machine Las Vegas can offer. One can play games on it for hours or pursue any subject on the Internet. Through chat rooms and e-mail, the user can contact people all over the globe. A computer provides access to a web of pure fun.

   b. A computer is a machine with many applications for work and play. Using word processing software, financial software, and databases, a person may run a small business from a home computer. Computer games and the Internet add recreational value, and educational software and online libraries provide tools for research.

4. **car**

   a. A car is a means of personal transportation. It comes in many different sizes, styles, and price ranges, and may be rented, leased, or bought outright. Many see a car as preferable to public transportation, and in many areas where mass transportation is unavailable, a car is a necessity.

   b. For many, a car is just a means of transportation, but for me, my 1969 Volkswagen beetle is a source of pride. The hours of work I put into lovingly restoring every detail pay off when heads turn as I drive down the road.

Wordsmith's Corner: Sample Definition Paragraphs

Read the two definition paragraphs below to see how two writers define two ordinary terms. Then answer the questions that follow each paragraph.

Definition Paragraph 1

In this paragraph, Shakira describes how her family experience affected the way she defines money.

Money

  Some people see money as evil, while others see it as something to spend on life's pleasures. My definition of money can be summed up in one word: security. My definition stems from my childhood experience. When I was growing up, my family was comfortable and my parents had good jobs, but I was always told that money was not important. It was family, love, and home that mattered. Then when I was fourteen, my father lost his job when his company downsized. My mother was carrying the financial load for the family, and my parents' marriage became more strained. Finally, my parents sat us down and told us we could no longer afford to keep the house we had lived in all my life. We moved to a cramped apartment. We were crowded together and it was much harder for my sister and me to avoid hearing the fights my parents had almost daily. When my father finally found a job two hundred miles away, he moved, but we stayed here. My parents called it a "trial separation," but it ended in divorce. I felt cheated, and I felt that everything my parents had told me about money was a lie. They had said money was not important, but without it, the things that were important were soon gone. Now, I see that money _is_ important. It can never replace family, home, and love, but it can help to make them more secure.

■ Questions

1. Underline the topic sentence of the paragraph. Does it state a personal definition?

   _____

2. Does the paragraph contain an introductory sentence?

   _____

3. Underline the two sentences that summarize the paragraph.

Definition Paragraph 2

Michael writes a definition that reveals his humorous view of his customers' shortcomings.

What Is a Customer?

Since I started working part time at a grocery store, I have learned that a customer is more than someone who buys something. To me, a customer is a person whose memory fails entirely once he or she starts to push a shopping cart. One of the first things customers forget is how to count. There is no other way to explain how so many people get in the express line, which is clearly marked "Fifteen items or less," with twenty, twenty-five, or even a cartload of items. Customers also forget why they came to the store in the first place. Just as I finish ringing up an order, a customer will say, "Oops! I forgot to pick up a big jar of pickles for my wife! I hope you don't mind waiting while I go get them." Five minutes later, the customer is back with pickles, a bottle of catsup, and three rolls of paper towels. Strange as it seems, customers also seem to forget that they have to pay for their groceries. Instead of writing a check or looking for a debit card while I am ringing up the groceries, my customer will wait until I announce the total. Then, in surprise, she says, "Oh! Now what did I do with my checkbook?" After five minutes of digging through her purse, she borrows my pen because she has forgotten hers. But I have to be tolerant of customers because they pay my salary—and that's something I can't afford to forget.

■ Questions

1. Underline the topic sentence of the paragraph. Does it state a personal definition?

   _____

2. What examples support the writer's definition?

_____

_____

_____

3. This paragraph contains an introductory sentence and a summary sentence. Underline those sentences.

TOPICS FOR PRACTICING DEFINITION

Definition Assignment 1: Dueling Definitions

Journal Entry

Topics 1 and 2 below require you to define the same word from two different points of view. Write two journal entries, one from each point of view.

Topic 1: Cookout. You live on a small farm, and every Fourth of July, you kill six fat chickens and roast them on an outdoor barbecue. You and your family and friends enjoy the feast, which has become a tradition. Write a definition of a cookout.

Topic 2: Cooked! You are a chicken, living on the small farm mentioned in Topic 1. As you peck around the chicken yard, you wonder where Uncle Albert is. You haven't seen him for a while. There seem to be some others missing, too. Suddenly, through the chicken wire, you see an outdoor barbecue. On it are six shapes, and one of them looks a lot like Uncle Albert. Write a definition of a cookout.

Definition Assignment 2: Defining Ordinary Terms

Paragraph

Write a paragraph giving your personal definition of one of the following ordinary terms.

jeans

a computer

dog

music

a particular food or beverage

Definition Assignment 3: Personal Definitions

Paragraph

Write a paragraph defining one of the types of people on the following list. Use a specific person (or persons) as an example if you wish, but be sure to give a precise personal definition before you give the example. See the sample topic sentences below for further help.

✘   My neighbor, Madeleine, is incredibly nosy.

The topic sentence above does not provide a definition.

✔   Some people might define a neighbor as a helpful friend, but to me, a neighbor is a person who always has her nose in other people's business.

This topic sentence works because it presents a definition. After the topic sentence has been stated, Madeleine the neighbor can be used as a supporting example.

Choose a term to define from the following list:

mother	son	daughter	teacher
father	minister	coach	neighbor
spouse	friend	boss	sister/brother

Definition Assignment 4: Defining an Activity

Paragraph

Write a paragraph defining one of the activities below, or substitute an activity of your own.

fishing	dancing	aerobics	shopping	running
reading	eating	jogging	driving	swimming
studying	working	cooking	gardening	sleeping

Classification

Whether you know it or not, **classification** comes naturally to you. From the time you are born, you explore, discovering that some things are pleasurable and others are painful, that some things are edible and others are not. Those are your first lessons in classification.

By the time you reach adulthood, you divide people, articles of clothing, words, teachers, and ways of behaving into different types or categories so automatically that you are barely aware of it. When you answer a classmate's question, "What kind of teacher is Dr. Burton?" or reply to a friend who asks what kind of day you have had, you are classifying.

When you write a classification paper, you must analyze this familiar process of classification to apply it to your writing.

Establishing a Basis for Classification

In the following list of kinds of shoppers, which item does not belong?

a. the spendthrift

b. the bargain hunter

c. the male shopper

If you chose c, "the male shopper," you are right. You have recognized, consciously or subconsciously, that the first two have the same basis for classification: attitude toward money. The third item has a different basis for classification: gender.

When you write a classification paper, it is important that your classification have a single basis or underlying principle.

Exercise 2   Classifying Items in a List

Part 1: Cross out the item that does not belong in each of the following lists. Then determine the basis for classification of the other items and write it in the blank to the right of the list. The first one is done for you.

1. sweaters   Basis for classification: _neckline style_____

   a. crew neck

   b. ~~wool~~

   c. v-neck

   d. turtleneck

2. dogs   Basis for classification: _____

   a. Dalmatian

   b. cocker spaniel

   c. toy

   d. Chihuahua

3. candy   Basis for classification: _____

   a. chocolate

   b. Halloween

   c. Easter

   d. Christmas

4. stars   Basis for classification: _____

   a. Sirius

   b. Castor

   c. Polaris
   d. Denzel Washington

5. paint   Basis for classification: _____
   a. arctic blue
   b. sun yellow
   c. semigloss
   d. leaf green

Part 2: To each list, add one item that fits the existing basis for classification and one item that does not fit.

6. drugs
   a. aspirin
   b. cough syrup
   c. antacid
   d. _____ (a drug that belongs on this list)
   e. _____ (a drug that belongs on another list)

7. games
   a. basketball
   b. softball
   c. tennis
   d. _____ (a game that belongs on this list)
   e. _____ (a game that belongs on another list)

8. car
   a. Toyota
   b. Renault
   c. Honda
   d. _____ (a car that belongs on this list)
   e. _____ (a car that belongs on another list)

9. clothing
   a. evening wear
   b. swimwear
   c. sportswear
   d. _____ (a type of clothing that belongs on this list)
   e. _____ (a type of clothing that belongs on another list)

10. shoes
    a. Reebok
    b. K-Swiss
    c. Adidas
    d. _____ (a shoe that belongs on this list)
    e. _____ (a shoe that belongs on another list)

EXERCISE 3   FINDING THE POINT THAT DOES NOT FIT

The following paragraph contains one point that has a different basis for classification than the other three. Read the paragraph and answer the questions that follow.

Types of Workers

At school and at work, I have noticed that people have different kinds of work habits. Some people are collaborators who like to work in groups. They find that doing a project with someone else makes the job more pleasant and the load lighter. Collaborators never work alone unless they are forced to. A second category I have noticed is the advice seeker. An advice seeker does the bulk of her work alone, but frequently looks to others for advice. When this worker has reached a crucial point in her project, she may show it to a classmate or coworker just to get another opinion. Getting the advice of others makes this worker feel secure about her project as it takes shape. Another type of worker I have noticed is the slacker. A slacker tries to avoid work whenever possible. If he seems to be busy at the computer, he is probably playing solitaire, and if he is writing busily, he's probably making his grocery list. Slackers will do anything except the work they are paid to do. The final type of worker is the loner. This type of worker prefers working alone. This type of worker has confidence in his ability and is likely to feel that collaboration is a waste of time. Loners work with others only when they are forced to. Collaborators, advice-seekers, slackers, and loners

have different work styles, but each knows the work
habits that help him or her to get the job done.

■ **Questions**

1. Which point does not have the same basis for classification as the
   others?

   _____

2. What is the basis for classification of the other three points?

   _____

   _____

Wordsmith's Corner: Sample Classification Paragraphs

Read the two classification paragraphs below. Then answer the questions
that follow.

Classification Paragraph 1

Danielle's paragraph classifies kinds of stress she experiences when she
goes on vacation.

Kinds of Vacation Stress

No matter how much fun I have on vacation, I
always experience several kinds of stress. Physical
stress is always part of the picture. If I take my
children to a theme park, the endless walking and
standing in line take their toll. In the mountains or
at the lake, insect bites, poison ivy, and sunburn
are often our traveling companions. In addition to
physical stress, the forced togetherness of a
vacation often causes emotional stress. After being
cooped up in a car together all day, my children
begin bickering. I lose patience and begin to think
how nice it would be just to have a quiet half hour by
myself. Finally, there is financial stress. Renting a
hotel room is just the beginning. We have to eat all
of our meals in restaurants, and even fast food is
more expensive than eating a meal at home. Tickets to
attractions are expensive, and souvenirs make the

hole in my wallet a little deeper. After a week, I am
ready to trade the stresses of vacation for the
everyday stresses of home and work.

■ Questions

1. Underline the topic sentence of the paragraph.
2. How many classifications of vacation stress are mentioned in the
   paragraph?

   _____

   _____

3. In this paragraph, vacation stress is classified of the basis of
   a. who causes it.
   b. how it affects the person.
   c. how long it lasts.
   d. who experiences it.

Classification Paragraph 2

Zack writes about the people he sees at his favorite arcade.

                    Kinds of Gamers

    When I go to the arcade, I play games, but I also
watch other people. I have noticed that my fellow
gamers fall into three categories. The first type
will try anything that the arcade has to offer,
from pinball and skeeball to a full-scale virtual
reality adventure. They may pause to sit in the
cybercafé and surf the Internet or drink a mocha
freeze. These adventurous types are there for the
entire experience, and they want to enjoy it all.
The next type of gamer has a narrower focus. This
group only plays games that print out tickets that
they can exchange for prizes. The prizes they can
win are small: glow-in-the-dark yo-yos, colorful
balls, and plastic dinosaurs. "Ticketheads" play to
collect long strings of tickets to claim the prize
they want. Finally, there are the obsessives. They
are there for one game and one game only, and they
play it again and again, trying to outdo their
personal best. They often come in pairs or groups,

all set on playing the same game, usually a traditional video arcade game. They cluster around the
machine for hours, feeding in money and encouraging
one another to beat the last high score. For me,
half the fun of visiting the arcade is watching other
players enjoying their own particular type of fun.

■ Questions

1. Underline the topic sentence of the paragraph.
2. What are the classifications of gamers in the paragraph?

_____

3. In this paragraph, gamers are classified of the basis of
    a. level of skill.
    b. number of different kinds of games played.
    c. appearance.
    d. number and type of prizes they win.

TOPICS FOR PRACTICING CLASSIFICATION

Classification Assignment 1: Classifying Your Moods

Paragraph or Journal Entry

Even people who seem cheerful most of the time have low moods occasionally.
How about you? Think about your moods, from high to low, and classify them
according to type in a paragraph or journal entry. You might arrange them from
low to high or from most frequent to least frequent.

Classification Assignment 2: Personal Style

Paragraph

Every day you see people eating, walking, taking tests, and having conversations.
Think about some of the ordinary (and not so ordinary) behavior you see on a
regular basis. Then, in a paragraph, classify people according to the way they perform a specific task or action. Use one of the suggestions below or come up with
an idea of your own.

Classify people by the way they:

eat	greet people	sit
drink	drive	study
chew gum	talk	dance
walk	sing	enter a classroom

Classification Assignment 3: Kinds of Kind People

Paragraph

Even kindness comes in more than one type. Some people will do a favor only if they receive something in return. Others are kind only when they receive recognition or praise for it. Others do kind acts in secret, when no one else will see. Write a paragraph classifying kinds of kind people. If you prefer, write your paragraph on kinds of mean people.

Classification Assignment 4: Fill in the Blank

Paragraph or Essay

Write a classification paragraph or essay on "Kinds of _____." Fill in the blank with one of the words below.

laziness	happiness	sadness	procrastination
tests	bosses	teachers	music
TV shows	games	sports fans	clothing

Process

When you write a **process** paragraph, you describe how to do something or how it works. Process writing surrounds you. Recipes, instruction manuals, and any of the many self-help books that promise to tell you how to become fit, lose weight, save money, or lead a more satisfying life are examples of how-to process writing. A chapter in an American government text describing how a bill becomes a law, the page in your biology text on the life cycle of the fruit fly, and the fine print on the back of your credit card statement explaining how interest is applied are examples of "how it works" process writing.

Organizing the Process Paper

Some processes are **fixed processes**—that is, ones in which the order of the steps cannot vary. If you tell someone how to change the oil in a car, for instance, you can't place the step "add new oil" before the step "drain old oil." If you explain how a bill becomes a law, you can't place "goes to president for signing or veto" before "approved by both houses of Congress." If you are describing a fixed process, list the steps in chronological order.

Other processes are **loose processes.** They have no fixed, predetermined order. Loose processes include such activities as handling money wisely or becoming physically fit. In describing these processes, it is up to you to choose the most logical order.

Imagine that you are writing a paper on handling money wisely. You decide that the steps involved include paying down debt, developing a spending plan, and saving for the future. Developing a spending plan seems logical as a first point, but you can't decide whether to place "saving" or "paying down debt" next in the order. You may say, "It's hard to save until debts are paid. Therefore, paying debt before saving is logical." Or you may reason like this: "Most people stay in debt for most of their lives. If it's not a credit card, it's a car loan or a mortgage. To save, pay yourself first, no matter what." Either order is logical. What is important is that you have thought about it and chosen the order that best suits your own philosophy.

One important point to remember when organizing the how-to process paper is that many processes require tools or certain conditions. Usually, then, step one of your process will direct the reader to gather tools and make preparations. Whether you're telling how to make a cake or how to defuse a bomb, your reader won't appreciate being led to a crucial point and then being instructed to use a tool that isn't handy. Ideally, a how-to paper is written so clearly and logically that the reader could carry out the process on the first read-through.

Wordsmith's Corner: Sample Process Paragraphs

In the next two paragraphs, look at the ways two other writers handle a process paragraph. Then answer the questions that follow each paragraph.

Process Paragraph 1

In this process paragraph, Ravi tells how to make a car an asset instead of an embarrassment.

```
How to Keep Your Car from Ruining Your Social Life

    If that cute guy or gal from your algebra class
just happened to walk out to the parking lot with
you after class, would you be embarrassed by the
appearance of your car? With a bit of attention and
```

a bit of work, you can have a car that is an asset
to your social life, not an obstacle. It all starts
inside your car, with the basic understanding that
a car is not a trash can or a file cabinet. Banana
peels and fast-food containers should not be tossed
in the back seat, and old test papers and handouts
should not be filed in the trunk. Instead, trash
and other items should be removed each day. If you
never leave anything in your car, it will never
start to look messy. Once the inside is neat, it's
time to make sure the outside is taken care of. It
is as simple as this: wash your car every week, or
at the very least, every other week. It does not
matter whether you wash it yourself with a hose and
sponge or whether you take it to a car wash. What
matters is that if you and the person from algebra
class go out together in your car, you will see the
blue sky or the golden moon through your windshield,
not two months' worth of dead bugs. There are
enough obstacles to a successful social life—don't
let your car be one of them.

■ Questions

1. Underline the paragraph's topic sentence.
2. Is the process described in this paragraph a fixed process or a loose
   process?

   _____

3. Underline the paragraph's summary sentence.

Process Paragraph 2

Sarah's process paragraph tells how she and her roommates eat well on
a budget.

How to Eat Well on a Budget

As poverty-stricken students sharing an
apartment, my roommates and I find eating well a
challenge. We have very little money, and, as
students carrying full-time class loads, we have
almost no time. But we have come up with some ways

to eat plentifully and somewhat nutritiously even on our small budget. Our first way of saving money and time is simple: noodles, noodles, noodles. They are cheap, low in fat, and are a basis for many easy-to-make meals. Spaghetti, chili mac, and macaroni and cheese are often on our menu. Baked ramen noodles are lower in fat than fried noodles and make a quick meal any time. When we tire of noodles, we turn to what we call our twenty-four-hour breakfast. Breakfast foods are cheap, tasty, and can be eaten at any meal. Scrambled eggs are quick to make, and a few pieces of toast complete the meal. Pancakes are filling, cheap, and satisfying. But the easiest breakfast of all is cereal. Any time of day, it's easy to pour a bowl of Cheerios or corn flakes, slice a banana over it, and pour on milk. Cereal and milk are always on our menu. Finally, on those days when we don't feel like cooking but want plenty to eat, we order the two-for-one special from the pizzeria down the road. It's the most affordable take-out food we can find, and sometimes we even have pizza left over. Refrigerated overnight, it makes a great cold breakfast in the morning. Our unconventional meals may break a few nutritional rules, but they are quick and easy and never break our budget.

■ Questions

1. Underline the paragraph's topic sentence.
2. Is the process described in this paragraph a fixed process or a loose process?

   _____

3. Underline the paragraph's summary sentence.

TOPICS FOR PRACTICING PROCESS WRITING

Process Assignment 1: The Small Stuff

Paragraph or Journal Entry

Write a paragraph or journal entry telling your reader how to do a simple, every-day process. Describe it so well and so completely that a reader could do it successfully based on your directions alone. Include at the beginning of the paper any tools that the reader will need. Below are a few suggestions.

tying a shoe	putting on and buttoning a shirt
brushing your teeth	feeding a pet
making toast	putting on makeup
making coffee	shaving
starting a car	reading a newspaper

Process Assignment 2: Advice Guru

Paragraph

You are an advice columnist, and you need to answer one more letter to complete tomorrow's column. Choose one of the following letters and write a process paragraph telling the letter writer how to solve his or her problem.

Dear Advice Guru,

I am twenty-three years old and plan to be married next month. My fiancé and I have planned a wonderful trip to the Bahamas as our honeymoon. The only problem is that my husband-to-be has announced that he wants to take his mother with us on our wedding trip! I love my fiancé and I like his mother, but I do not want her on our wedding trip. How can I resolve the situation without hurting anyone's feelings?

Signed,
Three's a Crowd

Dear Advice Guru,

I have a problem with my upstairs neighbors in the apartment where I live. Every day, all day, they play loud, obnoxious music. Even when they are gone, they leave the stereo blaring. At night, they watch television in bed with the volume up loud. They fall asleep and leave it on all night. I am hesitant to approach them because I am afraid of making the situation worse. What should I do?

Signed,
Quiet Please

Process Assignment 3: Getting Physical (or Mental)

Paragraph

Choose a physical or mental process and write an essay describing how it's done. Write about a process of your own choosing, or pick one from the lists below.

Mental Processes	Physical Processes
deciding between two job offers	working out with weights
studying	mowing a lawn
balancing a checkbook	washing a car
overcoming procrastination	packing belongings for a move

Process Assignment 4: You're the Expert

Paragraph or Essay

Write a paragraph or essay telling your reader how to do something that you do well. It might be a physical skill, like pitching a baseball, being a goalie on a hockey team, or doing an aerobic exercise routine. It might be a social skill, like making people feel comfortable or mediating an argument. Or it might be a practical skill or a craft, like getting the most for your money at the grocery store or making a stained-glass window. Whatever it is, you're the expert, so write with confidence.

TOPICS FOR COMBINING METHODS OF DEVELOPMENT

Definition, classification, and process are methods of showing the limits of a topic—the borders that define it—and of ordering it into steps, stages, or types. The following assignments ask you to combine one or more methods of development as you complete the assignment.

Mixed Methods Assignment 1: Courage

Definition and Classification

In this paragraph, your job is to define the term *courage* and to divide it into types. Your definition must be broad enough to cover all the types of courage that you explore in your paragraph. Then, list and define each type of courage. For example, you might discuss *moral courage,* the ability to stand up for what is right, or *physical courage,* the willingness to put oneself in danger for a cause. Since classification often incorporates examples, you may wish to provide examples that help the reader get a clear picture of each type of courage.

Mixed Methods Assignment 2: Problems and Solutions

Definition and Process

Define a particular problem that exists in your home, workplace, or school. It may be a problem that affects you or it may simply be a problem you have observed. Once you have defined the problem, your job is to suggest a process for solving it.

Mixed Methods Assignment 3: Classmates

Definition and Classification

As you observe the students in your classes, you probably classify some as serious students, others as perpetual latecomers, and still others as class clowns. Write a paragraph defining and classifying types of students in your classes. To make your paragraph more unified, discuss either students you enjoy having in class with you or students you dislike having in your classes.

9

Examining Logical Connections:

Comparison-Contrast, Cause-Effect, and Argument

A lawyer is summing up his defense for a jury. Let's listen in:

I know that you, members of the jury, have a lot of questions about this case. I have answers.

The defendant has admitted that he shot his grandmother as she slept in her bed. I am telling you to ignore my client's confession.

You may ask why you should ignore a legally obtained, video-taped confession. The answer is that this case is different from most. The differences are so obvious I won't insult you by going into them.

You may also ask why the defendant would shoot his defenseless grandmother. You can bet he had plenty of reasons!

You are rational people, ladies and gentlemen of the jury, and it will require a powerful argument to convince you to come back with a "not guilty" verdict. But I have the best argument of all: My client is innocent!

Do you think that the defense attorney in the example above was able to convince the jury? Without techniques of comparison-contrast, cause-effect, and argument, no lawyer would ever win a case and no salesperson would ever close a deal. These techniques of logical thought are also essential in the academic world.

When you compare alternatives, when you look for causes and effects, or when you argue for a particular course of action, you are using logic to explore connections between ideas. If your logic is thin or your connections weak, your reader will notice. The methods in this chapter call for rational thought and careful planning. The skills that go along with these methods of development—pinpointing differences and similarities, discovering reasons, predicting results, and arguing an issue logically—are essential. These higher-order tools of thought can help you in the college classroom and beyond.

Comparison-Contrast

One of the most effective ways of describing something that is unfamiliar to your reader is by comparing or contrasting it with something familiar. When you make a **comparison,** you show how two things are similar. If a friend asks you about a class you are taking, you may describe it by comparing it to a class that the two of you have taken together. When you **contrast** two things, you show how they are different. If you are asked on a political science exam to discuss the legislative and judicial branches of the government, you may contrast the ways each branch shapes the country's laws. In an English class, you might use both comparison and contrast to show how two writers develop similar themes in different ways. Used alone or together, comparison and contrast are useful tools for any writer.

■ Building Connections ■

When you make comparisons or draw contrasts, *examples* are often useful in making the similarities or differences clear to your reader.

Setting up a Comparison-Contrast Paragraph

The first step in setting up a comparison-contrast paragraph is to choose points of comparison or contrast and to decide whether to compare or contrast. One way to decide is through prewriting. Prewriting can help you determine whether your primary focus is on comparison or on contrast. Below is a sample brainstorming that sets the focus for a paragraph.

Brainstorming—Two Brothers

Eric	Rashad
✔ quiet	✔ outgoing
even-tempered, patient	easygoing
does not care what he wears	dresses well
✔ good student	✔ average student
✔ curious about ideas	✔ curious about people
likes music	likes music
good sense of humor	funny, always joking

Though there are points of comparison, there are even more points of contrast. The writer decides to focus on three contrasting points.

The next step in planning the comparison-contrast paragraph is to decide whether to use a point-by-point pattern or a block pattern to discuss the points. In a **point-by-point** pattern, each point of comparison or contrast is considered separately. Below is a point-by-point paragraph outline.

---

* Personality

Eric: Quiet

Rashad: Outgoing

---

* Academic Performance

Eric: Good student

Rashad: Average student

---

* Interests

Eric: Curious about ideas

Rashad: Curious about people

Another way of presenting a comparison or contrast is in a **block** pattern. In this pattern, information about one subject is presented in one big block, followed by information about the other subject in a second big block. A block paragraph outline is shown below.

Eric: Quiet—a listener rather than a talker

A good student—demands perfection

Interested in ideas

Rashad: Outgoing—keeps people entertained

Average student

Interested in people

EXERCISE 1   RECOGNIZING COMPARISON-CONTRAST PATTERNS

Below are two paragraphs written from the outlines shown earlier. Read each paragraph and decide which is the point-by-point paragraph and which is the block paragraph.

Paragraph A

My two brothers, Eric and Rashad, are from the same family, but they are different in many ways. Eric, my older brother, is the quiet one. He is a listener rather than a talker, and it takes a while to get to know him and see the friendly, funny person he is inside. He has always been a good and careful student. If he turns in a paper, it has been proofread several times, and he always checks math problems twice. He demands perfection of himself and isn't really happy unless he makes A's. Eric has always been interested in ideas, immersing himself in books and in the Internet and joining scholastic clubs like the Science Club. Rashad, on the other hand, is an outgoing person who makes friends easily. Maybe it is because he is the youngest child in our family and had to compete for attention, but he is a natural entertainer who keeps everyone laughing. As a student, he is just average. He procrastinates in studying, doing assignments, and preparing for tests. If he makes a C on an exam, he is satisfied. He is not so much intellectually curious as he is curious about people. He is always interested in what people are doing, and he wants to understand their behavior and know what motivates them. He would make a good counselor, coach, or psychologist. I have two wonderful brothers, but they are very different in their personalities, academic performance, and interests.

Paragraph B

My two brothers, Eric and Rashad, are from the same family, but they are different in many ways. Eric, my older brother, is the quiet one. He is a listener rather than a talker, so it takes a while to get to know him and see the friendly, funny person he is inside. Rashad, on the other hand, is an outgoing person who makes friends easily. Maybe it is because he is the youngest child in our family and had to compete for attention, but he is a natural entertainer who keeps everyone laughing. The two are also different in their approach to academics. Eric has always been a good and careful student. If he turns in a paper, it has been proofread several times, and he always checks math problems twice. He isn't really happy unless he makes A's. Rashad is more casual about studying. As a student, he is just average. He procrastinates in studying, doing assignments, and preparing for tests. If he makes a C on an exam, it does not bother him for too long. My brothers' interests are also different. Eric is idea-focused, immersing himself in books and in the Internet and joining scholastic clubs like the Science Club. Rashad, however, is not so much intellectually curious as he is curious about people. He is always interested in what people are doing, and he wants to understand their behavior and know what motivates them. He would make a good counselor, coach, or psychologist. I have two wonderful brothers, but they are very different in their personalities, academic performance, and interests.

■   **Questions**

1. The paragraph organized in point-by-point format is paragraph _____

2. The paragraph organized in block format is paragraph _____

3. Look at the two paragraphs. In which paragraph do you find more transitions? Why?

_____

_____

_____

Transitional Expressions

In setting up your comparison-contrast paragraph, you may find the following transitional expressions helpful. The transitions of contrast alert your reader to a change of direction, while transitions of comparison help to point out similarities.

Transitional Expressions Used to Compare and Contrast

* *Transitions of Contrast*				
although	even though	in contrast	in spite of	on the other hand
but	however	instead	nevertheless	yet

* *Transitions of Comparison*		
in the same way	like	similarly

Wordsmith's Corner: Sample Comparison-Contrast Paragraphs

Below, see how two writers handle topics using comparison-contrast. Read each paragraph and answer the questions that follow.

Comparison-Contrast Paragraph 1

Jesse's paragraph contrasts two different times of the week at the same car wash.

At the Car Wash

Once a week, on Friday night or Saturday morning, I take my car to the self-serve car wash. But the car wash on a Friday evening is quite different from the car wash on a Saturday morning. On Friday nights, as the sun goes down and the fluorescent lights come on, the car wash comes alive with sound. As I pull into the wash bay, I hear the thumping rhythms of rap and rock, and from somewhere, a smooth ballad. The people at the car wash are mostly in their teens or early twenties. Parked beside the vacuum with all four doors open wide, they clean their cars as their music competes with the sound coming from the other cars parked nearby. Laughter, flirting, and enthusiastic greetings among friends are as much a part of the scene as soap and water. The Friday night crowd is young, fun, and noisy. On Saturday mornings, the car wash attracts mostly families and older people. Children dart through the spray of the hose while their mothers scold. Older couples tackle the job together, while dads let their kids help with vacuuming the seats or polishing the tires. The only sounds are the spray of water on metal, the roar of the vacuum, and the shrieks and laughter of children. The bays and the vacuums remain the same, but the atmosphere of the car wash changes completely from Friday night to Saturday morning.

■ Questions

1. Underline the paragraph's topic sentence.
2. Is the paragraph comparison or contrast? What is being compared or contrasted?

   _____

   _____

3. Is the paragraph written in point-by-point or block format?

   _____

4. Underline the paragraph's summary sentence.

Comparison-Contrast Paragraph 2

Karen discusses how she functions in the morning and in the evening.

Morning and Evening

Most people function better at certain times of the day, but I take it to extremes. In the morning, I am a barely functioning human being, but when evening comes, I have energy to spare. Every morning, I stumble out of bed in a semiconscious state, only waking up after the second cup of coffee. My family knows that conversation with me before 10:00 A.M. is impossible. My end of the conversation consists of a few grunts, and whatever anyone else says does not stay in my sleep-fogged brain for more than a few seconds. I know better than to take an 8:00 A.M. class. Even if I could drag myself out of bed to get to class on time, I would never remember a word the professor said. By midafternoon, however, my engines start humming. When everyone else is in a midafternoon slump, I am out jogging around the lake or doing research for my term paper in the library. If I go out with friends, my energy increases as the night wears on, while my friends wilt like tired flowers as midnight approaches. If I am at home, I watch my family drift away to bed, one by one, in spite of my attempts to keep them awake with conversation and jokes. It's not easy to be a night owl when I am surrounded by larks.

■ Questions

1. Underline the paragraph's topic sentence.
2. Is the paragraph comparison or contrast? What is being compared or contrasted?

_____

_____

3. Is the paragraph written in point-by-point or block format?

_____

TOPICS FOR PRACTICING COMPARISON-CONTRAST WRITING

Comparison-Contrast Assignment 1: Two by Two

Paragraph or Journal Entry

Write a comparison-contrast paragraph or journal entry on one of the following topics.

> two brands of a product you use
>
> two classes
>
> two times of day
>
> two days of the week
>
> two television commercials

Comparison-Contrast Assignment 2: Family Traits

Paragraph

In a paragraph, discuss some of the ways in which two members of your family are alike.

Comparison-Contrast Assignment 3: What Would You Change?

Paragraph

What area of your life would you like to change, and how would you make it different from the way it is now? Make sure that your paragraph shows both sides: how it is now and how you would like it to be. Some possible areas of change are listed below.

> a family relationship
>
> relationship with a friend or significant other
>
> finances
>
> living conditions
>
> job
>
> transportation

Comparison-Contrast Assignment 4: Thumbs Up, Thumbs Down

Paragraph or Essay

Think of the best and the worst in any of the following categories. Then write a comparison-contrast paragraph or essay contrasting the two.

> the best/worst job you have held
>
> the best/worst date you have been on
>
> the best/worst place to go on a date

the best/worst place you have lived
the best/worst vacation
the best/worst TV show or movie

Cause and Effect

When you look for the **causes** of an event, you are looking for the reasons it happened. In other words, you are looking for answers to *why* questions. Why did your last romantic relationship end badly? Why is your Uncle Fred's car still humming along at 150,000 miles? Why are so many schools plagued by violence?

When you look for the **effects** of an action, you are looking for its results. You are answering the question *What would happen if?* What would happen if every community had a neighborhood watch? What would happen if you decided to devote just one hour a day to an important long-term goal? What is the effect of regular maintenance on an automobile?

When you explore both cause and effect, you look at both the reason and the result. You may explore actual cause and effect, as in "Uncle Fred performs all scheduled maintenance on his car and changes the oil every 3,000 miles; as a result, his car is still going strong at 150,000 miles." You may also explore hypothetical cause and effect, as in "Many members of my generation are bored and cynical because everything—material possessions, good grades, and even the respect of others—has come to them too easily."

Identifying Causes and Effects

A cause is a *reason.* If you are asking a "why" question, the answer is probably a cause. Why do toilets flush in a counterclockwise spiral above the equator and in a clockwise spiral below it? Why did I do so poorly on my history test? Why did the chicken cross the road? From the scientific to the silly, these "why" questions can be answered by finding reasons or causes.

An effect is a *result.* If you ask "What will happen if . . ." or "What were the results of . . ." then your answer is an effect. What would the results be if the speed limit were lowered by ten miles per hour? What would happen if I set aside an hour a day to exercise? What would happen if I threw these new red socks into the washer with my white underwear? When you answer these and other "what if" questions, your answer is an effect.

EXERCISE 2   CAUSES OR EFFECTS?

For each topic listed, indicate whether a paragraph on the topic would involve a discussion of causes (reasons) or effects (results).

_____ 1.   Why do so many people enjoy watching wrestling?

_____ 2.   What would the results be if attending college became mandatory?

_____ 3.   Why are so many American people overweight?

_____ 4.   Describe your reasons for choosing the career you are preparing for.

_____ 5.   What would happen if every television station in the United States stopped broadcasting for a one-month period?

_____ 6.   What effects does music have on you?

_____ 7.   What good habit have you taken up lately? Why?

_____ 8.   Why do so many people watch talk shows?

_____ 9.   What are the effects of habitual overuse of alcohol?

_____ 10.   Are you superstitious? Why or why not?

Wordsmith's Corner: Sample Cause-Effect Paragraphs

Below are two paragraphs dealing with causes and effects. Read each piece and answer the questions that follow.

Cause-Effect Paragraph 1

In this paragraph, Maria discusses obnoxious behavior at ball games.

Obnoxious Fans

The last time I went to a professional baseball game, a fan sitting near me shouted insults at the players until his voice was hoarse. Instead of enjoying the action on the field, I spent nine innings wondering why a fan would behave so obnoxiously at a game. One possible reason is that the fan is letting out pent-up aggression from some other, unrelated situation. Maybe his boss yells at him and insults him, and he can't yell back for fear of losing his job. So he takes out all his aggression for the price of a ticket to the ball game. Another possibility is that he is a coward who only strikes out at targets that won't strike back. Publicly humiliating people, shouting at them, or insulting their mothers is usually dangerous. However, ball players are relatively safe targets because their job is to focus on the game, and usually, they ignore abuse. Confrontational behavior might also be part of the fan's personality. Maybe he picks fights with everyone and sees no reason to behave differently just because he is at a ball game. While suppressed aggression, cowardice, or a confrontational personality could be the problem, there is one other possibility. Maybe the fan is just a jerk.

■ Questions

1. Underline the topic sentence of the paragraph.
2. Does the paragraph mainly discuss causes or effects? _____
3. Identify the effect(s) and the cause(s) in this paragraph.

_____

_____

_____

_____

Cause-Effect Paragraph 2

Anthony uses cause and effect to write about his credit card blues.

Credit Card Blues

Shortly after I enrolled in college, I received a credit card offer in the mail. My decision to accept had several negative effects. For one thing, having a credit card gave me the illusion of unlimited buying power. I would go into a store, see something I wanted, and pull out my shiny new credit card. Magically, that little piece of plastic gave me the power to buy, even if I had no money in the bank. When the first bill came, I was shocked to see that I had charged almost $300 on my card, almost as much as I cleared in a month on my part-time job. A second effect of having a credit card was the illusion that I could easily pay off my debt. On a $300 balance, the credit card company wanted only a $10 minimum payment. I paid the minimum, not realizing that it would take me well over two years to pay off my card at that rate. I continued charging, rationalizing that the $2,000 limit on my card would act as an automatic barrier and keep me from spending too much. But when I reached that amount, the credit card company raised my limit to $3,000. I felt proud, thinking I must really be a creditworthy person. I was more like a fish, attracted by a flashy plastic lure and caught on a line of credit. Finally, when my credit card balance reached $5,000, I called a halt to credit and cut up my card. But the card is still exercising its negative effects. I am now working extra hours at my part-time job to pay off my balance, and the amount I can spend day-to-day is reduced. Now, when envelopes come in the mail saying "preapproved" or "low interest," I tear them up without even opening them.

■ Questions

1. Underline the topic sentence of the paragraph.
2. Is the paragraph mainly about causes or effects?

_____

3. Identify the cause(s) and effect(s) discussed in the paragraph.

_____

_____

_____

_____

_____

_____

_____

_____

TOPICS FOR PRACTICING CAUSE AND EFFECT WRITING

Cause-Effect Assignment 1: Addictive Behavior

Paragraph or Journal Entry

Write a paragraph or journal entry about the causes or the effects of any type of addictive behavior. You may choose to write about addiction to substances such as alcohol, cigarettes, coffee, drugs, or chocolate. Or you may choose to focus on addiction to activities such as exercise, surfing the Internet, shopping, or watching television.

Cause-Effect Assignment 2: Just Causes

Paragraph

Discuss only the causes of one of the following in a paragraph.

> poor grades
>
> divorce
>
> financial problems
>
> shoplifting
>
> stress or burnout

Cause-Effect Assignment 3: Writing about Effects

Paragraph

Discuss the effects of one of the following in a paragraph.

> exercise
>
> violence in television programs, movies, and music
>
> technology on everyday life
>
> loss of a close friend or relative

Cause-Effect Assignment 4: A Painful Decision

Paragraph or Essay

Write a paragraph or essay discussing the reasons for a painful decision in your life. A decision to divorce, to have an abortion or to give up a child for adoption, to break off a friendship, or to quit a job are some possibilities.

Argument

Though the word **argument** is sometimes used to mean a heated discussion or even a shouting match, the argument you make in a paragraph is of a cooler sort. Using pen and paper to explain your stand on an issue has its advantages: no one will interrupt you or try to outshout you. However, a good argument is more than just your opinion on an issue. It is your convincing, well-supported opinion. What matters is not which side you take, but how well and how strongly you support your views. Logic, a strong regard for truth, and solid examples are your allies in constructing an argument paragraph.

Taking Sides

It has been said that there are two sides to every argument. Your paragraph, however, should favor just *one* side. In an argument paragraph, it is important to make your position clear, and that means starting with a strong topic sentence. Look at the examples below.

Examples

✗   Music education is often the first program to feel the axe when a budget crisis hits the public schools. (This topic sentence does not state a position.)

✗   Music education is considered essential by many, but others see it as a nonessential frill. (This topic sentence states two positions.)

✔   Music education is an essential part of a child's education. (This topic sentence states a clear position.)

✔   While some see music education as nonessential, I believe it should be a part of every child's education. (This topic sentence mentions the opposing viewpoint but makes it clear where the writer stands.)

EXERCISE 3   RECOGNIZING TOPIC SENTENCES THAT TAKE A SIDE

Look at the following pairs of topic sentences. Place a check beside the sentence that takes a side on the issue being discussed.

1.   _____ A museum is a place that houses artifacts and collections and educates and entertains the public.

     _____ The proposed science and technology museum would be an asset to our city.

2. _____ The death penalty, while unquestionably harsh, is justified in some instances.

   _____ The death penalty is an issue that generates much argument, both pro and con.

3. _____ Ever since I can remember, my family has always driven Toyotas.

   _____ The Toyota Corolla is the best car in its price range.

4. _____ Many people favor electing Ed Macklehouse as our next mayor, but then again, some people say he is a crook.

   _____ Ed Macklehouse should be our next mayor.

5. _____ Many people enjoy playing state lotteries that fund education and other state programs.

   _____ State lotteries are nothing more than a tax on people who don't understand math.

Will You Change Anyone's Mind?

A good argument is aimed at changing people's views. On some topics, a convincing argument may change someone's mind. On other topics, though, you will find it next to impossible to sway an opinion that may have been molded by a lifetime of experience. Particularly on such hot-button issues as abortion, assisted suicide, or the death penalty, the best you can realistically hope for is to open a window to your viewpoint. In this case, success means coaxing your reader to look through that window long enough to say, "I see what you mean, and I understand your point of view."

■ Building Connections ■

Arguing a point often involves *contrast* and *cause-effect*. Making an argument sometimes involves contrasting one side with another. An argument favoring a particular course of action (for example, making handgun ownership illegal) often involves examining both the positive and negative effects of that action.

Wordsmith's Corner: Sample Argument Paragraphs

Below are two examples of writing arguing a point. Read each piece and answer the questions that follow.

Argument Paragraph 1

Carmen argues for the usefulness of creatures that give some people the shivers.

Let Them Be

For many people, the immediate reaction to a spider, snake, or lizard is to yell, "Kill it!" But in most cases, the best thing to do is simply let it be. Spiders may look creepy, but they eat harmful insects. A wolf spider, for example, does not trap its prey, but actively hunts down ticks, cockroaches, and other insects. So when I see a wolf spider in my garage, I let it alone. Though it is ugly and its size is formidable, I know that it is beneficial. Occasionally, I see a snake in my yard or garden, but I do not run for a hoe to kill it. I know that snakes eat insects and small rodents that feed on plants. So if I have beautiful flowers or delicious tomatoes and squash, it is partly thanks to the snakes that keep pests from devouring my garden. Some creepy creatures are valuable just for their entertainment value. A resort hotel my family visited once was home to many geckoes, small darting lizards that lived in the bushes and in the spaces between the boards on the outside of the hotel. Instead of trying to eliminate them, the hotel made mascots of them. The gift shop and restaurant sold gecko keychains, gecko postcards, and small stuffed geckoes to take home as souvenirs. Snakes, lizards, and spiders may not be warm and cuddly, but they are mostly harmless and often helpful creatures that deserve a better fate than most people would allow them.

■ Questions

1. Underline the paragraph's topic sentence.
2. List the arguments that the writer makes in favor of spiders, snakes, and lizards.

_____

_____

3. Underline the paragraph's summary sentence.

Argument Paragraph 2

In this paragraph, the writer argues that curfews are a form of age discrimination.

```
      City Curfews: Legalized Age Discrimination

    The issue of whether a teenager had a curfew used
to be between the teen and his or her parents, but
lately, some cities have begun imposing curfews
on teenagers. The reasons for the curfews sound
convincing on the surface, but a closer look
shows that curfews are a form of legalized age
discrimination. Lawmakers say that teenagers are
responsible for more crime than other age groups,
and teens who are out late are more likely to
commit crimes. True, a teenager who is out late
might be committing a crime, but he also might be
returning home from work, coming back from a study
session, or simply having fun. Even convicted
felons, once their time is served, are allowed to
walk the streets freely. Keeping teenagers off the
streets because of crimes they might commit is
nothing more than discrimination. The same applies
to the argument that curfews cut down on drinking
and driving. A teen who drinks is violating the
law, and if he gets behind the wheel, he is doubly
guilty. But why should teens who are not drinking
and driving be penalized for the actions of those
who do? A better idea is to focus on those who do
wrong, and leave the innocent alone. A final
argument often made in favor of curfews is that
they keep teens safe. But concern for safety is
sometimes a convenient excuse for discrimination.
For instance, women were denied jobs as police
officers and firefighters for decades on the
grounds that those jobs were "too dangerous." But
```

danger, whether on the job or in the streets, is an
equal opportunity threat. If the streets are unsafe,
then they are unsafe for all age groups, not just
for teenagers. Cities should leave the power to set
curfews where it belongs—in the hands of parents.

■ Questions

1. Underline the paragraph's topic sentence.
2. What arguments does the writer use in saying that teen curfews are discriminatory?

_____

_____

_____

_____

_____

3. Underline the paragraph's topic sentence.

TOPICS FOR PRACTICING ARGUMENT WRITING

Argument Assignment 1: Seeing Both Sides

Paragraph or Journal Entry

Write a paragraph or journal entry arguing why one of your school's policies is unwise. Some students object to policies limiting the number of absences, while others fret at library policies that allow a book to be checked out for only two weeks. Still others object to exams that all students must pass before graduating. Brainstorming with other students will help to get your thoughts focused on your school's policies.

Argument Assignment 2: Child Care

Paragraph

Does attending day care while parents work harm children or help them? Write your argument in one paragraph.

Argument Assignment 3: Banned

Paragraph

Write a paragraph supporting the following fill-in-the-blank topic sentence:

"If I ran the world, _____ would be banned."

Note: On this topic, you might get a better paragraph from a small, concrete topic than a large, abstract one. For example, "television" or "open-toed sandals" might be more manageable topics than "hatred" or "racism."

Argument Assignment 4: Testing, 1, 2, 3 . . .

Paragraph

The topics below deal with testing in one form or another. Choose one of the topics and write a paragraph supporting one side of the issue.

1. Is the practice of employers testing job applicants for illegal drugs a good idea?
2. Should colleges require students to take a test demonstrating competence in reading and writing before issuing a diploma?
3. Should every newborn be tested for AIDS?
4. Should teachers be periodically tested in their subject area to make sure their knowledge is current?

TOPICS FOR COMBINING METHODS OF DEVELOPMENT

Comparison-contrast, cause-effect, and argument are methods of looking at the logical connections between ideas. How are they alike? How do they differ? How does one affect another, and what logical arguments can be made for or against an idea? The following assignments ask you to combine one or more methods of development as you complete the assignment.

Mixed Methods Assignment 1: Community Service

Argument and Cause-Effect

Some colleges are incorporating a community service component into the graduation requirements of the college or into the requirements of specific programs. As you argue for or against such a requirement in your own college, base your argument on the effects of mandatory community service on students or on the community at large.

Mixed Methods Assignment 2: Same or Different?

Comparison-Contrast and Cause-Effect

Write a paragraph that discusses ways in which you and a close friend or family member are alike or different. As you discuss each similarity or difference, describe the effect that it has on your relationship. Focus on either similarities or differences.

Mixed Methods Assignment 3: Givers and Takers

Argument, Comparison-Contrast, and/or Cause-Effect

Although most people fall somewhere between the two extremes, clearly some people are givers and others are takers. Givers work for the betterment of their community, give to their families, and always seem to be doing something for others. Takers rely on the help of others. It may even sometimes seem as though they are using other people to accomplish their own goals. If one has to make a choice, is it better to be a giver or a taker?

In this paragraph, you will answer the question with an argument—that is, your topic sentence will state that it is better to be a giver or better to be a taker. Although the paragraph is essentially an argument, structure it to include either comparison-contrast or cause-effect. If you include comparison-contrast, do so by showing the contrasts between being a giver and being a taker. If you include cause-effect, focus on one of the two alternatives (It is better to be a giver . . .) and show the effects choosing that particular alternative.

10
Writing an Essay

You are about to meet a form of writing that offers a ticket to just about anywhere in the academic world. When you master the fundamentals of the essay, you master a form of writing that can be used to express an opinion, analyze a poem, or compare two methods of government. Shrunk down a bit, it can be used to answer a question on an essay test or an employment application. Expanded a bit, it can be used to write a research paper, a term paper, or even a master's thesis. Even this textbook is, in many ways, an expansion of the essay format.

Parts of an Essay

Once you learn to write an essay, you can modify the essay form and length to suit your purpose for writing. Here's how an essay looks: First comes an introduction that catches the reader's attention, provides background, introduces the subject, and states the **thesis,** or the main idea of the essay.

Then come the **body paragraphs.** Each one discusses one aspect of your thesis. The topic sentence of each paragraph tells which thesis point the paragraph will develop.

The essay ends with a **conclusion** that sums up the points you have made and lets your reader know that you have ended the essay.

A diagram of a five-paragraph essay appears below. Study it to get a mental map of the essay, then use it for planning and checking your own essays.

Essay Diagram

Introduction
- The first sentence attracts the reader's attention.
- The introduction provides background and introduces the subject.
- The last sentence states the thesis (main idea) and may list the points of development.

First Body Paragraph
- The topic sentence states the first thesis point that you will develop.
- Support sentences give specific examples, information, and explanation of the topic sentence.
- A summary sentence (optional) sums up the entire paragraph.

Second Body Paragraph
- The topic sentence states the next thesis point that you will develop.
- Support sentences give specific examples, information, and explanation of the topic sentence.
- A summary sentence (optional) sums up the entire paragraph.

Third Body Paragraph
- The topic sentence states the third thesis point that you will develop.
- Support sentences give specific examples, information, and explanation of the topic sentence.
- A summary sentence (optional) sums up the entire paragraph.

Conclusion
- The first sentence of the conclusion is a broad, thesis-level statement. It may restate the thesis.
- The last sentence of the conclusion is satisfying and final-sounding.

Sample Essay

Like Father, Like Son

attention-getting opening — "Like father, like son," my aunt always said. Then her eyes would slide over to my mother in a secretive way, and I knew even as a child that it was not a compliment. Now that I have a child of my own, it is important to me to prove my aunt's *thesis statement* — words wrong. As a parent, I plan to be different from my own father in all of the ways that count.

topic sentence 1 — The first difference that my aunt—and my child—will see in me is that I will lead a more sober life than my father did. During all my growing-up years, my father abused alcohol and drugs. Since he and my mother were not together, I never saw *support* — the worst of it. But even on our rare visitation days, he could not take me to a ball game or a mall without stopping by a convenience store for a six-pack. Maybe because of that example—or maybe because I was young and stupid—I followed in my father's footsteps for a while. But now that I am older and have a son, my wild days are over. I realize the importance of setting a good example *summary sentence* — and of being a role model to him. Drugs and alcohol will never be a part of the image of me that my son Brandon carries through life.

topic sentence 2 — Another difference will be in my financial *support* — support of my child. My father drifted from job to job and had periods of unemployment, so his financial support was undependable. To make ends meet, my mother had to work two jobs, one in the mornings on a hotel janitorial staff and the other waiting tables on a part-time basis. Even then, times were often tough. Financial support is part of being a father. It is the reason that I work, *summary sentence* — and the reason I am enrolled in school. Brandon's mother will never have to work an extra job because I am not meeting my obligations.

(continued)

topic sentence 3 ——   Unlike my father, I am going to be there for my child. My father's visits were as unpredictable as

support —— his support checks. He was not there when I was six and had my tonsils taken out, and he was not there for my high school graduation. I will be there for Brandon. Brandon's mother and I have chosen to live separately, but both of us agree that I should have an active role in his life. When he was a baby, I held him and fed him and changed his diapers. Now, I am the one who takes him to t-ball practice and attends all his games.

summary sentence —— He can count on me to be there during the important moments in his life.

thesis restatement ——   I have never been a perfect person, and I won't be a perfect father. But I am determined to do better than my father did. I will be a good role model and support my son financially and emotion-

Closing thought —— ally. One day, someone may look at us and say, "Like father, like son." When that happens, I want Brandon to feel proud.

Meeting the Challenge of Essay Writing

How do you get from an idea or assignment to a polished, fully developed essay? It is sometimes difficult to make the transition from paragraph-length compositions to essays. The length and the format of your assignments have changed. But the basic principles you have been following have not changed. The writing process is still the same: you still prewrite, plan, draft, revise, and proofread.

Similarly, the characteristics of an effective paragraph also apply to the essay. **Direction, unity, coherence,** and **support** are part of the makeup of effective paragraphs *and* essays. Review those characteristics below, and see how these qualities of effective writing apply to the essay.

Characteristics of an Effective Essay

1. **Direction** means that the essay has a strong thesis sentence that states the main idea and sets the course that the essay will follow.

2. **Unity** means that the essay makes one main point and sticks to that point. Each body paragraph may discuss a different thesis point, but the essay never strays from the idea expressed in the thesis.

3. **Coherence** means that the essay is logically connected and easy to follow.

4. **Support** means that the essay contains specific and detailed discussion of the idea stated in the topic sentence.

Writing the Essay

Because the essay is so much longer than the paragraphs you have been writing, it may appear to be not so much a writing exercise as a major construction project. Like any major project, the construction of an essay is accomplished word by word, sentence by sentence, paragraph by paragraph. The next few sections of the chapter deal with the major parts of the essay and with how those parts fit together to form a coherent whole.

Providing Direction: Writing the Thesis Statement

Your **thesis statement** is the most important sentence in your essay. It states the main idea of your essay, often states or implies your attitude or opinion about the subject, and gives your essay **direction.** In an essay, the thesis statement is the controlling force behind every sentence and every word. It is a promise to your reader that you will discuss the idea mentioned in the thesis statement and no other.

Types of Thesis Statements

When constructing your thesis statement, you have a choice. You may write a **thesis with points** that lists the points the essay will cover or a **thesis without points** that does not list the points of development.

The Thesis with Points

A thesis with points presents the main idea and the points of development, listed in the order in which you will discuss them in the essay. The thesis with points has a long tradition in college writing. Listing your thesis points provides a road map that lets the reader see where the essay is headed.

Examples of a Thesis with Points

point 1   point 2
Playing with my children, shopping with my mother and sister, and
point 3
spending time with my husband are my weekend pleasures.

point 1
Older students may attend college to prepare for a new career, to
point 2   point 3
advance in their present career, or to satisfy a hunger for learning.

point 1   point 2   point 3
Action, an exciting plot, and strong characters are essential ingredients

for any movie.

EXERCISE 1   COMPLETING THESIS STATEMENTS

Complete the following thesis statements.

1. Our camping trip was a disaster. We were pelted by rain, bitten by _____,

   and _____ by _____.

2. Writing an essay requires good ideas, _____, and _____

   _____.

3. _____, _____, and _____ are my mother's best qualities.

4. These days, the best candidate for the job is usually the one _____

   _____, _____, and _____.

5. Some of the things people fear about getting old are _____, _____, and

   _____.

The Thesis without Points Listed

A thesis without points listed presents the central idea of the essay without enumerating the points of development. Without the "road map" that listing your points provides, it is even more important that your essay flow logically and smoothly. Therefore, topic sentences require careful planning so that they are clearly connected to the thesis. When you plan a thesis without points, plan each topic sentence, too, to ensure that you stay on track. Not listing thesis points does not mean that you do not plan them; it simply means that you do not list them.

Examples of a Thesis without Points Listed

Thesis: My weekend pleasures revolve around my family.

> **Topic sentence 1:** On Friday evenings, my husband and I often enjoy a movie.
>
> **Topic sentence 2:** On Saturdays, I take the children shopping or swimming.
>
> **Topic sentence 3:** Every Sunday, we visit my parents or my husband's parents.

Thesis: Starting an exercise program has made me a healthier person

> **Topic sentence 1:** For one thing, exercise has improved my aerobic capacity.
>
> **Topic sentence 2:** I also feel stronger since I began exercising.
>
> **Topic sentence 3:** Thanks to my exercise program, I have also dropped a few unwanted pounds.

Thesis: Losing my parents at the age of eighteen was the hardest thing I have ever gone through.

> **Topic sentence 1:** The accident was so sudden and my parents were gone so quickly that I was numb for weeks.
>
> **Topic sentence 2:** My parents' death left me with a tremendous amount of responsibility.
>
> **Topic sentence 3:** It is still difficult seeing the milestones ahead that my parents will never share with me.

EXERCISE 2   WRITING THESIS STATEMENTS

For each of the following topics, write a thesis statement without points.

1. What was the best (or worst) day of your life?

   _____

2. Should drivers and their passengers be required to wear seat belts?

   _____

3. Is there ever any justification for cheating?

   _____

4. If you could spend a week visiting any place in the world, where would you go?

_____

5. What popular activity do you consider overrated? Why?

_____

Getting Started: Introducing the Essay

It is said that you will never have a second chance to make a first impression. Because first impressions are so important, it pays to put extra effort into your introduction. However, an introduction is more than just a way to make a good impression. It does several jobs that no other part of the essay could do quite so effectively.

Purposes of an Introduction

1. **An introduction draws your reader into the essay.** The first sentence of your introduction should be irresistible. It won't always turn out that way, but aim high anyway.

2. **An introduction presents the general topic of your essay.** When you ease into the thesis by bringing up your general topic first, your reader has time to turn her thoughts away from whatever is on her mind—the price of gas or what to eat for lunch—and to get in the mood to listen to what you have to say.

3. **An introduction provides necessary background.** Background information is not always necessary. But if it is, the introduction is a good place for it. Background information tucked into the introduction gives the necessary details to set up the rest of the essay.

4. **The introduction presents your essay's thesis.** The most important job of an introductory paragraph is to present your essay's thesis. Every sentence in the introduction should follow a path of logic that leads directly to your thesis, which will be the last sentence of your introduction. Once you have stated the thesis, stop. Your body paragraphs will flow naturally from a thesis that comes at the end of the introduction.

Writing the Introductory Paragraph

Introductions that draw a reader in don't just happen; they are carefully crafted. Three common types of introduction appear below. Try them all, using the examples as models.

The Broad-to-Narrow Introduction

The *broad-to-narrow introduction* is a classic style of introduction. Sometimes called the *inverted triangle introduction*, it funnels your reader from a statement of your topic to the narrowest point in the introduction: your thesis.

Example

Driving is a great American pastime. Roads and highways swarm with drivers going back and forth from work, school, shopping, or recreation. And with so many drivers on the road, there are bound to be a few who should never have been trusted with that little plastic card called a license. The worst drivers on the road are those who tailgate, those who weave in and out of traffic, and those who drive drunk.

The Narrow-to-Broad Introduction

Instead of beginning with a statement of your general topic, the *narrow-to-broad introduction* begins at a point that is smaller than your thesis—often just a detail—and expands toward that thesis. With this method, you can create an unusual and intriguing opening.

Example

I see the tires first, grimed with the dirt of a long journey. Then I catch a glimpse of a face in the window of the long, boxy vehicle. The RV passes, giving me a last look at the bikes hooked to the back and "The Wanderer" painted above the rear window. I just don't get it. Why would anyone want an RV? An RV is a poor choice for vacationing because of its cost, size, and the chores that come along with it.

The Contrast Introduction

Gold placed on black velvet in a jeweler's window takes on extra luster against the contrasting background. In a *contrast introduction,* your ideas can shine through the drama of contrast. Starting with a contrasting idea is an easy and effective technique to use. Make sure that your introduction contains a change-of-direction signal such as *but* or *however* so that the two contrasting elements are clearly set apart.

Example

Modern life often means that people work long hours to buy possessions that they don't have time to enjoy. Sometimes, it means that children have too many toys and not enough of their parents' time.

But many people have decided to leave the rat race. Instead of striving for more, these families live on less in exchange for working fewer hours or sometimes quitting their jobs entirely and working for themselves. A simpler lifestyle can reduce stress, teach self-reliance, and encourage family unity.

The Body Paragraphs: Unity

Once you begin writing the body of your essay, you are in familiar territory once again. You already know how to write a topic sentence and support a paragraph. In writing the three body paragraphs of a five-paragraph essay, you are simply doing that familiar task three times. In an essay, however, each of the three body paragraphs is directly related to the thesis statement. Specifically, each body paragraph discusses one aspect of the thesis statement. This arrangement gives an essay **unity.** Look at the thesis from an earlier sample essay:

Thesis: As a parent, I plan to be different from my own father in all of the ways that count.

From reading the thesis, it is clear that the writer plans to discuss *ways his parenting style will be different from his father's.* Each body paragraph, then, will discuss one way in which the writer will be different from his own father.

Now look at the topic sentences from the sample essay and notice how each relates directly to the thesis (*being different from his father*) while at the same time discussing a distinct and separate point of that thesis:

Topic Sentence 1: The first difference that my aunt—and my child—will see in me is that I will lead a more sober life than my father did.

Topic Sentence 2: Another difference will be in my financial support of my child.

Topic Sentence 3: Unlike my father, I am going to be there for my child.

A thesis statement gives your essay direction. The topic sentences must follow that direction or the unity of the essay will be compromised.

EXERCISE 3   ELIMINATING FAULTY TOPIC SENTENCES

Each of the following thesis statements is followed by three topic sentences. Circle the letter of the topic sentence that does *not* support the thesis statement.

1. Football is my favorite sport.
    a. When I was in high school, I was on the football team three out of four years.
    b. During football season, I am glued to my television set to watch the games.
    c. Attendance at professional football games has risen in recent years, demonstrating the sport's popularity.

2. Like dogs themselves, there are several kinds of dog owners.
    a. Like the wolves they are descended from, dogs are pack animals and need to be part of a social structure.
    b. Some dog owners simply want a companion around the house or apartment.
    c. Another type of dog owner wants the protection that a dog can provide.

3. The city's new indoor skating park will have several positive effects.
    a. Skaters and skateboarders will have a place to call their own.
    b. Pedestrians will no longer be endangered by fast-moving skaters on downtown streets.
    c. Skating can be dangerous, so skaters and skateboarders should always wear safety equipment.

4. Our college should consider scheduling classes around a "Wonderful Wednesday" or a "Fabulous Friday," a day during the week when no classes meet.
    a. A weekly day off would give students time to go to the library and work on class projects.
    b. The idea has been rejected by the school's administration because students might not use the day productively.
    c. The day would also give professors a chance to catch up on grading and have conferences with students.

5. Looking at movies of the 1950s and movies of today, it is easy to see how their differences reflect social changes over the years.
    a. Romantic comedies of the 1950s almost always ended on marriage, but today's movies reflect a different social trend.
    b. Special effects in 1950s movies were unsophisticated, but today's advanced techniques produce impressive effects.
    c. Minorities and women were often stereotyped in 1950s movies, but today's films have fewer stereotyped characters.

The Body Paragraphs: Support

Once you have written the thesis and topic sentences, you have an outline composed of the main idea and major subpoints of the essay. All that remains is to flesh out the body paragraphs with strong, vivid, detailed support, just as you would in any paragraph. Review the principles of support by completing the exercise below.

EXERCISE 4   RECOGNIZING SPECIFIC SUPPORT

The introduction on recreational vehicles is extended here with three sets of body paragraphs. In the blank to the left of each paragraph, mark *S* if the paragraph contains specific support and *V* if the paragraph contains vague support.

Body Paragraph 1a

_____ First of all, an RV is extremely expensive. As anyone who has ever visited an RV dealer or an RV show can testify, the initial outlay for a new RV is considerable. In addition, there are numerous other expenses associated with RV ownership. Some of those expenses relate to traveling, while others relate to maintenance. For the cost involved in owning and maintaining an RV, a person might be able to enjoy a luxury vacation at the finest hotel.

Body Paragraph 1b

_____ First of all, an RV is extremely expensive. A new RV can cost $100,000 or more, as much as some houses. Add to that the cost of gas, maintenance, hookup at RV parks, storage, and repairs, and an RV becomes even more expensive. If a person put $100,000 in the bank at 5 percent interest instead of buying an RV, he would get $5,000 in interest each year, enough to take a vacation or two every year and still keep his $100,000.

Body Paragraph 2a

_____ Second, an RV is just too large. Its size makes it difficult to maneuver and gives it a greater stopping distance, thus requiring greater driving skill. It can't be parked just anywhere, nor can its driver just whip into a drive-through for a hamburger when the travelers get hungry. Its size also makes storage a problem during the months when it is not being used. My neighbors' RV is too large to fit into their garage, so they had to build a separate storage barn in their backyard just to keep their RV out of the weather. That's fine for people who have the money and the space to build a storage facility, but people who live in condominiums or who have small lots have to make other arrangements. An RV's size makes it more of a liability than an asset.

Body Paragraph 2b

_____ Second, an RV is just too large. The size of an RV is enormous, dwarfing every car on the road. Size has several disadvantages. Many of the maneuvers that drivers of smaller vehicles take for granted cannot be performed by an RV because of its size. Further, there is the consideration of RV storage, which must take size into account. An RV's size makes it more of a liability than an asset.

Body Paragraph 3a

_____ Finally, an RV is just too much work. People who travel in RVs have to clean, cook, make beds, and empty toilets. If they run out of food, they have to shop. If I have to take all that work on vacation with me, I might as well stay at home. When I go on vacation, I want to eat in restaurants and have my food brought to me perfectly prepared. I do not want to stand over a hot stove and know that I have to wash dishes after I eat. In the morning, I want to leave my bed unmade and my towels in the tub, walk on the beach, and come back to my room to find everything in perfect order. In an RV, I would have to do all the work myself.

Body Paragraph 3b

_____ Finally, an RV is just too much work. People who travel in RVs have to do all the work normally associated with a maintaining a house. In many

cases, there are other associated tasks that relate
to travel. Why would a person take all of those
household chores on vacation? It seems to me that
the purpose of a vacation is to leave everyday
chores behind. In a hotel these tasks are
accomplished by the hotel staff, so that the
traveler has little to do. That seems like the
ideal situation for any traveler. That way, when
the traveler returns home, he is rested and
refreshed, not worn out from trying to accomplish
all the tasks associated with traveling in an RV.

The Body Paragraphs: Coherence

An essay requires not only coherence *within* paragraphs, but coherence *between* paragraphs. That is, movement from one paragraph to the next should seem graceful, natural, and seamless.

Coherence within paragraphs is provided by transitional words, use of pronouns, and use of repetition. (To review these principles, glance back at the section on coherence in Chapter 5.) Look below for tips for making graceful transitions between paragraphs.

Tips for Smooth Transitions

1. In the first body paragraph, you do not necessarily need a transitional word. If you want to use one to indicate that this paragraph is making the first of several points, the choices are easy: *first of all, one reason* (*factor, cause,* or similar term), or *first.*

2. The second body paragraph gives you more choices. You can use a phrase like *a second reason* or a word such as *next, another,* or *also.* For variety, try slipping the word or phrase in the middle of your topic sentence instead of using it at the beginning: "Job security is *another* reason I have chosen a career in the medical field."

3. The third body paragraph gives you all of the transitional options of the second body paragraph and a few others as well. Since the third body paragraph is your last, you can use expressions like *finally* or *the last reason.* If you are using emphatic order (order of importance), you might want to try *most important, the major factor, best,* or *worst.*

4. Transitions of time and place are preferable in narrative or descriptive essays and can be used in any essay organized around time or place. Transitions of time might include phrases such as *after I had finished my*

classes for the day, the next morning, or *a few weeks later.* Transitions of place might include phrases such as *just down the hall, across the room,* or *on the other side of town.* (A more complete listing is found in Chapter 5.)

5. Avoid anything that would confuse your reader or make it seem as though you are just mechanically plugging in transitions instead of trying to write an artful essay. A reader would be confused, for instance, if you used a phrase such as *in conclusion* to begin your last body paragraph. The last body paragraph contains your last major point, but it is not your conclusion. (In fact, *in conclusion* is not even a recommended opening for conclusions.)

Any transitional sequence that uses counting throughout—*first, second, third; my first reason, my second reason, my third reason*—gives your reader the impression that you are using transitions mechanically and unthinkingly rather than choosing them for best effect. If you use numbers, combine them with other transitional expressions for best effect: *the first reason, another factor,* and *the final cause.*

A Graceful Exit: The Conclusion

The etiquette of concluding an essay, like that of ending a telephone conversation, is simple: keep the goodbye short and don't introduce any new information that keeps the other person hanging on too long.

After the specific and detailed support of the body paragraphs, the first sentence or two of your conclusion takes the reader back to a broad, thesis-level view of the topic. Often, this takes the form of a thesis restatement.

Then comes the closing statement, harder to write but vital because it is the last impression your reader takes away from the essay. The key requirement of a closing statement is that it should *sound* like a closing statement. It should sound as final as the slam of a door.

Sample Conclusion 1: A Summary Conclusion

The summary conclusion sums up the main points and ends with a sentence that provides a ring of finality.

Example

Recreational vehicles are too costly, too big, and too labor intensive. When I go on vacation, I'll drive my own car, stay at a reasonably priced motel, and let someone else do all the work.

Sample Conclusion 2: A Recommendation

A recommendation conclusion suggests a solution to a problem raised in the essay. A logical way to end an essay that discusses a problem is to offer a solution or suggest that one is on the horizon.

Example

In spite of a few problems, our school library is a valuable resource for all students. Extending weekend and evening hours, keeping the computer room open whenever the library is open, and setting aside a special group study area for students who need to converse will go a long way toward easing the frustrations many students experience when they visit the library.

Sample Conclusion 3: A Prediction

A look toward the future is another good way of ending an essay. The example below ends an essay discussing the advantages of online music stores with a summary and a prediction.

Example

Online music stores have a wide selection of merchandise, offer convenience, and allow customers to listen before they buy. With all of those advantages, it won't be long before a majority of people begin turning away from conventional music shops and taking their business online.

Wordsmith's Corner: Sample Essays

Below are two essays. One explores "inner space"—the writer's search for who she is—while the other discusses exploration of outer space. Read each essay and answer the questions that follow.

Essay 1

In the essay, Autumn discusses her lifelong search for her heritage.

A Mixed-up Kid

I opened the wedding invitation and read, "As we form a new union, we draw on the strength of our heritage and the unity of our family. Celebrate with us." A wave of longing and downright envy swept over me. I do not envy Kim her marriage. I envy her strong sense of who she is and where she comes from. It is a feeling I have never known. All my life, I have been searching for who I am.

When I look at the two people who adopted me twenty years ago, I feel lucky, secure, and loved, but I see nothing of where I came from. My mom's red hair and freckles tell of her Irish heritage, but say nothing of mine. She sets our Thanksgiving table with her great-grandmother's crystal and linen, and tells me to look forward, not back. She just doesn't understand. My dad, who has Scottish and Cherokee ancestry, understands a bit more. When I was younger, he would stretch his arm out, comparing his fawn-colored skin to mine. "That's a pretty close match," he'd say. "You might have a little Cherokee in you somewhere." Hearing him say that always made me feel connected and secure.

When I look in the mirror, I see no clear clues to my heritage. I see light caramel skin, coarse, wavy hair, and brown eyes. My face is wide, with a small, flat nose and delicate lips. I am short—just 5'2"—with a sturdy build. When I was in the sixth grade, a new girl at school asked me what race I was. I told her that my parents had told me my background was mixed, but I was adopted and not sure what the mixture was. "I'm a mixed-up kid, too," she said. I thought that was the perfect way of expressing how I felt—a mixed-up kid.

When I look to society to find out who I am, I get no answers. My adoption records are sealed, and my mom and dad know nothing about my birth parents. Was I given up by a teenage mother who loved me but couldn't keep me? Was I thrown in a dumpster by an uncaring parent or left on a doorstep by a desperate one? I may never know. Because I know so little about my background, I have tried to seek a mirror in many different social groups, and I have friends of all races. Yet there is still a part of me that feels like an outsider in any group because I am not sure where I come from.

For the most part, I am a happy person who feels fortunate in her family and friends. Mostly, I follow my mother's advice to look forward and not back. But when I look around me, hoping to see a reflection of who I am, all I see is a mixed-up kid.

■ Questions

1. Underline the thesis statement. Is it a thesis with points listed or without points listed?

_____

2. Underline the topic sentence of each paragraph.

Essay 2

Harley, the writer of this essay, discusses the value of the U.S. space program.

The Final Frontier

On the day that I was born, Neil Armstrong, the first person on the moon, took "one small step for man, one giant leap for mankind." I guess that is why I have always taken an interest in our space program. The space program, unlike many government programs, has something to give to every American.

The space program links every American to the mysteries that lie beyond Earth's atmosphere. Human beings have always looked to the heavens with a sense of wonder. Only in the last century have we actually been able to explore our moon and other planets. The Mars Pathfinder mission in 1997 gave us a closer look at the red planet with a mobile rover that took soil samples and pictures from all angles, even showing us a Martian sunset. The Voyager traveled outward among the planets, taking photographs of red Mars, ringed Saturn, and blue Neptune. In photographing the planet Jupiter and its moons, Voyager discovered ice on one of the moons, and where there is water or ice, there is the possibility of some form of life. What could be

more exciting than the discovery of life beyond
Earth's boundaries?

Another important contribution of the space
program is that it gives us heroes in a time when
heroes are few. Alan Shepherd, the first American
in space, had the courage to go "where no one had
gone before" as Americans sat mesmerized in front
of black-and-white TV sets. Neil Armstrong, the
first to set foot on the moon, was my hero for
many years. Sally Ride, the first woman in space,
inspired people all over the United States to cheer
her on with the words "Ride, Sally Ride!" And who
can forget Christa McAuliffe, the first teacher
in space, who died tragically in the explosion of
the space shuttle Challenger? John Glenn, a veteran
space traveler, was the first senior citizen to
test the effects of space travel on an aging body.
All of these people are heroes because they are
pioneers, among the first to travel where our
descendants may one day live.

The most important contribution of the space
program is the hope it gives for the future.
All around us, the earth's resources are being
depleted. If we don't replenish the forests, repair
the ozone layer, and repopulate endangered species,
life on Earth will be in danger. The growth of the
human population also raises the possibility that
one day, the earth may no longer have room for
everyone. The vast, cold reaches of space may hold
a solution to these problems. Human beings have
lived for months on the Mir space station, and that
is just the beginning. Self-sustaining space
colonies could eventually provide room for a
spreading human population. People may one day find
a way to populate the planets in the solar system
or even to reach other solar systems through
interstellar travel. In the future, space may hold
the key to human survival.

Space travel has fascinated me since I was old
enough to know that on my birthday, the first human
set foot on the moon. I believe that the space
program returns value for every penny that is spent

on it. It links us to the ancient mysteries of the
universe, it provides us with heroes, and it brings
hope for a brighter future for every human being.

■ Questions

1. Underline the thesis statement. Is it a thesis with points listed or without points listed?

_____

2. Underline the topic sentence of each paragraph.

TOPICS FOR WRITING ESSAYS

Essay Assignment 1: Reflections of You

In Sample Essay 1, "A Mixed-up Kid," the writer speaks of searching for her reflection in her parents, in her own mirror, and in society. Write an essay discussing who you are in your own eyes and in the eyes of two other groups or individuals. Possibilities include your parents, friends, teachers, members of your church, and children. Or you might move in a widening circle, first discussing how you see yourself, how your close friends see you, and how casual acquaintances see you. Another possibility, particularly if your view of yourself has changed radically over the years, is an essay explaining how you saw yourself in the past, how you see yourself now, and how you hope to see yourself in the future.

Constructing Your Essay

Step 1: Prewrite using one of the methods in Chapter 2. Prewriting is even more important in longer compositions, which usually require more thought. Try **freewriting** for ten minutes about the image that you have of yourself and that various other people or groups have of you. Or try a cluster diagram, with each branch of the cluster showing a different view of the person you are. Next, review your prewriting and choose the three viewpoints you want to include in your essay. Make sure that they are separate and distinct viewpoints. If all three viewpoints show you as the same exact person, your three body paragraphs will be nearly identical in content.

Step 2: Plan, making a brief outline of the essay you plan to write. Here's where you'll decide on the order in which to present your paragraphs and get some idea of the supporting examples you want to use. After you've done a scratch outline, write out your thesis statement and your three topic sentences. You may want to change the wording later, but completing a thesis statement and topic sentences prepares you for the next step.

Step 3: Draft your essay as completely as you can. If you have trouble with the introduction, start with your thesis and proceed from there. You can always come back and write your introduction later. Complete each paragraph as if it were an individual paragraph like the ones you have been writing in class, including plenty of specific support for each topic sentence. When you have completed your draft, including the introduction and conclusion, lay it aside for a while before proceeding to the next step.

Step 4: Revise your essay. First, do a visual check. Does your essay look balanced, with the three body paragraphs approximately equal in length? Are the body paragraphs framed by an introduction and conclusion that are shorter than the body paragraphs?

Next, check your word count. If you are writing on a computer, your word processor can check the count for you. If you have written in longhand, pick three lines at random. Count the number of words in each line, add them together, and then divide by three. The result is your average number of words per line. Count the number of lines, then multiply by the average number of words per line. The result is your approximate word count. If your word count is between 400 and 550, you are in the ballpark. If the count is over 600, check to make sure that everything you are saying supports your thesis and that you are not repeating yourself. If your word count is under 400, you probably need to add more support.

Finally, check the specific parts of your essay, using the Checklist for Revision at the end of this chapter.

Once you have completed the Checklist for Revision, you might want to show your essay to a classmate. Ask your classmate to focus on content and clarity. Does he or she understand everything you say? Are examples plentiful and specific?

Once you have looked at your essay, completed the revision checklist, and perhaps gotten a second opinion, rewrite the essay.

Step 5: Proofread after you have revised your essay and are satisfied that it is the essay you want to turn in. Correct any errors in grammar or spelling.

Essay Assignment 2: What Interests You?

In Sample Essay 2, "The Final Frontier," the writer discusses a lifelong interest in the space program. What interests you, either as an onlooker or a participant? Are you a movie buff, a music lover, or a follower of a particular sport? Do you read every book and watch every TV special about a particular historical period? Are you into collecting teacups, playing the alto sax, riding motorcycles, attending garage sales, or singing in a choir or chorus?

Whatever your interest, write about it, following the steps of the writing process as outlined in Essay Assignment 1. To get started, think of the following questions:

How long have you been pursuing your interest?

Who got you started?

What is it that inspires and fascinates you about it?

Are there people associated with it that you admire?

What activities do you participate in that involve your interest?

Checklist for Revision

The Introduction

✔ Does the introduction draw the reader in?

✔ Does the introduction provide background information, if needed?

The Thesis

✔ Is the thesis the last sentence of the introduction?

✔ If the thesis does not include points of development, does it state the main idea broadly enough to include all the points you raise in your body paragraphs?

✔ If the thesis lists points, does it list three separate and distinct points?

Topic Sentences

✔ Does each topic sentence raise one separate and distinct thesis point?

✔ If the thesis lists points, are body paragraphs arranged in the same order as thesis points?

The Body

✔ Does each body paragraph provide specific detail and examples for each thesis point?

✔ Have you provided enough specific support for each thesis point?

✔ Does each sentence of each body paragraph support the topic sentence?

The Conclusion

✔ Is the first sentence of the conclusion a broad, thesis-level statement?

✔ Is the conclusion short, with no new information introduced?

✔ Is the last sentence satisfying and final-sounding?

Checking Coherence

✔ Have you used transitional words effectively within paragraphs?

✔ Have you used transitional words effectively between paragraphs?

11

Writing Summary Reports

While the saying above is probably intended as a warning against short-cuts, it could just as easily apply to writing a summary. Summarizing is a painstaking process, involving fully understanding the material to be summarized, determining the most important ideas, and condensing them in your own words. A summary may be a shorter way of saying something, but writing one is a time-consuming process.

Writing a Summary Report

A **summary report** condenses and presents information, often from a single source. When you write a summary, your goal is to concisely present information from an essay, article, or book so that your reader understands the main points. In a summary, present the author's ideas objectively, without including your opinion of them. At the end of your report, if the assignment calls for it, write a brief evaluation of the essay, article or book.

Five Steps in Writing an Article Summary

The following section shows you the steps in summarizing an article.

Step 1: Choose a Topic and Find Sources of Information

Your instructor may assign a topic or area of investigation or you may be asked to choose your own topic. Choose a topic that interests you and on which information is readily available.

Articles on your topic may be found in periodicals, databases, or on Internet sites. An overview of each type of information source is provided below.

Periodicals are publications such as newspapers, magazines, and scholarly journals that are published on a regular basis—daily, monthly, or quarterly, for example. Newspapers and magazines are written for the general public, while journals are written for scholars in a particular field.

Subscription and CD-Rom Databases

Periodical articles are also available through subscription databases or CD Rom databases. Most college libraries subscribe to databases such as ABI/INFORM, Academic Search Premier, ERIC, and Research Library. These databases may contain full-text articles from journals, newspapers, or magazines, or they may contain article abstracts. **Full-text articles** are complete articles, exactly as originally published. **Article abstracts** are summaries intended to help you decide if a particular article is appropriate for

---

What Does the Suffix of an Internet Site Mean?

An Internet site's suffix can tell you a bit about the person or group behind the site. Here's a key to decoding Internet suffixes.

.org: A nonprofit organization

.edu: A college or university

.gov: A U.S. government site

.com: A business or private individual

your purposes. If it is, you will need to find the original article in the periodical in which it originally appeared.

Internet Sources

Some websites may contain articles previously published in print sources; others may contain articles written for and published on the Internet. Internet sources vary widely in quality; it is up to you to evaluate the credibility of each site you visit.

■ Advice for Online Researchers ■

Go Online

Research used to mean poring through stacks of books and periodicals. Today, it usually means sitting in front of a computer screen. Even print sources must be located through online catalogs, indexes to periodicals, and databases. Even if you are comfortable using a computer, these resources may seem alien to you at first. If you need help, do not hesitate to ask for it.

Find a Friend

Find someone in class who will agree to be your research partner. You don't need an expert, nor do you need someone who is working on the same topic. All you need is someone who is willing to go through the process with you. The two of you can work side by side and handle the rough spots together.

Ask a Librarian

Librarians are experts in finding information, and they are there to help. Explain your project and the kind of information you are looking for, and a librarian will point you in the right direction.

Print the Information

When you find useful articles online, print them so that you will not have to find them again. Documentation of online sources requires that you note the database you are using and the date you accessed the information.

Be Patient

Be patient with yourself and with the process of finding information—it always takes longer than you think it will.

Step 2: Evaluate Sources of Information

Once you have found articles on your chosen topic, evaluate them to make sure they are suitable for your summary. Use the following criteria for evaluation to find suitable articles.

- **Length.** If an article summary covers all the major points in the article, it will probably be 25 to 50 percent of the length of the article. Therefore, if you are assigned a five-hundred-word summary, choose an article of between one thousand and two thousand words. These figures are only an approximation. The idea is not to choose an article so short that a few sentences can summarize it or one so long that you cannot summarize the entire article.

- **Readability.** In any article that you choose, expect to find unfamiliar terminology and concepts that are new to you. After all, the purpose of research is to learn something new. However, some articles are written for experts in the field and may be hard for a layperson to understand. If you read the article three times and still feel as though you are trying to comprehend ancient Egyptian hieroglyphics, choose another article.

- **Publication Date.** A publication date helps you to evaluate the timeliness of the source. In fields where change is rapid, such as medicine or computer technology, finding up-to-date-sources is essential.

- **Author.** Is the author an authority in the field? If not—if the author is a journalist, for example—does the author consult and quote credible, authoritative sources? These questions help you evaluate the authority and credibility of your source.

Step 3: Read Your Article Thoroughly

Before taking any notes, read your article through once or twice. Then, highlighter in hand, look for the following information.

- **Main and major ideas.** Read through the article, highlighting main and major ideas. Remember, main ideas are often found at the beginning of an article and repeated at the end. Major ideas are often stated at the beginning of a paragraph or after a headline, and they are often supported by examples. Don't worry if this step takes more than one reading.

- **Examples and supporting details.** Once you have found the main and major ideas, go back and highlight the supporting details and examples that most directly support those ideas. A summary contains a minimum of the detail that fleshes out the main ideas, so be selective and choose only necessary and important details.

- **Information for the works cited list.** The final step in taking notes from your source is to write down the information you will need for your works cited list. In a summary of a single article, you have only one work to cite, but it is important to cite it correctly. A list of information needed for your works cited list follows.

For all sources
- Author
- Title of article
- Title of the magazine, journal, or newspaper in which the article was published.
- Date of publication
- Volume and issue number of periodical, if available
- Page numbers

For online sources, note the following additional information
- Date of access
- The URL (Universal Resource Locator, or complete web address) of an article from a website
- The name of the database for articles accessed from subscription databases through a college (or other) library, and the name of that library

Step 4: Draft Your Paper

Drafting a summary report is similar to drafting an essay. Your draft should contain the following elements:

- **Introduction.** The introduction includes the author's name, the title of the article, and the central idea of the article.

Example

Interviews are crucial for both employer and prospective employee. The employer needs to find the best person for the job; the prospective employee wants a fulfilling job and perhaps even a career. In his article, "The Interview: Rights and Wrongs," David Butcher describes techniques that can be employed by both interviewer and job-seeker to make the interview process easier and more productive.

- **Body paragraphs.** The body paragraphs outline the most important points in the article. The topic sentence of each body paragraph should state the idea that the paragraph will develop and incorporate a reference to the author.

Example

Smith believes that the Internet can be especially beneficial for senior citizens.

The inclusion of the author's name in each topic sentence makes it perfectly clear to the reader that you are still discussing the ideas of another person rather than your own ideas.

The body paragraph itself will paraphrase the author's ideas; that is, you will state the ideas in your own words. Quoting the author is also permissible, but use quotations sparingly. Most of the summary should be in your own words.

- **Conclusion.** The conclusion sums up the author's ideas and presents your evaluation of or reaction to the article. Placing your evaluation in the conclusion is a way of clearly separating your reaction to the article from the summary, but if your evaluation is lengthy, you may place it in a final body paragraph before beginning the conclusion

Step 5: Format, Proofread, and Cite Your Source

The final draft of your paper will include proper formatting and a works cited page. Use the documentation style recommended by your instructor or follow the brief guide to MLA style that appears later in this chapter. Your instructor may also ask you to provide a copy of the article you are summarizing.

Paraphrasing: An Essential Skill

One of the most difficult tasks of writing a summary is to put an author's ideas in your own words. When you **paraphrase,** you capture an idea using your own sentence structure and your own words. Here are some pointers to help you when you paraphrase:

- It's always permissible to repeat key terms. If the author uses the term "geriatric medicine," there's no need to rephrase it as "medical care of the elderly."

- Unusual phrasings should be reworded. If the author refers to a spider web as "a spider's gossamer trap," a paraphrase should simply call it a spider web.
- The sentence structure of a paraphrase should vary from that of the original material.

■ Making the Switch to Academic Writing ■

As you move from personal writing to academic writing, you need a new set of strategies. Here are five helpful strategies for academic writing.

A Learning Approach

While personal writing allows you to write about the things you know best, academic writing requires a willingness to read, understand, and evaluate the ideas of others.

Objectivity

Personal writing is *subjective*—that is, it allows you to express your own feelings and opinions. Academic writing, on the other hand, is *objective*. It requires you to put aside your own opinions and to look without bias at the ideas of another person—even if you disagree with those ideas.

Knowledge of Key Terms

When you read and write about academic subjects, understanding key terms is essential. Make an effort to learn the meanings of unfamiliar terms. This essential step will help your comprehension of the article you are reading and will help you to use the terms knowledgeably in your writing.

Use of Third Person

When you write from personal experience, you often use the *first-person* pronouns *I, me,* or *my*. In academic writing, *third person* is preferred, even when you are expressing your own opinion. Thus you would write, "Several of Emily Dickinson's poems reflect an obsession with death," not "I think that Emily Dickinson's poetry reflects and obsession with death."

Careful Acknowledgment of Others' Work

If you are quoting or using the ideas of other writers, it is important to acknowledge your sources both informally within the text of your paper and formally through parenthetical references and a works cited page. Failure to acknowledge sources is called **plagiarism** and is considered cheating.

EXERCISE 1   RECOGNIZING EFFECTIVE PARAPHRASES

For the numbered items below, circle the letter of the better paraphrase.

1. Original material:

    From retail buying to bargain hunting, the Internet has revolutionized shopping. Shoppers used to be limited to the retail stores in their area; now, online stores across the country or even across the world are open to them if they have an Internet connection and a credit card. Shoppers can find items that are not available locally and can compare prices to get the best deal. Bargain hunters no longer have to get up early and spend a Saturday morning scouring area yard sales. Now they can sign on to E-Bay or similar auction sites to find secondhand items in a variety of places, from Alaska to Nebraska and beyond. Both buyers and sellers have benefited from the availability of online shopping.

    a. Because of the Internet, shoppers are no longer limited to stores within driving distance. Online shopping has made a wider range of goods available to both retail shoppers and bargain hunters. Online stores and auction sites have benefited both buyers and sellers.

    b. The Internet has revolutionized shopping from retail buying to bargain hunting. Shoppers are not limited to items that can be bought locally. From Alaska to Nebraska, online shoppers can get better deals from E-Bay other auction sites as well as from online retail stores the world over.

2. Original material:

    A cat's eye is different from a human eye in several respects. The first and most obvious difference is the shape of the pupil as it contracts. The pupil in a human eye is round, and when exposed to light, it contracts, retaining its circular shape. The round pupil of a cat's eye, on the other hand, contracts from each side to form an ellipse. Unlike a human eye, a cat's eye shines in the dark. A cat's eye contains a reflective layer of cells that picks up and reflects available light, enhancing the vision of these nocturnal animals. A final feature that distinguishes the cat's eye from a human eye is the nictitating membrane, an inner eyelid that serves to clean and protect the cat's eye.

    a. A cat's eye is different from a human eye in the shape of the pupil as it contracts. The pupil in a human retains its circular shape when it contracts, but the round pupil of a cat's eye contacts from each side to form an ellipse. Unlike a human eye, a cat's eye shines in the dark. Finally, a cat's eye has a nictitating membrane, an inner eyelid that cleans and protects the cat's eye.

    b. Though they perform the same function, a cat's eye and a human eye are different in some ways. While the pupil of a human eye remains rounds as it contracts, a cats pupil becomes elliptical. Cats' eyes also reflect in the dark, something a human eye cannot do. In addition, cats' eyes possess a protective inner eyelid called the nictitating membrane.

EXERCISE 2   **PARAPHRASING SHORT PASSAGES**

Paraphrase the following short passages.

Passage 1

Aggressive driving is characterized by the tendency to view driving as a competition rather than
as a means of getting from one place to another.
While most drivers are content to move along with
the flow of traffic, aggressive drivers weave from
lane to lane, seeking any advantage that will place
them ahead of others. Aggressive drivers are also
more likely to tailgate and honk the horn in an
effort to intimidate other drivers or simply to
move them along faster. When confronted with
heavy traffic, aggressive drivers often engage
in dangerous behavior such as passing on the right,
using utility or turn lanes as driving lanes, and
ignoring traffic signals. Paradoxically, aggressive
drivers often pride themselves on their skill. They
see other, more cautious drivers as the problem,
not themselves.

_____

_____

_____

_____

_____

_____

_____

Passage 2

The National Academies' Institute of Medicine
now recommends an hour per day of total physical
activity such as walking, stair-climbing, or
swimming. Many Americans fall far short of reaching
this goal. Some are still trying to catch up to the
previous guidelines of thirty minutes of activity
five days per week. A century ago, Americans would
have found it easier to exercise for an hour per

day. Without cars, people walked more, and without
modern labor-saving devices, life required more
physical exertion. Today, however, many Americans
sit at a desk all day and come home to sit in front
of a TV or computer. Even those who make an effort
to exercise often find that they lack the time.

_____

_____

_____

_____

_____

_____

EXERCISE 3   SUMMARIZING A PASSAGE

In a paragraph, summarize the following longer passage. Use your paraphrasing
skills to condense the ideas in the original material.

Developing Focus

One of the most valuable skills a student can develop is focus. **Focus** is the ability to concentrate
on one thing for an extended period of time, shut-
ting out everything else. The person who is focused
has no trouble with homework; her mind is on the
task until it is finished. The focused person has
no trouble concentrating during a test. She does
not even notice the voice of the lecturer in an ad-
jacent classroom, the tapping pencil of the student
two rows over, or her instructor's squeaking chair.
People differ widely in their ability to
concentrate. Some seem capable of laserlike focus
on any job until it is completed. Other are easily
distracted, jumping up from homework to do a
hundred small but suddenly urgent tasks as the
homework gets pushed further into the background.
Like any other skill, the ability to focus can be
learned and reinforced through practice. To improve

your ability to concentrate, start by establishing a set time and place to study. If possible, study at the same time and in the same place every day. Establishing a routine gives study the importance it deserves and helps make studying a habit. Then, to keep yourself on task, set a small timer as you begin studying. Start by setting the timer to go off after fifteen minutes. Until the timer goes off, give studying your full attention. If your mind wanders—and it will—pull it back to the task. Then reward yourself with something small: five minutes of solitaire on your computer or a trip to the refrigerator for a glass of iced tea. Time your reward, too—about five minutes should be sufficient. Then set the timer for another fifteen minutes.

As concentration becomes a habit, that habit will spill over into the classroom, too. You will be better able to focus on your instructor's words or on the test you are taking. If extraneous noises during test still distract you, invest in a pair of earplugs to shut out noise as you take your test.

The ability to concentrate is a necessary skill. Fortunately, it is a skill that can be improved with effort.

_____

_____

_____

_____

_____

_____

_____

_____

_____

_____

_____

Brief Guide to MLA (Modern Language Association) Style

The following section outlines a few basic principles of MLA style. For complete information on MLA style, consult the *MLA Handbook for Writers of Research Papers*, available in most college libraries and bookstores.

Formatting Your Paper

- Double-space the paper, including the works cited page.
- Use one-inch margins.
- Indent paragraphs one-half inch.
- Do not use a title page. Instead, put your name, your instructor's name, your course name, and the date at the top of the first page, each on a separate line, each line flush with the left margin. Center the title above the first paragraph. This material, like the rest of your paper, should be double-spaced.

Price 1

Ferris Price

Dr. Ruby S. Acres

Business Administration 101

22 April 2003

Summary of "The Interview: Rights and Wrongs"

Referencing Sources Within Your Paper

Within your paper, MLA style requires **parenthetical references,** not footnotes. For a paragraph in which you mention the author's name, the only parenthetical reference necessary is a page number placed at the end of the paragraph. If you use a direct quotation, place a page number after the quotation.

Example

✔ According to Steven Pinker, the idea that parents are at fault if children turn out badly is an outgrowth of the "tabula rasa" or "blank slate" theory. This theory holds that cultural influence, not genetics, determines personality and character(16).

The Works Cited List

Use the following model entries as a guide to preparing your works cited list.

Journal Article

> Shipman, Harry L. "Hands-on Science, 680 Hands at a Time." Journal of College Science Teaching 30.5 (2001): 318-21.

Magazine Article

> Pinker, Steven. "The Blank Slate." Discover Oct. 2002: 34-40.

Newspaper Article

> Hummer, Steven. "Surviving the Sweet Science." Atlanta Journal-Constitution 13 Oct. 2002: E-9.

Article on a Website

> Dunleavy, M. P. "Twenty Ways to Save on a Shoestring." MSN/Money 29 Dec. 2001. 16 Oct. 2002. <http://moneycentral.msn.com/articles/smartbuy/basics/8677.asp.>

Note that the date of publication is followed by the date of access. The complete Internet address of the article is enclosed within carets.

Article Accessed from an Online Database

> Zimbardo, Phillip G. "Time to Take Our Time."
>   Psychology Today 35: 2 Mar/Apr 2002 Psychology
>   and Behavioral Sciences Collection. EbscoHost.
>   10 Oct. 2002. Metro College Library.

Include the name of the database through which you accessed the article, the date of access and the library where you accessed it (if applicable).

> Jackson, Carol D., and R. Jon Leffingwell. "The
>   Role of Instructors in Creating Math Anxiety in
>   Students from Kindergarten through College."
>   Mathematics Teacher 92.7 (1999). ERIC.
>   EbscoHost. 2 May 2003. GALILEO.

If your college is part of a larger university system that has a systemwide set of databases, reference that systemwide set of databases rather than the individual library.

A Model Summary Report

For her summary report, Sandra chose an article dealing with the evolutionary reasons behind negative emotions such as fear and anxiety. The article, along with Sandra's highlighting and annotations, appears on page 193, followed by the final draft of her summary report.

The Fears that Save Us
Diane Ackerman

main idea

Anxiety, dread, panic, aversion, depression—a small demonology of our age. It makes one anxious just to name them, and most people will eagerly perform any ritual, intone any magic that might keep such demons at bay. But, despite the disruptions that they cause us today, these demons once had a life-saving purpose. Just as physical pain warns us of potential damage to the body, emotional pains helped us avoid more complicated threats to life and limb.

Indeed, the full bouquet of our cherished traits and tastes, as well as the bestiary of our negative behaviors, evolved at a time when humans lived in small bands of hunter-gatherer scavengers. To us, their lives seem arduous and uncertain, but heaven knows what they would make of ours. The only thing is, we still navigate by their maps, still respond according to their instincts, still act like hunter-gatherers, though we grapple with problems they would not have encountered, understood, or valued.

anxiety — major point

example — usefulness of anxiety

Anxiety, that masochistic terrier of one's own devising, played a life-saving role in our ancestors' lives by alerting them to potential threats so they could plan a response. "A tiger may be in that grass," one instinctive train of thought might go. "It looks like the same sort of tall grass tigers hide out in. If a tiger is hiding there and attacks me, what would I do? Did I just see the grass move? Maybe not. On the other hand, maybe I'd better check again." Obsessive worry about nonexistent tigers might burn up needed calories, interfere with work and damage the body by flooding the tissues with cortisol, a stress hormone. Costly strategy, that, but one hungry tiger could result in instant death.

Evolution wagers risk against advantage. Better to agonize at every opportunity about a tiger than be wrong that one lethal time. The grinding down of one's spirit, hope, health, and sense of well-being doesn't matter; only one's ability to survive long enough to launch heirs. We face profound and trivial uncertainties: the possible effects of fluoride, a nuclear test in the South Pacific, deciding what to wear on a first date. Our penchant for anxiety doesn't sift what's important from that civilized heap. Worry kicks in even when we don't need it, want it or know how to stop it.

another type of anxiety

example — usefulness of r'ship anxiety

Anxiety about a relationship feels the worst of all, but ultimately it's a lifesaver. When you're faced with hunger, the elements, and wild animals, belonging to a loyal family group is your only hope.

Not belonging is one of those things to dread and worry endlessly about. You keep checking to be sure you won't be abandoned, won't be sacrificed if wild animals attack, won't be left to starve. Most of the time, these may be unfounded neurotic fears, but misread the situation once, overlook a warning sign, and you're dead.

Small wonder that loneliness frightens us. Even though being excluded isn't deadly today, the nerve it touches stretches down the arms of time to a world of distant relations who left us a bag of tricks we barely understand but which we enjoy, puzzle over and often misuse.

depression — major point

Faced with horrible adversity or nameless anxiety, the more vulnerable among us become depressed. In a sense, it's a form of temporary hibernation. Overloaded, a person winds down to a low-energy state, speaks and moves very little. Famine produces the same inert, energy-saving response. Depression also elicits concern and nurturing, and people tend to make allowances for the depressed person who may ignore the normal give-and-take of society, not meet the same schedules or obligations. "I'm helpless as a child," the posture says "Protect me, embrace me, tell the world I'm not available for a while."

usefulness of depression

low self-esteem — major point

We think of low self-esteem as an affliction, but it had important benefits too. Self-esteem helps one seize opportunities. But if our ancestors had been confident in every circumstance, they would have taken too many risks—like venturing alone into the wilderness—or they might have been tempted to pick fights, challenge leaders, not bother negotiating or create some other social havoc.

usefulness of low self-esteem

point — fewer positive emotions

Besides serenity, joy, excitement, thrill and desire, it may seem that we've evolved few positive emotions, or at least a wider and subtler range of negative ones. That may be because, when things are going well, only a few responses are needed. Everything is dandy, and we get on with tracking happiness like the elusive quarry it is.

possible reason

How odd to live in a country whose Constitution guarantees us the right to pursue happiness. In a recent study of thirty-nine cultures reported in Psychology Today, the U.S. ranked twelfth in perceived happiness. Citizens of Denmark, Finland, Norway, and Sweden were the happiest despite their gloomy weather. Surprisingly, people in France and Japan said they were among the least happy. Many cultures don't expect to be happy, though they're thankful for its state of grace. In collectivist countries such as China, an individual's wishing to be happy is thought selfish and therefore not a high priority. But we expect happiness, pursue it, feel wretched in its absence and experience sadness as a failure.

usefulness
of happiness

We sometimes feel serene, quiet, at rest—what we label "happy." When you're happy, the world is breaking someone else's heart. Of course, it may be nothing more than a sort of biological idle, the body being thrifty with its limited energy. Negative feelings burn up precious calories, so not to be in pain or at red alert feels good.

What continues to amaze me is how such mind-binding forces, ancient and powerful as glaciers, can be modified by circumstance to produce quirky individuals living unique and unpredictable lives. However tempting it may be to think evolution stopped with us—its crowning glory—in the grand scheme of things, we're new-comers.

prediction—
more evolutionary
changes

Our evolution isn't happening fast enough to be visible in our lifetime, but it's still under way as we eat, sleep, play, lust, worry, learn, work, dream. Heaven only knows what we will become.

1 inch

1/2 inch

Lopez 1

Sandra Lopez

Psychology 1101

Dr. Wilder

7 February 2004

Double-spaced
throughout

Title Centered ———————————————

Article Summary: "The Fears that Save Us"

Most people have heard of the "fight or flight" response, the rush of

adrenalin that is blamed for everything from road rage to panic attacks.

Most people have also heard that this response is left over from

prehistoric days when a tiger might attack at any moment and a quick

response could save a life. In her article, "The Fears That Save Us," Diane

Ackerman takes the idea even further. She believes that a whole range of

negative emotions can be traced to the prehistoric past, and that those

emotions were once necessary to the survival of our earliest ancestors.

The first emotion that Ackerman discusses in terms of evolutionary

value is anxiety. While constant worry may not seem useful today, our

ancestors needed it. Ackerman points out that anxiety wastes time that

might be used on more valuable pursuits, floods the body with stress

hormones, and wears down an individual's sense of well-being. How

could such a negative emotion have been useful to our ancestors?

Ackerman suggests that constant anxiety about a tiger hiding in tall

grass might have a big payoff if, just once, there really was a tiger and

the watchfulness caused by anxiety saved a life. Ackerman also points

out that anxiety over relationships can be traced to a very real threat. In

prehistoric times, a person left alone might not survive.

Ackerman also has evolutionary explanations for depression and

low self-esteem. Depression is an emotional retreat from the world, but

it also saves the body's energy and brings a nurturing response from

Lopez 2

others, both of which could make survival more likely. Low self-esteem, seen as negative today, could have helped groups stay together by making it less likely that someone would challenge authority or fight.

Ackerman points out that, compared to the wide range of negative emotions, we seem to have developed few positive emotions. She suggests that positive emotions are not necessary for survival—when things are going fine, there's no need for a response. Happiness may be nothing more than a form of "biological idle"—a way of saving energy when there is no imminent danger. These responses are not the end of the evolutionary road, according to Ackerman. Evolution is a slow process, and while we will not see changes in our lifetime, they are certain to come.

Ackerman's article was valuable to me because it helped me to see negative emotions in a new light. This article also makes me wonder if I should evaluate my own negative emotions in terms of their usefulness. If I am worrying over a test or over a relationship, maybe that anxiety is a sign that I should take some action—or maybe not. Diane Ackerman's article, "The Fears That Save Us," was a fascinating look at how negative emotions may actually have had survival value for our earliest ancestors.

Lopez 3

Centered

Works Cited

First line is flush with left margin; any subsequent lines are indented one-half inch.

Ackerman, Diane. "The Fears That Save Us." <u>Parade</u> 26 Jan. 1997: 18.

SUMMARY REPORT ASSIGNMENTS

Summary Report Assignment 1: Summarizing an Article about Your Career or Major

Write a summary of an article that deals with some aspect of your chosen career or major. The article may be one about job opportunities in your field, or it may focus on a particular issue central to your field. Follow the step-by-step process outlined in this chapter to find your article, evaluate it, read it to find the main ideas, and write your summary.

Summary Report Assignment 2: Summarizing an Article That Solves a Problem

Write a summary of an article that helps you solve a problem in your life. Whether you are trying to find ways to save more money, impress an interviewer, organize your time, choose an automobile, or eat more nutritiously, dozens of articles await you in the library or on the Internet. Because articles of this type vary widely in length, be sure to choose an article substantial enough to lend itself to summarizing. Follow the step-by-step process outlined in this chapter to find your article, evaluate it, read it to find the main ideas, and write your summary.

Summary Report Assignment 3: Summarizing an Article That Explores a Social Issue

Write a summary of an article that explores a current social problem. You will find articles on homelessness, drug abuse, domestic violence, school violence, and many more issues of current concern in the library or on the Internet. Articles may vary in length, so be sure to choose and article substantial enough to lend itself to summarizing. Follow the step-by-step process outlined in this chapter to find your article, evaluate it, read it to find the main ideas, and write your summary.

Part 2
Grammar

12

Verbs and Subjects

If there were no verbs or subjects, the top two items in the list of traditional journalist's questions would be eliminated. Verbs tell *what* was done, while subjects tell *who or what* the sentence is about.

The **verb** of a sentence carries the action, if any, and directs that action to and from the other words in the sentence. Some verbs, called **linking verbs,** function as connectors for related words.

A **subject** is what the sentence is about. It is usually a noun or a pronoun. It is probably not the only noun or pronoun in the sentence, but it is the only one that enjoys such a direct grammatical connection to its verb. If you ask, "Who or what _____?" putting the verb in the blank, the answer to your question is always the subject of the sentence.

Action and Linking Verbs

Verbs work in two ways within a sentence. They show the action, physical or mental, of the subject of the sentence, or they link the subject with other words in the sentence.

Action Verbs

Action verbs show physical or mental action performed by a subject. Look at the action verbs below, highlighted in italic type.

Examples

✔ Beth *sat* at her desk. (physical action)

✔ She *noticed* that her clock *had stopped*. (mental action, physical action)

✔ She *wondered* how long she *had been studying*. (mental action)

PRACTICE 1   RECOGNIZING ACTION VERBS

Underline the action verb in each sentence.

1. Buzz leaped for the volleyball.
2. Pilar quickly ate her tuna salad sandwich.
3. A crop duster droned overhead.
4. The dog barked loudly at the stranger's approach.
5. Melvina returned two books to the library's drop box.

Linking Verbs

A **linking verb** links its subject with a word that describes or renames it. The most common linking verb in English is the verb *to be*, in all its various forms: *is, are, was, were, has been, will be,* and so on. Look at the following examples to see how the verb *to be* functions as a linking verb.

Examples

✔ The glass *is* empty.

The verb *is* links the subject, *glass,* with an adjective describing it.

✔ Li *has been* student body president for the past year.

The verb *has been* links the subject, Li, with a noun, *president*, that renames him. In other words, he could be referred to as either "Li" or "the student body president." ("Student" and "body" are adjectives.)

Other common linking verbs include the verbs *to seem, to appear, to grow,* and *to become.* Verbs of the senses, such as *to smell, to taste, to look, to sound,* and *to feel,* can be action or linking verbs depending on how they are used.

Examples

L   The book *seems* interesting. (The verb links *book* with an adjective that describes it.)

L   The burned potatoes *looked* terrible. (*Looked* is a linking verb. The potatoes are performing no action.)

A   Terralyn *looked* at the schedule of classes. (The verb shows Terralyn's physical action.)

L   The sliced turkey *smelled* bad. (The verb links *turkey* with an adjective that describes it.)

A   The dog *smelled* his owner's pockets, hoping for a treat. (The verb shows the dog's physical action.)

The Linking Verb Test

To tell if a verb is a linking verb, see if you can substitute *is* or *was* in its place. If the substitution works, the verb is probably a linking verb.

Examples

?   The drone of the engine *grew* louder as the plane approached the airport.

L   The drone of the engine ~~grew~~ *was* louder as the plane approached the airport.

The substitution makes sense; therefore, *grew* is used here as a linking verb.

?   The friendship between Della and Miriam *grew* quickly because they shared many interests.

A   The friendship between Della and Miriam ~~grew~~ *was* quickly because they shared many interests.

The substitution does not makes sense; therefore, *grew* is used as an action verb.

?   After drinking four cups of coffee, Martin *felt* jittery.

L   After drinking four cups of coffee, Martin ~~felt~~ *was* jittery. (linking verb)

?   Casey *felt* someone tap her shoulder and turned to see who it was.

A   Casey ~~felt~~ *was* someone tap her shoulder and turned to see who it was. (action verb)

PRACTICE 2   RECOGNIZING ACTION AND LINKING VERBS

Underline the verbs in each sentence. In the blank to the left, write *A* if the verb is an action verb, *L* if it is a linking verb.

_____ 1.   The picture on the wall is crooked.

_____ 2.   Lu Ana smelled the milk to see if it was fresh.

_____ 3.   This crossword puzzle looks difficult.

_____ 4.   The squirrel scampered up the trunk of the tree.

_____ 5.   Kim prepared her report carefully.

_____ 6.   The company's representative asked for Zelda's account number.

_____ 7.   The scrambled eggs tasted good.

_____ 8.   Anna tasted the eggs cautiously.

_____ 9.   Two young men lounged against a car in the parking lot of the fast food place.

_____ 10.   The mail carrier seemed cheerful.

Recognizing Verbs and Subjects

Finding the Verb

Finding the subject and verb of a sentence is easier if you look for the verb first. Below are some guidelines to help you spot the verb in a sentence.

1.   **A verb may show action.**
   ✔ Laney <u>laughed</u> aloud at the cartoon.
   ✔ Kirsten <u>wondered</u> what was so funny.

2. **A verb may link the subject to the rest of the sentence.**

   ✔ The inspection sticker in the elevator <u>was</u> four years old.

   ✔ The broken glass on the floor <u>looked</u> dangerous.

3. **A verb may consist of more than one word. Some verbs include a main verb and one or more *helping verbs.***

   ✔ Zeke <u>has been working</u> in the campus bookstore for three months.

   ✔ Melanie <u>had</u> not <u>planned</u> to attend a commuter college.

   ✔ Gavin <u>might have been expecting</u> me to return his call.

4. **Some verbs are compound verbs.**

   ✔ Nick <u>pulled</u> a muscle in his shoulder and <u>went</u> to see the doctor.

   ✔ The loan officer <u>calculated</u> the payments and <u>handed</u> the customer a loan agreement.

   ✔ Angelo <u>ate</u> octopus once but <u>did</u> not <u>know</u> what it was.

5. **An infinitive (*to* + verb) cannot act as a verb in a sentence.**

   ✘ Kendall has begun <u>to accept</u> too many credit card offers.

   The phrase *to accept* is an infinitive and cannot be the main verb of the sentence. The verb in this sentence is *has begun*.

   ✘ The advertiser's claims about the new skin cream sounded too good <u>to be</u> true.

   The phrase *to be* is an infinitive, not the verb of the sentence. The verb in this sentence is *sounded*.

6. **A verb form ending in *-ing* cannot act as a verb in a sentence unless a helping verb precedes it.**

   ✘ The smell of baking bread drifted into the street, <u>inviting</u> passersby into the bakery.

   Inviting cannot be the verb because a helping verb does not precede it. The verb in this sentence is *drifted*.

   ✘ The basset hound's <u>drooping</u> jowls gave him a mournful appearance.

   Drooping cannot be the verb because a helping verb does not precede it. The verb in this sentence is *gave*.

   ✔ Elaine's mother <u>was waving</u> from the porch.

   The verb in this sentence is *was waving* (helping verb + main verb).

   ✔ Jeff said he <u>had</u> not <u>been sleeping</u> well for the last few months.

   The verb in this sentence is *had been sleeping* (helping verb + main verb).

Underline the verbs in each sentence.

1. Vernon shared his hamburger with a stray dog.
2. Melanie noticed a footprint on the kitchen wall.
3. The woman's hair was long enough to brush the pockets of her jeans.
4. April did not move except to turn a page of her book now and then.
5. The employee guided a long line of grocery carts, pushing them through the parking lot toward the store.
6. The governor announced a new program to help preschool children.
7. The photograph on the calendar showed a polar bear relaxing on an ice floe.
8. Sleepily, Tony poured a cup of coffee and popped a frozen waffle into the toaster.
9. My grandmother believes that people behave more irrationally during a full moon.
10. A rumor about the company's closing had been circulating for some time.

Finding the Subject

A subject answers the question "*Who* or *what* _____?" To find the subject of a verb, ask the question, "Who or what _____?" The verb fills in the blank. *Note*: Be sure the words *who* or *what* are stated *before* the verb, or you will find the object rather than the subject.

✔ Inside Maurice's briefcase, his cell phone rang.

Who or what rang? The cell phone rang. *Cell phone* is the subject of the verb *rang*.

✔ The hot coffee burned Adrienne's tongue.

Who or what burned? The hot coffee burned. *Coffee* is the simple subject of the verb *burned*. (The words *the* and *hot* are modifiers and are part of the complete subject.)

✔ Katelyn and Marie wanted to ride the ferris wheel.

Who or what wanted? Katelyn and Marie wanted. *Katelyn and Marie* is the compound subject of the verb *wanted*.

✔ Carefully, Tom <u><u>measured</u></u> the olive oil and <u><u>folded</u></u> it into the pizza dough.

Who or what measured? Tom measured. Who or what folded? <u>Tom</u> folded. *Tom* is the subject of the compound verb *measured and folded*.

✔ Carefully, Tom <u><u>measured</u></u> the olive oil while Ruthie <u><u>kneaded</u></u> the pizza dough.

Who or what measured? Tom measured. *Tom* is the subject of the verb *measured*. *Who* or what *kneaded*? Ruthie kneaded. *Ruthie* is the subject of the verb *kneaded*.

PRACTICE 4   RECOGNIZING VERBS AND SUBJECTS

Double underline the verb in each sentence. Then find the subject by asking "Who or what _____?" Underline the subject once.

1. Marvin squeezed behind the wheel of the small sports car.
2. A candy jar sat on top of the filing cabinet.
3. The photograph showed a much thinner Bert.
4. The computer emitted a strange clunking noise.
5. Gwyn opened the door and called the dog.

Recognizing Prepositional Phrases

A subject will not be part of a prepositional phrase. In many sentences, prepositional phrases intervene between subject and verb.

✔ The top *of the refrigerator* was covered with dust.

When we pick out the subject of the verb by asking "What is covered with dust?" it is tempting to say, "The refrigerator is covered." But *refrigerator* cannot be the subject of the verb in this sentence. Grammatically, it already has a job: it is the object of the preposition. The subject of this sentence is *top*.

To avoid mistakes in picking out the subject of the sentence, cross out prepositional phrases before picking out subject and verb.

Below are a few tips for recognizing prepositional phrases:

- **Prepositional phrases always *begin* with a preposition.** Prepositions are often short words like *of, to, by, for,* or *from.* They are often words of location, such as *behind, beside, beneath, beyond,* or *below.* Below is a list of common prepositions.

Frequently Used Prepositions

about	beneath	in	to
above	beside	into	toward
across	between	like	under
after	beyond	near	underneath
along	by	next to	until
along with	down	of	up
around	during	off	upon
at	except	on	with
before	for	outside	within
behind	from	over	without

- **Prepositional phrases always *end* with a noun or pronoun.** The object of a preposition, always a noun or pronoun, comes at the end of a

---

■ Famous Prepositional Phrases ■

The prepositional phrases below have been used as titles for songs, television shows, movies, and books. How many do you recognize? Can you think of others?

Above Suspicion	In Living Color
Against the Wind	Of Mice and Men
Around the World in Eighty Days	On Golden Pond
At Long Last Love	On the Waterfront
At the Hop	Over the Rainbow
Behind Closed Doors	Under the Boardwalk
Behind Enemy Lines	Under the Yum Yum Tree
Beneath the Planet of the Apes	Up a Lazy River
Beyond the Sea	Up on the Roof
In Cold Blood	Up the Down Staircase

---

* Real-World Writing: Is it okay to end a sentence with a preposition?

How else would you say, "Will you pick me up?" or "I feel left out"?

Sometimes, what seems to be an objection to a preposition at the end of a sentence is really an objection to an awkward or redundant construction. "Where are you at?" will bring a scowl to any English teacher's face—not because it ends in a preposition, but because it is redundant: *where* and *at* are both doing the same job—indicating location.

But by all means, say "I have nothing to put this in" or "The dog wants to go out." Except in the most formal writing, ending sentences with prepositions is something almost everyone can live with.

---

prepositional phrase: of the *ceiling*, beside the *restaurant*, with *us*, to *Rita and Dean*, within *four months*.

- **Prepositional phrases often have a three-word structure.** Often, prepositional phrases have a three-word structure: preposition, article (*a, an,* or *the*), noun. Thus phrases like *of an airplane, under the bleachers,* and *with a frown* become easy to recognize. But prepositional phrases can also be stretched with modifiers and compound objects: Everyone made fun *of Sam's extra-distance, glow-in-the-dark, Super-Flight golf balls and his tasseled, monogrammed golf club covers*. More often, though, the three-word pattern prevails.

PRACTICE 5   ELIMINATING PREPOSITIONAL PHRASES

Cross out prepositional phrases in the each sentence. Underline subjects once and verbs twice.

1. The smell of cough drops and the sound of sneezing filled the waiting room of the doctor's office.
2. Siren blaring, the fire truck pulled into the street.
3. The cracked and uneven cement walk in front of the science building posed a danger to students and faculty walking to class.
4. The sugary taste of the cereal and the bright colors on the box were appealing to children.
5. The smell of fried chicken drifted from the kitchen, tantalizing Fran.

Regular and Irregular Verbs

Regular verbs follow a predictable pattern in the formation of their **principal parts.** Every verb has four principal parts: the present-tense form, the past-tense form, the past participle (used with helping verbs), and the present participle (the *-ing* verb form used with helping verbs). Regular verbs add *ed* to form their past tense and past participles. Some examples of regular verbs follow.

Regular Verb Forms

Present	Past	Past Participle	Present Participle
walk	walked	(have) walked	(are) walking
change	changed	(have) changed	(are) changing
add	added	(have) added	(are) adding
pull	pulled	(have) pulled	(are) pulling

Irregular verbs, on the other hand, follow no predictable pattern in their past and past participle forms. Sometimes a vowel changes: *sing* in the present tense becomes *sang* in the past tense and *sung* in the past participle. Sometimes an *n* or *en* will be added to form the past participle: *take* becomes *taken, fall* becomes *fallen.* Some verbs, such as *set,* do not change at all. Others change completely: *buy* in the present tense becomes *bought* in the past and past participle.

Below are some common irregular verbs and their principal parts. If you are unsure about a verb form, check this list or consult a dictionary for the correct form.

Principal Parts of Common Irregular Verbs

Present	Past	Past Participle	Present Participle
become	became	(have) become	(are) becoming
begin	began	(have) begun	(are) beginning
blow	blew	(have) blown	(are) blowing
break	broke	(have) broken	(are) breaking
bring	brought	(have) brought	(are) bringing
burst	burst	(have) burst	(are) bursting
buy	bought	(have) bought	(are) buying

Present	Past	Past Participle	Present Participle
catch	caught	(have) caught	(are) catching
choose	chose	(have) chosen	(are) choosing
come	came	(have) come	(are) coming
cut	cut	(have) cut	(are) cutting
do	did	(have) done	(are) doing
draw	drew	(have) drawn	(are) drawing
drink	drank	(have) drunk	(are) drinking
drive	drove	(have) driven	(are) driving
eat	ate	(have) eaten	(are) eating
fall	fell	(have) fallen	(are) falling
feel	felt	(have) felt	(are) feeling
fight	fought	(have) fought	(are) fighting
find	found	(have) found	(are) finding
fly	flew	(have) flown	(are) flying
freeze	froze	(have) frozen	(are) freezing
get	got	(have) gotten (or got)	(are) getting
give	gave	(have) given	(are) giving
go	went	(have) gone	(are) going
grow	grew	(have) grown	(are) growing
have	had	(have) had	(are) having
hear	heard	(have) heard	(are) hearing
hide	hid	(have) hidden	(are) hiding
hold	held	(have) held	(are) holding
hurt	hurt	(have) hurt	(are) hurting
keep	kept	(have) kept	(are) keeping
know	knew	(have) known	(are) knowing
lay (put)	laid	(have) laid	(are) laying
lead	led	(have) led	(are) leading
leave	left	(have) left	(are) leaving
lend	lent	(have) lent	(are) lending
lie (recline)	lay	(have) lain	(are) lying
lose	lost	(have) lost	(are) losing

Present	Past	Past Participle	Present Participle
put	put	(have) put	(are) putting
ride	rode	(have) ridden	(are) riding
rise	rose	(have) risen	(are) rising
run	ran	(have) run	(are) running
see	saw	(have) seen	(are) seeing
set (place)	set	(have) set	(are) setting
sing	sang	(have) sung	(are) singing
sit (be seated)	sat	(have) sat	(are) sitting
speak	spoke	(have) spoken	(are) speaking
swim	swam	(have) swum	(are) swimming
take	took	(have) taken	(are) taking
tear	tore	(have) torn	(are) tearing
throw	threw	(have) thrown	(are) throwing
write	wrote	(have) written	(are) writing
be, am, are, is	was, were	(have) been	(are) being

PRACTICE 6   USING IRREGULAR VERBS

Fill in the blank with the correct form of the verb shown to the left of each question. For help, consult the list of irregular verbs above.

(become)   **1.**   Tamiki has _____ an avid baseball fan.

(break)   **2.**   Before putting the eggs in his grocery cart, Ed opened the carton to make sure none were _____.

(drink)   **3.**   Someone has _____ all the orange juice.

(eat)   **4.**   Did you _____ breakfast this morning?

(go)   **5.**   The secretary said Mr. Cavanaugh had _____ for the day.

(lead)   **6.**   The kindergarten teacher _____ the children down the hall in single file.

(lend)   **7.**   A classmate _____ me a pen, but I forgot to return it.

(run)   **8.**   The cashier _____ to catch the customer who had forgotten his keys.

(see)   **9.**   When David's parents _____ his grade report, they told him they were proud.

(swim)   **10.**   When Jennifer had _____ fifteen laps, she stopped to rest.

Puzzling Pairs

Some irregular verbs are easily confused with other words. The following section will help you make the right choice between *loan* and *lend*, *lie* and *lay*, and *sit* and *set*.

Lend and Loan

Lend is a verb meaning "to allow someone to borrow," as in "*Lend* me ten dollars until payday," or "She *lent* her book to another student." *Loan* is a noun meaning "something borrowed," as in "He went to the bank for a mortgage *loan*."

> ### * Real-World Writing: Lend? Loan? Who Cares?
>
> People who care about English also care about the distinction between *lend* and *loan*. Though the use of *loan* as a verb is widespread, it is not considered acceptable by careful writers and speakers of English.
>
> Therefore, it's best to avoid such constructions as "Loan me a quarter for the telephone," or "He loaned me his car."

Examples

✘ I hoped my neighbor would *loan* me his lawnmower.

✔ I hoped my neighbor would *lend* me his lawnmower.

✘ Shakespeare wrote, "Friends, Romans, countrymen, *loan* me your ears."

✔ Shakespeare wrote, "Friends, Romans, countrymen, *lend* me your ears."

✔ Without a good credit record, it's hard to get a *loan*.

PRACTICE 7   USING *LEND* AND *LOAN*

Underline the correct word in each sentence.

1. Calvin wanted a car, but knew he could not afford payments on a (lend, loan).
2. We can get the job finished quickly if Andrew (lends, loans) a hand.

3. Before Josh went to camp, his mother warned him not to (lend, loan) his toothbrush or comb.

4. "Before you can get a (lend, loan) from a bank," said Portia, "you have to prove you don't need the money."

5. Would you mind (lending, loaning) me a dollar?

Lay and Lie

Lay and lie are often confused, partly because their forms overlap. The present-tense form of lay and the past-tense form of lie are both the same: lay. Look at the chart below to see the different forms of each verb.

Present	Past	Past Participle	Present Participle
lay (put)	laid	(have) laid	(are) laying
lie (recline)	lay	(have) lain	(are) lying

- The verb *lay* means "to put or place." It always takes an object: that is, there will always be an answer to the question, "Lay what?"

Examples

Whenever I need help, Manuel lays his work aside to assist me.

Carol laid her purse on the table and went to answer the phone.

Spiros has laid the brick for his patio.

The company is laying the groundwork for further expansion.

- The verb *lie* means "to recline." It does not take an object.

Examples

When Morgan had the flu, she lay in bed for almost two days.

The town lay in a little valley surrounded by hills.

Grady's back was aching because he had lain too long in one position.

The dog has been lying on the sofa again; his fur is all over the cushions.

PRACTICE 8   USING *LAY* AND *LIE*

Underline the correct verb forms in the paragraph below.

When Jack came home from work, he found his wife ¹(laying, lying) unconscious on the kitchen floor. He ²(laid, lay) his briefcase on the table and quickly dialed 911, wondering how long she had been ³(laying, lying) there. He listened numbly as the operator said, "Don't move her, just let her ⁴(lay, lie) there until the ambulance arrives. ⁵(Lay, lie) the phone down and check her breathing, but don't hang up." When the ambulance arrived, the paramedics ⁶(lay, laid) Arlene on a stretcher and put her in the ambulance. At the hospital, Jack paced the small waiting room, ⁷(laying, lying) in wait for the doctor and news of Arlene. Dr. Rodriguez finally emerged from the treatment room and told Jack that his wife had a mild concussion. "We'd like to observe her and make sure she ⁸(lays, lies) quietly for a day or two," the doctor said. Later, Jack brought his overnight bag and ⁹(lay, laid) it on the spare bed in Arlene's hospital room. "Stay with her if you like," said the nurse, "but it's not necessary. She will be fine." "I'll stay," said Jack. "I have ¹⁰(laid, lain) beside that woman every night for thirty-two years, and I see no reason to stop now."

Sit and *Set*

The verb *sit* means "to take a seat" or "to be located." It does not take an object.

verb
The class members sit in a circle to discuss what they have read.

verb
The dog sat on the porch, waiting for her owner to return.

verb   verb
We had just sat down to dinner when the telephone rang.

Set means to "put" or "place." The verb *set* always takes an object; that is, you will always find an answer to the question, "Set what?"

　　　　　　 verb　　　 object
Please <u>set</u> the <u>pizza</u> on the kitchen counter.

　　　　　　　　　 verb　　　　　　　　　　 object
The company <u>has set</u> minimum sales <u>goals</u> for its staff.

　　　　　　　　　 verb　　 verb　　 object
The instructor <u>has</u> not <u>set</u> a <u>due date</u> for the research paper.

PRACTICE 9   USING *SIT* AND *SET*

Underline the correct verb form in each sentence.

1. "I can't (sit, set) any longer in this uncomfortable chair," said Leo.
2. Carrie and Josh are engaged but have not (sat, set) a date for their wedding.
3. Two old men were (sitting, setting) at a small table playing checkers.
4. Michael says that he was never able to meet his goals until he (sat, set) them down in writing.
5. "I used to have a crock pot," said Camille, "But I never used it. It just (set, sat) on a shelf."

Review Exercises

Complete the Review Exercises to see how well you learned the skills addressed in this chapter. As you work through the exercises, go back through the chapter to review any of the rules you do not understand completely.

REVIEW EXERCISE 1   FINDING SUBJECTS AND VERBS

Cross out prepositional phrases in each sentence. Then underline the subject once and the verb twice.

1. In many theaters, advertisements for local businesses are shown before the movie.
2. More rain is forecast throughout next week.
3. Because of an unusually high number of accidents at the intersection of Kay Street and Brennan Avenue, the city installed a traffic light.
4. The bulletin board was covered with memos, reminders, and photographs.
5. The math quiz had not been announced in advance.

6. Across the top of Nan's computer monitor sat a row of small stuffed animals.

7. The noise of a lawnmower could be heard in the distance.

8. Warren accidentally spilled coffee on his computer keyboard.

9. By five o'clock, the office was deserted.

10. Junk mail and a few bills were stuffed into Kevin's mailbox.

REVIEW EXERCISE 2   FINDING SUBJECTS AND VERBS

Cross out prepositional phrases in each sentence. Then underline the subject once and the verb twice.

1. The cover of the book had been torn by accident.

2. Some of the store's customers complained about the potholes in the parking lot.

3. Wearing a yellow raincoat and carrying a red umbrella, the child walked toward the bus stop.

4. Every student at the college has an e-mail address.

5. Bananas are tasty and high in potassium.

6. Abraham Lincoln was carrying two pairs of glasses and a penknife on the night of his death.

7. On his way to work, George stopped for gas.

8. A pen had leaked into Randy's pocket, leaving a blue ink stain on his shirt.

9. The plastic bag in the bottom of the refrigerator contained bean sprouts in the final stages of decomposition.

10. The sign advertised sweaters at 50 percent off.

REVIEW EXERCISE 3   PUZZLING PAIRS

Choose the correct form of *lend* or *loan, lay* or *lie*, and *sit* or *set*.

1. The sign in the veterinarian's office said, "(Sit!, Set!) Stay! The doctor will be with you in a moment."

2. Despite the risk of sunburn or skin cancer, many people spend their vacations (laying, lying) in the sun.

3. Fernando (lent, loaned) a set of socket wrenches to his brother.

4. Linda has promised to (lend, loan) a hand when I try to repair the washer.

5. Discarded cans, fast food wrappers, and cigarette butts (lay, laid) alongside the road.

6. "I need to be doing something," said Jacquelyn. "I can't just (lay, lie) around the house."

7. His mother's calm in the face of the thunderstorm (lay, laid) Timmy's fears to rest.

8. "I have great news!" Kelly told her mother. "Are you (sitting, setting) down?"

9. "Would you (loan, lend) me a dollar until tomorrow?" Craig asked.

10. "My roommate leaves her stuff (laying, lying) all over the place," said Ebony.

REVIEW EXERCISE 4   USING IRREGULAR VERBS

Fill in the blank with the correct form of the verb shown to the left of each question. For help, consult the list of irregular verbs in this chapter.

(lie)   1. Several motorists stopped to help gather the boxes that _____ scattered around the overturned truck.

(burst)   2. After the meal, James leaned back in his chair and said, "I feel like I am about to _____."

(fly)   3. "Have you ever _____ before?" the flight attendant asked?

(put)   4. Alison asked her daughter if she had _____ away her toys.

(hurt)   5. "I think I _____ my ankle, coach," said Ben.

(begin)   6. The student apologized for entering after class had _____.

(leave)   7. "Has Mr. Simmons already _____?" asked Mandy.

(buy)   8. Kali _____ four boxes of Girl Scout cookies this year.

(fight)   9. For as long as they could remember, the couple had _____ over money.

(throw)   10. The student said he had _____ away the rough draft of his paper.

REVIEW EXERCISE 5   USING IRREGULAR VERBS

Fill in the blank with the correct form of the verb shown to the left of each question. For help, consult the list of irregular verbs in this chapter.

(bring)   1. The councilwoman said that the year had _____ many changes to the town of Newton.

(rise)   2. The morning was so cloudy and dark that it seemed as if the sun had not _____.

(ride)   3. Amiko said that she had never _____ a subway.

(see)   4. Paco did not come with us because he had already _____ the movie.

(drink)   **5.** Who _____ all the orange juice?

(lay)   **6.** For warmth, the cat _____ on top of the television.

(break)   **7.** Harold was fired because he had _____ the company's rules.

(go)   **8.** "I would never have _____ to the party if I had known Amanda would be there," said Tom.

(lose)   **9.** Sherrod has _____ his computer password again.

(drive)   **10.** Carol and Monty were bleary-eyed on their first day of vacation because they had _____ all night

13

Subject-Verb Agreement

The Question

How can I get on with writing
When subjects and verbs are always fighting?

The Answer

Plural paired with singular
Can't seem to get along,
And singular with plural
Just doesn't quite belong.

But singular and singular
Will need no referee,
And plural paired with plural
Is in perfect harmony.

In grammatical relations
You'll achieve tranquility
By using combinations
That never disagree.

Fortunately, the rules for agreement between subjects and verbs are much simpler than the rules for human relationships. All of the rules for subject-verb agreement presented in this chapter have the same idea behind them: **A singular subject requires a singular verb, and a plural subject requires a plural verb.**

The Basic Pattern

Most subject-verb agreement problems occur in the present tense. Look at the conjugation of the present-tense verb *speak*. You can see exactly where trouble is likely to occur if you ask the question, "Where does the verb change its form?"

	Singular	Plural
First person	I speak	we speak
Second person	you speak	you speak
Third person	he, she, it speaks	they speak

As you see, the verb changes its form in the third person by adding an *s* to the singular form. As a result, the third-person verb has two forms, a singular form and a plural form. The third-person singular verb ends in *s*; the third-person plural verb does not. Most problems with subject-verb agreement in the present tense occur in the third person.

PRACTICE 1   CONJUGATING A VERB

All regular verbs follow the pattern above. Using the previous sample as a model, fill in the forms of the verb *look* in the spaces below.

	Singular	Plural
First person	I _____	we _____
Second person	you _____	you _____
Third person	he, she, it _____	they _____

Did you remember to put the *s* on the third-person singular form? Notice that the pattern of third-person verbs is exactly the opposite of the pattern seen in nouns. When you look at the noun *dog*, you know that it is singular and that the plural form is *dogs*. But verbs in the third person, present tense, work in exactly the opposite way. The third-person singular form of the verb ends in *s*, not the plural form. When you see the verb *walks*, you know it is singular because it ends in *s*.

Examples

A third-person singular subject and verb usually follow this pattern:

The *dog walks*. (The singular noun does not end in *s*; the singular verb does end in *s*.)

A third-person plural subject and verb usually follow this pattern:

The *dogs walk.* (The plural noun ends in *s;* the plural verb does not end in *s.*)

---

* *Memory Jogger*

If you have trouble with third-person verbs, remember the following verse.

The Singular S
When verbs are in the present tense,
You never need to guess.
The singular third-person verb
Always ends in s.

PRACTICE 2   CONJUGATING VERBS

On your own paper, fill in the first-, second-, and third-person forms of the regular verbs *install, shop, play, insist,* and *enjoy.* Remember to add the *s* to the third-person singular form.

	Singular	Plural
First person	I _____	we _____
Second person	you _____	you _____
Third person	he, she, it _____	they _____

Verbs Ending in -*es*

Now look at the regular verb *impress* in the present tense. Here, when the verb already ends in *s,* the third-person singular form also changes, adding an *es.*

	Singular	Plural
First person	I impress	we impress
Second person	you impress	you impress
Third person	he, she, it impress**es**	they impress

Using Third Person

Third person is sometimes confusing. One reason is that it is the only person where the verb form changes. The biggest reason, however, is that third person includes much more than just the pronouns *he, she, it,* and *they.* Third-person singular also includes any noun or pronoun that can be replaced by *he, she,* or *it. Janis, Mr. Brown, otter, desk, toddler, someone, convenience store clerk, one,* and *George Washington* are all third-person singular. Thus each requires a present-tense verb ending in *s* or *es.*

Any noun or pronoun that can be replaced by *they* is third-person plural. *The Smiths, both, gas and groceries, poodles, sport utility vehicles,* and *many* are words that could be replaced by *they.* Thus all are third-person plural and require a present-tense plural verb, the form that does not add *s* or *es.*

The Verb *to be*

Now look at the most common irregular verb, the verb *to be.*

	Singular	Plural
First person	I am	we are
Second person	you are	you are
Third person	he, she, it is	they are

Notice that the pattern still holds: the third-person singular form of the verb always ends in *s* or *es.*

A Fundamental Rule

Knowing the pattern that present-tense verbs follow should make it a bit easier to apply the fundamental rule of subject-verb agreement:

A singular subject requires a singular verb, and a plural subject requires a plural verb.

Examples

    S   V
<u>Angela</u> <u>phones</u> home every day to check on her dog Hector. (singular subject, singular verb)

    S   V
<u>Halloween</u> <u>is</u> celebrated across the United States. (singular subject, singular verb)

      S   V
Many <u>students</u> <u>have</u> some difficulty adjusting to college life. (plural subject, plural verb)

    S   V
<u>Strawberries</u> <u>give</u> Clifford hives. (plural subject, plural verb)

PRACTICE 3   MAKING SUBJECTS AND VERBS AGREE

Underline the correct verb form in each sentence.

1. Like most people, Norma (resists, resist) trying new things.
2. Michael (impress, impresses) everyone with his determination and hard work.
3. The candy jar (holds, hold) only paper clips and spare change since Cecile decided to eat more nutritiously.
4. Two cups of coffee (is, are) barely enough to keep Roberto alert during his eight o'clock class.
5. Wolves (lives, live) in closely knit social groups, just as humans do.

Problems in Subject-Verb Agreement

Prepositional Phrase between Subject and Verb

When a prepositional phrase comes between subject and verb, it is easy to make mistakes in subject-verb agreement. Crossing out prepositional phrases will help you avoid errors and will help you to remember this important rule:

The subject of a verb is never found in a prepositional phrase.

Example 1

Consider the following problem in subject-verb agreement:

The members of the chorus (rehearses, rehearse) in the auditorium every Tuesday.

Which verb is correct? If you try to find the subject without crossing out prepositional phrases, you might ask the question, "Who or what rehearses or rehearse?" It seems logical to say, "The *chorus* rehearses, so *chorus* is the subject of the sentence and *rehearses* is the verb." However, *chorus* cannot be the subject of the sentence because it already has a job: it is the object of a preposition, and *the subject of a sentence is never found in a prepositional phrase.*

Incorrect Solution

✗   The members of the <u>chorus rehearses</u> in the auditorium every Tuesday.

Correct Solution: Cross out prepositional phrases to find the subject.

✔ The <u>members</u> of the chorus <u>rehearse</u> in the auditorium every Tuesday.

Example 2

The <u>bumper stickers</u> on Nat's car <u>reveal</u> his changing political attitudes over the years.

The verb agrees with its subject, *stickers,* not with the object of the preposition.

PRACTICE 4   MAKING SUBJECTS AND VERBS AGREE

In the sentences below, cross out prepositional phrases to find the subject of the sentence. Then underline the subject and double-underline the correct verb.

1. Several signs in front of the store (warns, warn) that cars parked in the fire lane will be towed.
2. The popularity of some brands of athletic shoes (makes, make) some people willing to pay high prices.
3. The driving beat of the music in the fitness center (helps, help) people exercise longer.
4. Writing in her journal every day (is, are) difficult for Susan.
5. The free samples of food in the supermarket on Saturday (attracts, attract) many shoppers.

Indefinite Pronouns as Subjects

Problems in subject-verb agreement are also likely to occur when the subject is an **indefinite pronoun,** a pronoun that does not refer to a specific person or thing. The following indefinite pronouns are always singular and require singular verbs.

each	everybody	anyone	anything
either	somebody	everyone	everything
neither	nobody	someone	something
anybody	one	no one	nothing

> * *Memory Jogger*
>
> Remember the singular indefinite pronouns more easily by grouping them:
>
> Each, either, neither
>
> All the bodies (anybody, everybody, nobody, somebody)
>
> All the ones (anyone, everyone, one, no one, someone)
>
> All the things (anything, everything, nothing, something)

Examples

subject verb

Janna answered the telephone, but <u>no one</u> <u>was</u> on the other end.

The subject, *no one,* is singular, as is the verb, *was.*

subject   verb

<u>Each</u> of the cupcakes <u>has been decorated</u> with a jack-o'-lantern face.

The singular verb, *has been decorated,* agrees with the singular subject, *each.* The plural object of the preposition, *cupcakes,* does not affect the verb.

PRACTICE 5   MAKING VERBS AGREE WITH INDEFINITE PRONOUNS

In each sentence, cross out prepositional phrases and underline the verb that agrees with the indefinite pronoun subject.

1. Neither of the cars (has, have) all the features that Carl wants.
2. Everybody in the apartment complex (believes, believe) the manager is doing a poor job of groundskeeping.
3. Someone in one of Helen's classes (is, are) organizing a study group.
4. Everything in the store (has, have) been reduced to half price.
5. Each of the barbers (pays, pay) rental to the shop owner.

Subject Following the Verb

In most English sentences, the subject comes before the verb. However, the subject follows the verb in these situations:

1. when the sentence begins with *here* or *there*
2. when the sentence begins with a prepositional phrase that is immediately followed by a verb
3. when the sentence is a question

Examples

        verb   subject
There <u><u>are</u></u> several <u>oranges</u> left ~~in the bowl~~.

The plural subject, *oranges,* requires the plural verb, *are.* The word *there* is not the subject of the sentence.

                  verb   subject
~~In front of the fireplace~~ <u><u>sit</u></u> two comfortable <u>chairs</u>.

The prepositional phrases *in front* and *of the fireplace* are immediately followed by a verb. Since the subject is never found in a prepositional phrase, it must be somewhere *after* the verb. The plural verb, *sit,* agrees with the plural subject, *chairs.*

         verb   subject
What <u><u>was</u></u> the <u>price</u> ~~of the small soft drink~~?

The singular subject, *price,* follows the singular verb, *was.*

        verb   subject
What <u><u>were</u></u> those strange <u>noises</u> that I heard outside?

The plural subject, *noises,* follows the plural verb, *were.*

PRACTICE 6   MAKING VERBS AGREE WITH SUBJECTS THAT COME AFTER VERBS

Cross out prepositional phrases in each sentence. Then underline the subject and double-underline the correct verb.

1. Nestled in the crawl space under the house (was, were) a mother cat and four fat kittens.
2. Why (does, do) Rodney have two cars when he can drive only one at a time?
3. There (is, are) a package outside Jamie's front door.
4. (Does, Do) anyone know where to get a parking permit?
5. There (wasn't, weren't) any seats available for Friday night's concert.

Compound Subjects

Compound subjects may also cause confusion in subject-verb agreement. The rules for subject-verb agreement with compound subjects are outlined in the sections that follow.

Compound Subjects Joined by *and*

Because *and* always joins at least two elements, compound subjects joined by *and* require a plural verb. Remember this rule:

Compound subjects joined by *and* require a plural verb.

Examples

                    compound subject   verb
A <u>pizza</u> *and* a rented <u>video</u> <u>are</u> Kim and Anthony's way of relaxing on Friday nights.

            compound subject   verb
<u>Winning</u> modestly *and* <u>losing</u> gracefully <u>are</u> two ways of demonstrating good sportsmanship.

                        compound subject
A prickly <u>cactus</u>, a <u>pot</u> of geraniums, *and* a <u>doormat</u> that says "Go
      verb
Away" <u>sit</u> on my neighbor's front porch.

                    compound subject   verb
Discarded beer <u>cans</u> *and* cigarette <u>butts</u> <u>dot</u> the convenience store's parking lot.

PRACTICE 7   MAKING VERBS AGREE WITH SUBJECTS JOINED BY *AND*

Cross out prepositional phrases, then double-underline the verb that agrees with each compound subject.

1. A trip to the mall with three children and a visit to a fast-food restaurant (was, were) not Harriet's idea of relaxation.
2. A tight waistband and the numbers on his scale (tells, tell) Arthur that it's time to start a diet.
3. At the movie theater, a giant soft drink, a large bag of popcorn, and a candy bar (costs, cost) more than the price of admission.
4. Finishing on time and remembering all the material (is, are) just two of the pressures of taking tests.

5. A timer shaped like a hen and a glass jar filled with spare change (sits, sit) on top of the microwave in Natalie's kitchen.

Compound Subjects Joined by *or, either/or,* or *neither/nor*

When subjects are joined by *or, either/or,* or *neither/nor,* it is not always possible to use logic to determine whether the verb will be singular or plural. Therefore, one rule applies to all compound subjects joined by *or, either/or,* or *neither/nor:*

When a compound subject is joined by *or, either/or,* or *neither/nor,* the verb agrees with the part of the subject closer to it.

Consider the following sentence:

Seth or his brother (is, are) opening the shop on Saturday morning.

How many will open the shop? The answer is "just one": either Seth *or* his brother. Therefore, using the singular verb is logical. The singular verb *is* also agrees with *brother,* the part of the subject closer to the verb.

Seth *or* his <u>brother</u> <u>is</u> opening the shop on Saturday morning.

Now, let's change the sentence a bit.

Seth's brothers or his assistants (is, are) opening the shop on Saturday.

How many will open the shop? In this sentence, *more than one:* either Seth's brothers or his assistants. It makes sense, then, to use a plural verb. The plural verb *are* also agrees with *assistants,* the part of the subject closer to the verb.

Seth's <u>brothers</u> *or* his <u>assistants</u> <u>are</u> opening the shop on Saturday.

The next two sentences do not respond to logical examination.

Seth or his assistants (is, are) opening the shop on Saturday.

Seth's assistants or his brother (is, are) opening the shop on Saturday.

How many will open the shop? There is no way to tell. Simply follow the rule and make the verb agree with the part of the subject closer to it.

Seth *or* his <u>assistants</u> <u>are</u> opening the shop on Saturday.

Seth's assistants *or* his <u>brother</u> <u>is</u> opening the shop on Saturday.

Examples

A five-dollar donation *or* two nonperishable food <u>items</u> <u><u>are</u></u> required for admission to the concert.

Two nonperishable food items *or* a five-dollar <u>donation</u> <u><u>is</u></u> required for admission to the concert.

Either two nonperishable food items *or* a five-dollar <u>donation</u> <u><u>is</u></u> required for admission to the concert.

Neither the alarm clock *nor* her two <u>cats</u> <u><u>were</u></u> successful in getting Kendra out of bed.

PRACTICE 8   **MAKING VERBS AGREE WITH SUBJECTS JOINED BY *OR*, *EITHER/OR* OR *NEITHER/NOR***

Cross out prepositional phrases, then double-underline the verb that agrees with each compound subject. Some subjects are joined by *and* while others are joined by *or, either/or,* or *neither/nor.*

1. Soup or a microwaveable pizza (was, were) all that Elton had on hand for lunch.
2. Either a sweatshirt or a warm sweater (feels, feel) good on a cool day.
3. Strawberries or a sliced banana (tastes, taste) good over cereal.
4. Neither Deon nor his two brothers (talks, talk) about anything except sports.
5. Taking drugs or drinking alcohol to escape problems often (leads, lead) to even bigger problems.

Review Exercises

Complete the Review Exercises to see how well you learned the skills addressed in this chapter. As you work through the exercises, go back through the chapter to review any of the rules you do not understand completely.

REVIEW EXERCISE 1

Underline the correct verb in each sentence.

1. The room (was, were) too warm, and Larry found it difficult to stay awake.
2. Only one of the members of the jury (believe, believes) the defendant committed the crime.

3. When Emily or her brothers (needs, need) money, their father tells them to get it the old fashioned way—to earn it.

4. Each of the cashiers (has, have) a good reason for being late.

5. Long hours and her supervisor's habit of calling her in on weekends (is, are) forcing Shayna to consider quitting her job.

6. Running and weight lifting (keeps, keep) Brandon in shape and feeling good.

7. There (was, were) too many distractions in the room during the test, and Andy had a hard time concentrating.

8. Inside Marcie's lunch bag (is, are) a diet soft drink, an apple, and a gooey snack cake.

9. Why (does, do) Cathy and Dennis bother to come to class when they never do any of the assigned work?

10. The Mason jars sitting on the table (is, are) filled with homemade jam.

REVIEW EXERCISE 2

Write C in the blank to the left of the sentence if the italicized verb agrees with its subject. If the verb is incorrect, write the correct form in the blank. Two of the sentences are correct.

_____ 1. The large crowd in the doctor's waiting room *make* me think I will be here a while.

_____ 2. The noise from the washers, the dryers, and the television *makes* it hard to hold a conversation in the laundromat.

_____ 3. "One of the mechanics *are* going to call me when my car is ready," said Ann.

_____ 4. Everybody in the path of the hurricane *have* been warned to prepare for evacuation.

_____ 5. A jacket, a hat, and a pair of gloves *was* lying on the kitchen floor.

_____ 6. "Either the telephone bill or the cable bill *have* to wait till next week," said Burton.

_____ 7. The bright sunshine and the music on her car radio *were* not enough to lift Natasha's gloomy mood.

_____ 8. There *is* the keys that Nathan was looking for a few minutes ago.

_____ 9. Why *have* the professor changed the due date of the assignment?

_____ 10. Andrea says everyone *give* her strange looks whenever she wears her purple outfit.

REVIEW EXERCISE 3

Cross out the two incorrect verb forms in each item. Then write the correct forms on the lines provided.

1. Julie says she does not mind if her husband spend his Saturdays working on his old motorcycle. However, she refuse to stand around and hand him tools while he works.

   Sentence 1: _____   Sentence 2: _____

2. John's full-time job and his heavy class schedule makes it almost impossible for him to find enough time to study. "Either full-time work or full-time school are okay," he says, "but not both."

   Sentence 1: _____   Sentence 2: _____

3. The lenses in Margaret's glasses turns darker when she goes outside in the sun. The lenses were expensive, but Margaret says she come out ahead because she does not have to buy sunglasses.

   Sentence 1: _____   Sentence 2: _____

4. As she grows older, Hal's grandmother live increasingly in the past. She remembers what she wore to her high school graduation party but do not recall whether she ate breakfast or not.

   Sentence 1: _____   Sentence 2: _____

5. Above the flat, sandy beach rise a large, dome-shaped sand dune. Small bushes or tufts of grass grows from the smooth sand dune, looking like patches of hair on an otherwise bald head.

   Sentence 1: _____   Sentence 2: _____

REVIEW EXERCISE 4

In each numbered item, cross out the two verbs that do not agree with their subjects. Then write the corrected verbs on the lines provided.

1. Sonya has never met the people in the apartment next door to her, but she has already decided she don't like them. Their music, pounding from the other side of the wall at all hours, annoy her.

   Sentence 1: _____   Sentence 2: _____

2. Inside the huge grocery superstore is a bank, a dry-cleaning shop, a fast-food restaurant, and a hair salon. "A person need hiking boots to get around in that huge store," Josh complained.

   Sentence 1: _____   Sentence 2: _____

3. In the fall, the leaves on the oak tree in our front yard bursts into a beautiful blaze of red. They are not so beautiful when they fall off the tree and my brother and I has to rake them up.

   Sentence 1: _____   Sentence 2: _____

4. There are no faculty member or staff person on duty in the grammar lab on Saturday. However, Sunday through Friday, computer tutorials and help with grammar is available for students of the college.

   Sentence 1: _____   Sentence 2: _____

5. The twins' mother is angry because their membership in several of the school's clubs and activities require them to sell merchandise to raise funds. "It is bad enough that I end up buying most of it," she says, "but even worse, each new item that I buy seem tackier and more expensive than the last."

   Sentence 1: _____   Sentence 2: _____

REVIEW EXERCISE 5

Underline the ten subject-verb agreement errors in the following paragraph. Then write the corrected verbs on the lines provided.

[1]In my rural neighborhood, at the end of a long gravel driveway, sit a house that is a mystery to everyone. [2]It was built over a year ago, but neither I nor my neighbors has ever seen it. [3]A chain, heavy and made of metal, run between two thick posts at the end of the driveway. [4]Hanging from the chain and nailed to the posts is several signs: "Keep Out," "No Trespassing," "Private Property." [5]Though it is customary in our area to welcome new neighbors with a visit and a basket of fruit, nobody in the neighborhood have dared to go past those unfriendly signs. [6]Instead, everyone speculate. [7]Maybe the woods that hug the property conceal a drug manufacturing plant, or perhaps the residents is growing marijuana. [8]Or they could be members of a militia group, stockpiling guns and preparing for war with anyone who venture beyond that chain at the end of the driveway. [9]There is many possibilities, but one thing is certain. [10]Our new neighbors prefers to keep to themselves.

1. _____
2. _____
3. _____
4. _____
5. _____

6. _____
7. _____
8. _____
9. _____
10. _____

14

Verb Shifts

A Shifty Excuse

"Professor, I brought my term paper with me, but when I opened my notebook, it's gone. I can't print out another copy because the file was erased by me."

The excuse above is shifty—but not just because it is unconvincing. It contains two common types of **verb shifts.** The first sentence contains an unnecessary shift from past tense to present tense, and the second contains an unnecessary shift from active voice to passive voice.

In this chapter, you will learn to correct unnecessary shifts from past to present tense and to make necessary shifts into the past perfect tense. You will also learn to recognize active voice and passive voice and to correct unnecessary shifts between the two.

Shifts in Tense

Verb tenses give the English language its sense of time, its sense of *when* events occur. The timeline below shows six verb tenses, and the chart that follows the timeline briefly explains how each tense is used.

Verb Tense Timeline

	past I walked	present I walk	future I will walk

past ◊←- - - * - - - - - - * - - - - - * - - - - - - - - * - - - * - - - - →◊ future

	I had walked	I have walked	I will have walked
	past perfect	present perfect	future perfect

Verb Tense Chart

◊◊◊	Furthest in the past; happened before another past action	past perfect *had* + *-ed* verb form	I *had walked* up the stairs, and I was out of breath.
◊◊	In the past; happened before now.	past *-ed* verb form	I *walked* all the way around the nature trail.
◊•	In the past but extending to the present	present perfect *have* or *has* + *-ed* verb form	I *have walked* every day for the last month. He *has walked* a mile already.
•	Happens regularly or often, or is happening now.	present base verb form or base verb + *-s*	I *walk* at least five miles a week. She *walks* quickly.
◊	Happens in the future but before another future event	future perfect *will have* + *-ed* verb form	By the time you join me on the track, I *will have walked* at least two miles.
◊◊	Happens at some time in the future	future *will* + base verb	I *will walk* with you tomorrow if we both have time.

Avoiding Unnecessary Tense Shifts

With so many ways to designate time, writers of English are bound to slip up occasionally. The most common error in verb tense is an unnecessary shift from past tense to present tense. Writers easily become so caught up in the past event they are describing that it becomes, at least temporarily, a part of "the now." Unnecessary shifts from present to past, while not quite as common, are also avoidable.

Examples

Necessary Shift:

✔ James <u>was</u> sick yesterday, but he <u>is feeling</u> better today.

past ... *present*

Unnecessary Shift from Past to Present:

✘ Cameron <u>was driving</u> on Route 42 when all of a sudden a bus <u>pulls</u> out in front of her.

past ... *present*

Unnecessary Shift Corrected:

✔ Cameron <u>was driving</u> on Route 42 when all of a sudden a bus <u>pulled</u> out in front of her.

past ... *past*

Unnecessary Shift from Past to Present:

✘ When we <u>arrived</u> at the theater, we <u>notice</u> that the line <u>stretches</u> all the way around the building.

past ... *present* ... *present*

Unnecessary Shift Corrected:

✔ When we <u>arrived</u> at the theater, we <u>noticed</u> that the line <u>stretched</u> all the way around the building.

past ... *past* ... *past*

Unnecessary Shift from Present to Past:

✘ Jerry <u>comes</u> home every day and <u>turned on</u> the television set to watch the news.

present ... *past*

Unnecessary Shift Corrected:

✔ Jerry <u>comes</u> home every day and <u>turns on</u> the television set to watch the news.

present ... *present*

PRACTICE 1   MAINTAINING CONSISTENT TENSE

Underline the correct verb in each sentence.

1. When Ralph came home, he saw that his puppy had chewed the sofa pillows and (is, <u>was</u>) hiding under the bed.
2. I thought Abby had quit smoking, but when I went outside for my break, there she (stands, stood), smoking a cigarette.
3. The boat towed the skier to the far end of the lake, then (turns, turned) around and headed back toward the dock.

4. Every afternoon, the children play outside until their mother (calls, called) them in for dinner.

5. The cat was sleeping on the arm of a chair, but when the doorbell rang, he (darts, darted) under the sofa.

PRACTICE 2   CORRECTING UNNECESSARY TENSE SHIFTS

In each sentence, correct the unnecessary shift from past to present.

1. Valerie fills her gas tank on Monday, but by Friday it was empty again.

   _____

2. Michael had been working all morning in the heat, and when he came in, he seems dizzy and ill.

   _____

3. Lynn woke up in the middle of the night and could not go back to sleep, so she decides to clean out the refrigerator.

   _____

4. The score was tied at the bottom of the ninth, and McGriff comes up to bat amid the cheers of the fans.

   _____

5. Sylvester thought he no longer loved Carmen until he sees her at the laundromat on a Tuesday night in April.

   _____

Active and Passive Voice

Active voice means that the grammatical subject of a sentence performs the action described by the verb, as in the following sentence:

Before the game began, Cynthia sang the national anthem.

In this sentence, *Cynthia*, the grammatical subject, performs the action described by the verb *sang*.

Rewritten in **passive voice,** the sentence looks like this:

Before the game began, the national anthem was sung by Cynthia.

What has changed? Simply put, the grammatical subject of the sentence is not acting, but is acted upon. The subject *anthem* performs no action, but instead is acted upon by the person who sings it. Notice, too, another hallmark of the passive voice: the verb contains a helping verb that is a form of the verb *to be*. Though an active voice verb also may have a helping verb such as *is, was, were, have been, will be*, or another form of *to be*, a passive voice verbs *always* does. Another hallmark of the passive voice is the "by" construction (*by* Cynthia) that sometimes tells who or what acted upon the subject.

---

* Memory Jogger

In *active voice*, an action is done *by* the grammatical subject.

In *passive voice*, an action is done *to* the grammatical subject.

PRACTICE 3   EXAMINING ACTIVE AND PASSIVE VOICE

Answer the questions about each set of sentences. The first one is done for you.

Set 1

   Active: The police arrested the suspected bank robbers on Thursday morning.

   The subject of the verb is _____.

   The verb that shows the action done *by* the subject is _____.

   Passive: The suspected bank robbers were arrested by the police on Thursday morning.

   The subject of the verb is _____.

   The verb that shows the action done *to* the subject is _____.

Set 2

   Active: Samantha watered her house plants.

   The subject of the verb is _____.

   The verb that shows the action done *by* the subject is _____.

   Passive: The house plants were watered by Samantha.

   The subject of the verb is _____.

   The verb that slows the action done *to* the subject is _____.

Set 3

Active: Marcus caught the ball before it could reach the plate glass window.

The subject of the verb is _____.

The verb that shows the action done *by* the subject is _____.

Passive: The ball was caught by Marcus before it could reach the plate glass window.

The subject of the verb is _____.

The verb that shows the action done *to* the subject is _____.

Set 4

Active: Claude took the mud-spattered Chevrolet to the car wash.

The subject of the verb is _____.

The verb that shows the action done *by* the subject is _____.

Passive: The mud-spattered Chevrolet was taken to the car wash by Claude.

The subject of the verb is _____.

The verb that shows the action done *to* the subject is _____.

Set 5

Active: After the restaurant closes, the employees clean the tables and vacuum the carpet.

The subject of the verb is _____.

The verb that shows the action done *by* the subject is _____.

Passive: After the restaurant closes, tables are cleaned and the carpet is vacuumed.

In this sentence, the subjects of the verbs are _____.

The verbs that show the actions done *to* the subjects are _____ and _____.

Uses of Active and Passive Voice

Active voice, with its directness and vitality, is stronger than passive and is preferred in most situations. Sometimes, however, passive voice is appropriate. For example, you would use passive voice in a sentence like "The furniture will be delivered on Tuesday" because you don't care who delivers it, you just care that it arrives.

However, try to avoid awkward shifts between active and passive voice. Look at the following example:

✗ The professor $\overset{\text{active}}{\underline{\text{wished}}}$ us luck, and at exactly 8:10, the tests $\overset{\text{passive}}{\underline{\text{were handed}}}$ out.

✔ The professor $\overset{\text{active}}{\underline{\text{wished}}}$ us luck, and at exactly 8:10, he $\overset{\text{active}}{\underline{\text{handed}}}$ out the tests.

Writing Sentences in Active and Passive Voice

To avoid unnecessary shifts between active and passive voice, you need to be able to recognize and write sentences in both voices.

Switching from Passive to Active Voice

To switch from passive voice to active voice, determine *who* or *what* acts upon the subject of the sentence, and rewrite the sentence to make that actor the subject.

Examples

Passive: The car was driven by Mario's brother.

To switch this passive voice sentence to active voice, look for the word or phrase that tells who performs the action described in the subject-verb sequence. In this sentence, look for a word or phrase that tells *who drove the car. Mario's brother* drove the car. To put the sentence into active voice, make *Mario's brother* the subject of the sentence and work from there.

Active: Mario's brother drove the car.

Sometimes, the *by* construction is omitted, and you need to mentally fill in the blank to put an actor into the sentence.

Passive: The prisoner was sentenced to life without parole.

The sentence does not say who sentenced the prisoner, but logic tells you that it must have been a judge. To rewrite the sentence in active voice, put a judge into the sentence.

Active: The judge sentenced the prisoner to life without parole.

PRACTICE 4   WRITING SENTENCES IN ACTIVE VOICE

Rewrite each of the following sentences in active voice.

1. The pizza was delivered by a man with red hair.

    the man delivering the pizza has red hair.

2. Evidence was collected by two uniformed officers.

    Two Officers in uniform is collecting evidence.

3. The concert was attended by a small, enthusiastic crowd.

    A small enthusiatic crowd attends the concert.

4. After eight rings, the telephone was answered by a man who sounded as though he had been sleeping.

    A man who sounded as though he had been sleeping answered the phone.

5. At the park's entrance, hot dogs were sold by a vendor.

    At the Park's entrance, a vendor sold hotdogs

Switching from Active to Passive Voice

To switch from active voice to passive voice, reverse the position of the actor (the subject of the verb) and the recipient of the action (the object of the verb).

Examples

Active: The technician expertly cleaned and repaired the old lawnmower.

The actor (the subject of the verb) is *technician.* The recipient of the action is *the old lawnmower.* To convert the sentence to passive voice, switch the positions of the two.

Passive: The old lawnmower was expertly cleaned and repaired by the technician.

Here is a second example:

Active: The meteorologist predicted rain and temperatures in the seventies.

Passive: Rain and temperatures in the seventies were predicted by the meteorologist.

PRACTICE 5   WRITING SENTENCES IN PASSIVE VOICE

Rewrite each of the following sentences in passive voice.

1. The dog ate the rest of the leftovers.
   The rest of the leftovers were ate by the dog

2. Hundreds of cattle ate the contaminated feed.
   The contaminated feed was ate by hundreds of cattle

3. The school board took a firm stand against the banning of books.
   _____

4. The gardening expert gave a presentation on leaf mold.
   A presentation was given on leaf mold by a gardening expert

5. The sound of his mother's voice calmed and reassured the child.
   The child was calmed + reassured by his mother's voice.

Correcting Shifts in Voice

When an unnecessary shift in voice occurs within a sentence, rewrite the sentence so that it is in one voice. Active voice is usually preferred.

Examples

Unnecessary Shift:

          active   passive

✗ Before Clayton <u>took</u> the test, his notes <u>were reviewed</u> quickly.

Corrected:

          active   active

✔ Before Clayton <u>took</u> the test, he quickly <u>reviewed</u> his notes.

Unnecessary Shift:

    active   passive

✗ Camille <u>lost</u> her battered old umbrella, so a new one <u>was purchased</u>.

Corrected:

✔ Camille lost her battered old umbrella, so she purchased a new one.

active (above "lost")   *active* (above "purchased")

PRACTICE 6   CORRECTING SHIFTS IN VOICE

Each of the following sentences contains a shift in voice. Underline the passive-voice portion of each sentence. Then rewrite each sentence in active voice.

1. Cody's parents <u>were firm</u> with him, but he <u>was spoiled</u> by his grandparents.

   Cody's parents are firm w/ him, but his g.p. spoiles him.

2. Kelly made soup, and bread <u>was baked</u> by Tom and Kara.

   Kelly made soup, and Tom + Kara baked bread.

3. Although many other job offers <u>were received</u>, Shenita has decided to work for Collins Corporation.

   Although she received other job offers, Shenita has decided to work for Collins Corporation.

4. Because the garden was carefully tended by Sean, it thrived.

   Because Sean carefully tended the garden it thrived.

5. After the newspaper had been read by everyone in the family, Cliff put it in the recycling bin.

   _____

   _____

6. Ramon was angry when he found out that a trick had been played on him by his friends.

   _____

7. Connie wanted to monitor her food intake, so everything she ate was written down.

   _____

8. In the doctor's office, a nurse took Glenn's vital signs, and then he was examined by the doctor.

   _____

   _____

9. After Nelson wrote a cover letter, it was mailed along with his resumé.

   _____

10. As if the instructor had not given us enough work, an additional book was added to our reading list by her at midterm.

_____

_____

Review Exercises

Complete the Review Exercises to see how well you learned the skills addressed in this chapter. As you work through the exercises, go back through the chapter to review any of the rules you do not understand completely.

REVIEW EXERCISE 1

The italicized portions of the following sentences contain unnecessary shifts in voice or tense or verbs that need to be shifted from the past to the past-perfect tense. For each sentence, circle _a, b,_ or _c_ to indicate the type of problem in the sentence. Then correct the problem in each sentence.

1. In the morning, Tom left his car at the dealership. When he returned at five-thirty, the mechanics _replaced the brake pads and tuned the engine._
   The problem in this sentence is
   a. a shift in voice
   b. a shift between past and present tense
   c. past-tense verbs that need to be further in the past (past perfect).

   _____

2. Marie's parents sat on the couch and _hold_ hands as if they were teenagers.
   The problem in this sentence is
   a. a shift in voice
   b. a shift between past and present tense
   c. a past-tense verb that needs to be further in the past (past perfect).

   _____

3. In the stands, baseball fans stood for the seventh-inning stretch while _hot dogs, soft drinks, and beer were sold by vendors._
   The problem in this sentence is
   a. a shift in voice
   b. a shift between past and present tense
   c. a past-tense verb that needs to be further in the past (past perfect).

   _____

4. In the shelter of the carport, the cats dismembered a small bird that *had been caught by them.*

    The problem in this sentence is

    a. a shift in voice

    b. a shift between past and present tense

    c. a past-tense verb that needs to be further in the past (past perfect).

    _____

5. When Adam reached his hotel room, he realized he *left* his toothbrush and toothpaste at home.

    The problem in this sentence is

    a. a shift in voice

    b. a shift between past and present tense

    c. a past tense verb that needs to be further in the past (past perfect).

    _____

REVIEW EXERCISE 2

The italicized portions of the following sentences contain unnecessary shifts in voice or tense, or verbs that need to be shifted from the past to the past-perfect tense. Correct the problem in each sentence.

1. The letter said Gary was a winner if the winning number *was held by him.*

    _____

2. When I saw Anita, *she says,* "Why weren't you at the meeting yesterday?"

    _____

3. Bonita asked Alan to join our study group, but he said *he studied already.*

    _____

4. Hank shook the salesman's hand and said, "I'll let you know when *a decision has been reached by me.*"

    _____

5. In the computer store, Julia bought the new keyboard she needed, and just as she was ready to leave, she *decides* to get a mouse pad, too.

    _____

6. Since *bids were signaled by the buyers* with a nod or a slight hand movement, the auctioneer had to be alert.

    _____

7. Rowe *already finished* his report and was ready to turn it in, so he was irritated when the instructor granted the class a last-minute extension.

    _____

8. Darrell and Ellie had just fallen asleep when *the baby starts crying*.

    _____

9. Bill held his burned finger under cold running water, and then *ice was applied*.

    _____

10. Kim looked at the clock and realized she *worked* for half an hour.

    _____

REVIEW EXERCISE 3

The italicized portions of the following sentences contain unnecessary shifts in voice or tense, or verbs that need to be shifted from the past to the past-perfect tense. For each sentence, circle *a, b,* or *c* to indicate the type of problem in the sentence. Then correct the problem in each sentence.

1. On the first day of class, the instructor handed each student a syllabus and *says*, "Everything you need to know about the course content, exams, and assignments is in this document."
    The problem in this sentence is
    a. a shift in voice
    b. a shift between past and present tense
    c. a past-tense verb that needs to be further in the past (past perfect).

    _____

2. When Ralph arrived at home, the mail carrier *left* a note, "Package on front porch."
    The problem in this sentence is
    a. a shift in voice
    b. a shift between past and present tense
    c. a past-tense verb that needs to be further in the past (past perfect).

    _____

3. When Stephanie fed Rover, the dog *eats* an entire can of food in one gulp.
    The problem in this sentence is
    a. a shift in voice
    b. a shift between past and present tense
    c. a past-tense verb that needs to be further in the past (past perfect).

    _____

4. Ray won the race today, *and another school record was set by him.*
   The problem in this sentence is
   a. a shift in voice
   b. a shift between past and present tense
   c. a past-tense verb that needs to be further in the past (past perfect).

   _____

5. After the exam, Carolyn walked into the hall and said she was certain *she did well.*
   The problem in this sentence is
   a. a shift in voice
   b. a shift between past and present tense
   c. a past-tense verb that needs to be further in the past (past perfect).

   _____

REVIEW EXERCISE 4

Underline the voice or tense problem in each sentence. Then write the correct voice or tense on the lines provided.

1. The server asked if I tried the house dressing before.

   _____

2. The hair stylist had almost finished styling Sue's hair when the hair dryer erupts in flames.

   _____

3. The snow fell thickly and soon it covers everything in a blanket of white.

   _____

4. If the job was done by Joel, he did it right.

   _____

5. Margaret saw that she had e-mail, so she opens her mailbox.

   _____

6. When Elliott reached the bench where he planned to meet Ann, she left already.

   _____

7. Carl tried to hail a cab, but it just passes him by.

   _____

8. Justine said that we should not worry, arrangements had been made by her.

    _____

9. The lake was shrouded in mist, but one small boat is visible near the shore-line.

    _____

10. Rosie loves to paint. The oil painting on her living room wall and the water-colors in her bedroom were painted by her.

    _____

    _____

REVIEW EXERCISE 5

Each sentence in the paragraph contains a voice or tense problem. First, underline the problem. Then correct it by rewriting a verb in past tense or past-perfect tense or by changing a passive voice construction to active voice.

[1]At my ten-year high school class reunion last week, I saw many people I did not see in years. [2]One old classmate seen by me was Patrick, the class clown. [3]Many tricks had been played by him on the teachers at Truman High School, but now, he is a teacher himself. [4]Another former classmate I saw was Heather, who is the homecoming queen ten years ago. [5]Her bubbly personality did not change since high school. [6]She remembered everyone's name and greets them with a hug and a warm hello. [7]The person that surprised everyone was Wanda, who in high school is a computer nerd. [8]Then, she was quiet and shy, but today, a major software company is owned by her. [9]Many of the guys probably wished they paid more attention to Wanda back then. [10]The reunion was fun; I enjoy myself and can't wait to see what changes the next ten years will bring.

1. _____

2. _____

3. _____

4. _____

5. _____

6. _____

7. _____

8. _____

9. _____

10. _____

15

Sentence Variety

Dear Friend,

   This is a chain letter. It is composed of a chain of simple sentences. Each sentence has one subject and one verb. Each sentence conveys one idea. Each idea is expressed in the same way. The writer has fallen into a pattern. This pattern becomes monotonous. The reader wants to scream.

   If you break the chain, you will have good luck. Your writing will flow more smoothly, and your reader will not scream. In this paragraph, for instance, the chain of simple sentences has been broken using techniques that you will learn in this chapter. Break the chain and set your writing free!

Sincerely,
One Who Wishes You Well

Power Tools for Writing Sentences

When you learned to write, you started by expressing one idea per sentence. But as your ideas become more complex, so should your writing. Use this chapter to strengthen your ability to write varied, interesting sentences. You can vary your sentences by using these four "power tools": Be concise, vary sentence openings, connect ideas through coordination, and connect ideas through subordination.

Power Tool 1: Be Concise

The poet Robert Browning said, "Less is more." This simple idea has been repeated in connection with everything from architecture to zoology, and it is also one of the cornerstones of good writing. In other words, use as few words as it takes to do the job well.

Examples

✗   I bought a used car. It is a Chevrolet Malibu. It is blue. It has only eighteen thousand miles on it. (five sentences, twenty-one words)

✔   I bought a blue Chevrolet Malibu with only eighteen thousand miles on it. (one sentence, thirteen words)

The second sentence in the example above represents a savings of eight words. In the omission of those eight words, has any of the substance been left out? True, the word *car* is left out in the second version, but most Americans old enough to read the word "Chevrolet" know that a Chevrolet is a car. The word *used* is also left out, but the reader knows that if the car has eighteen thousand miles on it, someone has used it.

Examples

✗   Charles was wearing a t-shirt. It was an old shirt. It was white. It had ketchup stains across the front. (four sentences, twenty words)

✔   Charles was wearing an old, white t-shirt with ketchup stains across the front. (one sentence, thirteen words)

PRACTICE 1   WRITING CONCISE SENTENCES

Combine the four ideas in each set of sentences into one concise sentence. Make sure that the sentence expresses the idea fully but uses as few words as possible.

1.   Alicia read her horoscope.

   The horoscope was in the newspaper.

   The newspaper was called *The Daily Spectator*.

   The horoscope said that Alicia's persuasive powers were strong.

   _____

   _____

2.   Rashad picked up an empty soft drink can.

   The can was in the parking lot.

The parking lot was a student parking lot.

Rashad put the can in a trash container.

_____

_____

3. The window on the driver's side of the car was rolled down.

   The car belonged to Rosa.

   The window had been open during a thunderstorm.

   The seat on the driver's side of the car was wet.

   _____

   _____

4. Someone in the classroom was chewing gum.

   The same person was popping the gum.

   Some students were annoyed.

   The class was taking a test.

   _____

   _____

5. There was a calendar on the wall.

   The wall was in the machine shop.

   The calendar showed women.

   The women were wearing bathing suits.

   _____

   _____

Power Tool 2: Vary Sentence Openings

The most common sentence pattern in English is one that opens with a subject followed by a verb, as in the following sentences:

      S   V

Imana dashed across the finish line.

     S   V

Cattle grazed peacefully in a field of bright green.

This pattern is common because it is strong and dynamic and gets the job done quickly. When you read a sentence in this pattern, you know immediately who the actors were and what they did. But too many sentences in this pattern can make for dull reading, especially if they are short sentences like the ones in the "chain letter" you read at the opening of this chapter. So while you never want to give up writing strong sentences with the subject and verb at the beginning, occasional variation strengthens your writing. Two ways to vary your sentence openings are with prepositional phrases and verbal phrases.

Prepositional Phrases to Begin Sentences

You are probably used to ending sentences with prepositional phrases.

A yellow light shone *from the window.*

Bob went to the deli *during his lunch hour.*

A candy wrapper had been dropped on the floor *near the front of the room.*

Occasionally, try beginning a sentence with a prepositional phrase:

From the window, a yellow light shone.

During his lunch hour, Bob went to the deli.

Near the front of the room, a candy wrapper had been dropped on the floor.

PRACTICE 2   BEGINNING SENTENCES WITH PREPOSITIONAL PHRASES

Rearrange each sentence to begin with a prepositional phrase.

1.   Anna made a note of the appointment on a page of the calendar.

_____

2.   Michael picked up a rain-soaked newspaper from the driveway.

_____

3.   Perry heard laughter from the next room.

_____

4.   A child was playing hopscotch in the street.

_____

5.   Bryan seemed quiet and shy in the office.

_____

Verbal Phrases to Begin Sentences

A verbal phrase is a word group that begins with an *-ing* verb or an *-ed/-en* verb:

> *Riding into the sunset,* the cowboys sat tall in the saddle.

> *Eating quickly,* Arturo hoped he would get back to work on time.

> *Written in haste,* the paper was barely legible.

> *Coated with flour,* the cockroach scurried across the floor of the restaurant's kitchen.

Opening Sentences with *-ing* Verbal Phrases

Sometimes, an idea expressed in two sentences can be compressed by converting one of the sentences into an *-ing* phrase. Be sure to put the *-ing* phrase as close as possible to the person or thing it describes:

> Samuel walked into the room.

> He was trying not to attract attention.

> *Trying not to attract attention,* Samuel walked into the room.

> Amelia was expecting to be laid off.

> She was shocked when she was offered a promotion.

> *Expecting to be laid off,* Amelia was shocked when she was offered a promotion.

PRACTICE 3   USING *-ING* PHRASES

In each sentence pair below, convert one of the sentences to an -ing verbal phrase to make one sentence.

1. The blue van sped past at a high rate of speed.
    It was swerving dangerously on the wet pavement.

    _____

    _____

2. Vernon was planning to cut his English class.
   He was dismayed to meet his instructor in the hall.

   _____

   _____

3. Renita was opening her mailbox.
   She was surprised to see a spider inside.

   _____

   _____

4. Allen was reaching for a piece of candy.
   He spilled the whole bag on the floor.

   _____

   _____

5. My neighbor woke me up in the middle of the night.
   She was ringing the doorbell and pounding on the door.

   _____

   _____

Opening Sentences with *-ed* Verbal Phrases

Sometimes, an idea expressed in two sentences can be compressed by converting one of the sentences into an *-ed/-en* phrase:

The grass was covered with dew.

It was impossible to mow.

Covered with dew, the grass was impossible to mow.

The television was broken beyond repair.

It was placed beside the curb for trash pickup.

Broken beyond repair, the television was placed beside the curb for trash pickup.

PRACTICE 4   USING *-ED* PHRASES

In each sentence pair, convert one of the sentences to an *-ed* verbal phrase to make one sentence.

1. The interviewer was impressed by the candidate's credentials.
    She decided to offer him a job.

    _____

    _____

2. Alonzo was inspired by the speaker's message.
    He decided to pursue his dream of becoming a veterinarian.

    _____

    _____

3. Tia promised herself she would do better on her next test.
    She was disappointed by her grade on the chapter test.

    _____

    _____

4. Jon was annoyed by the telephone's constant ringing.
    He decided to buy an answering machine.

    _____

    _____

5. The sand castle was swept from the shore.
    It was engulfed by a huge wave.

    _____

    _____

Power Tool 3: Connect Ideas through Coordination

Often, ideas expressed in short, simple sentences can be joined to make a more effective sentence. One way to join sentences is called **coordination.** Coordination can be done in two ways: by using a comma and a coordinating (FANBOYS) conjunction or by using a semicolon and a joining word.

Comma and FANBOYS

FANBOYS conjunctions, more commonly called *coordinating conjunctions*, are used with a comma to join two independent clauses. If you can remember the nonsense word FANBOYS, you can remember all seven coordinating conjunctions: *for, and, nor, but, or, yet, so.*

This is the pattern used when a FANBOYS conjunction is used with a comma to join two clauses. The comma goes before the FANBOYS conjunction.

Independent clause , and independent clause .

Example

John worked the math problem twice.

He came up with a different answer each time.

The two independent clauses above can be joined with a FANBOYS and a comma:

John worked the math problem twice, **but** he came up with a different answer each time.

A list of FANBOYS conjunctions appears below:

* FANBOYS Conjunctions						
for	and	nor	but	or	yet	so

PRACTICE 5   JOINING SENTENCES WITH *FANBOYS* CONJUNCTIONS

Join each sentence pair below with a comma and a FANBOYS.

1. The telephone was ringing on the secretary's desk.
   No one bothered to answer it.

   _____

2. Harlan's suitcase had a broken handle.
   He decided to buy another one before his vacation.

   _____

3. The mall's parking lot was crowded.
   The store was packed with shoppers.

   _____

4. Lisa did not have time to make coffee at home.
    She bought a cup of flavored coffee from a machine in the convenience store.

    _____

5. Allen may go skiing on his vacation.
    He may stay home and paint his house.

    _____

Semicolon and Joining Word

Another method of coordination is using a semicolon and a joining word. As with a comma and FANBOYS conjunction, a complete sentence (or independent clause) will appear on both sides of the semicolon.

__Independent clause__ ; therefore, __independent clause__ .

Example

Anthony would like to make more money.

He fears that working more hours would interfere with his studies.

The two separate sentences can be combined with a semicolon and a joining word.

Anthony would like to make more money; **however,** he fears that working more hours would interfere with his studies.

The joining words also function as *transitional expressions,* underscoring the relationship between the two clauses. A list of joining words commonly used with semicolons appears below.

Joining Words Used with a Semicolon

accordingly	however	nevertheless
also	in addition	of course
as a result	in fact	on the other hand
besides	instead	then
finally	meanwhile	therefore
furthermore	namely	thus

PRACTICE 6   JOINING SENTENCES WITH SEMICOLONS AND TRANSITIONAL WORDS

Join each sentence pair with a semicolon, a joining word from the list on page 261, and a comma.

1. The child knew that there were no monsters in the closet.
   He thought his mother should check anyway.

   _____

2. The instructor was ill on Tuesday.
   The class was canceled.

   _____

3. The citizen firmly refused to remove the junked cars from his yard.
   He argued that the city should pay him for his "art."

   _____

4. Felicia hoped that her tax refund would arrive before the weekend.
   She did not get it until the following Wednesday.

   _____

5. Al had locked his keys in the car twice during the past month.
   He had an extra set made.

   _____

Power Tool 4: Connect Ideas through Subordination

Placing a **dependent word** such as *because, although, if, when,* or *after* in front of an independent clause makes it a **dependent** or **subordinate clause,** one that can no longer stand on its own as a sentence. It must be connected to another idea that is stated as a complete sentence. It will then depend on the sentence it is attached to and can no longer be separated from it. A sentence containing a dependent clause may be written in two ways: dependent clause first or dependent clause last.

Dependent Clause First

Place a comma after a dependent clause that introduces a sentence.

Example

Dan realized that he was paying over fifty dollars for cable TV.

He decided to drop his premium channels.

If a dependent clause acts as an introductory clause, a comma follows it.

When <u>dependent clause</u> , <u>independent clause</u> .

When Dan realized that he was paying over fifty dollars for cable TV, he decided to drop his premium channels.

Dependent Clause Last

Another way to connect ideas through subordination is to place an independent clause first and follow it with a dependent clause.

<u>Independent clause</u> when <u>dependent clause</u> .

Example

Traffic on the interstate was rerouted for two hours.

A tractor trailer overturned in the southbound lane.

Traffic on the interstate was rerouted for two hours **when** a tractor trailer overturned in the southbound lane.

A list of dependent words is shown below.

Commonly Used Dependent Words

after	how	what
although	if	whatever
as	once	when
as if	since	whenever
as long as	so that	where
as soon as	that	wherever
as though	though	which
because	unless	while
before	until	who
even though		

PRACTICE 7 JOINING SENTENCES WITH DEPENDENT WORDS

Choosing from the list of dependent words above, connect each sentence pair using the following pattern:

<u>Dependent clause</u> , <u>independent clause</u> .

1. My little brother turned sixteen.
   He took the test for his driver's license.

   _____

   _____

2. Quinton was not sure he was good enough to make the team.
   He decided to try out anyway.

   _____

   _____

3. Mika had lived in the same town all her life.
   She was eager to attend college in a different city.

   _____

   _____

4. The weather forecaster had predicted morning rain.
   The day dawned sunny and clear.

   _____

   _____

5. Fredo was accepted at a technical school.
   He changed his mind and decided to apply to a four-year college.

   _____

   _____

PRACTICE 8   JOINING SENTENCES WITH DEPENDENT WORDS

Choosing from the list of dependent words above, connect each sentence pair using the following pattern:

<u>Independent clause</u>   when   <u>dependent clause</u> .

The first one is done for you.

1. A small house was swept away by the flood. Onlookers watched in horror.
   A small house was swept away by the flood as onlookers watched in horror.

   _____

2. Sarah let out a sigh of relief.
   She saw that she had passed her midterm exam.

   _____

   _____

3. Trenton was angry.
   He had to wait almost an hour for his job interview.

   _____

   _____

4. Brandy did not finish her research project.
   She became distracted exploring the Internet.

   _____

   _____

5. The workers were confident they would finish the project on time.
   They were three weeks behind their planned schedule.

   _____

   _____

Creating Emphasis through Subordination

Dependent words also act as transitional words, showing the relationship between the ideas. Using dependent clauses helps to downplay one idea while emphasizing another. Usually, the idea expressed in the independent clause is of greater importance, while the idea in the dependent clause is of lesser importance.

Examples

Although Diana had no money in her bank account,

emphasis on the check
she wrote a check for two hundred dollars.

Although Diana wrote a check for two hundred dollars,

emphasis on empty account
she had no money in her checking account.

emphasis on the cheer
A cheer went up from the crowd as Hank Aaron strode onto the field.

emphasis on the Hank Aaron
Hank Aaron strode onto the field as a cheer went up from the crowd.

PRACTICE 9   EMPHASIZING IDEAS WITH DEPENDENT WORDS

Choosing from the list of dependent words on page 263, connect each sentence pair. Emphasize the idea marked with a check. Do not introduce the emphasized idea with a dependent word. The first one is done for you.

1. Jonas seldom spoke up in class.

    He was obviously an intelligent person. ✔

    Although Jonas seldom spoke up in class, he was obviously an intelligent

    person.

2. Jordan took vitamins every day.

    She was sure her diet was nutritionally adequate. ✔

    _____

    _____

3. Lu-Chen struggled to stay awake. ✔

    She tried to read just one more chapter.

    _____

    _____

4. The cottage cheese smelled sour and unpleasant. ✔

    The expiration date was five days away.

    _____

    _____

5. Katelyn said she was too full to eat her broccoli.

    She had plenty of room for dessert. ✔

    _____

    _____

Review Exercises

Complete the Review Exercises to see how well you have learned the skills addressed in this chapter. As you work through the exercises, go back through the chapter to review any of the rules you do not understand completely.

REVIEW EXERCISE 1   WRITING CONCISE SENTENCES

In each problem, combine the four ideas into one concise sentence. Make sure that the sentence expresses the idea fully but uses as few words as possible.

1. Gordon looked at a dent.
   He looked at it unhappily.
   The dent was in the door of his car.
   His car was new.

   _____

   _____

2. A pleasant aroma drifted through the air.
   It came from the restaurant.
   The restaurant was called Myra's Kitchen.
   It was on the corner.

   _____

   _____

3. Bill saved his pocket change.
   He saved it in a jar.
   The jar had once held pickles.
   The jar sat on the table.

   _____

   _____

4. The telephone rang.
   It rang several times.
   Michaela ignored it.
   She ignored it until the ringing stopped.

   _____

   _____

5. Tom ate a ham sandwich.
   It was on rye bread.
   He also ate an apple.
   He ate the sandwich and the apple for lunch.

   _____

   _____

Review Exercise 2   Using Prepositional Phrases to Begin Sentences

Rearrange each sentence to begin with a prepositional phrase.

1. Two children were playing catch in the middle of the street.

    _____

2. A cement truck slowly rumbled along in the lane ahead of us.

    _____

3. It was dark and deliciously cool in the movie theater.

    _____

4. Jake has lived in the same house for twenty years.

    _____

5. Claudia sounded charming and capable over the telephone.

    _____

Review Exercise 3   Using Verbal Phrases to Begin Sentences

Join each sentence pair by converting one of the sentences to an *-ed* or *-ing* verbal phrase.

1. The washing machine stopped in the middle of its cycle.
    It was clogged by lint from a cotton blanket.

    _____

    _____

2. Myesha was sitting on a bench in the park.
    She found it difficult to concentrate on the book she was reading.

    _____

    _____

3. Elena was annoyed at Roberto's self-centeredness.
    She finally decided to end their relationship.

    _____

    _____

4. Michael ran into the parking lot and leaped into his car.
    He was hoping he would not be late for the meeting.

    _____

    _____

5. Elliot was chilled by the icy wind.
   He decided to stop and get a cup of coffee.

   _____

   _____

REVIEW EXERCISE 4   CONNECTING IDEAS THROUGH COORDINATION

Connect each sentence pair using a coordination. Use a comma and a FANBOYS *or* a semicolon, a joining word, and a comma.

1. There was nothing that Tina wanted to see at the movie theater.
   She rented a video.

   _____

2. Horton realized the cashier had given him five dollars too much.
   He knew he should return it.

   _____

3. The laundromat was crowded.
   Sam decided to do his laundry some other time.

   _____

4. The job required extensive travel.
   Deloris decided not to take it.

   _____

5. The woman was trying to walk at a brisk pace.
   Her little dog kept stopping to sniff at the ground.

   _____

REVIEW EXERCISE 5   CONNECTING IDEAS THROUGH SUBORDINATION

Connect each sentence pair using a subordination. Use a dependent word (and a comma if necessary).

1. Brendan should have been writing his English paper.
   He was playing Solitaire on his computer.

   _____

   _____

2. Nancy cleaned out her refrigerator.
    She found six half-empty containers of cottage cheese.

    _____

    _____

3. Alexa headed for the last parking space in the lot.
    A battered Volkswagen rounded a corner and zipped into the space.

    _____

    _____

4. The building looked like a toy from a distance.
    It boasted twenty floors and state-of-the art environmental controls.

    _____

    _____

5. Burton hated to fly.
    He never went anywhere that his car would not take him.

    _____

    _____

16

Run-on Sentences

"Hi. How are you?"

"Oh, you wouldn't believe the things that have been happening lately I got a job did I tell you that the last time I saw you I don't remember and anyway I'm working with Angela you remember her from high school she sat in the second row near the window in our homeroom well she and I are dating now can you believe it my old car you know the one I was driving last year the transmission just tore up completely and I had to get rid of it my dad cosigned for a loan though and I got a Honda it's parked over there walk on over with me and I'll show it to you hey, are you listening to me?"

What Is a Run-on Sentence?

A **run-on sentence** is not one sentence, but two or more, run together without proper punctuation, like the sentences in the box above. Reading a run-on sentence is like listening to a person speaking so quickly that the words pour out in a breathless jumble. You may get the general idea, but you may lose track of where one thought ends and the next begins. The sentence below is a run-on.

✗ Tasha worked slowly and carefully she had trouble finishing tests on time.

By examining the sentence, you can probably figure out where the first thought ends and the second begins: between *carefully* and *she*.

Grammatically, too, you can figure out why the thoughts should be separate. Each has a subject and a verb and is an **independent clause,** a clause that can stand alone as a sentence or that can be combined with other clauses in specific patterns.

Another type of run-on is called a **comma splice** because two independent clauses are spliced, or joined, with a comma.

✘ Tasha worked slowly and carefully, she had trouble finishing tests on time.

The run-on can be corrected in a variety of ways. Here are two of them.

✔ Tasha worked slowly and carefully, so she had trouble finishing tests on time.

✔ Because Tasha worked slowly and carefully, she had trouble finishing tests on time.

The first step toward writing paragraphs and essays that are free of run-on sentences is to learn to recognize run-ons and comma splices. When you see a sentence that you believe is a run-on, test it. Read the first part. Is it a sentence that could stand alone? If your answer is "yes," read the second part, asking the same question. If your answer is again "yes," the sentence is probably a run-on.

PRACTICE 1   RECOGNIZING RUN-ONS AND COMMA SPLICES

In each sentence, underline the spot where the run-on or comma splice occurs. Mark *RO* in the blank to the left of the sentence if the sentence is a run-on, *CS* if it is a comma splice.

_____ 1. Harold had one claim to fame he could wiggle his ears without moving his face.

_____ 2. The renovated theater was beautiful, the plush seats and velvet curtains recalled a more elegant era.

_____ 3. Leonard was seasick he stayed in his cabin on the first evening of the cruise.

_____ 4. "All I do is work and go to school, I feel like I'm on an endless treadmill," said Angelica.

_____ 5. Kaya stopped at a convenience store for gas she also bought a cup of coffee and a doughnut.

Correcting Run-ons

Five methods of correcting run-ons are presented in the following sections. The first three methods are simple; the final two are more complex. Learning all five methods will give you more than just ways to correct run-ons; it will give you a variety of sentence patterns and transitional words to use in your writing.

Method 1: Period and Capital Letter

Correcting a run-on with a period and capital letter is the easiest method to use. The hard part is knowing when and how often to use it. Short, single-clause sentences can emphasize ideas by setting them apart. However, too many short sentences can make your writing seem choppy and disconnected.

Pattern: <u>Independent clause</u>. <u>Independent clause</u>.

Put a period between the two sentences. Use a capital letter to begin the new sentence.

Example

✗ Leon looked glumly at the blank sheet of paper he could not think of a thing to write.

✔ Leon looked glumly at the blank sheet of paper. He could not think of a thing to write.

PRACTICE 2   CORRECTING RUN-ONS WITH A PERIOD AND CAPITAL LETTER

In each sentence, underline the spot where each run-on or comma splice occurs. Write *RO* in the blank to the left of the sentence if it is a run-on, *CS* if it is a comma splice. Then correct each sentence using a period and a capital letter.

_____ 1. Carol plans to study audiology she wants to help people with hearing problems.

_____

_____ 2. Sally and Layla have been friends for years now they plan to go into business together.

_____

_____ 3. Scientists have developed a new drug it can help grow new blood vessels.

_____

_____ 4. The short-term memory holds only five to seven bits of information, that is one reason people need grocery lists.

_____

_____ 5. The baby's hair had not come in, she had a faint peach fuzz all over her head.

_____

Method 2: Comma and FANBOYS Conjunction

Coordinating conjunctions, or FANBOYS conjunctions, are among the most useful and powerful connecting words in the English language. If you can remember the nonsense word FANBOYS, you can remember the seven coordinating conjunctions: *for, and, nor, but, or, yet, so.*

Pattern: <u>Independent clause</u>, and <u>independent clause</u>.

When a FANBOYS conjunction is used with a comma to separate two clauses, the comma goes before the FANBOYS conjunction.

Example

✗ Greg had not eaten breakfast, he cooked some instant oatmeal in the microwave.

✔ Greg had not eaten breakfast, so he cooked some instant oatmeal in the microwave.

* FANBOYS Conjunctions						
for	and	nor	but	or	yet	so

PRACTICE 3   **CORRECTING RUN-ONS WITH A COMMA AND *FANBOYS***

In each sentence, underline the spot where each run-on or comma splice occurs. Write *RO* in the blank to the left of the sentence if it is a run-on, *CS* if it is a comma splice. Correct each run-on or comma splice by using a comma and a FANBOYS conjunction.

_____ 1. The address label was shaped like a teacup, the sender's address was on the saucer.

_____

_____ 2. Victoria tried to tell Jim his plan would not work he did not want to hear her criticism.

_____

_____ 3. Tyler's neighbors had three new cars and a recently installed hot tub, they each worked two jobs to pay for them.

_____

_____ 4. Sabrina felt stylish in her new coat, there was a little bounce in her walk.

_____

_____ 5. A cat rested on the porch rail it scampered away as a visitor approached.

_____

Method 3: Semicolon

Using a semicolon to join clauses works best with ideas that are closely connected and need no transitional word to explain the connection between them. The semicolon, as used here, is the grammatical equivalent of a period, but the first letter of the clause after the semicolon is *not* capitalized.

  Pattern: <u>Independent clause;</u> <u>independent clause</u>.

The semicolon goes between the two clauses.

Example

✗ The book had been assigned for two weeks, Emily had not read a single page.

✔ The book had been assigned for two weeks; Emily had not read a single page.

PRACTICE 4 CORRECTING RUN-ONS WITH A SEMICOLON

In each sentence, underline the spot where each run-on or comma splice occurs. Write *RO* in the blank to the left of the sentence if it is a run-on, *CS* if it is a comma splice. Then correct the sentences using a semicolon alone.

_____ **1.** The drama club held a car wash in a grocery store parking lot, cars lined up to take advantage of the low prices.

_____

_____ **2.** Bruce thought he was typing in the Internet address of a government agency he accessed a page of nude photographs instead.

_____

_____ **3.** Fashion trends exist in language, new words come into fashion as old ones go out.

_____

_____ **4.** Valerie had several errands to run, her first was to go by the dry cleaners.

_____

_____ **5.** The mailbox was filled with colorful sale flyers and catalogs Terry threw them in the trash.

_____

Method 4: Semicolon and Joining Word

A run-on sentence may also be corrected with a joining word. These joining words also function as transitional expressions, underscoring the relationship between the two clauses.

Pattern: <u>Independent clause</u>; therefore, <u>independent clause</u>.

A semicolon precedes the joining word and a comma follows it. With the words *thus* and *then,* the comma is often omitted.

Example

✗ The bananas on the produce department's display were turning brown, the lettuce looked wilted.

✔ The bananas on the produce department's display were turning brown; furthermore, the lettuce looked wilted.

Joining Words Used with a Semicolon

accordingly	finally	however
also	for example	in addition
as a result	for instance	in fact
besides	furthermore	instead

meanwhile	of course	therefore
namely	on the other hand	thus
nevertheless	then	

PRACTICE 5   CORRECTING RUN-ONS WITH A SEMICOLON AND JOINING WORD

In each sentence, underline the spot where each run-on or comma splice occurs. Write *RO* in the blank to the left of the sentence if it is a run-on, *CS* if it is a comma splice. Then correct the sentence using a semicolon and an appropriate joining word.

_____ **1.** The elevator did not come Mina pushed the button again.

_____

_____ **2.** The deli clerk was daydreaming, he cut nearly two pounds of meat instead of one.

_____

_____ **3.** Shane finally finished his phone call and returned to his soup it had gotten cold.

_____

_____ **4.** Sarah noticed a telephone number written inside the cover of her psychology book, she could not remember whose number it was.

_____

_____ **5.** The movie theater was dark Michelle almost sat on someone's lap.

_____

Method 5: Dependent Word

Placing a dependent word in front of an independent clause makes it a dependent clause, a clause that can no longer stand on its own as a sentence. It now *depends* on the sentence it is attached to and can no longer be separated from it.

Two variations of the dependent word method are shown below.

Example

✗ The restaurant was dark Martha could barely read her menu.

Pattern: Because <u>dependent clause</u>, <u>independent clause</u>.

When the dependent clause acts as an introductory clause, a comma follows it.

✔ Because the restaurant was dark, Martha could barely read her menu.

Pattern: <u>Independent clause</u> because <u>dependent clause</u>.

When the dependent clause comes last in the sentence, no comma is used.

✔ Martha could barely read her menu because the restaurant was dark.

Commonly Used Dependent Words

after	if	whatever
although	once	when
as	since	whenever
as if	so that	where
as long as	that	wherever
as soon as	though	which
as though	unless	while
because	until	who
before	what	whoever
even though		

PRACTICE 6   CORRECTING RUN-ONS WITH A DEPENDENT WORD

In each sentence, underline the spot where each run-on or comma splice occurs. Write *RO* in the blank to the left of the sentence if it is a run-on, *CS* if it is a comma splice. Correct each sentence using a dependent word.

_____ 1. Every computer in the lab was busy, Nelson put his name on the waiting list.

_____

_____ 2. The truck rumbled past, Veronica gripped the steering wheel of her small car.

_____

_____ 3. Phil pumped gas into his car he noticed that the station across the street had lower prices.

_____

Five Ways to Correct Run-on Sentences

Method 1: Period and Capital Letter

Pattern: Independent clause. Independent clause.

Method 2: Comma and FANBOYS Conjunction

Pattern: Independent clause, and independent clause.

A comma goes before the FANBOYS conjunction in this pattern.

FANBOYS Conjunctions

for	and	nor	but	or	yet	so

Method 3: Semicolon

Pattern: Independent clause; independent clause.

Method 4: Semicolon and Joining Word

Pattern: Independent clause; therefore, independent clause.

A semicolon goes before the joining word and a comma follows it. With the words *thus* and *then*, the comma is often omitted.

Joining Words Used with a Semicolon

also	however	of course
as a result	in addition	on the other hand
besides	in fact	then
finally	instead	therefore
for example	meanwhile	thus

Method 5: Dependent Word

Pattern 1: Although dependent clause, independent clause.

When a dependent word begins the sentence, a comma is used between the dependent and independent clause.

Pattern 2: Independent clause when dependent clause.

When the dependent clause ends the sentence, a dependent word separates the clauses.

Dependent Words

although	because	that	whenever
as	before	though	where
as if	if	unless	wherever
as long	once	until	which
as soon as	since	whatever	while
as though	so that	when	who

_____ **4.** Rita's week had been long and tiring, she did not feel like going out.

_____

_____ **5.** A little flag began to wave at the bottom of Joe's computer screen he knew he had e-mail.

_____

Review Exercises

Complete the Review Exercises to see how well you have learned the skills addressed in this chapter. As you work through the exercises, go back through the chapter to review any of the rules you do not understand completely.

REVIEW EXERCISE 1

In each sentence, underline the spot where the run-on or comma splice occurs. Then correct the ten run-on sentences, using each of the five methods at least once.

1. The rain poured down in sheets Nell could barely see the road in front of her.

_____

2. The edges of the wooden desk were once square and sharp now they are rounded from wear.

_____

3. The lasagna was frozen solid, Linda knew it would take too long to reheat it.

_____

4. Jemal tried to answer the telephone he dropped the receiver on the floor.

_____

5. The delivery truck was behind schedule the hardware store employee said he did not think our order would be delivered today.

_____

6. Fred bit into a crisp toasted marshmallow, delicious white goo slid onto his tongue.

_____

7. Representatives from businesses and industries visited campus today, students crowded around to sign up for interviews.

_____

8. Bootsie was due for her rabies shot, the vet sent a reminder in the mail.

   _____

9. The loud pounding beat of the music in the aerobics room gave Jill a headache she wished someone would turn down the sound.

   _____

10. Brian fell asleep in front of the television he woke up at 2:00 A.M. with a crick in his neck.

   _____

REVIEW EXERCISE 2

In each sentence, underline the spot where the run-on or comma splice occurs. Then correct the ten run-on sentences, using each of the five methods at least once.

1. Channing knew it was getting late he could not seem to stop playing his computer game.

   _____

2. The children visited the museum some of them petted a boa constrictor.

   _____

3. Heather likes parties and people her husband prefers quiet evenings at home.

   _____

4. Jim bought highlighters, pens, index cards and a notebook he still had trouble motivating himself to study.

   _____

5. Vijay had his term paper stored on disk, however, he could not find the disk.

   _____

6. The lines were long the fast-food place was giving free fries to everyone.

   _____

7. The deli clerk asked how the customer wanted his bologna sliced he replied, "I want it so thin that I can read my newspaper through it."

   _____

8. Under the porch, a patch of flowers grew apparently the amount of sunlight was just right for them to thrive.

   _____

9. I saw Tom just a minute ago, where is he now?

   _____

10. A storm came through last night two trees were uprooted, and power lines were down.

_____

REVIEW EXERCISE 3

In the following exercise, underline the spot where each run-on or comma splice occurs. Then correct the two run-ons in each sentence group.

1. A line of cars waited at the toll booth Alec impatiently craned his neck to see what was holding up traffic. A dog had jumped out of a car window the owner was frantically trying to coax it back.

_____

_____

2. Trevor fixed himself a plate of spaghetti he piled it high on the plate. As he carried it back to the table, a meatball fell then the whole plateful slid off onto the floor.

_____

_____

3. The children complained that there was nothing to do, their mother told them they could help her with the laundry. They decided they weren't bored after all they suddenly found plenty of games to play.

_____

_____

4. Colonial Americans used brightly colored "witch balls" to prevent evil spirits from entering their homes the witch balls were made of glass. Threads within the ball were supposed to trap evil spirits, once entangled in the threads, the spirits could not fly out.

_____

_____

5. Terrell says he never watches the news any more it only depresses him. He says he does not need to hear about the meanness in the world, he would rather focus on the good.

_____

_____

REVIEW EXERCISE 4

In the following exercise, underline the spot where each run-on or comma splice occurs. Then correct the two run-ons in each sentence group.

1. Marian browsed through the video store the only selections left were children's movies. She decided to watch *The Lion King* one more time, she had always liked it.

    _____

    _____

2. Fran rushed through the grocery store, she wished that the man in front of her would hurry. Then she noticed that the man was walking with a cane, she was ashamed of her impatience.

    _____

    _____

3. The Gullah people are descendants of slaves they speak their own unique language. Their music incorporates the rhythms of clapping hands and stamping feet, their songs date back to the days of slavery.

    _____

    _____

4. The Tomlinsons have just one television, they own two computers. They believe that their time is better spent on the computer, watching television does not engage their minds.

    _____

    _____

5. At the barbecue place, Samuel ordered a quart of barbecue then he decided to add a rack of ribs to his order. He might be sorry tomorrow, at least he would eat well tonight.

    _____

    _____

REVIEW EXERCISE 5

In the following paragraph, underline the spot where each run-on or comma splice occurs. Then correct the ten run-on sentences or comma splices, using the five methods presented in this chapter. Try to use each method at least once.

> [1]David woke up and squinted at the clock, the blue numbers on its face read 8:35. [2]Immediately, he

was filled with panic he had to be at work at nine.
^{3}He leaped out of bed then he ran quickly to his
son's room. ^{4}"Get up, Jason, it's time for school,
and Daddy's running late." he said. ^{5}When David saw
that his son was awake, he turned on the shower as
the water warmed up, he thought of all the things
he had to do. ^{6}He would grab a shower and get
dressed, then he would make sure Jason got ready
for school. ^{7}He would make a quick call to his
office to say he would be a few minutes late he
and Jason could take off, eating their breakfast
in the car. ^{8}After showering and dressing quickly,
David went to check on Jason his son was still in
his pajamas, eating Cheerios from the box and
watching television. ^{9}He stopped, astonished that
his son was not getting ready for school Jason
looked up at him and said, "Dad, it's Saturday."
^{10}David laughed and flopped on the couch beside his
son "Pass the Cheerios," he said.

1. _____

2. _____

3. _____

4. _____

5. _____

6. _____

7. _____

8. _____

9. _____

   _____

10. _____

17

Sentence Fragments

To whoever finds this—

I know I am dying. But the secret of my family's treasure shall not die with me. I pass it on to you now.

Here are specific directions to reach it. It is buried in the Oza
on a piece of land deeded to me by my grandfather. Take Rout
en turn left, walk four paces, and dig beside the old well.

But beware the curse. If you do not
it means certain death.

Good luck—you will need it.

Whoever finds the letter above is likely to be frustrated because it is only a fragment. Important elements are missing. Readers are similarly frustrated by sentence fragments because they leave out important elements of a sentence.

What Is a Sentence Fragment?

✗ Susan finished reading the last section of the newspaper. *And dropped it on the floor beside her chair.*

✗ *When gasoline prices rise dramatically and stay high for a long time.* Automobile companies see a rise in the sale of smaller, more fuel-efficient cars.

The italicized word groups are **sentence fragments:** pieces of sentences that cannot stand alone. A sentence fragment is an incomplete sentence. It may be a dependent clause that cannot stand on its own, or it may lack a subject, a verb, or both. If you read a fragment by itself, without the other sentences that surround it, you will usually recognize that it does not express a complete thought. It is only a part, or fragment, of a sentence.

Dependent Clause Fragments

✗ *Because Javarez had missed the first bus.* He stood on the corner shivering and hoping that another one would come along soon.

✗ No one answered Alicia's knock. *Although someone was obviously at home.*

Each of the italicized fragments above is a **dependent clause fragment.** A dependent clause fragment always begins with a dependent word. To fix a dependent clause fragment, attach it to a complete sentence.

✔ Because Javarez had missed the first bus, he stood on the corner shivering and hoping that another one would come along soon.

✔ No one answered Alicia's knock although someone was obviously at home.

Dropping the dependent word or changing it to another type of transitional expression is an alternative to connecting the fragment to the sentence.

✔ Javarez had missed the first bus. He stood on the corner shivering and hoping that another one would come along soon.

✔ No one answered Alicia's knock. However, someone was obviously at home.

> **** Punctuation Pointer***
>
> In general, use a comma to attach a dependent clause fragment at the begin-
> ning of a sentence.

Commonly Used Dependent Words

after	how	whatever
although	if	when
as	once	whenever
as if	since	where
as long as	so that	whenever
as soon as	that	which
as though	though	while
because	unless	who
before	until	whoever
even though	what	

PRACTICE 1   CORRECTING DEPENDENT CLAUSE FRAGMENTS

Correct the dependent clause fragments by attaching them to an independent
clause.

1. While several of her friends planned to go out of town over the long week-
    end. Sarah preferred to stay at home, relax, and save her money.

    _____

2. Tyrell was put off by a salesman. Who placed an arm around his shoulder
    and greeted him like an old friend.

    _____

3. Because Mary slept through her alarm. She missed her 10:00 A.M. class.

    _____

4. As Dan unloaded the groceries from the car. He realized that the gallon of
    milk he had bought was not in the trunk.

    _____

5. My grandparents say they have never considered divorce as a solution to their
    problems. Although Grandma says she has occasionally considered murder.

    _____

Verbal Phrase Fragments (*to, -ing,* and *-ed*)

✘ *To keep gasoline costs down.* Many people carpool to work or school.

✘ *Worrying about damage to his car.* Jonathan ran out into the hailstorm to pull it into the garage.

✘ *Curled in a protective ball in the corner of his cage.* Jo's hedgehog looked unhappy.

The examples above are **verbal phrase fragments.** A verbal phrase fragment begins with a verb form that is not used as a main verb. Verbal phrase fragments include *to* fragments, *-ing* fragments, and *-ed/-en* fragments.

Correct verbal phrase fragments by attaching them to a complete sentence.

✔ To keep gasoline costs down, many people carpool to work or school.

✔ Worrying about damage to his car, Jonathan ran out into the hailstorm to pull it into the garage.

✔ Curled in a protective ball in the corner of his cage, Jo's hedgehog looked unhappy.

to Fragments

Correct *to* fragments by connecting them to a sentence or by adding a subject and verb.

Examples

✘ To keep her children entertained on the long trip home. Kayla challenged them to see who could spot license plates from the largest number of states.

✔ To keep her children entertained on the long trip home, Kayla challenged them to see who could spot license plates from the largest number of states.

✘ Last Friday, Ron invited his friends over. To help him celebrate his graduation from college.

✔ Last Friday, Ron invited his friends over to help him celebrate his graduation from college.

✗ Joann practiced for hours over the weekend. To make sure everything would go well during her interview on Monday.

✔ Joann practiced for hours over the weekend. She wanted to make sure everything would go well during her interview on Monday.

---

* Punctuation Pointer

A *to* fragment attached to the beginning of a sentence is followed by a comma because it is an introductory phrase. A *to* fragment connected to the end of the sentence needs no comma.

PRACTICE 2   CORRECTING *TO* FRAGMENTS

Underline and correct the *to* fragments.

1. To strengthen her back and improve her posture. Shauna began a weight-lifting program.

   _____

2. The cook used a wide metal spatula. To turn the pancakes on the grill.

   _____

3. To give himself time to review for the exam. Damon set his clock a half hour early.

   _____

4. The networks schedule popular movies and special shows. To attract viewers during "sweeps week."

   _____

5. To unwind at the end of the day. Marcy took a walk and watched the sun set.

   _____

-ing Fragments

To correct an *-ing* fragment, connect it to the rest of the sentence with a comma. You may also correct it by adding a subject and a helping verb.

Examples

✗ Eating the hearty bean soup that he had made. Ed decided that he was becoming a good cook.

✔ Eating the hearty bean soup that he had made, Ed decided that he was becoming a good cook.

✘ The decorator stepped back from the paintings she had hung. Checking to make sure they were precisely aligned.

✔ The decorator stepped back from the paintings she had hung, checking to make sure they were precisely aligned.

✔ The decorator stepped back from the paintings she had hung. She was checking to make sure they were precisely aligned.

> ### * Punctuation Pointer
>
> Usually, *-ing* fragments can be connected to the rest of the sentence with a comma.

PRACTICE 3   CORRECTING *-ING* FRAGMENTS

Underline and correct the *-ing* fragments.

1. Realizing that the high noise level could damage employees' hearing. The factory's management required workers to wear earplugs.

   _____

2. Hearing a commotion in the living room. Rita wondered whether she should check on the children.

   _____

3. Samantha quickly locked the door and left. Knowing she was probably going to be late for work.

   _____

4. Swinging their bare feet and gazing down into the green water. The two children amused themselves while their father fished from the dock.

   _____

5. The police officer raised a white-gloved hand. Stopping traffic to let a group of children cross the street.

   _____

Missing-Subject Fragments

Fragments beginning with a joining word such as *and, or, but*, or *then* followed by a verb are **missing-subject fragments.** The subject of the verb is usually in a previous sentence. Connect the fragment to the sentence or add a subject to begin a new sentence.

Examples

✘ The crowd grew silent when the player clutched his leg and fell. Then cheered as he was helped off the field.

✔ The crowd grew silent when the player clutched his leg and fell, then cheered as he was helped off the field.

✘ Kara mailed her telephone bill. But forgot to enclose a check.

✔ Kara mailed her telephone bill, but she forgot to enclose a check.

✔ Kara mailed her telephone bill. But she forgot to enclose a check.

PRACTICE 4   CORRECTING MISSING-SUBJECT FRAGMENTS

Underline and correct the missing-subject fragments.

1. Anthony started to fill out the questionnaire. Then decided that it asked too many nosy questions.

    _____

2. The snow began to stick around 10:00 in the morning. And was four inches deep by 5:00 in the afternoon.

    _____

3. Tanisha longed for a double cheeseburger with a side order of fries. But decided to have a plain chicken sandwich on whole wheat.

    _____

4. Narcissus was a mythological character who bent to look at himself in a pool of water. And fell in love with his own image.

    _____

5. Beth jumped at a strange noise that seemed to come from her living room. Then decided it was her imagination and turned back to her computer.

    _____

---

* *Real-World Writing: Is it okay to start a sentence with* but?

Yes and no. Grammatically, it is correct to start a sentence with *but* or any other FANBOYS conjunction. However, your instructors may discourage the practice, for two good reasons.

1. Beginning a sentence with *but* is an informal technique. It may work in personal essays but should not be used in formal compositions such as research papers. (This text, you may have noticed, takes an informal, conversational approach, addressing you directly and occasionally using a FANBOYS conjunction to begin a sentence.)
2. Using *but* to begin a sentence can be addictive. *But* is the strongest contrast signal in our language, and it's easy to overuse.

The bottom line: Use conjunctions to begin sentences only if your instructor gives the green light, and then use them sparingly.

Example and Exception Fragments

Fragments often occur when a writer adds an example or notes an exception. Example fragments often begin with *such as, including, like, for example,* or *for instance*. Exception fragments often begin with *not, except, unless, without,* or *in spite of*. To fix the fragment, connect it to the sentence with which it logically belongs. If the fragment begins with *for example* or *for instance*, it is often best to make the fragment into a separate sentence.

Examples

✗ Holly remained focused on the paper she was writing. In spite of her little brother's constant interruptions.

✔ Holly remained focused on the paper she was writing, in spite of her little brother's constant interruptions.

✗ Ed signed up for the Great American Smokeout, but he was not sure he could make it through the day. Without smoking a cigarette.

✔ Ed signed up for the Great American Smokeout, but he was not sure he could make it through the day without smoking a cigarette.

✗ Clayton says that there are many things he cooks well. For example, instant breakfasts and microwaveable dinners.

✔ Clayton says that there are many things he cooks well. For example, he does a great job with instant breakfasts and microwaveable dinners.

> ### * Punctuation Pointer
>
> Usually, you can connect fragments beginning with *such as, including, not, especially,* and *in spite of* with a comma and fragments beginning with *except, unless, without,* and *like* with no comma.
>
> A fragment beginning with *for example* or *for instance* may be attached with a comma if it immediately follows the idea it illustrates: **The chef enjoyed cooking with beans, for example, lima beans, garbanzo beans, and kidney beans.** If the idea that the example illustrates is expressed earlier in the sentence, place the example in a new sentence: **Beans are the specialty of the house at Rizzoli's Restaurant. For example, the chef makes delicious dishes from lima beans, garbanzo beans, and kidney beans.**

PRACTICE 5   CORRECTING EXAMPLE AND EXCEPTION FRAGMENTS

Underline and correct the example and exception fragments.

1. Stacie says she never takes her children anywhere. Without bringing along water, juice, and snacks.

    _____

2. Kendrick complains that his wife has a few bad habits. For example, never turning a light off when she leaves a room.

    _____

3. The dentist told Sharon she did not need to floss. Unless she wanted to keep her teeth.

    _____

4. During the holidays, the department store where Amy works takes extra security measures. Such as hiring store detectives who pose as shoppers.

    _____

5. With a new pair of athletic shoes, a stationary bike, and a membership in a fitness center, Kyle had everything he needed. Except willpower.

    _____

Prepositional Phrase Fragments

A prepositional phrase, alone or within a series, cannot function as a sentence. Correct a prepositional phrase fragment by connecting it to a sentence with which it logically belongs.

Examples

✘ Kelsey rented a small, one-bedroom apartment. In a complex that offered a pool and other recreational facilities.

✔ Kelsey rented a small, one-bedroom apartment in a complex that offered a pool and other recreational facilities.

✘ On the day of his first political science test. Lee woke up with a pounding headache and a fever of 101 degrees.

✔ On the day of his first political science test, Lee woke up with a pounding headache and a fever of 101 degrees.

---

* Punctuation Pointer

Use a comma behind an introductory prepositional phrase. No punctuation is required to connect a prepositional phrase to the end of a sentence.

PRACTICE 6   CORRECTING PREPOSITIONAL PHRASE FRAGMENTS

Underline and correct each prepositional phrase fragment.

1. In the vacant lot beside the convenience store. Someone had discarded an old recliner.

   _____

2. It was such a pleasant day that we decided to study. Under a tree beside the lake.

   _____

3. Beneath the smooth-looking, freshly painted surface. Hundreds of termites were gnawing at the wood.

   _____

4. Hassan thought he needed a new car, but he decided against it after he checked prices. In the classified ads section of the newspaper.

   _____

5. On a Greyhound bus headed toward New Jersey. Channa's woolen gloves, forgotten under the seat, traveled on without her.

   _____

Review Exercises

Complete the Review Exercises to see how well you have learned the skills addressed in this chapter. As you work through the exercises, go back through the chapter to review any of the rules you do not understand completely.

REVIEW EXERCISE 1

Underline and correct each fragment.

1. A puzzled frown creased Martin's brow. As he studied the recipe in front of him.

   _____

2. When he investigated the strange lump on his bed. Walter found the cat curled up underneath the bedspread.

   _____

3. During the storm, a rotting tree toppled. And lay across the road, blocking two lanes of traffic.

   _____

4. The police have set up a roadblock in front of the bridge. To catch drivers who don't have current tags or insurance.

   _____

5. With its arched doorways and intricate stained glass windows. The old church was a beautiful place to hold a wedding.

   _____

6. Speaking no English and with little savings. Kim's grandparents came to the United States to begin a new life.

   _____

7. Eduardo and Maria built a successful business. And sent their five children to college.

   _____

8. Harry says that he never reads tabloids. Except when he is standing in line at the grocery store.

   _____

9. Grover sat in line at the drive through for fifteen minutes at the hamburger place. Wondering how fast food could be so slow.

    _____

10. As she looked at the clutter on top of her desk. Corinne wondered how she would ever sort it all out.

    _____

REVIEW EXERCISE 2

Underline and correct each fragment.

1. After it was cleaned and pressed. Ryan's old sport coat looked like new.

    _____

2. Following in her older sister's footsteps. Natalie decided she would go into the medical field, too.

    _____

3. The career fair next week is open to all students. And is hosted by the college's career counseling office.

    _____

4. Athough the car's bumper sticker read "Have a Nice Day." The driver's angry gesture carried a different message.

    _____

5. Yellowing and nearly falling apart. The newspaper clippings were obviously very old.

    _____

6. Trembling from the near-collision. Jeff pulled his car to the side of the road.

    _____

7. With a dissatisfied grunt and a shake of his closely shaven head. The unhappy customer left Mack's Barber Shop.

    _____

8. Because the line of cars at the gas station was so long. Anita decided to wait and buy gas another day.

    _____

9. The speaker asked us to imagine what we could accomplish if we did not waste so much time on trivial activities. For example, watching television for hours on end.

    _____

10. Spiros found it strange staying at his grandparents' house. Because they had no computer and no VCR.

_____

REVIEW EXERCISE 3

Underline and correct the two fragments in each numbered item.

1. When Nora and A. J. returned from their vacation. They noticed a strange, unpleasant odor in the kitchen. They tried to find the source of the smell. And discovered a package of pita bread covered in dark green mold.

_____

_____

2. Antwan bought everything he needed for his backyard cookout. Including three kinds of meat and two varieties of barbecue sauce. He had thought of everything. Except the possibility of rain.

_____

_____

3. Joseph spent many hours at his kitchen table. Building and painting a delicate model ship. When he was finally finished, he set it out to dry. In a place that he hoped was too high for his three-year-old to reach.

_____

_____

4. Whenever she was almost finished with a task. Such as reading a novel, writing a paper, or doing a set of math problems, Jennifer was anxious to get the job done. Yet always put off reading the last few pages, writing the conclusion, or finishing the last few problems.

_____

_____

5. Though Paul was an expert at many things, such as carpentry and music. He had trouble functioning in daily life. He sometimes seemed unable to perform the simplest tasks. Such as balancing his checkbook or remembering to fill his car with gas.

_____

_____

REVIEW EXERCISE 4

Underline and correct the two fragments in each numbered item.

1. Neil bought a small car a few years ago. But kept his old pickup truck, too. Neil is glad he kept the pickup. Especially when he needs to transport a piece of furniture or some other large item.

    _____

    _____

2. As the logs in the fireplace began to burn. Ebony realized she had forgotten to open the damper. When smoke started pouring into the living room. She began to cough.

    _____

    _____

3. Maria had lived in the South all her life. But had never eaten grits. When she finally tried them. She said they tasted like buttered sand.

    _____

    _____

4. Some drivers' behavior on the road would be funny. If it were not so dangerous. For example, some drivers put on makeup while driving. Or talk on a cell phone as if they are at home.

    _____

    _____

5. In his glove compartment, Will found several items he had thought were lost. Such as an old address book and the good pen his grandmother had given him when he graduated from high school. But he did not find his license and registration. To give to the police officer who was standing patiently beside his car.

    _____

    _____

REVIEW EXERCISE 5

Underline and correct the ten fragments below.

    Jessie walked through the house, looking under
    chairs and behind sofa pillows. And trying to find
    her cellular phone. "When did you see it last?" her

mother asked. Jessie said she had taken it with her the night before. When she went out to walk Bruce, her big Newfoundland dog. Then had thrown it into an armchair as she walked into the family room. Jessie and her mother searched every crevice of the armchair. But did not find the phone. Jessie's brother suggested that she dial the cell phone's number. Then locate the phone by its ringing. When Jessie dialed the number. She heard a faint ringing. Leaving the phone off the hook, Jessie walked into the family room. Where Bruce was lying asleep in front of the fireplace. "It's under Bruce!" she called, trying to roll the dog over. Then she realized that the sound was not coming from underneath Bruce. But from inside him. Her dog had somehow swallowed her cell phone. Immediately, she ran back to the kitchen and called the veterinarian. As soon as the vet stopped laughing. He told Jessie not to worry. "Bruce is a big dog." he said. "The cell phone should pass through his system in a day or two." Jessie was relieved. That her dog would be all right. She could get another cell phone, but Bruce was irreplaceable.

_____

_____

_____

_____

_____

_____

_____

_____

_____

_____

_____

18

Pronoun Case

No matter what the verse above seems to suggest, pronouns are not simply nouns that have turned professional. **Pronouns** are words that stand in for nouns or for other pronouns. They are useful words that keep writers and speakers from tediously repeating words. The rules that govern them are complex, however, and confusion over pronoun usage is common. If you have ever hesitated over "Carlton and me" or "Carlton and I" or wondered whether to say "between you and I" or "between you and me," this chapter will help you find the answers.

Subject and Object Pronouns

Personal pronouns (*I, we, you, he, she it, they*) refer to specific people or things. These pronouns take different forms, called **cases,** as they perform various jobs in a sentence. Look at the example that follows to see how the first person pronoun *I* changes form as its role in a sentence changes.

301

✔ When *I* went to the post office to pick up *my* mail, the clerk said there was a package for *me*.

Subject pronouns (the *subjective case*) include pronouns such as *I, we, you, he, she, it*, and *they*.

✔ *They* were up until midnight trying to put up the wallpaper.

✔ *We* tried to call you, but your line was busy all evening.

✔ The winners were Bryan and *she*.

Object pronouns (the *objective case*) are pronouns such as *me, us, you, him, her, it*, and *them*.

✔ If you are through with the book, please pass it on to *me*.

✔ The cats are waiting for Hilary to feed *them*.

✔ I looked for the flashlight but could not find *it* in the dark.

Subject Pronouns

In most instances, you probably use the subject form of the pronoun correctly without thinking about it. You probably haven't said, "Me went to the park" since you were three. However, using the subject form becomes trickier when a *compound subject* is used. Is it "Tiffany and her went to the concert" or "Tiffany and she went to the concert"? Usually, trying the sentence with the pronoun alone helps you hear the correct answer. Without "Tiffany and" the sentence becomes clear. "*She* went to the concert" is correct, not "*Her* went to the concert."

Example

? *Her and Liz* worked in the same office.

Step 1: To determine if the sentence is correct, try the pronoun alone.

✘ *Her ~~and Liz~~* worked in the same office.

✘ *Her* worked in the same office.

Step 2: If the pronoun alone sounds incorrect, try changing the form.

✔ *She* worked in the same office.

✔ *She and Liz* worked in the same office. (corrected sentence)

PRACTICE 1   USING SUBJECT PRONOUNS

Underline and correct the errors in each sentence. To determine the correct pronoun form, try the pronoun alone, without the compound element.

1.   Joel and me took the afternoon off to go fishing.

   _____

2.   When I left for the day, Lynda and them were still working.

   _____

3.   I heard that Monica and him made the two highest grades on the test.

   _____

4.   You and me should work on our grammar homework together.

   _____

5.   Have you and him known each other for very long?

   _____

Subject Pronouns after Linking Verbs

"Hello?"

"May I speak to Tanisha Jones, please?"

"This is she."

"Hello, Tanisha, this is Randall Groover from your biology class. I was wondering . . ."

This polite exchange is typical of the way many telephone conversations begin, and it illustrates a rule that many people use in telephone conversations but ignore otherwise: When a pronoun renames the subject (that is, when it is a *subject complement*) and follows the verb *to be* or any *linking verb*, that pronoun takes the subject form.

Examples

✔   subject   linking verb   subject complement
    The recipient of the award   will be   he.

✔ It is *I*. (not *me*)

✔ I had not seen Sheldon since grade school, so I was not sure that it was *he*. (not *him*)

✔ If you want to see Ms. Long, that is *she* in the hat and sunglasses. (not *her*)

Underline the correct pronoun in each sentence.

1. I enjoyed Dr. Barker's English 100 class, so when I found out the teacher for English 200 would be (he, him), I signed up.

2. For many years, my closest friend was (she, her).

3. The speaker at our club's luncheon will be (he, him).

4. As he answered the phone, Leon said "Who is this?" "It is (I, me)," said Pete.

5. If there is anyone who deserves a promotion, it is (she, her).

Object Pronouns

Object pronouns are used as objects of verbs and prepositions. As with subject pronouns, problems with object pronouns commonly occur in compound constructions. These problems can usually be resolved by isolating the pronoun.

Example

?   The instructor agreed to give *Tran and I* a makeup exam.

✗   The instructor agreed to give ~~Tran and~~ *I* a makeup exam.

✗   The instructor agreed to give *I* a makeup exam.

✔   The instructor agreed to give *me* a makeup exam.

Object Pronouns with *between*

Object pronouns always follow the preposition *between*. Thus, it is always *between you and me, between us and them, between him and her, between Larry and him.*

---

* Grammar Alert!

Pronouns are often misused with *between*. Remember to use the object form: between you and *me, him, her,* or *them.*

Examples

✗   Just between you and *I,* I think Sara is planning to quit school and work full time.

✔ Just between you and *me,* I think Sara is planning to quit school and work full time.

✘ The agreement was between Anita and *he;* I had nothing to do with it.

✔ The agreement was between Anita and *him;* I had nothing to do with it.

PRACTICE 3   USING OBJECT PRONOUNS

Underline the correct pronoun in each sentence.

1. The man behind the counter at the convenience store gave Yolanda and (I, me) directions, but we got lost anyway.
2. We aren't sure who will be elected president of the club, but the choice is between Calvin and (she, her).
3. The office barely had enough room for Leo and (he, him).
4. At the grocery store, an employee gave my husband and (I, me) a handful of coupons.
5. The table was small, but it was perfect for Tracy and (he, him).

Intensive and Reflexive Pronouns

Personal pronouns also take on forms known as *intensive* and *reflexive* forms. These pronouns are the *-self* pronouns: *myself, ourselves, yourself, himself, herself, itself,* and *themselves.*

Intensive Pronouns

Intensive pronouns are used for emphasis. They let a reader know that an action was performed by or directed toward *only* the person or thing that the pronoun refers to. It is easy to identify intensive pronouns. Since they are used strictly for emphasis, a sentence would make perfect sense and have the same meaning if the intensive pronoun were left out.

✔ The district attorney *himself* recommended that the charges be dropped.

✔ In spite of severe damage in outlying areas, the town *itself* was untouched by the tornado.

✔ Although the project was supposed to be a group effort, Sharon did every bit of the research *herself.*

Reflexive Pronouns

Reflexive pronouns show that an action was performed by someone on himself or herself (or by something on itself).

✔ Erica cut *herself* as she was slicing an onion.

✔ Brian forced *himself* to finish the job.

✔ The machine monitors *itself* for problems in functioning.

PRACTICE 4   RECOGNIZING INTENSIVE AND REFLEXIVE PRONOUNS

Underline the *-self* pronoun in each sentence below. Then, in the blank provided, write *I* if the pronoun is an intensive pronoun and *R* if it is a reflexive pronoun.

_____ **1.** The President himself called to congratulate the soccer team.

_____ **2.** Phyllis treated herself to dinner and a movie.

_____ **3.** The building itself needs extensive repairs.

_____ **4.** Hal bought himself a new car.

_____ **5.** The instructor herself told Charles that the course was cancelled.

Problems with Intensive and Reflexive Pronouns

Intensive and reflexive pronouns are often used incorrectly in compound subjects or objects. Look at the examples below.

★ Grammar Alert!

The *-self* pronouns are never used as subjects.

Example

✗ *Jake and myself* went to the auto parts store to pick up an oil filter.

When you leave out the compound element, the problem is easier to spot:

✗ *Myself* went to the auto parts store to pick up an oil filter.

A subject pronoun is needed to correct the sentence:

✔ *I* went to the auto parts store to pick up an oil filter.

✔ Jake and *I* went to the auto parts store to pick up an oil filter.

Example

✘ "Janie makes *her mother and myself* very proud," said Mr. Smith.

✘ "Janie makes *myself* very proud," said Mr. Smith.

✔ "Janie makes *her mother and me* very proud," said Mr. Smith.

---

* Grammar Alert!

Never use *hisself, theirself,* or *theirselves.* They are not words. *Himself* and *themselves* are the proper forms.

PRACTICE 5   AVOIDING ERRORS WITH *-SELF* PRONOUNS

Underline the correct pronoun in each sentence.

1. The Andersons were proud because they had built the deck (them, themselves).
2. Brad and (I, me, myself) have agreed to meet at my house at six A.M. on Sunday.
3. When Roy looked at (him, himself) in the mirror, he realized he needed to comb his hair.
4. The supervisor assigned the task to Jondrea and (me, myself).
5. "If you do the job (you, yourself), you can save nearly five hundred dollars," said the contractor.
6. "Just between you and (I, me, myself)," said Brandon, "I did not study for the test at all."
7. Sandra decided to give (she, her, herself) a break from studying, so she took a walk.
8. "Would you like to go out to lunch with Natisha and (I, me, myself)?" said Gloria.
9. "No, thanks. I made lunch for (I, me, myself) before I left home," said Morgan.
10. The governor (he, him, himself) came over to shake Miguel's hand.

Review Exercises

Complete the Review Exercises to see how well you have learned the skills addressed in this chapter. As you work through the exercises, go back through the chapter to review any of the rules you do not understand completely.

REVIEW EXERCISE 1

Underline the correct pronoun in each sentence.

1. The coach complained that the unfavorable stories written about (he, him, himself) had led to his firing.
2. (I, Me) and my family have decided that we will try to spend more time together this year.
3. When Angie saw the quilt, she asked if Trina had made it (her, herself).
4. The winner of the scholarship was (he, him).
5. Tabitha promised (her, herself) that if she studied for one more hour, she would take the next hour off to watch her favorite program.
6. Since no one else wanted the funny-looking black and white kitten, we decided to keep it (us, ourselves).
7. Julie and (he, him) found it hard to survive on such a small paycheck.
8. Russell and (he, himself) decided that they would sand and stain the old desk over the weekend.
9. When I called Dad, he said that mother and (he, himself) were taking a vacation next month.
10. Leigh bought (her, herself) a used car with the money she earned over the summer.

REVIEW EXERCISE 2

Underline and correct the pronoun error in each sentence.

1. Rudy and me are going to take a walk if the rain has stopped.

   _____

2. Katrina said she had e-mailed both Teresa and myself about the meeting.

   _____

3. "May I speak to Mr. Smith?" asked the caller. "This is him," replied Andrew.

   _____

4. Bruce showed Mary and I the hand-tied fishing flies his uncle had sent him.

5. Mr. Jones and her said they would not mind working late on Thursday evening.

6. Merrill and myself will stay with Aunt Beatrice when we visit New York.

7. Elaine wondered why the most trivial and boring jobs were always given to José and she.

8. My little brother always wants me to take he and his friends to the mall on Saturdays.

9. Amanda said that Morris and her had fixed the computer themselves.

10. "I am glad that you and me are not fighting anymore," Al told his girlfriend.

Review Exercise 3

Underline and correct the two pronoun case errors in each sentence or sentence group.

1. Lonnie and myself went to the baseball game with Harold and he.

2. Please give the photographs to Anna and they, and be sure to say that they are from myself.

3. "Can you pick the man who robbed you from the lineup?" asked the police officer. "Officer, it was him!" said Mr. Smith, pointing to a tall red-haired man. "He pulled a gun on the night manager and I."

4. Nicole's mailbox was stuffed with catalogs addressed to her husband and she. "We need to buy us a bigger mailbox," said Nicole.

     _____

     _____

5. "Can you give Willie and I a ride?" asked Minardo. "Him and I will appreciate it."

     _____

     _____

REVIEW EXERCISE 4

Underline the correct pronoun in each sentence.

[1]Hiromi, a student from Japan, told me that (she, her, herself) and her family had been living in the United States for the past five years. [2]When she first came here, she knew barely enough English to make (she, her, herself) understood. [3]After taking courses in English for several years, however, (she, her, herself) and her brother are excelling in their college classwork. [4]Hiromi says that for (she, her, herself) and her family, one of the biggest differences between living in Japan and living in the United States is the amount of space. [5]"Our house here is twice as big as the one (we, us, ourselves) had in Japan, and the streets here are far less crowded" she says. [6]She told (I, me, myself) that the Japanese politeness is born out of necessity. [7]"People are so crowded together in Japan, that it would be hard for (they, them, themselves) to get along if they did not follow rules of etiquette," she said. [8]Another necessity in Japan is neatness—when people live in small spaces, (they, them, themselves) are forced to be tidy. [9]"I am not very neat (I, me, myself)," says Hiromi. [10]"Maybe living here in the United States has spoiled (I, me, myself).

19

Pronoun Agreement, Reference, and Point of View

Abbott and Costello's classic comedy routine deliberately causes confusion through use of pronouns. Sometimes, writers unintentionally cause confusion through errors in pronoun reference, agreement, and point of view. Each sentence below contains a pronoun error. Can you figure out why the pronouns in bold type are incorrect?

✗ The new grocery store closes on Christmas day, but **they** are open every other day of the year.

✗ Leo told Jim that **he** needed to clean up the work area.

✗ "I have looked everywhere," said Shelly, "but **you** just can't find an affordable apartment in this area."

Each of the sentences above contains a pronoun error that could confuse the reader. The first sentence contains an error in pronoun agreement.

The pronoun *they* is plural, but the word it refers to is singular. The corrected sentence is shown below.

✔ The new *grocery store* closes on Christmas day, but *it* is open every other day of the year.

The second sentence contains an error in pronoun reference. The reader cannot be sure whether *he* refers to Leo or Jim.

✔ Leo told Jim, "*I* need to clean up *my* work area."

The third sentence contains an error in pronoun point of view. The speaker switches from the first person (*I* have looked) to the second person (*you* can't find).

✔ "*I* have looked everywhere," said Shelly, "but *I* just can't find an affordable apartment in this area."

Keeping your writing free of errors in pronoun agreement, reference, and point of view helps your reader move through your work smoothly and without confusion.

Pronoun Agreement

Pronoun agreement means that a pronoun agrees in number with the word it refers to. In other words, a singular pronoun can refer only to a singular noun or pronoun, and a plural pronoun can refer only to a plural noun or pronoun.

The word that a pronoun refers to is called its **antecedent.** An antecedent may be a noun such as *table* or *ideas,* a pronoun such as *everyone* or *they,* or even a compound construction such as *cars and buses* or *Ferdinand and Isabella.*

Examples

singular antecedent   singular pronoun
✔ The dog caught the <u>Frisbee</u> in midair and brought <u>it</u> back to Julie.

In the sentence above, the singular pronoun *it* refers to one word in the sentence, the singular word *Frisbee.*

plural antecedent   plural pronoun
✔ Todd gathered up the <u>bills</u> he needed to mail and took <u>them</u> to the mailbox.

Here, the plural pronoun *them* refers to the plural antecedent *bills*.

plural antecedent   plural pronoun

✔ Todd gathered up the bills and letters he needed to mail and took them to the mailbox.

Above, the plural pronoun *them* refers to the compound antecedent *bills and letters*.

Problems in Pronoun Agreement

Errors in pronoun agreement occur when a singular pronoun is used to refer to a plural word or when a plural pronoun is used to refer to a singular word.

Examples

singular   plural

✘ Mary pulled in to her bank's drive-through, but they had closed for the day.

singular   singular

✔ Mary pulled in to the bank's drive-through, but it had closed for the day.

plural   singular

✘ The teller was carrying several rolls of coins, but when she tripped it flew out of her hands and spilled onto the floor.

plural

✔ The teller was carrying several rolls of coins, but when she tripped,
plural
they flew out of her hands and spilled onto the floor.

Practice 1   Making Pronouns Agree

Underline the correct pronoun in each sentence.

1. The photographs on display were so striking that people lingered for a long time to look at (it, them).
2. As snow gathered on the branches of the tree, Harold watched the limbs sag under (its, their) weight.
3. Mr. Smith banks with First City Bank because (it is, they are) locally owned.
4. Every restaurant is required to display (its, their) health inspection certificate.

5. After the hailstorm, the dented cars on the dealership's lot had price reduction stickers on (its, their) windshields.

Singular Indefinite Pronouns

The following indefinite pronouns are always singular.

each	everybody	anyone	anything
either	somebody	everyone	everything
neither	nobody	someone	something
anybody	one	no one	nothing

✻ *Memory Jogger*

Remember the singular indefinite pronouns more easily by grouping them:

Each	either	neither
all the *bodies*	all the *ones*	all the *things*

Examples

       singular   *plural*
✗ <u>Somebody</u> called you, but <u>they</u> didn't leave a message.

       singular   *singular*
✔ <u>Somebody</u> called you, but <u>he</u> didn't leave a message.

       singular   *plural*
✗ <u>Each</u> the team members has <u>their</u> own particular strength.

       singular   *singular*
✔ <u>Each</u> the team members has <u>her</u> own particular strength.

PRACTICE 2   MAKING PRONOUNS AGREE WITH INDEFINITE PRONOUN SUBJECTS

Underline the correct pronoun in each sentence.

1. Somebody had parked (his, their) new car so that it took up two spaces in the parking lot.
2. Each of the treasured photographs had (its, their) own place of honor on the mantel.
3. Each of the children brought (her, their) lunch on the field trip.
4. Nobody in the room would admit that (he, they) had voted for the losing candidate.

5.   When the hosts of the party began to argue loudly, everyone mumbled ex-
     cuses and said that (they, he) had to go.

As you probably noticed when you did the previous practice exercise, the use of singular indefinite pronouns often raises a problem. Words like *everybody, somebody, anyone,* and *everyone* often designate both males and females. Saying "Each of the team members has her own particular strength" works only if we know that all team members are female. The use of indefinite pronouns raises not only the question of pronoun agreement, but also the question of gender fairness.

Pronouns and Gender Fairness

Gender fairness means using gender-neutral terms such as *server, police officer,* and *firefighter.* It means not stereotyping professions: Gary Kubach is a *nurse,* not a *male nurse;* Sarita Gray is a *doctor,* not a *woman doctor.* Naturally, gender fairness also includes avoiding describing women solely in terms of their looks or men solely in terms of their bank accounts. Those things are fairly simple. The area of gender fairness and pronouns, however, requires more thought. Using *he or she* or *his or her* is often awkward, and constructions such as *he/she* or *(s)he* are downright ungraceful. How, then, can a writer's language be unbiased, graceful, and grammatically correct, all at the same time? There are several possible solutions.

Example

✗   *Nobody* has received *their* grades from the last term yet.

This sentence contains an error in pronoun agreement. The singular indefinite pronoun *nobody* does not agree with the plural pronoun *their.* Below are several ways to correct pronoun agreement errors such as this one while remaining gender-fair.

Solution 1: Choose a gender and stay with it throughout a single example or paragraph. Then, in your next example or paragraph, switch to the other gender.

✗   *Nobody* has received *their* grades from the last term yet.

✔   *Nobody* has received *his* grades from the last term yet.

✔   *Nobody* has received *her* grades from the last term yet.

Solution 2: Use a "his or her" construction. Because this solution is grammatically correct but stylistically awkward, use it in situations where you will not have to repeat the construction.

✘ *Nobody* has received *their* grades from the last term yet.

✔ *Nobody* has received *his or her* grades from the last term yet.

Solution 3: Use plural rather than singular constructions.

✘ *Nobody* has received *their* grades from the last term yet.

✔ The *students* have not received *their* grades from the last term yet.

Solution 4: Remove the pronoun agreement problem by removing the pronoun.

✘ *Nobody* has received *their* grades from the last term yet.

✔ *Nobody* has received grades from the last term yet.

PRACTICE 3   MAKING PRONOUNS AGREE

Underline and correct the pronoun agreement error in each sentence, using the solutions listed above.

1. Each of the class members received a folder with their name on it.

    _____

2. The driver discovered that someone had left their camera on the tour bus.

    _____

3. Has everyone in the class decided on their major?

    _____

4. The table grew quiet as everyone began to enjoy their meal.

    _____

5. No one in the apartment building where the murder occurred wanted to give their name or talk to reporters.

    _____

6. Everybody is entitled to their own opinion.

    _____

7. Each person in the discussion group was eager to express their ideas.

    _____

8. "If one of those postal clerks puts their 'Next Window' sign up, I think I'll scream," said a woman carrying a bulky package.

   _____

9. When the driveway was poured, somebody put their handprint in the cement before it dried.

   _____

10. "I need to page someone. Would you call their name over the loudspeaker?" Anita asked the store clerk.

    _____

Pronoun Reference

If a sentence has problems with **pronoun reference,** then either a pronoun has no antecedent or it has more than one possible antecedent.

Pronoun Reference Problem: No Antecedent

If a pronoun has no antecedent, your reader may become confused.

Examples

✗ When Melanie went to pick up her son's birthday cake, *they* told her it wasn't ready.

Who are *they?* Replacing the pronoun *they* with a more specific word makes the sentence's meaning clear.

✔ When Melanie went to pick up her son's birthday cake, *the bakery clerk* told her it wasn't ready.

✗ Because his brother is on the basketball team, Derrick wants to be *one*, too.

What does Derrick want to be? A brother? A basketball? A team? The word that should logically be the antecedent of *one*—the word *player*—appears nowhere in the sentence. The simplest way to correct the problem is to replace the word *one* with a more specific word.

✔ Because his brother is on the basketball team, Derrick wants to be *a basketball player,* too.

PRACTICE 4   CORRECTING PROBLEMS IN PRONOUN REFERENCE

Underline and correct the pronoun reference problems in each sentence.

1. The instructions said the form had to be filled out in ink, but Fred had not brought one with him.

   _____

2. When Brett applied to the college, they told him he was exempt from physical education courses because he was a military veteran.

   _____

3. When she arrived at her house, Andrea called the auto mechanic and told him it was still making a funny noise.

   _____

4. Eric applied for a car loan, but they told him he would need a cosigner since he had no credit history.

   _____

5. Giselle said that from the time she first saw The Nutcracker as a child, she fell in love with ballet and knew she wanted to be one.

   _____

Pronoun Reference Problems with *This*

The pronoun *this* is so often used incorrectly that you should check it every time you see it in your writing.

When you see the pronoun *this* in a sentence, particularly if it begins the sentence, ask the question, "This what?" If you cannot put your finger on a noun that answers that question, then *this* probably has no antecedent.

Examples

✗ In some neighborhoods, people are afraid to go out after dark. Increased police presence in high-crime neighborhoods could help to prevent *this.*

✗ In the twenty-first century, parents are spending more time at work and children are increasingly involved in school, sports, and social activities. *This* means that families have less time to spend together.

There are two quick ways to fix the problem. The first is to place a noun that answers the question "This what?" immediately after the word *this.*

✔ In some neighborhoods, people are afraid to go out after dark. Increased police presence in high-crime neighborhoods could help to prevent *this fear.*

✔ In the twenty-first century, parents are spending more time at work and children are increasingly involved in school, sports, and social activities. *This increase in outside activity* means that families have less time to spend together.

The second solution is to take out the pronoun and replace it with an appropriate word or phrase. This solution takes a bit more time but is usually more graceful and exact.

✔ In some neighborhoods, people are afraid to go out after dark. Increased police presence in high-crime neighborhoods could help *citizens feel safer.*

✔ In the twenty-first century, parents are spending more time at work and children are increasingly involved in school, sports, and social activities. *As a result,* families have less time to spend together.

PRACTICE 5   CORRECTING VAGUE USES OF *THIS*

Underline and correct the vague uses of *this.*

1. Edward closed his math book and put his calculator aside with a sigh. "This makes no sense to me," he said.

   _____

2. The courthouse, the oldest county building still in use and a local landmark, was burned down last year by a man who did not like the terms of his divorce. This saddened and outraged many people in the community.

   _____

3. The lack of a traffic signal at the intersection of Wilroy Road and Broad Street creates a danger to drivers and pedestrians alike. Can't something be done about this?

    _____

4. After gaining five pounds on the Chocolate Lover's Diet, Lisa tried counting calories and fat grams and exercising every day. This was more effective but not nearly as much fun.

    _____

5. Joe dug his toes into the warm sand and watched the waves roll in. "This is great," he said.

    _____

Pronoun Point of View

It is important to avoid unnecessary shifts in **point of view,** that is, shifts from one person to another. The chart below shows common **first-, second-, and third-person** pronouns in their singular and plural forms.

Point of View	Singular	Plural
First person (the person speaking)	I	we
Second person (the person spoken to)	you	you
Third person (the person spoken about)	he, she, it singular indefinite pronouns (everybody, anybody, etc.)	they

Examples

       1st person   2nd person

✗ I enjoy going to auctions and flea markets because you can find bargains and unusual items.

The sentence contains an unnecessary shift in point of view. In this sentence, *you* do not find bargains and unusual items; *I* find them.

       1st person   1st person

✔ I enjoy going to auctions and flea markets because I can find bargains and unusual items.

         3rd person   1st person   1st person

✗ When someone studies all night for a test, I am disappointed if I don't make at least a B.

1st person   1st person   1st person

✔ When I study all night for a test, I am disappointed if I don't make at least a B.

           3rd person   3rd person

✔ When someone studies all night for a test, he is disappointed if

3rd person

he doesn't make at least a B.

PRACTICE 6   CORRECTING PROBLEMS IN PRONOUN POINT OF VIEW

Underline and correct the point of view problems in each sentence.

1. Dennis has decided to pursue a double major because you don't know what opportunities life will present.

_____

2. You should always drive defensively because I see all sorts of crazy drivers on the road.

_____

3. People enjoy the Corner Café because it's a friendly place where you can always find someone to talk to.

_____

4. Javarez likes many types of music, but he says that when he is feeling down, you might as well listen to the blues.

_____

5. Kayla looked out the window and shivered; you could tell it was cold just by looking at the low, gray clouds and the white-frosted ground.

_____

Review Exercises

Complete the Review Exercises to see how well you have learned the skills addressed in this chapter. As you work through the exercises, go back through the chapter to review any of the rules you do not understand completely.

REVIEW EXERCISE 1

Underline the correct alternative in each sentence. Then in the blank to the left of the sentence, indicate whether the problem is one of *agreement* (singular with plural, plural with singular), *reference* (no clear antecedent), or *point of view* (shifts in person).

_____ 1. Claire begins her drive to work at 6:30 A.M. because (you miss, she misses) rush-hour traffic that way.

_____ 2. At his job interview, (they, the interviewer) asked Richard to write a sample memo.

_____ 3. Neither of Kim's uncles is sure that (he, they) can fly in for her wedding.

_____ 4. When Renee walked into the clothing store with her shopping bag, (they, a store employee) told her she would have to leave it at the customer service desk.

_____ 5. Each member of the women's bowling team brought (her, their) own ball and shoes to the tournament.

_____ 6. The Community Trust Bank has named Madeleine R. Bowen as (its, their) new president.

_____ 7. Rick told Mr. Flanders (that the supplies he had ordered were ready for pickup, "The supplies you ordered are ready for pickup.")

_____ 8. As he rubbed the clear liquid into his thinning hair, James said, "(They claim, The company claims) that this mixture will regrow hair in 70 percent of men. I hope I am one of the 70 percent."

_____ 9. Glen stood over the crib making strange faces and funny noises because (this, his clowning) seemed to amuse the baby.

_____ 10. Roderick had a security system installed in his home because, as a firefighter, (he has, they have) to sleep at the fire station every other week.

REVIEW EXERCISE 2

Underline and correct the pronoun reference, agreement, or point of view error in each sentence.

1. The tuna salad and the sliced turkey had been left on the counter since lunchtime, so Ian decided that the safest thing to do was to throw it away.

   _____

2. When a poll was taken, everyone in the room said that they knew someone who abused drugs or alcohol.

   _____

3. Hannah says she loves being a musician. Even when she is alone, music is your constant companion.

_____

4. Jacob sat on a bench and watched the skateboarders. You could tell that some of them were inexperienced because they wobbled uncertainly and some-times fell.

_____

5. Many experts advise breaking long-term goals into smaller steps. This makes the goals seem less distant and unreachable.

_____

6. Someone had left their smelly gym socks on a bench in the men's locker room.

_____

7. The shovel and the trowel rusted because Oscar had left it out in the rain.

_____

8. Tanya told Carol that she would make a good spokesperson for the group.

_____

9. "I don't know why I play the lottery," Jason said. "You have two chances of winning—slim and none."

_____

10. Each of the horses has their mane braided neatly against its neck.

_____

REVIEW EXERCISE 3

Underline and correct the two errors in pronoun agreement, reference, or point of view in each numbered item.

1. When Frank goes to the health club, they always ask him for his ID. But you don't always keep an ID in the pocket of your gym shorts.

_____

_____

2. Karalyn does not drink, so when anyone offers it to her, she says, "No, thanks." If someone tries to pressure her, she tells them that she has to drive.

_____

_____

3. Everyone said they did not think the ventriloquist was very talented. This was evident in the way his lips moved when the dummy was supposed to be talking.

_____

_____

4. Noelle refuses to take money from her parents because she thinks she should be independent once you have a job. "Everyone eventually needs to take care of themselves," she says.

_____

_____

5. Tyler told Dewayne that his car and his son's bicycle were blocking the driveway. "I'll move it right away," said Dewayne.

_____

_____

REVIEW EXERCISE 4

Underline and correct the two errors in pronoun agreement, reference, or point of view in each numbered item.

1. When the car's engine overheated, Andrew pushed it to the side of the road. He called a tow truck, but they did not come for two hours.

_____

_____

2. In my sociology class today, everyone said they had done the assigned reading. But you could tell that Professor Dunham suspected otherwise.

_____

_____

3. When Paige received her first paycheck, she thought they had made a mistake. Then she realized how much money you had to pay toward taxes, insurance, and retirement benefits.

_____

_____

4. When Dolores saw that they had brought her mail, she went eagerly to get it. But she came back with a frown on her face, asking "Why do they send me so many credit card offers?"

_____

_____

5. As Paul drove past the dumpster, he noticed that someone had left a small, shivering puppy along with their bag of trash. This made him angry; he could not understand how people could be so cruel.

_____

_____

REVIEW EXERCISE 5

Underline and correct the error in pronoun agreement, reference, or point of view in each numbered sentence.

[1]When I started college, everybody told me that registration would be difficult and time-consuming, but I did not believe them. [2]All you have to do is sign up for classes, I thought, and that can't be too difficult. [3]But registration turned out to be an all-day job that started when you walked onto the huge campus. [4]I tried asking for directions, but everybody was so new that they could not help me. [5]When I finally made it to orientation, they loaded me down with handouts and confusing information. [6]Finally, I was told to see an academic advisor in another building, but this turned out to be more difficult than I had anticipated. [7]I was herded into a big room with at least fifty other students, and it was half an hour before a harried secretary called my name and said he would see me. [8]When I had my prized class schedule in hand, I went to the business office where you had to stand in another line to pay. [9]Finally, they sent me to the bookstore to buy my books, an expensive and time-consuming process. [10]When I finally made it home, I decided that they were right: registration was a big hassle.

1. _____

2. _____

3. _____

4. _____

5. _____

6. _____

7. _____

8. _____

9. _____

10. _____

20

Adjectives, Adverbs, and Articles

> Verbs supply the muscle
> That helps a sentence go,
> And prepositions are the veins
> that help control its flow.
>
> Nouns and pronouns form the bones
> That make it stand upright.
> Conjunctions are the sinews
> That help its parts unite.
>
> But adjectives and adverbs
> Are the flesh upon the bone.
> They give each sentence its own face
> And make its meaning known.

Nouns are the bones of a sentence and verbs are the muscles that move them, but adjectives and adverbs provide the flesh and the cartilage, the color and the texture. Without adjectives and adverbs, you could convey only the basics: what happened and to whom. You could not show how and why, how many and what kind. This chapter provides a brief overview of adjectives and adverbs and reviews three useful words called articles.

Adjectives

Adjectives are words that give information about nouns or pronouns. They answer the questions, "What kind?" "How many?" and "Which one?" Usually, adjectives within a sentence come before the noun or pronoun they modify (*Fido nuzzled Horace's hand with his* cold, clammy, nose) or after a verb that *links* them to the noun or pronoun (*Fido's nose was* cold *and* clammy).

Examples

A *scented* candle burned on the table.

The toffee was *smooth* and *creamy*.

Kasim looks *unhappy*.

Nick is the *smartest* person I know.

PRACTICE 1   FINDING ADJECTIVES AND THE NOUNS THEY MODIFY

Underline the two adjectives in each sentence and draw an arrow connecting each with the word it modifies.

1.   The cookies were warm and delicious.

2.   Holly wore a heavy coat and a pair of warm gloves.

3.   The shivering dog huddled in a sheltered doorway.

4.   Ben looked anxious and uncertain.

5.   Comfortable benches had been placed alongside the winding pathway.

Adjective Forms: Positive, Comparative, and Superlative

Each adjective has three forms: the positive form, the comparative form, and the superlative form.

Positive

The *positive* form is the base form of the adjective. It is used when you are describing something but not comparing it to anything else.

Examples

The floor was *dirty*.

The ice cream tastes *good*.

Brenda was driving a *beautiful* car.

Comparative

The *comparative* form is used to compare two things or to compare one thing to a group of similar items.

Examples

When the two children came in, Emily was *dirtier* than Leslie.

The ice cream tastes *better* than the yogurt.

Violet thought that France was even *more beautiful* than Italy.

Donna is *more efficient* than her coworkers.

Superlative

The *superlative* form is used to compare one thing with all others in its group.

Examples

Ryan gave his grandmother a t-shirt that read, "World's *Best* Grandma."

Sam was the *least expensive* private detective we could find.

Chief was just a brown and white mutt, but to Jody, he was the *most beautiful* dog in the world.

Emily is the *most efficient* person in her office.

Adjective Forms

	Positive	Comparative	Superlative
One syllable		add -*er*	add -*est*
	cool	cooler	coolest
	smooth	smoother	smoothest
Two syllables ending in *y*		change *y* to *i*, add -*er*	change *y* to *i*, add -*est*
	happy	happier	happiest
	tardy	tardier	tardiest

	Positive	Comparative	Superlative
Most words of two or more syllables		use *more* or *less*	use *most* or *least*
	solemn	more solemn	most solemn
	intense	more intense	most intense
	inventive	more inventive	most inventive
	slippery	more slippery	most slippery
	important	less important	least important
Irregular adjectives	good	better	best
	bad	worse	worst

PRACTICE 2   REVIEWING ADJECTIVE FORMS

Fill in the comparative and superlative forms of each adjective. Use the Adjective Forms chart as your guide.

	Positive	Comparative	Superlative
1.	full	_____	_____
2.	crisp	_____	_____
3.	pesky	_____	_____
4.	trendy	_____	_____
5.	toxic	_____	_____
6.	pleasant	_____	_____
7.	humorous	_____	_____
8.	colorful	_____	_____
9.	good	_____	_____
10.	bad	_____	_____

---

* Grammar Alert!

Be sure to use *more* and *most* only in combination with base (positive) adjective forms, not with *-er* or *-est* forms. *More significant* is correct, but *more happier* or *most best* is not.

PRACTICE 3   USING ADJECTIVE FORMS

In each sentence below, decide whether the positive, comparative, or superlative form is needed. Then convert the adjective in parentheses to the proper form, using the Adjective Forms chart as your guide.

(careful)   1. Elaine is a _____ driver than her husband.

(big)   2. The hotel was the _____ that Chim had ever seen.

(attentive)   3. The children, seated in a circle, watched the storyteller with _____ faces.

(small)   4. Maggie carried a _____ notebook in her purse to jot down ideas and record her thoughts.

(brilliant)   5. Few scientists are _____ than Dr. Otto Schummer, but his work habits are erratic and his personality unconventional.

(tasty)   6. As the server described the items on the dessert cart, each one sounded _____ and more tempting than the last.

(ugly)   7. "Frank, I do believe that is the _____ tie I have ever seen," said his wife.

(young)   8. Glenn was the _____ of the three brothers.

(old)   9. Glenn was _____ than his sister Jackie.

(good)   10. Roberta has many good friends, but Ashley has been her _____ friend since grade school.

Adverbs

Adverbs give information about verbs (skated *gracefully*), adjectives (*extremely* slippery), or other adverbs (*very* badly). Often, but not always, adverbs are *ly* forms of the adjective. *Graceful* becomes *gracefully*, *bad* becomes *badly*, *quick* becomes *quickly*. The easiest way to tell an adverb from an adjective is to see what question the word answers. An adjective tells *how many, what kind*, or *which one*. An adverb tells *how, when*, or *to what degree*.

Examples

After her run, Kerri was breathing *rapidly*. (how)

Don nodded *coldly* when he passed Al in the hall. (how)

The performance was *extremely well* done. (to what degree/how)

The check will be sent *immediately*. (when)

PRACTICE 4   RECOGNIZING ADVERBS

Underline the adverb in each sentence.

1. The turtle slowly made its way across the sandbar.
2. Secretly, the old man had taken fifty dollars from each check he received and hidden it under his mattress.
3. Geneva artfully braided her daughter's hair and tied a small bow at the end of each braid.
4. Arthur seldom had headaches, but the loud music in the nightclub made his head pound.
5. Samantha waited anxiously for the plane to arrive.

Adverb Forms

	Positive	Comparative	Superlative
adverbs ending in *ly*		use more	use most
	smoothly	more smoothly	most smoothly
	happily	more happily	most happily
	solemnly	more solemnly	most solemnly
	intensely	more intensely	most intensely
Irregular adverbs	well	better	best
	badly	worse	worst

---

* Memory Jogger

Adjectives tell *how many, what kind,* or *which one.*

Adverbs tell *how, when,* or *to what degree.*

PRACTICE 5   RECOGNIZING ADJECTIVES AND ADVERBS

Underline the correct word in each phrase below. Decide whether the word tells *how many, what kind, which one, how, when,* or *to what degree,* and write your response in the first blank. In the second blank, write the part of speech: *adjective* or *adverb.* The first one is done for you.

1. sang (loud, loudly)

    The word tells _____ and is an _____.

2. a (beautiful, beautifully) dress

    The word tells _____ and is an _____.

3. walked (slow, slowly)

    The word tells _____ and is an _____.

4. a (slow, slowly) dance

    The word tells _____ and is an _____.

5. a (complete, completely) turnaround

    The word tells _____ and is an _____.

6. turned around (complete, completely)

    The word tells _____ and is an _____.

7. (several, severally) reasons

    The word tells _____ and is an _____.

8. (happy, happily) agreed

    The word tells _____ and is an _____.

9. (responsible, responsibly) behavior

    The word tells _____ and is an _____.

10. behaved (responsible, responsibly)

    The word tells _____ and is an _____.

PRACTICE 6   USING ADJECTIVES AND ADVERBS

Underline the correct word in each sentence.

1. Jason read the article (quick, quickly).
2. Mr. Smith made a (quick, quickly) trip to the grocery store.
3. The children had a (good, well) time at the museum.
4. "Please proceed (calm, calmly) to the exit," said the theater manager.
5. The coffee was (bare, barely) warm.
6. "Your presentation could not have gone more (smooth, smoothly)," Rick said.
7. Julia's (helpful, helpfully) attitude made everyone more cooperative.
8. The man was (angry, angrily).

9. The man was (angry, angrily) gesturing at passing cars.
10. The card wished Kevin a (speedy, speedily) recovery.

Puzzling Pairs

Certain adjective and adverb pairs are confused more often than others. The next sections explain the differences between the pairs *good* and *well*, *bad* and *badly*, and *worse* and *worst*.

Good and *well, bad* and *badly*

Good and *bad* are adjectives that tell *what kind; well* and *badly* are adverbs that tell *how.*

Examples

Since she has been using the Mavis Beacon typing software, Clare has become a *good* typist. (tells *what kind* of typist)

Since she has been using the Mavis Beacon typing software, Clare has learned to type *well*. (tells *how* she types)

Todd bought *good* tires that will perform *well* even in bad weather. (tells *what kind* of tires and *how* they perform)

---

* *Grammar Alert!*

Well can be an adjective when it refers to health, as in "He is not a *well* man" or "I am not feeling *well.*"

Ross had never been around children, and he was afraid he would
adjective
be a *bad* parent. (tells *what kind* of parent)

The dog was so timid that the animal shelter workers wondered if it
adverb
had been treated *badly*. (tells *how* it may have been treated)

adverb   adjective
Helen slept *badly* after having a *bad* dream. (tells *how* she slept and *what kind* of dream)

PRACTICE 7   USING *GOOD* AND *WELL*, *BAD* AND *BADLY*

In each sentence, choose *good* or *well*, *bad* or *badly*.

1.   Anita has a (good, well) job that pays her (good, well).
2.   Because it was (bad, badly) prepared, the souffle did not taste very (good, well).
3.   Lev is not a (bad, badly) tennis player; in fact, he plays rather (good, well).
4.   "(Good, Well) boy, Rex!" Mac told his dog. "Let's go to the vet so you can get (good, well)."
5.   "I react (bad, badly) when I lose," said Franklin, "but I don't think that makes me a (bad, badly) person."

Worse and *worst*

Worse and *worst* are both adjectives, but they are often confused. *Worse* is the comparative form, the form you use to compare one thing to another or one set of things to another set. *Worst* is the superlative form, used to compare one thing to all (or many) others in its class.

Examples

"I am disappointed in my grade," said Matt, "but I guess I could have done *worse*."

Matt is comparing two things: his actual grade and a hypothetical lower grade.

"This coffee tastes even *worse* with cream and sugar in it," said Kelly.

Kelly is comparing two things: the coffee before the addition of cream and sugar, and the same coffee after the flavorings were added.

Kelly made a face. "This is the *worst* coffee I have ever drunk," she said.

Kelly is comparing the coffee she is drinking to all others she has drunk.

The *worst* meal I ever ate in a restaurant was at the No Way Café.

The meal is being compared to all others in its class.

PRACTICE 8   USING *WORSE* AND *WORST*

Choose *worse* or *worst* in each sentence.

1. "I don't know which of them is (worse, worst)," said Kate, looking at her twin sons.
2. Not only did Adam lose the tennis match, but he probably turned in his (worse, worst) performance ever.
3. "I am your (worse, worst) nightmare," the drill sergeant snarled.
4. Nell's arthritis always gets (worse, worst) during rainy weather.
5. Meteorologists said that the hurricane was the (worse, worst) of the last century.

Articles

The **articles** in the English language are *a, an,* and *the.* Articles are small, easy-to-overlook words, but they are so often used that it is important to use them correctly. When a writer uses the word *pen,* for example, an article can reveal whether the writer is talking about a specific pen (the pen) or any pen (a pen).

Using *a* and *an*

The most common mistake people make with articles stems from uncertainty over when to use *a* and when to use *an.* Use *a* before a **consonant sound**—that is, before any word that sounds as if it begins with anything other than *a, e, i, o,* or *u.*

> *a* **b**owl
>
> *a* **p**eeled onion
>
> *a* **y**outh
>
> *a* **u**seful tool (*Useful* begins with the sound of the consonant **y**—the *yoo* sound. Therefore, the article *a* is used.)

Use *an* before a **vowel sound**—that is, before any word that sounds as if it begins with *a, e, i, o,* or *u.*

an **u**nderstanding

an **a**ble-bodied person

an **o**melet

an **h**onor (*Honor* begins with the *ah* sound often associated with the vowels **o** and **a.** Therefore, the article *an* is used.)

PRACTICE 9 USING *A* AND *AN*

Put *a* in front of words that begin with a consonant sound. Put *an* in front of words that begin with a vowel sound.

1. _____ calendar

2. _____ eraser

3. _____ hard-boiled egg

4. _____ bottle of shampoo

5. _____ orange t-shirt

6. _____ apple pie

7. _____ honest opinion

8. _____ young man

9. _____ utility pole

10. _____ unbelievable story

11. _____ sour taste

12. _____ usable item

13. _____ unusable item

14. _____ polar bear

15. _____ irritating noise

16. _____ ambidextrous person

17. _____ can of oil

18. _____ humorous remark

19. _____ oil can

20. _____ argument

PRACTICE 10 USING *A* AND *AN*

Put *a* or *an* in the blank in each sentence.

1. Gaby bought _____ chocolate milk shake.

2. Cho went to the store for _____ half gallon of orange juice.

3. _____ orange mouse pad sat to the right of the computer keyboard.

4. Looking into his refrigerator, Esteban saw _____ egg, a bottle of store-brand grape juice and a four day-old fast-food sandwich.

5. _____ open container of gasoline can be dangerous.

6. Since it was warm, Stacie decided to wear _____ short-sleeved shirt.

7. Peeling _____ onion always makes Shika cry.

8. The pages of the calendar were held together by _____ small plastic clip shaped like an airplane.

9. Jiro, do you have _____ opinion on the subject?

10. When _____ car pulled out in front of him, Erik blew the horn.

Review Exercises

Complete the Review Exercises to see how well you have learned the skills addressed in this chapter. As you work through the exercises, go back through the chapter to review any of the rules you do not understand completely.

REVIEW EXERCISE 1

Underline the correct article in each sentence.

1. In the newspaper, Rita saw (a, an) announcement of (a, an) new furniture store's grand opening.

2. Harvey saved the big coffee can, knowing he would find (a, an) use for it at (a, an) later date.

3. In (a, an) health magazine, Carly read (a, an) article called "The Hidden Dangers of Vitamins."

4. When she had a question about her taxes, Cheryl sent (a, an) e-mail to her father, who was (a, an) accountant.

5. For breakfast, Pat ate (a, an) scrambled egg and drank (a, an) glass of orange juice.

REVIEW EXERCISE 2

In each sentence, decide whether the positive, comparative, or superlative form is needed. Then convert the adjective in parentheses to the proper form. Use the Adjective Forms chart in this chapter as your guide.

(bad)   1. Traffic is much _____ than it was five years ago.

(large)   2. "I want the _____ size that you have," Carl told the ice cream store clerk.

(sick)   3. When Tom woke up, he felt _____.

(small)   4. Although Tiffany is the older of the two children, she is the _____ of the two.

(cloudy)   5.   The meteorologist said to expect a _____ day.

(good)   6.   Each of the ice cream flavors seemed _____ than the last.

(good)   7.   Anya's grade on the final test was the _____ grade she had made.

(reliable)   8.   Mr. Morton said that Ed was the _____ employee he had ever had.

(old)   9.   Rosetta said that her house was _____ than she was.

(roomy)   10.   When the company moved its office into the new building, the three supervisors bickered over who should get the _____ office.

REVIEW EXERCISE 3

Underline the correct modifier in each sentence.

1.   Looking at the huge stone in Mrs. Smythe-Buffington's ring, Michelle wondered if it was a (real, really) diamond.
2.   The blues musician said that before a person could (real, really) sing the blues, he had to live the blues.
3.   The children tried to catch the squirrels, but the squirrels were too (quick, quickly) for them.
4.   "If the appointment does not suit you," said the secretary, "we can reschedule at a (more convenient, most convenient) time."
5.   Hajel was ambidextrous, but the writing he did with his left hand was (neater, more neatly) than the writing he did with his right hand.
6.   The professor moved through the material so (rapid, rapidly) that the class complained.
7.   Brendan ran so (quick, quickly) that his little brother found it hard to keep up.
8.   The school bus driver said that she was (grateful, gratefully) for weekends and holidays.
9.   One advantage of oil over coal is that oil burns (cleaner, more cleanly).
10. Hal's car always looks (cleaner, more cleanly) than mine.

REVIEW EXERCISE 4

Underline the correct modifier in each sentence.

1.   Duncan reads very (quick, quickly), but he is a (slow, slowly) writer.
2.   Looking at the CD his daughter had (recent, recently) bought, Jim asked if there was (real, really) a band called Bunnygrunt.
3.   Though the critics agree that the movie is a (good, best) one, few would call it the (better, best) movie of the year.

4. Even though she did not do (bad, badly) on the exam, Rose knew she could have done (better, more better).

5. Real estate agents say it is a good idea to buy the (smaller, smallest) house in the (more, most) expensive neighborhood you can afford.

REVIEW EXERCISE 5

Underline and correct the errors in adjectives, adverbs, and articles. Each sentence contains one error.

[1]My friends envy me because I have an healthy bank account. [2]However, they could save money easy if they would just give up some of their wasteful spending habits. [3]My friend Abby, for instance, drinks only the most fanciest bottled water. [4]She says it is pure than tap water. [5]She may be right, but bottled water is also a expensive luxury she could probably do without. [6]Another friend, Jennifer, spends a great deal of money to dress fashionable. [7]If Jennifer waited for clothing to go on sale, then she could dress good for a lower price. [8]Toni, my best friend, is always complaining about her lack of money, but when she gets her paycheck, she heads for the bookstore for the most recently novels. [9]With an library card, Toni could read the latest bestsellers for free. [10]If I have more money than my friends, it is only because I spend more careful.

1. _____

2. _____

3. _____

4. _____

5. _____

6. _____

7. _____

8. _____

9. _____

10. _____

21
Capital Letters

```
i LOv yOu
mOM!!!!
MaX
AgE 4
```

When you learned to print your first awkward letters as a child, you slowly began to learn the rules of capitalization. You learned to capitalize your own name, the first letter of a sentence, and the pronoun *I*. Later came other rules for capitalizing names of places and things. This chapter reviews these fundamentals and introduces many of the fine points of capitalization.

Capital Letters to Begin Sentences

Capitalize the first word of a sentence or a direct quotation.

Examples

Sarita placed her coffee cup on the windowsill.

On the roof of the house lay a lime-green Frisbee.

"What time does the next bus come?" Frankie asked impatiently.

341

Capitalization of Words Referring to Individuals

Names and the Pronoun *I*

Capitalize people's names and the pronoun *I*.

> May I have that last doughnut if you aren't going to eat it?
>
> Mr. Bittenton gave Harold an old model train set.

Family Relationships

Family Designations Used in Place of a Name

Capitalize a word that designates a family relationship if it is used in place of a name. To make sure that the word is used as a name, try substituting a name for the word. If the word is used as a name, the substitution will sound natural.

Examples

> I took Grandma out to lunch at the mall.
>
> I took ~~Grandma~~ Betty Smith out to lunch at the mall.

"I took Betty Smith out to lunch" sounds natural, so *Grandma* is correct.

Try your own substitution in the next sentence. If substituting a name for *Dad* sounds natural, the capitalization is correct.

> "I am taking a course," Dad said, "because if I don't use my mind, I may lose it.

Family Designations Used with Possessives and Articles

When family designations such as *father, mother,* or *great-uncle Elmo* are preceded by a possessive pronoun (*my, her, his, their*), a possessive noun (*Ted's, Penny's*), or an article (*a, an,* or *the*), they are not capitalized. For additional proof, try directly substituting a name for the family designation. It will sound awkward.

Examples

I took my grandma out to lunch at the mall.

I took my ~~grandma~~ Betty Smith out to lunch at the mall.

The phrase "my Betty Smith" sounds awkward, so *grandma* is correct.
    Try substituting a name for *dad* in the next sentence, making sure to leave the pronoun *my* in the sentence. If the name does not sound natural, then the lower-case *dad* is correct.

"I am taking a course," my dad said, "because if I don't use my mind, I may lose it."

Professional Titles

Do not capitalize professional titles unless they are used immediately before a name.

Pandita Gupta is the doctor on duty in the emergency room.

The accident victims were treated by Dr. Pandita Gupta.

James Solkowski is my English professor.

I am taking American literature with Professor James Solkowski.

PRACTICE 1   CAPITALIZING WORDS REFERRING TO PEOPLE

Underline and correct the two capitalization mistakes in each sentence.

1. Uncle Ed took grandpa to the Doctor for a flu shot.

    _____

2. My Aunt always said, "Experience is the best Teacher."

    _____

3. Latrelle and jason are in professor Langley's Tuesday biology lab.

    _____

4. Nathaniel, my Cousin, is an Attorney with the firm of Vogel and Krantz.

    _____

5. Mr. peabody called his Senator to complain about taxes.

Capitalization of Words Referring to Groups

Religions, Geographic Locations, Races, and Nationalities

Capitalize words that refer to specific religions, geographic locations, races, and nationalities.

Examples

People of many races attend school with me. I have classmates who are Asian, Caucasian, African American, Latino, and Native American.

Though Bjorn is originally from Sweden, he considers himself a Los Angeleno.

Alan drives an American car, drinks German beer, and collects Mexican glassware.

Rashid was brought up Baptist, but he converted to Islam when he was twenty-six.

Organizations, Businesses, and Agencies

Capitalize specific names of organizations, businesses, and government agencies.

Examples

Harley belongs to the Meadow Community Chorus, the Spanish Club, and the Association of Nursing Students.

Perry works at the Campbell Corporation and his wife works for AT&T.

After Lenore finished her accounting degree, she went to work for the Internal Revenue Service.

Do not capitalize nonspecific or generic organization names.

Examples

Clarissa is active in church and is also a member of the choir.

As an executive in a large corporation, Simone often travels.

When Claud finishes college, he wants to work for the government.

PRACTICE 2 CAPITALIZING WORDS REFERRING TO GROUPS

Underline and correct the two capitalization mistakes in each sentence.

1. Janet went to the Library to find information on the american red cross.

   _____

2. The first methodist children's choir sold candy to benefit a charity called kids yule love.

   _____

3. When he began working for ford, Dwight joined the Union.

   _____

4. One of the most active clubs at the College is the association of nontraditional students.

   _____

5. I heard that our Company chairperson was offered a job at the federal trade commission.

   _____

Capitalization of Words Referring to Time and Place

Dates, Days, Holidays, and Seasons

Capitalize months of the year, days of the week, and names of holidays.

Examples

Thanksgiving Day is always celebrated on the last Thursday in November.

October holidays include Halloween and Columbus Day.

Do *not* capitalize the names of the four seasons.

> Marvin wants to take one last summer trip before his children go back to school in the fall.

Place Names

Capitalize specific place names.

Examples

> On our trip to Orlando, we visited Disney World, Sea World, Universal Studios, and Wet 'n' Wild.
>
> We also ate at King Arthur's Feast.
>
> When Sandra attended Glendale Community College, she worked part-time at Pizza Hut.
>
> The robber ran out of the Kwickie Food Mart and tore down Lemon Street.

Do not capitalize *general, nonspecific* place names.

Examples

> On our trip to Orlando, we visited three theme parks and a water park.
>
> We also ate at two expensive and entertaining restaurants.
>
> When Sandra attended college, she worked for a pizza place.
>
> The robber ran out of the convenience store and tore down the street.

Do not capitalize compass points unless they refer to a specific geographical area.

Examples

> The car traveled north on the interstate before turning east toward the city.
>
> Having lived on the East Coast all her life, Deb found it hard to adjust to the mountainous West.

PRACTICE 3   CAPITALIZING WORDS REFERRING TO TIME AND PLACE

Underline and correct the two capitalization mistakes in each sentence.

1. Cathryn had always lived in the south, but when she was eighteen, she moved to california.

   _____

2. The bus was headed South on peachtree street.

   _____

3. People living in new mexico sometimes have trouble convincing people that they live in the united states.

   _____

4. Kim's family celebrates both kwanzaa and Christmas in the Winter.

   _____

5. The state of north Carolina is known for its beaches as well as its beautiful blue ridge mountains.

   _____

Capitalization of Words Referring to Things and Activities

School Subjects

Do not capitalize subjects studied in school unless they are part of a *specific* course title.

Examples

Sandro is taking physics, French, and sociology this term.

Sandro is taking Physics 101, French 102, and Sociology 208 this term.

Sandro is taking Principles of Physics, Intermediate French, and Social Problems this term.

Titles

In general, capitalize titles of novels, short stories, poems, newspapers, magazines, articles, works of art, television shows, movies, songs and other musical works. There are exceptions to many rules in English, and this rule has more exceptions than most. Some newspapers and journals capitalize only the first word in the title of an article. Some writers, like e. e. cummings, do not follow the conventional rules of capitalization. When you write about an article, a poem, or any other piece of writing, preserve the title as it was published.

Otherwise, follow these rules: Capitalize the first word of a title. Do not capitalize articles (*a, an,* and *the*) or short prepositions (*to, of, from,* and similar short prepositions) unless they are the first word in a title. Capitalize all other words.

Examples

Hisako read an article in *Sky and Telescope* called "Radio Astronomy in the 21st Century."

Kelly's literature class read Anton Chekhov's play, *The Cherry Orchard*.

Isabel wrote her paper on "Sorting Laundry" by Elisavietta Ritchie and "Snow White and the Seven Deadly Sins" by R. S. Gwynn.

Myra tried to keep the children busy by teaching them to sing "Row, Row, Row Your Boat."

Consumer Products

For consumer products, capitalize the brand name but not the general product name.

Examples

At the college bookstore, Roger bought a Paper Mate highlighter, a roll of Scotch tape, a Bic pen, and a Mead notebook.

A Toyota broke down in front of the drive-through at Burger King.

Abbreviations

Abbreviations of organizations, corporations, and professional designations are capitalized. Some examples include NBC, AFL-CIO, FBI, NAACP, CIA, UPS, CPA, M.D., Ph.D., D.D.S. The disease AIDS is always written in all capitals.

PRACTICE 4   CAPITALIZING WORDS REFERRING TO THINGS AND ACTIVITIES

Underline and correct the two capitalization mistakes in each sentence.

1. Al pulled his toyota into the convenience store parking lot and ran over an empty Coke Bottle.

2. Mollie opened a can of alpo dog food, but when Taffy refused to eat it, she shared her mcDonald's cheeseburger with him.

3. Ann reads the miami herald or watches cbs to get the latest news.

4. Since he was out of Maxwell House Coffee, Ed decided to have some Lipton Tea.

5. Leshan read an article in new woman called "how I lost fifty pounds."

Review Exercises

Complete the Review Exercises to see how well you have learned the skills addressed in this chapter. As you work through the exercises, go back through the chapter to review any of the rules you do not understand completely.

REVIEW EXERCISE 1

Underline and correct the two capitalization mistakes in each sentence.

1. When Mimi couldn't find what she needed at foodmax, she went to kroger.

2. Alton bought a flower arrangement for his Mother to celebrate mother's day.

3. When grandpa tried to cut the thanksgiving turkey, it slipped off the platter and shot across the table.

4. When Randy went to his High School reunion, he borrowed a friend's lexus instead of driving his old Chevy truck.

5. It was late march before Andrew received his letter of acceptance from the College.

REVIEW EXERCISE 2

Underline and correct the two capitalization mistakes in each sentence.

1. Sonia wore her mickey mouse t-shirt and her nike shoes to the picnic.

    _____

2. The bus pulled into the town of east point at 6:00 A.M., then headed West on Route 27.

    _____

3. Before the baseball game started, the crowd at turner field stood to sing "the star-spangled banner."

    _____

4. Kelsey munched on a bag of Frito's Corn Chips as she watched a rerun of the munsters.

    _____

5. Some birds live in north america during the summer and migrate to south america in the winter.

    _____

REVIEW EXERCISE 3

Underline and correct the two capitalization mistakes in each sentence.

1. Harry and his Dad went on a two-week fishing trip to Crystal Lake last Spring.

    _____

2. Scientists who do aids research get a portion of their funding from the Government.

    _____

3. Kim said, "a few years ago, I used to smoke Marlboro Cigarettes. Now my worst vice is Hostess Ho Hos."

    _____

4. Kaya bought a half gallon of breyer's Strawberry frozen yogurt.

    _____

5. Gary is from the midwest, but he has lived in south Carolina for three years.

    _____

Underline and correct the capitalization errors in the paragraph below.

[1]A friend recently asked me, "how would you define success?" [2]The term means different things to different people, so i wasn't sure how to answer. [3]For some people, it means a new ford explorer in the driveway. [4]Or it means a big screen Sony Television in the den. [5]For others, it's a fat bank account at first national bank. [6]Some want a chauffeur-driven limousine stocked with bottles of Cristal Champagne. [7]To some people, success is improved health—money and possessions can't outweigh good health to a person with aids or Alzheimer's. [8]Still others aspire to fame and measure success by the number of times their faces appear on the cover of People or time. [9]Perhaps bertrand russell gave the best definition of success and its relationship to happiness. [10]He said, "success is getting what you want. Happiness is wanting what you get."

1. _____

2. _____

3. _____

4. _____

5. _____

6. _____

7. _____

8. _____

9. _____

10. _____

22

Words Commonly Confused

Poor Kevin. Although his e-mail has no misspelled words, it contains several errors involving words that are commonly confused. This chapter helps you avoid the kinds of errors that Kevin has made—errors that a spelling checker will not catch.

Words Commonly Confused

a, an   The article *a* is used before consonant sounds. The article *an* is used before vowel sounds. Thus you would write **a** dog, **a** rocky shoreline, **a** patch of ice, **an** icy road, **an** oblong box, **an** office. But you must base your choice on the consonant or vowel *sound*. Some words, such as those beginning with a silent *h* or with a *u* that is pronounced like *y*, require careful treatment: **an** honest person, but **a** hat; **an** uncle, but **a** used car.

✔ At the market, Trinh bought **an** eggplant, **a** large basket of crisp apples that came with **an** apple corer, and **a** few squash.

✔ The actor said that it was **an** honor to receive such **a** prestigious award.

accept, except   To *accept* is to take or believe; the word *except* means *but* or *with the exception of.*

✔ The company will **accept** applications, but **except** for a few clerical positions, no jobs are available.

advice, advise   *Advice* is a noun; one gives advice or asks for it. *Advise* is the verb form; one person may *advise* another.

✔ The psychic **advised** Abby to seek further **advice** at only $2.95 per minute.

affect, effect   *Affect* is the verb form. It means *to cause a change or variation.* *Effect* is the noun form. It means *outcome or result:*

✔ Jacob's illness does not seem to **affect** his mood.

✔ Even though Janice studied hard, the **effect** on her grades was not immediate.

all right, ~~alright~~   *All right* is the only correct spelling. It is never all right to write *alright.*

✔ The computer was not working this morning, but it seems to be **all right** now.

a lot, ~~alot~~, allot   *A lot* (never *alot*) is always written as two words when you mean *much* or *many,* but it's preferable to use a word such as *much, many, several,* or a specific amount instead of *a lot.* The word *allot* means *to allow or set aside* for a special purpose: *Erica allotted fifty dollars per month to her vacation fund.*

✔ **Acceptable:** It took **a lot** of work to get the old house in livable condition.

✔ **Better:** It took **months** of work to get the old house in livable condition.

among, between   *Among* is used with three or more persons or things; *between* is used with two.

✔ At the banquet, Governor Albright was seated **between** the mayor and Senator Jones. Later, however, she walked **among** the tables, chatting with her constituents.

breath, breathe   *Breath* is the noun form: a person can take a *breath* or be out of *breath*. *Breathe* is the verb form: someone may *breathe* heavily after exercising.

✔ "I can't take a vacation," said Pierre. "I am so busy I can't even take a **breath.**"

✔ "First, you need to learn how to **breathe,**" said the yoga instructor.

by, buy   *By* means *beside* or *through*. *Buy* means *to purchase*.

✔ "If you go **by** the ice cream shop," said Brandon, "**Buy** me a pint of strawberry."

fewer, less   Use *fewer* when writing about things you count; *less* when writing about things you measure. Specifically, if you can put a number in front of a word (five dollars), use *fewer*. If you cannot put a number in front of a word (five money), use *less*. You would write *fewer* rocks but *less* sand, *fewer* cookies but *less* flour.

✔ Anita noticed that when she used **less** fertilizer, her plants produced **fewer** tomatoes.

good, well   *Good* is an adjective that answers the question "What kind?" *Well* is an adverb that answers the question "How?" or "In what manner?" Therefore, a person writes a *good* essay. (*Good* answers the question, "What kind of essay?") But he writes it *well*. (*Well* answers the question, "How did he write it?")

✔ Carlisle has a **good** arm, but he does not pitch very **well** under pressure.

himself, hisself   The word is always *himself*, never *hisself*.

✔ Rico was proud that he had done the repairs **himself.**

its, it's   If you mean *it is* or *it has,* use *it's* (with the apostrophe). Otherwise, use *its*.

✔ "**It's** a pleasure to drive my old Ford," said Daniel, "because **it's** been taken care of."

✔ The inchworm, bending double then stretching full length, slowly made **its** way across the walkway.

knew, new   *Knew* is the past tense of *know; new* means *not old.*

✔ The owner of the small hardware store **knew** that he faced stiff competition from the **new** Handy Andy down the street.

know, no   *Know* means *to understand; no* means *not any* or the opposite of *yes.*

✔ "I do not **know** why there are **no** gas stations along this stretch of highway," said Joan.

loose, lose   *Loose* is the opposite of *tight; lose* is the opposite of *find.*

✔ Althea's clothes are getting **loose,** but she says she plans to **lose** more weight.

past, passed   *Past* (an adjective) means *beyond* or *before now. Passed* (a verb) means *went by.*

✔ More and more, Aunt Emma seems to talk about the **past.**

✔ Every time Tammy **passed** a fast-food place, her son yelled, "Want fries!"

peace, piece   *Peace* means *calm* or *tranquility; piece* means *a part.*

✔ Sam knew he would get no **peace** until he gave Cujo a **piece** of his hamburger.

plain, plane   *Plain* means *clear* or *simple.* A *plane* is a form of air transportation, a carpenter's tool, or a geometric surface.

✔ Joseph's **plain,** simple office belied the fact that he had a company **plane** at his disposal.

principal, principle   *Principal* means *chief* (principal reason) or *a person in charge of a school* (principal of Westmore High). A *principle* is a policy, a moral stand, or a rule.

✔ The **principal** said she hoped to encourage solid values and strong **principles** in her students.

✔ Pete's inability to get along with his coworkers was the **principal** reason he was fired.

quit, quite, quiet   *Quit* means *to stop*. *Quite* means *entirely* or *very*, and *quiet* means *hushed*.

✔ "I am not **quite** through with my homework," Anna told her daughter. "If you will **quit** banging on that pot and be **quiet** for just a few minutes, I will play with you when I'm through."

regardless, ~~irregardless~~   Regardless of the number of times you may have seen it, *irregardless* is not a word. The word is *regardless*.

✔ **Regardless** of the setbacks and problems that Aldo had, his term paper turned out well.

themselves, ~~themself~~, ~~theirself~~, ~~theirselves~~   The word is always *themselves*.

✔ After they did their Saturday chores, Tina and Frank decided to give **themselves** a treat and order a pizza.

then, than   *Then* is used to show time or cause and effect; *than* is used to compare.

✔ If you are going to the library tomorrow, maybe I will see you **then.**

✔ If Jerrald moves to the new apartment complex, **then** he will have a longer commute to work.

✔ The new copier takes up much less space **than** the old one did.

there, their, they're   *There* is used to mean *in that place* or to start a sentence or clause. *Their* means *belonging to them*, and *they're* means *they are*.

✔ "**They're** not for you," Kim warned as the dog nosed the bag of sandwiches.

✔ "**There** are not enough places in this mall to sit down," said Alberta.

✔ Valorie took her children to the health department for **their** school vaccinations.

through, threw   *Through* means *within, between,* or *finished*. *Threw* is the past tense of *throw*.

✔ After Jim was **through** with his newspaper, he **threw** it in the recycling bin and sat looking **through** the window.

two, too, to   *Two* refers to the number two; *too* means *also* or indicates an excessive amount, as in the phrase *too much.* Any other use requires *to.*

✔ Alfredo said he wanted **to** go **to** the beach **too,** but I told him we had **too** many people unless someone else agreed **to** drive so that we could take **two** cars.

weather, whether, rather   *Weather* includes natural phenomena such as temperature, rainfall, and wind velocity. *Whether* means *if* and indicates the existence of two possibilities. It is often paired with *or not. Rather* indicates a preference.

✔ The **weather** is expected to turn warm after the weekend.

✔ We aren't sure **whether** we can afford a vacation this year.

✔ Would you **rather** have ice cream or frozen yogurt?

where, were   *Where* rhymes with *air* and refers to *place. Were* rhymes with *fur* and is a past tense form of *to be.*

✔ When Cari did not see you, she asked **where** you **were.**

Review Exercises

Complete the Review Exercises to see how well you have learned the skills addressed in this chapter. As you work through the exercises, go back through the chapter to review any of the rules you do not understand completely.

REVIEW EXERCISE 1

Refer to the explanations in this chapter to choose the correct words in each sentence. Underline the correct choice.

1. Jiro made (a, an) egg noodle soup that his guests agreed was (quite, quiet) good.
2. Leo was not sure (rather, whether) he would (rather, whether) take a biology course or an anthropology course.
3. Dorothy went (threw, through) every drawer in the kitchen because she could not remember (were, where) she had put the can opener.

4. Michael blamed (himself, hisself) for his financial troubles. He knew that he should not (buy, by) so many things on credit.

5. The twins (were, where) known around the apartment complex as "the terrible (too, to, two)."

REVIEW EXERCISE 2

Underline the correct words in each sentence.

1. After her children left for school in the morning, Monica enjoyed the (piece, peace) and (quite, quiet).

2. The singer flashed a (piece, peace) sign and said, "Everything is uptight, (alright, all right), and out of sight."

3. Lakeisha wore (a, an) caftan that was flowing and (loose, lose).

4. James could not (except, accept) Laurie's declaration that she was (through, threw) with him.

5. Aimee decided to take her conservative grandmother's (advice, advise) and print her resume on (plain, plane) white paper instead of hot pink.

REVIEW EXERCISE 3

Cross out the two word choice errors in each sentence. Then write the correct words on the line provided.

1. At the paint store, Marie found it hard to chose between the forty different shades of yellow.

_____

2. "I used too wish I was smarter then my brother," said Joseph, "until I realized that I was."

_____

3. "The coffee tasted very well," said Owen, "but I'm not sure weather I should have drunk it so late at night."

_____

4. Dwight and Hakim reminded theirselves that they had meant too go to the library to study.

_____

5. Carol couldn't except our invitation because she had alot of work to do.

_____

REVIEW EXERCISE 4

Cross out the two word choice errors in each sentence. Then write the correct words on the line provided.

1. Steve said that the principle reason he quit his job was that his supervisor asked him to falsify financial records. Dishonesty was against Steve's principals.

   _____

2. Ellen's goldfish was floating lifelessly in it's bowl Thursday morning. She wondered weather she had overfed it the night before.

   _____

3. Brian had told no one accept Courtney that he was planning to quit his job. He was surprised to find that all of his coworkers new about it.

   _____

4. When a wasp landed on her magazine, Susan held her breathe. Then she quickly through the magazine over the porch railing.

   _____

5. When Zack woke up screaming from his nightmare, his mother came to make sure he was alright. Then she rocked him and sang to him until he was quite.

   _____

REVIEW EXERCISE 5

Cross out the ten word choice errors in the paragraph below. Then correct them on the lines provided.

^{1}One of the best things about technology is that it offers a host of knew excuses for not turning in assignments on time. ^{2}If you have a computer and a printer, you have access to excuses that almost any professor will except. ^{3}Just before the class period when the assignment is due, run breathlessly into the professor's office and say that your printer cartridge quite printing just as you were trying to print your paper. ^{4}Or tell the instructor that your computer's hard drive crashed and made you loose all your files. ^{5}Even if you do not own a computer, technology still gives you alot of excuses. ^{6}If you need another day on your paper, call the professor, say you are sick, and ask if it is alright for your mother (or some other person) to fax in the assignment. [7]The next day, take in your paper, apologize, and say that your mother kept getting disconnected because their was a poor line condition on the fax. [8]Another good excuse is that you tried to make a extra copy of your paper, but the copier had a paper jam as your paper went through. [9]If you fill bad about lying to your professor or think that he or she won't accept your excuse, there is another way. [10]You can take the safe, dull route and get threw with your paper in time to turn it in on the due date.

1. _____   6. _____

2. _____   7. _____

3. _____   8. _____

4. _____   9. _____

5. _____   10. _____

23

Word Choice

Carlton is interviewing for his first postcollege job. When he is ushered into the office of the interviewer, what should he say?

    a. "Yo! Got any jobs, man?"
    b. "Allow me at this point in time to present and introduce myself to you."
    c. "Good afternoon. I'm Carlton Smith."
    d. "If you're looking for the cream of the crop, it's as plain as the nose on your face that I am a cut above the rest."

If you answered *c* to the question in the box above, you have shown good judgment in word choice. But when you write, word choice is not always so clear-cut. This chapter helps you to fine-tune your judgment and to recognize categories of word choice that are generally not appropriate for college writing: slang, clichés, and wordiness.

Slang

People enjoy using **slang** because it is informal, up-to-the-minute, and fun. Just as a common language forms a bond among those who speak it, slang reinforces the bond within the groups that use it. Yet the very things that make slang appealing in conversation make it unsuitable for writing to a broad audience. Writing requires a common language and is usually more formal than conversation. In addition, no writer wants to use words that may be out of date if an audience reads them years later. Slang expressions such as *the bee's knees, hunky-dory,* and *groovy* may have sounded up-to-the-minute decades ago, but now they are relics of another time.

Group Exercise 1   Discussing Slang Terms

Form small groups. Try to include both sexes and as many different ages and ethnic groups as possible. Each group member should write down five slang terms and then share the list with other group members. Are some of the terms different? (The more diverse the group, the more likely that it will generate a variety of slang.) Are there any slang expressions that not all group members are familiar with? What conclusions can the group draw about the use of slang? Choose one spokesperson to report the group's findings, along with a few of the most interesting slang terms, to the class.

PRACTICE 1   AVOIDING SLANG EXPRESSIONS

Replace the italicized slang expressions in each sentence with more traditional word choices.

1. Vince was wearing a *cool* new pair of *shades* with round lenses.

   _____

   _____

2. Shara *flipped out* when she *eyeballed* the scratch on her car door.

   _____

   _____

3. Dolores went on a huge shopping spree and *maxed out* her *plastic*.

   _____

   _____

4. Instead of studying, Frank decided to *chill out* in front of the *tube* for a few hours.

   _____

   _____

5. Lucinda's brother is going with her to buy her car because he thinks she is so *clueless* that she would probably be *ripped off*.

_____

_____

Clichés

While slang is fresh and new, **clichés** are expressions used so often for so long that they have become worn out. The cliché *burn the midnight oil,* for instance, is a relic of a time when working until midnight meant lighting an oil lamp. Because they are easy to remember and widely used, clichés are often the first expressions that come to mind. It takes a deliberate effort to recognize them and eliminate them from your writing.

Look at the following list of clichés. Can you think of others?

apple of my eye	dead as a doornail	live and let live
as good as gold	easy as pie	once in a blue moon
as old as Methuselah	flat as a pancake	pretty as a picture
at the drop of a hat	in the lap of luxury	raining cats and dogs
cream of the crop	light as a feather	sick as a dog

PRACTICE 2 AVOIDING CLICHÉS

Rewrite each sentence to eliminate the two italicized clichés.

1. The job bagging groceries was as *easy as pie,* but Tom was fired because he was *slow as molasses.*

   _____

   _____

2. During the interview, Sally looked *as cool as a cucumber,* but inside she was *shaking like a leaf.*

   _____

   _____

3. Keisha says her job keeps her *as busy as a bee* and that she gets a vacation *once in a blue moon.*

   _____

   _____

4. Because Kevin has *worn so many hats* at Acme Tool and Die, he knows the company *like the back of his hand*.

_____

_____

5. My next-door neighbor is *as old as Methuselah*, but he seems to be *fit as a fiddle*.

_____

_____

Wordiness

Wordiness sometimes happens when writers do not take the time to be concise. The shortest and simplest way of expressing an idea is usually the best way.

The words and phrases below contribute to wordiness and can usually be omitted.

basically	~~basically~~ performs no function in most sentences
definitely	is ~~definitely~~ a space-waster
in my opinion	usually weakens a sentence ~~in my opinion~~
the fact is that	~~The fact is that~~ facts, like opinions, can usually be stated without preamble.
totally	usually ~~totally~~ unnecessary
very	can ~~very~~ often be omitted

The phrases below are wordy and can usually be shortened and strengthened.

Wordy	Concise
at the present time	now, today
due to the fact that	because, since
for the reason that	because, since
in point of fact	in fact
in today's society	today
long in length	long

Examples

✘ I dreaded taking the course, but *in point of fact*, I needed a course in the *basic fundamentals* of English.

✔ I dreaded taking the course, but in fact, I needed a course in the fundamentals of English.

✘ *Due to the fact that at this point in time* I don't have a car, I ride the bus every day.

✔ Since I don't have a car, I ride the bus every day.

PRACTICE 3   ELIMINATING WORDINESS

Each sentence contains two italicized wordy expressions. Rewrite the sentences to eliminate wordiness.

1. I stayed awake until *1:00 A.M. in the morning* to watch the *lunar eclipse of the moon*.

   _____

   _____

2. Because of the high crime rate *in today's society*, many people are *basically* distrustful of other people.

   _____

   _____

3. *Annually each year*, an employees' picnic is held to reward the workers for the hard work they do *each and every day*.

   _____

   _____

4. *In my opinion, I think* that *financial decision-making about money matters* should be taught in high school.

   _____

   _____

5. James was *totally and completely dedicated* to *the best on-the-job performance he could deliver to his employer in the workplace*.

   _____

   _____

Group Exercise 2   Eliminating Slang, Clichés, and Wordiness   Confident? Go solo!

In small groups, "translate" the sentences written here in slang, clichés, or wordy language. Then rewrite the same thought in clear, concise language.

Sentence Group 1

Slang: Leo had the pedal to the metal, but he thought his radar detector would keep him from being busted by the fuzz.

Wordiness: Leo was definitely exceeding the speed limit posted upon the signs beside the road, but he thought having a radar detector in his car to alert him to police presence would prevent the authorities from detecting or stopping him.

Your revision: _____

_____

Sentence Group 2

Slang: Catherine flipped out when she saw her main squeeze hanging out with another woman.

Cliché: When Catherine saw the apple of her eye with another woman, she hit the ceiling.

Your revision: _____

_____

Sentence Group 3

Cliché: Joanna eats like a horse, but she is still as thin as a rail.

Wordiness: Joanna eats a great deal of food of all kinds and types, but she somehow manages to maintain a thin slenderness of body that is surprising.

Your revision: _____

_____

Sentence Group 4

Slang: Jake really dug his new ride to the max.

Wordiness: Jake received a great deal of enjoyment and pleasure from his Nissan automobile, which was red in color.

Your revision: _____

_____

Sentence Group 5

Slang: I pulled out my plastic, but the clerk said I had to lay some green on him.

Wordiness: I retrieved my Visa credit card from its place within my wallet, but the store clerk in the convenience store said that the store accepted only cash money, not a Visa credit card, or for that matter, a MasterCard or American Express credit card.

Your revision: _____

_____

Review Exercises

Complete the Review Exercises to see how well you have learned the skills addressed in this chapter. As you work through the exercises, go back through the chapter to review any of the rules you do not understand completely.

REVIEW EXERCISE 1

In the blank to the left of each sentence, indicate whether the italicized expressions are slang (*S*), clichés (*C*), or wordy expressions (*W*). Then replace the italicized words to correct the problem in word choice.

_____ 1. Ben *freaked out* when he saw the parking ticket on his windshield.

_____

_____ 2. It was *raining cats and dogs* by the time Tasha got out of her political science class.

_____

_____ 3. *In point of fact,* trees prevent soil erosion, produce oxygen, and provide cooling shade.

_____

_____ 4. Because he had *prearranged plans that he had made at an earlier time to at-tend a conference,* the professor canceled Friday's class.

_____

_____ 5. Samantha was *born with a silver spoon in her mouth* and has lived *in the lap of luxury* all her life.

_____

_____ 6. Professor Adams was *ticked off* because the class did so poorly on the last test.

_____

_____ 7. Because it was raining, the game was *postponed until a later time.*

_____

_____ 8. At the restaurant, we *pigged out* on hamburgers and fries, so we were too full to order dessert.

_____

_____ 9. Without her friends from high school, Amy was *like a fish out of water* during her first few months at college.

_____

_____ 10. The speaker *concluded his speech with a wrap-up that summarized his major points.*

_____

REVIEW EXERCISE 2

Underline and correct the two word choice problems in each sentence.

1. Because Hal has a heart of gold, he agreed to take care of his sister's two rug rats while she was out of town.

_____

_____

2. Rollo thought he would cop some z's during class, but the professor became angry and threw him out on his ear.

_____

_____

3. When the strange noise persisted in continuing, Alissa put on her bedroom slippers, grabbed a flashlight, and went outdoors to examine the outside exterior of the house.

_____

_____

4. Since Anna has wheels, I asked her if we could ride with her, and she said she was cool with that.

_____

_____

5. Laurie is basically tired of Sam, but she is definitely interested in Paul.

_____

_____

REVIEW EXERCISE 3

Some slang expressions have alternate meanings that are not slang. For each sentence pair, choose the expression from the word list that best fits both sentences. Then write the slang meaning and the standard meaning of the expression in the blanks provided.

Word list: cool, bust, bug, shaft, gross

1. Sentence pair 1

   a. The store manager was sorry he had ordered a _____ of glow-in-the-dark yo-yos. In six months, he sold just 10 and had 134 left in stock.

   b. Jason's mother bought a gelatin mold in the shape of a human brain. She thought it was _____, but she knew Jason would love it.

   Slang meaning: _____

   Standard meaning: _____

2. Sentence pair 2

   a. Ever since a _____ crawled into his shoe one night, Bobby shakes out both shoes before putting them on in the morning.

   b. "Don't _____ me, squirt," Al said to his little brother.

Slang meaning: _____

Standard meaning: _____

3. Sentence pair 3

   a. On the piano, Mr. Schoenmeyer had a small _____ of Mozart.

   b. The drug dealer peddled his wares from a bench in the park, seemingly unafraid of a police _____.

   Slang meaning: _____

   Standard meaning: _____

4. Sentence pair 4

   a. After his divorce, Raymond's favorite song was "She Got the Gold Mine, I Got the _____."

   b. Through a high window, a single _____ of sunlight fell into the cheerless room.

   Slang meaning: _____

   Standard meaning: _____

5. Sentence pair 5

   a. The candy, called Boogers, came in a plastic nose. "_____!" said the delighted twins.

   b. When the rest of us are comfortable, Pat always shivers and says it is too _____.

   Slang meaning: _____

   Standard meaning: _____

REVIEW EXERCISE 4

Underline and correct the two word choice problems in each sentence.

1. The Chinese tea was pale green in color and deliciously fruity in taste.

   _____

   _____

2. Arthur was as mad as a wet hen because the car's battery was as dead as a doornail.

_____

_____

3. The dude in the gross-looking work boots is my cousin Malcolm.

_____

_____

4. Due to the fact that she had not found a job Luanne was basically broke.

_____

_____

5. Reginald was hip to the fact that the exam would be a bummer.

_____

_____

REVIEW EXERCISE 5

Rewrite the letter below, correcting the errors in word choice in the salutation, body, and close of the letter.

[1]Yo, Professor Smith,

[2]What a major bummer it was to miss the midterm exam in your class yesterday. [3]I know that your syllabus definitely states that you basically do not give make-up exams. [4]However, I am absolutely certain beyond a shadow of a doubt that in my case you will see fit to make an exception to this policy. [5]You see, I became as sick as a dog after a late-night study session with some friends over at the Keg and Barrel.

[6]I know that we have had our differences, but aside from the unfortunate incident of the fake vomit, you have to admit that I have been as good as gold in your class. [7]I swear I am as innocent as a lamb in the matter of the stolen exam key.

[8]Let me say prior to concluding this letter that in my opinion, I think you are one of the best and

most fair-minded professors on this campus. [9]I hope that you will forgive and forget, let bygones be bygones, and allow me to make up the exam.

[10]Later, teach!

Desmond Kruger

_____

_____

_____

_____

_____

_____

_____

_____

_____

_____

_____

_____

_____

24

Commas

There are so many comma rules that, in desperation, people often resort to makeshift rules like the ones above. Unfortunately, these blanket statements don't always work. When it comes to commas, rules—and exceptions—abound. The rules presented in this chapter help you cope with the complexities of comma usage.

Commas to Set off Introductory Words, Phrases, and Clauses

Use commas after an introductory word, phrase, or clause.

Examples

Later, we walked on the beach and watched the sun set.

In the long run, getting an education pays.

375

When Ethan saw the giraffe, he laughed and clapped his hands.

In the spaces between the keys on her computer keyboard, Kim could see dust.

PRACTICE 1   USING COMMAS AFTER INTRODUCTORY ELEMENTS

Insert commas after introductory words, phrases, and clauses.

1. Painfully the man rose to his feet and walked toward us.

    _____

2. To Arlene's irritation a little sports car slipped into the parking place she had been waiting for.

    _____

3. By the time the pizza arrived it was cold.

    _____

4. Without apology or explanation Eric strolled in two hours late.

    _____

5. After Mary's coupons were deducted her grocery bill came to $34.95.

    _____

Commas to Join Items in a Series

When a series of three or more words, phrases, or clauses is connected with *and*, *or*, or *nor*, place a comma after each item except the last one. The final comma will come before *and*, *or*, or *nor*.

> ### * Real-World Writing
>
> In journalism, it is becoming customary to omit the comma before *and*, *or*, or *nor*. Academic usage is more traditional and favors keeping the final comma.

Examples

Ferrell said his car needed a wash, a wax job, and an oil change.

Apples, oranges, and bananas filled a wooden bowl on the kitchen counter.

Nell said she would consider herself successful if she graduated from college, opened her own business, and had a happy family.

Ellie said she knew Brett was smart because he was a good Scrabble player, he read a lot, and he had a good sense of humor.

If only two items appear in the series, no comma is used.

The old farmer said he had cut his livestock to just a few cows and three dozen pigs.

The toll collector said that there was a traffic tie-up in the tunnel and a wreck near the downtown connector.

On his new diet, Uncle Frank said he was hungry just twice a day: when he was awake and when he was asleep.

PRACTICE 2   USING COMMAS TO JOIN ITEMS IN A SERIES

Insert commas to join words, phrases, and clauses in a series of three or more. One sentence has only two items in the series and does not require a comma.

1. Jason's summer job with a lawn maintenance firm helped him learn that he hates grass dirt and heat.

    _____

    _____

2. Mom makes her special orange cookies only at Christmas because of the cost and the labor involved in making the cookies.

    _____

    _____

3. The receptionist said that Dr. Brantley was booked solid during June July and August.

    _____

    _____

4. The white-hatted chef pulled the souffle from the oven set it on the counter and watched as it slowly deflated.

    _____

    _____

5. At the opening of the ice-skating rink, skaters leaped twirled wobbled or fell, according to their level of expertise.

    _____

    _____

Commas to Join Independent Clauses

Use a comma with a FANBOYS conjunction (*for, and, nor, but, or, yet, so*) to join independent clauses. Recall that an independent clause has a subject and a verb and can stand alone as a complete sentence.

Examples

Evelyn needed to go to the post office, so she left the house twenty minutes early.

Thad felt an uncomfortable twinge in his right ankle, but he kept running anyway.

The temperature is expected to drop, and snow is predicted.

Do not use a comma if the FANBOYS connects a verb to a clause rather than a clause to a clause. That is, do not use a comma unless there is a complete sentence (subject *and* verb) on both sides of the FANBOYS.

subject verb   verb
Carrie put her tea in the microwave and made a tomato sandwich.

The dog stood by the door and waited for Vince to come out.

Fernando can take a new job at lower pay or stay with the old job he hates.

PRACTICE 3   USING COMMAS WITH *FANBOYS* TO JOIN INDEPENDENT CLAUSES

Place commas before FANBOYS conjunctions that join two independent clauses. One sentence contains a compound verb, not two clauses, and does not need a comma.

1. Grass and weeds grew tall around the unpainted house and shutters hung haphazardly from its windows.

    _____

2. The sun was hot but a cool breeze occasionally brought relief.

    _____

3. A police car circled the block several times but did not stop.

    _____

4. Laurie woke up early so she decided to work on her term paper.

_____

5. Ralph thought he could fix the sink easily but it took him most of the afternoon.

_____

Commas around Interrupters

An **interrupter** is a word, phrase, or clause inserted into a sentence to give more information about some element within the sentence. An interrupter is never essential to the structure of the sentence. If you took the interrupter out, the sentence would still make perfect sense.

Examples

The road, freshly paved, was no longer pitted with dangerous potholes.

The bag, crumpled and stuffed under a bench, held the remains of someone's lunch.

PRACTICE 4   USING COMMAS AROUND INTERRUPTERS

Insert commas around interrupters in the following sentences.

1. The song one of Bryan's favorites was first recorded over thirty years ago.

_____

2. Mr. Cartwright the building's custodian retired because of poor health.

_____

3. The child sulking unhappily picked up his toys.

_____

4. The container of cottage cheese still sealed was two months past its expiration date.

_____

5. The highway long and lonely stretched through the trees and over the hill.

_____

Commas with Direct Quotations

A **direct quotation** is an exact repetition of the words that someone speaks or thinks. When a comma is used with a direct quotation, the comma is always placed in front of the quotation mark.

1. When a direct quotation is followed by a **tag** (such as *he said*), a comma goes after the quoted words and *in front of the quotation mark:*

    "I would like to go on a cruise ship someday," said Maria.

2. When a tag leads into a direct quotation, a comma goes after the tag and *in front of the quotation mark:*

    Spencer asked, "Where is the best place to buy a used car?"

3. When a sentence is written as a split quotation, commas are placed *in front of the quotation marks:*

    "If our dog had not awakened us," the woman told the reporter, "we might have died in the fire."

PRACTICE 5   USING COMMAS WITH DIRECT QUOTATIONS

Insert commas to set off direct quotations in the following sentences.

1. Tiffany asked "Which bus will take me to the library?"

    _____

2. "Since I started walking every day" said Dee "I feel like a different person."

    _____

3. "Can someone help me? I have locked my keys in the car" said Nando.

    _____

4. "If I could choose the color of grass" said the child "I would pick purple."

    _____

5. Oscar Wilde said "I can resist everything except temptation."

    _____

Commas in Names and Dates

When a professional title follows a name, it is set off with commas.

The clerk's name tag read, "Bettye, Associate."

Samuel Spencer, M.D., is the Holtons' family doctor.

When you write the month, day, and year, a comma goes between the day and year.

The Declaration of Independence was signed on July 4, 1776.

When you write just the month and year, no comma is used.

The Declaration of Independence was signed in July 1776.

PRACTICE 6   USING COMMAS IN NAMES AND DATES

Insert commas as needed in the following sentences. One sentence needs no comma.

1. The letter was dated September 1 1999.

    _____

2. Stephanie Bascomb D.V.M. did the surgery on Sparky's paw.

    _____

3. Kwame was born in May 1982.

    _____

4. Burton Fellstone C.P.A. has opened an office on Grant Street.

    _____

5. The sign on the door read Anne Grossman M.D.

    _____

Review Exercises

Complete the Review Exercises to see how well you have learned the skills addressed in this chapter. As you work through the exercises, go back through the chapter to review any of the rules you do not understand completely.

REVIEW EXERCISE 1

Insert commas where they are needed in each sentence.

1. The theater gave away t-shirts movie tickets and coupons for soft drinks at its grand opening.

   _____

2. Predictably there was a crowd in the video store by the time Stan got there.

   _____

3. The Pet Stop a motel for animals takes care of pets while their owners are on vacation.

   _____

4. In October 1929 the stock market crashed after a long period of prosperity and excess.

   _____

5. When the pizza delivery car pulled into the driveway the children stampeded to the door.

   _____

6. Fast food wrappers soft drink cans and empty bottles littered the picnic area.

   _____

7. The personal ad had led Lauren to expect a tall man so she was surprised when Roy approached her.

   _____

8. A lighted neon sign blaring music and laughter spilling from the open door told Alfredo that the Dew Drop Inn was still open for business.

   _____

9. "Thanks for waiting. I hope I'm not too late" Leona said breathlessly.

   _____

10. Kevin Nguyen my brother's roommate is majoring in chemistry.

    _____

REVIEW EXERCISE 2

Insert commas where they are needed in each sentence.

1. Before leaving his car in the stadium's huge parking lot Ron tied a bright orange flag to the antenna.

   _____

2. Elmont Morrison M.D. sleepily fumbled for the ringing telephone.

   _____

3. Muttering angrily under her breath Juanita retrieved her soggy newspaper from the puddle where it lay.

_____

4. The well-dressed woman unaware of the store detective's presence slipped the silver necklace into her handbag.

_____

5. In the basement dusty jars of Grandma's vegetables and preserves lined the shelves.

_____

6. After the hurricane residents slowly emerged to assess the damage to houses and cars.

_____

7. The bookstore's comfortable chairs were filled with people reading chatting or even sleeping.

_____

8. The directory on the wall beside the elevator said that Carl Smith D.D.S. was in Suite 205.

_____

9. Andrew saw billboards advertising motels restaurants and nightclubs.

_____

10. With a powerful leap the cat lunged after the bird.

_____

REVIEW EXERCISE 3

Insert commas where they are needed in each sentence. Each numbered item contains two problems that can be fixed with the addition of a comma or commas.

1. When she tried to unlock the door with her arms full of groceries Leslie dropped her keys into the bushes beside the front steps. She set the groceries on a chair took a flashlight from her purse and hunted through the bushes for her keys.

_____

_____

2. Even though he was tired Joshua tried to stay up to watch the movie. However he soon fell asleep on the couch.

_____

_____

3. A stuffy head a runny nose and a sore throat told Ashley that she was coming down with a cold. She decided to stop at the drugstore on the way home for tissues cough drops and decongestant tablets.

    _____

    _____

4. Pretending to read a newspaper the detective sat outside the apartment complex for an hour and watched the door. "I never thought this would be such a boring line of work" he thought.

    _____

    _____

5. The date on the letter was April 13 1932. "This letter was written by my great-grandfather" said Michael.

    _____

    _____

REVIEW EXERCISE 4

Insert commas where they are needed in each sentence.

1. The t-shirt was old ragged and stained with paint. "It's still too good to throw away" Mia said.

    _____

    _____

2. Containers on a table beside the hot dog stand held catsup relish and even chopped onions. However there was not a drop of mustard.

    _____

    _____

3. Jeff made just one New Year's resolution but it was one he wanted to keep. He said "I want to pay off all my credit card debt."

    _____

    _____

4. Tacked to the bulletin board were several old receipts two greeting cards and a yellowed newspaper article. On the desk a calendar was still turned to July 2003.

    _____

    _____

5. Arthur wearing only his bathrobe and his underwear slipped out of the house to get his newspaper. Halfway down the driveway he realized he had accidentally locked himself out.

_____

_____

REVIEW EXERCISE 5

Insert commas where they are needed in the paragraph below. Each sentence contains one comma problem.

[1]Stephanie who used to share my apartment with me likes to hoard things. [2]When she was living with me we never had an empty closet or cabinet. [3]In the kitchen cabinet Stephanie would store all the items she had bought on sale. [4]The cabinet under the counter was jammed with bricks of coffee five-pound bags of sugar and rolls of paper towels that had been too good a bargain to resist. [5]Under the bathroom sink Stephanie stored the many boxes of toothpaste and bars of soap she had purchased at bargain prices. [6]"You'll be old enough to wear dentures before you use all that toothpaste" I told her once. [7]Stephanie however paid no attention to my teasing. [8]She said "It makes me feel secure to have enough of everything." [9]When Stephanie moved to another city she packed up all her carefully hoarded items to take with her. [10]I was sorry to see her go but I'm glad to have a little more room to store things now.

1. _____

2. _____

3. _____

4. _____

5. _____

6. _____

7. _____

8. _____

9. _____

10. _____

25

Other
Punctuation

$$.\,?\,!\,;\,:\,-\,(\,)$$

Punctuation marks other than the comma are the focus of this chapter. Some of these punctuation marks, such as the period and the question mark, are familiar. Others, such as the dash and the colon, are more exotic and less often used. This chapter reinforces the familiar marks of punctuation and introduces the less familiar.

End Punctuation: Period, Question Mark, and Exclamation Point

The period, the question mark, and the exclamation point are all forms of **end punctuation;** that is, they signal the end of a sentence.

The Period

The **period** is used to mark the end of a sentence that makes a statement.

Examples

✔ The car was less than two years old, but it already had nearly 35,000 miles on the odometer.

✔ The peacock unfurled its tail in a colorful display of blue and green.

Periods are also used to signal an appropriate abbreviation. Except for abbreviations in courtesy titles, such as *Mr., Ms., Dr.,* or *Rev.* used before proper names, spell out words in your paragraphs and essays. Most abbreviations should be reserved for only the most informal usage, such as your class notes or e-mail to a friend.

Examples

✘ Marg. is going to Fla. w/ her bro. in Apr. of next yr.

✔ Margaret is going to Florida with her brother in April of next year.

✔ Ms. O'Neill refuses to take Dr. Moore's advice.

The Question Mark

A **question mark** is used at the end of a direct question.

Examples

✔ Who borrowed my stapler?

✔ Does the tan Saturn belong to you?

No question mark is used with an indirect question.

✔ "I wonder if animals dream, too," said Jamie.

✔ Judge Gronsky asked if anyone objected to postponement of the hearing.

The Exclamation Point

Exclamation points are used to show extreme excitement or surprise and are seldom needed in college writing. Unless you are quoting someone who has just discovered that the building is on fire, there will be few opportunities to use an exclamation point. Interjections such as "Ouch!" or

"Yikes!" are followed by exclamation points but are seldom needed for college writing. Use exclamation points when you quote someone who is shouting or speaking excitedly. Otherwise, let your words, not your punctuation, carry the excitement of your essay.

Examples

✗ Samantha noticed smoke streaming from under the hood of her car! She realized her engine was on fire!

✔ Samantha noticed smoke streaming from under the hood of her car. She realized her engine was on fire.

✗ She pulled to the side of the road! Now she could see flames coming from under the hood!

✔ She pulled to the side of the road. Now she could see flames coming from under the hood.

✔ She heard a bystander yell, "Get away from the car!"

PRACTICE 1   USING ABBREVIATIONS AND END PUNCTUATION

In each sentence, correct an inappropriate abbreviation or place a period after an appropriate abbreviation. Then place end punctuation (period, question mark, or exclamation point) where needed.

1. Janice asked, "Do you know why the door to the study rm. is locked"

   _____

   _____

2. I asked the dr. if she would prescribe something for my cold

   _____

   _____

3. Dr Miller told me that if she prescribed medication, my cold would be gone in two weeks. Without medication, it would take fourteen days

   _____

   _____

4. Aunt Rachel wants to know if you will come to her Xmas Eve breakfast

   _____

   _____

5. "Come back" Jason yelled, as the thief ran away with the $$ he had earned.

_____

_____

The Semicolon

Semicolon to Join Independent Clauses

A **semicolon** may be used with a transitional expression between independent clauses or alone between independent clauses that are closely related. (For a more detailed discussion of this use of the semicolon, see Chapter 15, "Sentence Variety," and Chapter 16, "Run-On Sentences.")

Examples

✔ The copier was out of order this morning; it seems to be working now, though.

✔ The cell phone was convenient and fun to use; however, the monthly fees were high.

Semicolon to Join Items in a List

Ordinarily, items in a list are joined by commas. However, if the items themselves contain commas, avoid confusion by using semicolons to join the items.

Examples

✔ Arlene has relatives in Richmond, Virginia; Atlanta, Georgia; and Houston, Texas.

✔ The new book on heart-healthy eating was written by James Hobson; Carletta Berry, Ph.D.; and Lazarus Salter, M.D.

PRACTICE 2   USING SEMICOLONS

Use semicolons in the following sentences to join independent clauses or items in a series.

1. The coffee was too strong Karla felt jittery throughout the morning.

    _____

    _____

2. Andrew says he rejects his parents' materialistic values he would rather serve others than enrich his bank account.

    _____

    _____

3. Michael's three children were born on April 1, 1995 May 3, 1997 and July 29, 1999.

    _____

    _____

4. Our city's tap water is of high quality in fact, it tastes better than most bottled water.

    _____

    _____

5. At its first meeting, the club elected the following officers: Amy Gray, President Juanita Gonzales, President-elect Perry Malden, Treasurer and Kim Park, Recorder.

    _____

    _____

Colons and Dashes: Formal and Informal Punctuation

The Colon

The **colon** is used to introduce a list, a restatement, or a clarification. The most important thing to remember when you use a colon is that the words that come before the colon must always be a complete sentence.

1. A colon is sometimes used to introduce a list. A complete sentence must come before the colon.

Examples

✘ On his overnight trip, Jamal carried only: a toothbrush, a change of clothes, and a good book.

✔ On his overnight trip, Jamal carried only the necessities: a toothbrush, a change of clothes, and a good book.

It is also correct—and sometimes simpler—to integrate a list into a sentence without using a colon.

✔ On his overnight trip, Jamal carried only a toothbrush, a change of clothes, and a good book.

2. A colon is used to introduce a restatement or clarification of an idea. A complete sentence must come before the colon.

Examples

✔ Ed says there are two reasons he stays broke: Visa and MasterCard.

The words *Visa and MasterCard*, preceded by a colon, restate and clarify the "two reasons" that Ed stays broke.

✔ Vera was never out of her family's reach: she carried a cellular phone and wore a pager wherever she went.

The colon introduces a clarification of the idea "never out of her family's reach."

The Dash

While the colon is a formal mark of punctuation, the **dash** is informal. The first two uses of a dash are exactly like those of the colon: to introduce a list, a restatement, or a clarification. A dash is also used to set off material that a writer wants to emphasize.

1. A dash introduces a list or restatement. When used in this way, a dash must be preceded by a complete sentence. A dash is typed as two hyphens, with no spaces before or after.

Examples

✔ On his overnight trip, Jamal carried only the necessities—a toothbrush, a change of clothes, and a good book.

The dash introduces a list.

✔ Ed says there are two reasons he stays broke—Visa and MasterCard.

The dash is used here to introduce a restatement and clarification of "reasons he stays broke."

2. A dash is used to set off material that the writer wants to emphasize.

✔ It was his easygoing personality—not his money—that made him popular.

A more formal way of punctuating this sentence would be to use commas to set off the interrupter: *It was his easygoing personality, not his money, that made him popular.*

✔ There was so much to do—bills to pay, errands to run, and yard work to finish—that Tom did not know where to begin.

One way of expressing the idea in the sentence more formally would be to use two sentences: *There was so much to do that Tom did not know where to begin. He had bills to pay, errands to run, and yard work to finish.*

Parentheses: Tools of Understatement

While dashes emphasize, **parentheses** downplay. Parentheses are used to enclose material that a reader could skip over without missing the more important ideas.

Examples

✔ Miss Clara, my elderly neighbor, says there is no better way to spend a Sunday afternoon than listening to Handel (her favorite composer) and drinking a cup of tea.

✔ Harlan told the salesman he loved driving the car. He liked the color (maroon) and he loved the interior (a rich, tan leather). But he hated the price.

PRACTICE 3 USING COLONS, DASHES, AND PARENTHESES

Rewrite each sentence as indicated, punctuating the italicized portion of the sentence with a colon, a dash (or dashes), or parentheses.

1. Analida says that staying sane on rainy weekends at home with her children requires just three things. It requires *plenty of patience, a good supply of games and songs, and a pair of heavy-duty earplugs.*

   Directions: Rewrite as one sentence, with a colon introducing the list. Remove words as needed.

   _____

2. The professor said that the price of the hardback dictionary, *just eighteen dollars*, was small, considering all the words we would get for our money.

   Directions: Rewrite so that the price of the dictionary is deemphasized. You will need to remove the commas.

   _____

3. Allan says if his house were on fire and he could save just one possession, the choice would be easy: *his computer.*

   Directions: Rewrite so that the restatement is set off in an informal way rather than a formal way.

   _____

4. Dad's shoes (*tan loafers he has had since his college days*) are so old they are coming apart at the seams.

   Directions: Rewrite so that the parenthetical material is emphasized. Assume that the sentence can be written informally.

   _____

5. The half-gallon carton contained three flavors of ice cream: *chocolate, vanilla, and strawberry.*

   Directions: Rewrite so that the list is introduced in an informal way.

   _____

Review Exercises

Complete the Review Exercises to see how well you have learned the skills addressed in this chapter. As you work through the exercises, go back through the chapter to review any of the rules you do not understand completely.

REVIEW EXERCISE 1

Look at the punctuation printed in color in each sentence; then briefly explain the rule that justifies its use. The first one is done for you.

1. After the unexpected frost, the plants on Mrs. Kowalski's porch turned brown and died.

   A period is used to end a sentence that makes a statement.

   _____

2. Gary asked whether I had ever been to Disney World.

   _____

   _____

3. The scientist revealed his formula for success: perseverance, hard work, and a little luck.

   _____

   _____

4. The movie (which has set box-office records) contains scenes of extreme violence: two explosions, a hanging, and seventeen deaths by shooting.

   _____

   _____

5. The salesperson—who must have been in a bad mood that day—was surly and unhelpful.

   _____

   _____

6. Traffic was backed up for miles on the interstate; hundreds of cars and trucks had slowed to a crawl.

   _____

   _____

7. "Hey! Watch out for that open manhole!" the worker called to the pedestrian.

   _____

   _____

8. The company had offices in Seattle, Washington; London, England; and Tokyo, Japan.

   _____

   _____

9. The mailbox contained only two pieces of mail—a drug store flyer and a credit card offer.

_____

_____

10. At 5:00 A.M., a garbage truck rumbled past Ed's house; Ed woke suddenly, wondering if he had remembered to take the trash to the curb.

_____

_____

REVIEW EXERCISE 2

Fill the blank(s) in each sentence with a period, question mark, exclamation point, semicolon, colon, dash (or dashes), or parentheses. On some questions, more than one answer may be possible. Be sure you can justify the answer you choose.

1. Dawn slammed on brakes when the dog ___ a slow-moving basset hound ___ lumbered into the road.

_____

2. Steve could not remember the accident that had totaled his car and put him in the hospital, but he was sure of one thing ___ he was lucky to be alive.

_____

3. "Call 911 ___" yelled Andrea as she ran past the door.

_____

4. The lease states that any resident who has a pet ___ either a dog or a cat ___ must pay a nonrefundable pet deposit of two hundred dollars.

_____

5. "Do you mind if I cut in line ___ I have only two items," the woman said.

_____

6. The company's employees will be off on Thursday, November 27 ___ Friday, November 28 ___ Thursday, December 26 ___ and Friday, December 27.

_____

7. After Tiana loaded a new program ___ a virus scanner ___ on her computer, she felt safer downloading material from the Internet.

_____

8. "I won ___ I won! ___" the red-haired woman yelled, waving her Bingo card in the air.

_____

9. The company vice president said that three things would kill a job candidate's chances ___ late arrival, poor language skills, and a sloppy appearance.

10. The woman rolled down her window and handed something ___ probably a dollar bill ___ to the man standing at the interstate exit.

REVIEW EXERCISE 3

In each sentence, add a period, question mark, exclamation point, semicolon, colon, dash (or dashes), or parentheses.

1. From the street, John could hear the persistent whoop of a car alarm

2. "Could you repeat the fourteen flavors of ice cream again" Millie asked the server.

3. The Simmonses were devastated when the house their first home together burned to the ground.

4. "Come out with your hands on your head" the police officer yelled.

5. After pulling a twelve-hour shift, Kelvin wanted only one thing sleep.

6. The headline read, "Con Artists Foiled in Aluminum Siding Scam"

7. The part for the dishwasher had to be ordered the salesperson said it would take two weeks.

8. William's parents told him he had two choices go to school or get a job.

9. "Why didn't you call me if you needed help" Natasha asked.

10. "Hey, mister, you left your wallet" the clerk called.

REVIEW EXERCISE 4

Fill in the blanks with the correct punctuation.

[1]When he twisted his knee playing softball, Jack made his own diagnosis__just a muscle pull. [2]There was a sharp pain as he slid into second__when he tried to get up, he could not. [3]"We need help here__" the second baseman called, and his teammates came running to help him off the field. [4]"Do you want me to take you to the emergency room__" his coach asked. [5]But Jack insisted that all he needed was an ice pack and a good night's sleep__ [6]The next morning, Jack's knee was a rainbow of colors__mostly black, blue, and yellow__and was swollen to the size of a grapefruit. [7]He called a friend__his softball buddy Levon__to drive him to the doctor's office. [8]His doctor said nothing was broken but told Jack his softball days were over__at least for a while. [9]Now, Jack walks with the help of crutches__ [10]Jack won't be sliding into second for a while, but he will be at every game to support his teammates__

26

Apostrophes

The florist may sell wonderful flowers, but her use of the apostrophe leaves a great deal to be desired. Can you pinpoint the two apostrophe problems in the sign? If you can't now, you will be able to after reading this chapter, which outlines the two main uses of apostrophes: forming contractions and showing possession.

Apostrophes in Contractions

Contractions are informal or conversational shortenings of words: *doesn't* for *does not*, *won't* for *will not*, and *it's* for *it is* or *it has*. Contractions are used in informal writing, but are generally inappropriate for formal or scholarly writing. You will find them in some journalistic writing, in some textbooks, in works of fiction, and in informal essays. However, contractions are considered inappropriate in reports of academic research or in legal documents. Your instructor will specify the level of formality you should use in your essays and other writings.

To form a contraction, replace omitted letters with a single apostrophe. Close any spaces between words.

Examples

couldn't = could not

don't = do not

hasn't = has not

isn't = is not

won't = will not (Won't is an irregular contraction: the *i* in *will* changes to an *o*.)

wouldn't = would not

PRACTICE 1   FORMING CONTRACTIONS

Make a contraction of each expression. Be sure to place an apostrophe where letters are omitted, not in the space between the words.

1. she is   _____

2. I am   _____

3. would not   _____

4. does not   _____

5. he is   _____

6. it is   _____

7. we are   _____

8. I will   _____

9. they are   _____

10. cannot   _____

PRACTICE 2   USING CONTRACTIONS

Underline the error in each sentence. Then supply the missing apostrophe in the contraction and write the contraction in the blank provided.

_____ 1. Mariko says shes well enough to play in the hockey game next week.

_____ 2. Arthur hasnt applied for either of the jobs I told him about.

_____ 3. It isnt unusual for Tabitha to bring home dead birds and mice.

_____ 4. Its going to be hot and sunny tomorrow, just in time for our trip to the beach.

_____ 5. "After Ive found a job," said Roberta, "I have to worry about paying back my student loan."

_____ 6. "Sorry," said the teller, "but were not supposed to cash out-of-town checks."

_____ 7. "Isnt Karen planning to drop this class before midterm?" said Dean.

_____ 8. Art had no money, but he couldnt resist visiting the electronics store in the mall.

_____ 9. The children dont like couscous; they want hamburgers instead.

_____ 10. "Give me a minute," said Ella. "Ill be right back."

Apostrophes to Show Possession

If you could not use apostrophes to show **possession,** you would have to rely on long, tedious constructions such as "I drove the car of my father to the house of Ray to study for the test of tomorrow," instead of "I drove my father's car to Ray's house to study for tomorrow's test."

Making Nouns Possessive

There are two rules for making nouns possessive.

Rule 1: Add an apostrophe and *s* (*'s*) to form the possessive of singular nouns and of plurals that do not end in *s*.

Examples

the dish that belongs to the dog = the *dog's* dish

the pages of the magazine = the *magazine's* pages

the work of a day = a *day's* work

the flower garden belonging to Carlton = *Carlton's* flower garden

the toys that belong to the children = the *children's* toys

the office of my boss = my *boss's* office

PRACTICE 3   FORMING POSSESSIVES OF SINGULAR NOUNS

Convert the ten expressions to possessives using *'s*.

1.   The glow of the flashlight = _____

2.   The blue shirt belonging to Charlie = _____

3.   the office of Dr. Bell = _____

4.   the career of the pianist = _____

5.   the schedule of next week = _____

---

* Grammar Alert!

When a singular word ends in *s*, it is also acceptable to use an apostrophe alone to make it possessive: *Mr. Jones'* job, *Dickens'* novels, the *boss'* office, the *crabgrass'* rapid growth.

Rule 2: If a plural noun already ends in *s*, add an apostrophe after the *s* to make it possessive.

Examples

the lawn belonging to the Smiths = the *Smiths'* lawn

the brightness of the stars = the *stars'* brightness

PRACTICE 4   FORMING POSSESSIVES OF PLURAL NOUNS

Convert the ten expressions to possessives using an apostrophe.

1.   the jobs of my sisters = _____

2.   the leashes of the dogs = _____

3. the energy of the dancers = _____

4. the determination of the athletes = _____

5. the appearance of the cupcakes = _____

6. the test grades of two classes = _____

7. the keyboards of the computers = _____

8. the overseas trip of the Joneses = _____

9. the barking of the dogs = _____

10. the movements of the actors = _____

PRACTICE 5   FORMING POSSESSIVES OF SINGULAR AND PLURAL NOUNS

Convert the ten expressions to possessives by adding 's or by adding an apostrophe after the s.

1. the whir of the ceiling fan = _____

2. the tick of the clock = _____

3. the smiles of the children = _____

4. the sale of Sports World = _____

5. the disgust of Mrs. Bliss = _____

6. the impact of the suggestion = _____

7. the hairstyles of the women = _____

8. the strong belief of Gina Terrino = _____

9. the glow of the streetlights = _____

10. the web site of the college = _____

Distinguishing Possessives from Simple Plurals

To use apostrophes correctly, it is important to distinguish between possessives and simple plurals. A plural may be followed by a verb, a prepositional phrase, or by nothing at all. Words that show possession end in *s* like plurals, but they are immediately followed by something that is being possessed, as in "Mom's *homemade chicken and dumplings*" or the "*horse's mane.*"

Possessive (apostrophe used)	Plural (no apostrophe used)
Amy's computer	computers used in class
a day's work	days in a month
Mother's Day	Mothers Against Drunk Driving
a king's ransom	kings in the seventeenth century
Placido's lost wallet	the wallet Placido lost
the tornadoes' fury	several tornadoes
the washer's spin cycle	the broken washers

PRACTICE 6   DISTINGUISHING POSSESSIVES FROM PLURALS

In each sentence, underline the noun that ends in *s'* or *'s*. If the noun is possessive, write *possessive* in the blank provided. If the noun is simply a plural, remove the apostrophe and write the corrected plural form in the blank. The first one is done for you.

_____   1. Sometimes I think my parents' are hopelessly old fashioned.

_____   2. The dog's expression was mournful.

_____   3. The speaker's voice was so soothing that Kim nearly fell asleep.

_____   4. Anthony visited several schools' before making his decision.

_____   5. Many years ago, most offices had typewriters' instead of computers.

_____   6. Amy had never liked the carpet's color.

_____   7. The Smith's host a neighborhood party every Fourth of July.

_____   8. The youngest employee in the library is thirty year's old.

_____   9. The manatee's large gray body moves gracefully in the water.

_____ 10. The benefit's of a good breakfast include increased alertness and improved mental function during the morning hours.

Possessive Forms of Pronouns

Personal pronouns (*I, we, you, he, she, it,* and *they*) have their own possessive forms that never require an apostrophe. These forms include *my, mine, our, ours, your, yours, his, hers, its, their,* and *theirs.*

The pronoun that is the focus of the most confusion is *its*. Since the possessive form of a pronoun never takes an apostrophe, *its* is the possessive form, meaning *belonging to it. It's*, the form with the apostrophe, always means *it is* or *it has*.

Examples

The lawnmower seems to have lost *its* pep. (belonging to it)

It's too hot to mow, anyway. (it is)

That old paring knife has outlived *its* usefulness. (belonging to it)

It's time to buy a replacement. (it is)

PRACTICE 7   CORRECTING APOSTROPHE ERRORS WITH *ITS* AND *IT'S*

Underline and correct the apostrophe errors in the following sentences.

1. "Its essential that you come to class every day," Professor Vanta told the class.

    _____

2. The house was old, and it's owner had not painted or repaired it for many years.

    _____

3. Ted is committed to getting in shape; its his first priority.

    _____

4. The salmon swiftly made it's way upstream.

    _____

5. Because Lindsay has not had time to finish her report, its sitting unfinished on her desk.

    _____

Proofreading for Apostrophe Errors

Apostrophes Incorrectly Omitted from Possessives

To find apostrophes incorrectly omitted from possessives, check each noun ending in *s* to see if it is followed by something it possesses.

✗   The *cars brakes* made a squealing sound whenever Vashti came to a stop.

Cars is followed by the word *brakes*. Do *brakes* belong to *cars*? Yes. But does the apostrophe go before or after the *s*? Look for clues to whether the original word (before it was made possessive) was intended to be singular or plural. The main clue in this sentence lies in the words *whenever Vashti came to a stop*. There is one driver, therefore also one car.

Brakes is followed by *made*, a verb, so it is plural, not possessive.

✔ The car's brakes made a squealing sound whenever Vashti came to a stop.

✘ The *employees paychecks* were small, but their work was strenuous.

Does anything belong to *employees*? Yes, *paychecks* belong to *employees*, but does the apostrophe go before or after the *s*? Since there is more than one paycheck, and since the pronoun *their* is used to refer to employees, the word *employees* is clearly plural. Therefore, the apostrophe goes after the *s*.

Does anything belong to *paychecks*? No, a verb follows the word, so *paychecks* is simply a plural.

✔ The employees' paychecks were small, but their work was strenuous.

PRACTICE 8   CORRECTING APOSTROPHE ERRORS

Supply the omitted apostrophe in each of the following sentences.

1. The driveways concrete surface had cracked in several places.

_____

2. The speakers voice could not be heard clearly in the back of the auditorium.

_____

3. The books ending was disappointing to many of its readers.

_____

4. Sam and Elaine said they spent two weeks salary in one weekend.

_____

5. The doctor said Elizabeths shoulder should begin to feel better in about two weeks.

_____

Apostrophes Placed Incorrectly in Possessives

An incorrectly placed apostrophe is usually a confusion of singular and plural. As you proofread, target words ending in *'s* or *s'* and look for clues that tell you whether the word is singular or plural.

✗ For the landowner, the *tree's* beauty outweighed their value as lumber.

The pronoun *their* suggests more than one tree.

✔ For the landowner, the trees' beauty outweighed their value as lumber.

✗ The *buildings'* roof leaked and was in need of repair.

Only one roof is mentioned, so there is just one building.

✔ The building's roof leaked and was in need of repair.

PRACTICE 9   CORRECTING APOSTROPHE ERRORS

Underline and correct the apostrophe errors in the following sentences.

1. The airplanes' wings glinted in the sunlight as it flew overhead.

   _____

2. The twin's grade point averages are nearly identical.

   _____

3. Andre swept a days' accumulation of litter and cigarette butts from the sidewalk in front of the restaurant.

   _____

4. At her husbands' urging, Valerie decided to enroll in college.

   _____

5. As the tennis player's skills improved, they enjoyed the game more.

   _____

Review Exercises

Complete the Review Exercises to see how well you have learned the skills addressed in this chapter. As you work through the exercises, go back through the chapter to review any of the rules you do not understand completely.

REVIEW EXERCISE 1

Convert the ten expressions in the exercise to possessives using *'s* or an apostrophe.

1. the beam of the searchlight = _____
2. the call of a mockingbird = _____
3. the opening of the museum = _____
4. the covers of the books = _____
5. the weed trimmer belonging to Jacob = _____
6. the craters of the moon = _____
7. a rest of three days = _____
8. the voice of Ms. Bradshaw = _____
9. the route of the truck driver = _____
10. the faded color of the blankets = _____

REVIEW EXERCISE 2

Each sentence has an omitted apostrophe in a contraction or a possessive form. Underline the error; then, in the blank, write the word with the apostrophe placed correctly.

_____ 1. After turning his ankle, Allen couldnt complete his run.

_____ 2. The restaurants lunch menu featured a variety of homemade soups.

_____ 3. Using an ice pack helped to ease the pain in Ronitas knee.

_____ 4. The tabloids headline read, "I Married a Space Alien!"

_____ 5. Amin stood on a dock at the rivers edge and watched the sun set.

_____ 6. "Work is important," said Dana. "But its my family that really matters."

_____ 7. Memos, notes, and papers entirely covered the desks surface.

_____ 8. The office buildings immense lobby was obviously created to impress visitors.

_____ 9. The letter said that Freds car payment was overdue.

_____ **10.** A pirates treasure was said to be buried on one of the small islands.

Review Exercise 3

Each sentence contains two omitted apostrophes. Underline the error; then, in the blank, write the words with the apostrophes placed correctly.

1. Phillip says that he hasnt had a good nights sleep in two weeks.

_____

2. The hospitals smoke alarms were checked twice a month for the patients safety.

_____

3. To the children waiting for Santas arrival, the clocks hands seemed to move slowly.

_____

4. The students grades were not high enough for their instructors satisfaction.

_____

5. "Ive put in two days work on this group project and not one person has helped me," Melissa said angrily.

_____

Review Exercise 4

Each numbered item contains two apostrophe errors, one omitted apostrophe in a contraction or a possessive form and one misplaced or unnecessary apostrophe. Underline the error; then write the correct form of each word below.

1. Lees garage is piled high with tools and bag's of fertilizer.

_____

2. "Its been warm for October," said Max. "Usually, temperature's are in the fifties by now."

_____

3. An old sofa and several bundles of clothes' sat on the porch, awaiting the Goodwill trucks arrival.

_____

4. The cough remedys price was high, but it's performance was disappointing.

_____

5. Tom said his VCRs feature's include a remote control and a preprogramming feature that he has never learned how to use.

_____

REVIEW EXERCISE 5

Underline and correct the ten apostrophe errors in the restaurant review, writing your answers in the numbered spaces. Each numbered section of the review contains one error. Apostrophes may be misplaced, missing, or unnecessary.

[1]Restaurant Review: Eds R. K. Café

[2]When I told a friend I was reviewing Ed's R. K. Café on Interstate Drive, he whispered, "No! Havent you heard the rumors about how Ed gets his meat?" [3]I told my friend that rumor's were common in small towns, and I offered to treat him to dinner and put those rumors to rest. [4]There were no line's on Monday night at Ed's, and as we sat down, Ed himself came in with a large cloth sack. [5]He looked surprised to see customers but said, "Youre lucky, I was just bringing in some groceries." [6]I decided on Steak Michelin, which I assumed to be a French dish, and ordered "Sunday Drivers Stew" for my friend, who had suddenly excused himself from the table. [7]When it came, the Steak Michelin, pounded very flat with some sort of tool that left an attractive zigzag pattern on it's surface, met all my expectations. [8]My friends' stew smelled delicious, and looked as if it contained several kinds of meat, but he said he was not feeling well and that he could not eat. [9]In any case, its a pleasure to recommend Ed's, which is close enough to the highway to be convenient for everyone. [10]Service is slow, but worth the wait, and the meat taste's wonderfully fresh.

1. _____   6. _____

2. _____   7. _____

3. _____   8. _____

4. _____   9. _____

5. _____   10. _____

27

Quotation Marks

Quotation marks are visual signals that give a reader information that would otherwise have to be conveyed in words. They are a kind of academic shorthand that says, "Someone else wrote, said, or thought these words" or "These words are the title of a short work." Underlining and italics say, "These words are the title of a long work." Learning to use quotation marks, underlining, and italics adds another dimension to your ability to communicate within the academic world.

Quotation Marks to Signal Quotations

Direct Quotations

Quotation marks are used to signal **direct quotation;** that is, they are placed around the exact words that someone speaks, writes, or thinks. As you look at the examples, notice that when a comma or period comes at

413

the end of a quotation, it is always placed inside the quotation mark.
When a direct question is quoted, the question mark also goes inside the
quotation marks.

Examples

"I'll pick up the dry cleaning on my way home," said Pat.

Keiko said, "I don't need to go to the gym. I stay in shape lugging all
these books around the campus."

The child asked, "Why don't people have wings?"

"Did you bring the doughnuts?" asked David.

PRACTICE 1   USING QUOTATION MARKS WITH DIRECT QUOTATIONS

Place quotation marks around direct quotations.

1. I am sorry I'm late, said Al.

   _____

2. Is this something we need to know for the test? Karen asked the professor.

   _____

3. The bumper sticker said, If you can read this, thank a teacher.

   _____

4. Alicia said, I think there's a gas station at the next exit.

   _____

5. I get a headache whenever it rains, complained Rosa.

   _____

Split Quotations

Some direct quotations are **split quotations.** Below are two rules for splitting quotations.

1. When you split a sentence, use commas to set off the *tag* (such as *she
   said*) that tells who said, thought, or wrote the words you are quoting.

   "When you come through the door," Raven told her son, "please
   try not to slam it."

2. When there is a complete sentence before and a complete sentence after the tag, put a comma after the first sentence and a period after the tag.

> "I couldn't turn in my paper yesterday," Alex told the professor. "I wasn't here."

PRACTICE 2   USING QUOTATION MARKS AND COMMAS WITH DIRECT QUOTATIONS

Place quotation marks around direct quotations, and add commas where they are needed.

1. Your stock clerks need to be more careful the customer told the manager. This milk was expired when I bought it.

    _____

    _____

2. My job as a human cannonball is great said the circus performer. Business is booming.

    _____

    _____

3. If you can't say something nice Aunt Dolly said come over here and talk to me.

    _____

    _____

4. You have won third prize in a beauty contest the Monopoly card read. Collect $10.

    _____

    _____

5. For Mother's Day this year Charlotte told her husband I'd like a day of peace and quiet.

    _____

    _____

PRACTICE 3   USING QUOTATION MARKS AND COMMAS WITH DIRECT QUOTATIONS

Place quotation marks around direct quotations, and add commas or question marks as needed.

1. Are you new to this area the real estate agent asked.

   _____

   _____

2. I hate roller coasters said Anthony. I am afraid of heights.

   _____

   _____

3. Spreading his arms wide, the singer shouted Hello, Philadelphia!

   _____

   _____

4. I know you love your hunting dogs Janice told her husband but do we have to take them on vacation with us?

   _____

   _____

5. You have been preapproved for a $10,000 line of credit the letter began.

   _____

   _____

Indirect Quotations

An **indirect quotation** is a paraphrase. It repeats the essence of what a person said. It may repeat some or all of the words, but it is not a word-for-word quotation. The word *that* is stated or implied before an indirect quotation. An indirect quotation is not set off by quotation marks.

Examples

Ashley said that she needed a vacation.

Ashley said she needed a vacation.

The two examples above are indirect quotations. They do not repeat Ashley's exact words (Ashley did not use the word *she*). The word *that* is stated in the first example and implied in the second. Therefore, no quotation marks are used.

PRACTICE 4   IDENTIFYING DIRECT AND INDIRECT QUOTATIONS

On the line provided, label each quotation as direct (*D*) or indirect (*I*).

_____ 1. Ellen said, "I would have caught the ball if the sun had not been in my eyes."

_____ 2. Ellen said that she would have caught the ball if the sun had not been in her eyes.

_____ 3. The customer in the drive-through said he wanted extra ketchup.

_____ 4. The bumper sticker said, "In case of alien abduction, driver's seat will be empty."

_____ 5. "If you are going to lunch," said Zoe, "would you bring back a sandwich for me?"

_____ 6. Brandon said, "Here, Mom. I made this clay volcano for you."

_____ 7. Jan asked, "Has anyone watered the fern?"

_____ 8. Jan asked if anyone had watered the fern.

_____ 9. The salesperson told Bill that the tires should last for the life of the car.

_____ 10. Brad said that he could live without his car but could not get along without his bike.

PRACTICE 5   WORKING WITH DIRECT AND INDIRECT QUOTATIONS

On the line provided, label each quotation as direct (*D*) or indirect (*I*). Place quotation marks around direct quotations, and leave indirect quotations as they are.

_____ 1. Ray said, Mr. Bartlett, I can work nights but not weekends.

_____

_____ 2. Ray told Mr. Bartlett that he could work nights but not weekends.

_____

_____ 3. The headline read, Too Few Americans Exercise.

_____

_____ 4. Two out of three people surveyed said they were better off financially than they had been last year.

_____

_____ 5. Perry said, I wish I could afford a new truck.

_____

_____ 6. The article said Americans received fewer vacation days than
          Europeans.

_____

_____ 7. The child said she knew nothing about the broken cookie jar.

_____

_____ 8. I'm not in the mood to watch a video, said Theo.

_____

_____ 9. Would you like dessert? asked the server.

_____

_____ 10. The salesperson said that she could order any color we wanted.

_____

Quotation Marks, Underlining, and Italics to Set off Titles

Quotation marks, underlining, and italics act as academic shorthand to signal a title. **Quotation marks** are used around titles of short works or works that are contained within other works. The following types of titles are set off by quotation marks:

1. Chapter title (short works contained within a longer work)

    "Subject-Verb Agreement"

    "Sentence Variety"

2. Essays

    "Barbie Madness"

    "Neat People vs. Sloppy People"

---

* *Grammar Alert!*

When you write *about* an essay, place the title of the essay within quotation marks. When you type the title of *your* essay on a cover sheet or at the head of the essay, do not use quotation marks.

---

3. Individual episodes of a TV series (short works contained within the longer series)

> "Phil Silvers: Top Banana" (in the series Biography)
>
> "The Slicer" (an episode of Seinfeld)

4. Song titles (short works, often contained within a longer album of works)

> "The Star-Spangled Banner"
>
> "Georgia on My Mind"

5. Newspaper articles

> "NFL injury list grows"
>
> "Hungry for Housing"

6. Poems

> "I Wandered Lonely as a Cloud"
>
> "Fern Hill"

7. Short stories

> "Sonny's Blues"
>
> "The Ones Who Walk Away from Omelas"

Underlining and italics are used to set off the title of a long work, a continuing work (such as a comic strip or television series) or a complete published work such as a pamphlet or brochure. Use underlining or italics with the following types of titles:

---

* Grammar Alert!

Italics are used instead of underlining published materials, and modern word processors have italic capability. However, the MLA (Modern Language Association) recommends underlining for clarity.

---

1. Books

> The Color Purple
>
> There Are No Accidents

2. Comic strips (a series containing individual daily or weekly strips)

> Dilbert
>
> Jumpstart

3. Newspapers

> The New York Times
>
> The Macon Telegraph and News

4. Anthologies (collections) of poetry or short stories

> The Poem: An Anthology
> Discovering Literature: Stories, Poems, Plays

5. Compact discs

> La Pipa de la Paz
> Hung Down Head

6. Television programs

> Pop-Up Video
> Inside the Actors Studio

7. Movies

> E.T.
> Titanic

PRACTICE 6   USING QUOTATION MARKS AND UNDERLINING WITH TITLES

In each sentence, use quotation marks and underlining to set off titles.

1. Tonight's episode of Wild Discovery is entitled Cheetah.

   _____

   _____

2. For next week, the professor assigned a chapter called Using Critical Thinking Skills in the book College Success.

   _____

   _____

3. Rita's favorite song on Joan Baez: From Every Stage is Love Is Just a Four-Letter Word.

   _____

   _____

4. From a book called Poetry: An Introduction, the class read The Ballad of Birmingham by Dudley Randall.

   _____

   _____

5. The headline in the Wall Street Journal read Economy on the right track, but Sam did not feel any richer.

   _____

   _____

Review Exercises

Complete the Review Exercises to see how well you have learned the skills addressed in this chapter. As you work through the exercises, go back through the chapter to review any of the rules you do not understand completely.

REVIEW EXERCISE 1

Rewrite the following sentences, placing quotation marks around direct quotations.

1. I need just one extra hour in the day, said Althea.

   _____

   _____

2. Patrick Henry said, Give me liberty or give me death.

   _____

   _____

3. I wish people wouldn't throw trash out their car windows, said Alphonso, especially since most of it seems to land in my yard.

   _____

   _____

4. You should have been at the game, said Claudius. We won fourteen to two.

   _____

   _____

5. The car's bumper sticker read, I may be slow, but I'm ahead of you.

   _____

   _____

6. The slip of paper on Gaia's fortune cookie said, Wherever you go, there you are.

   _____

   _____

7. I am sorry your goldfish died, said Andi's mother. Let's hold its funeral in the bathroom so we can send it back to the sea.

   _____

   _____

8. Let's pick up a copy of *Consumer Reports* before we buy a washer, said Nicole.

_____

_____

9. I like Joseph, but he's not very reliable, said Paula.

_____

_____

10. I wish I could lose weight without dieting, Betty sighed.

_____

_____

REVIEW EXERCISE 2

Rewrite the following sentences, placing quotation marks around direct quotations. Four of the sentences are indirect quotations that do not require quotation marks.

1. The loan officer told Brad and Lexie that she hoped they hadn't had to wait too long.

_____

_____

2. Why are your paws so wet? Alfreda asked her dog.

_____

_____

3. If he could have talked, Alfreda's dog might have said that he had walked through a puddle on the way home.

_____

_____

4. When she came back from the All-Night Moonlight Sale-a-Thon, Bernice said, Never again.

_____

_____

5. What is this disgusting-looking bug? asked Phillip.

_____

_____

6. Patrick said he had already finished his paper.

7. If I have to eat spaghetti one more time, said Nick, I'll turn into a meatball.

8. Too late, said his wife.

9. I've got it, said the worker as he grabbed one end of the sofa.

10. The disk jockey said that he would play audience requests for the next two hours.

REVIEW EXERCISE 3

Correct the following sentences, using underlining or quotation marks to set off titles.

1. Wendy took out a library book called Cold Mountain.

2. Before Chet left for the video store, his wife said she would leave him if he rented Men in Black again.

3. Chapter 10, Taking Care of Yourself, discusses stress and nutrition.

4. Meghan's Irish grandfather believes there's no sweeter sound than Danny Boy sung by an Irish tenor.

5. Luis bought an album by Los Fabulosos Cadillacs called Fabulosos Calavera.

    _____

    _____

6. Derek swears there is a country song called If My Nose Were Full of Nickels, I'd Blow It All on You.

    _____

    _____

7. The Complete Works of Shakespeare, Bjorn's text for English 210, must weigh at least ten pounds.

    _____

    _____

8. After new special effects were added to the 1970s movie Star Wars, it was brought out again for a new generation.

    _____

    _____

9. When it came out, the movie Titanic broke box-office records.

    _____

    _____

10. A small headline at the top of the page said No clues in hit and run.

    _____

    _____

REVIEW EXERCISE 4

In the following sentence groups, place quotation marks around direct quotations. Use underlining or quotation marks to set off titles. Do not place indirect quotations in quotation marks.

1. Karen said her trip over spring break was a disaster. The hotel claimed to have no record of our reservation, she said.

    _____

    _____

    _____

2. Give me just a minute to finish getting ready, said Aimee. You've already had an hour, said her husband.

    _____

    _____

    _____

3. Chloe bought a bumper sticker that read, I Never Eat Anything with a Face. That's disgusting, said Chloe's mother.

    _____

    _____

    _____

4. David clipped an article called Walk off pounds for good from Tuesday's paper. The article said that people who combine diet with exercise keep weight off longer than those who only diet.

    _____

    _____

    _____

5. Yesterday, Sophie bought a book called The Complete Idiot's Guide to Reaching Your Goals. It sounds like it was written just for you, her friend joked.

    _____

    _____

    _____

Eight Editing Exercises

Find and correct the ten sentence errors in the paragraph below. In the blanks provided, write the number of the sentence in which you find each error, followed by your correction. Two of the sentences are correct.

2 errors in words commonly confused
2 sentence fragments
2 run-on sentences
4 subject-verb agreement errors

[1]I read an article not long ago that claimed that the weather effects the human body. [2]Since I can link both my headaches and my moods to the weather. [3]I can support the claim made by the author of the article. [4]My headaches begins with the drop in barometric pressure that precedes a storm. [5]The clouds roll in a throbbing pain that no aspirin can completely relieve begins on one side of my head. [6]As soon as the clouds dissipate. [7]My headache slips away like a forgotten memory. [8]Additionally, winter affect my state of mind like no other season. [9]With the falling of the leaves, my generally upbeat attitude begins to fall as well I slide into a gloomy mood. [10]According to the article, the changes in my mood is symptomatic of a condition called Seasonal Affective Disorder, or SAD. [11]Plenty of sunshine eventually lifts my spirits. [12]The whether does play an important role in my well-being.

_____

_____

_____

_____

_____

_____

_____

_____

_____

_____

Editing Exercise 2   Commas, Words Commonly Confused, and Comma Splices

Find and correct the ten sentence errors in the paragraph below. Each sentence contains an error.

1 comma omitted after introductory element
2 commas omitted in a series of three items
3 errors in words commonly confused
4 comma splices

[1]When I look back over the jobs I've held none of them taught me more about responsibility and hard work than my summer job at Tossi's Bakery. [2]My principle responsibility was to arrive at the bakery at 5:20 every morning and prepare the machines and the ingredients for the baker. [3]One Saturday morning I turned off the alarm rolled over for just one more minute under the covers, and drifted back to sleep. [4]On that day, disappointed customers did not get there fresh bread and breakfast rolls when the bakery opened at 7:00. [5]Ashamed of my irresponsibility, I promised Mr. Tossi that I would never be late again, I never was. [6]I also learned too perform hard physical work. [7]I hauled huge sacks of flour, sugar and other ingredients from the storehouse in the back of the bakery to a platform near the large machines that blended the ingredients into dough. [8]At first, I dragged myself home each day and barely moved until the next morning, however, I soon adjusted to the hard work. [9]The huge bags of flour seemed lighter, the workday no longer

seemed to last forever. [10]My job at the bakery lasted just one summer, it helped mold me into the responsible person that I am today.

1. _____   6. _____

2. _____   7. _____

3. _____   8. _____

4. _____   9. _____

5. _____   10. _____

Editing Exercise 3   Apostrophes, Commas, Subject-Verb Agreement

Find and correct the ten sentence errors in the paragraph below. Each sentence contains an error.

1 apostrophe error
3 commas omitted after introductory element
6 subject-verb agreement errors

[1]At one time, seasonal displays and products appeared on retailers shelves near their actual season. [2]Halloween costumes and candy, for example, was placed on shelves a month or so before pint-sized ghosts and witches canvassed the neighborhood in search of as much sugar as they could carry. [3]In mid-January Valentine candy would appear, allowing sufficient time for children to purchase boxes of pastel conversation hearts and for adults to buy heart-shaped boxes of chocolate. [4]Traditionally Christmas displays appeared only after the Thanksgiving turkey had been digested. [5]Lately, however, stores seems to have lost their sense of time. [6]Halloween costumes and candy is on display from Labor Day through the end of October. [7]Christmas catalogs and advertisements begins to arrive in mailboxes in September. [8]By October, Christmas merchandise slowly appear on store

shelves. ⁹When Christmas items are removed in late
December, the red hearts of Valentine's Day
appears. ¹⁰For retailers every day is a holiday.

1. _____   6. _____

2. _____   7. _____

3. _____   8. _____

4. _____   9. _____

5. _____   10. _____

Editing Exercise 4   Pronoun Point of View, Pronoun Agreement, Subject-Verb Agreement, Pronoun Case

Find and correct the ten sentence errors in the paragraph below. Each sentence
contains an error.

2 shifts in pronoun point of view
3 pronoun agreement errors
4 subject-verb agreement errors
1 pronoun case error

¹As an intern for a television station, I see
firsthand how strangely some people behave when
point a camera at them. ²Once, when I accompanied
the camera crew to a local mall, we had trouble
interviewing the manager because of all the
teenagers who stood behind him, waving, grinning,
and yelling out comments as if he or she were the
reason the cameras were there. ³Among my favorite
assignments is street interviews. ⁴When the
interviewer tries to stop someone on the street to
ask them a question, some people just shake their
heads and walk on. ⁵Other people look at their
shoes and mumbles the briefest possible answer.
⁶There is always at least one star quality
interviewee who looks directly into the camera and
gives a polished answer that sounds as if they have
rehearsed it for hours. ⁷But the strangest people

of all are the ones who act as if they has something to hide. [8]Once, when the camera operator and me were setting up the camera for the shot, a man covered his face with his jacket and actually ran from us. [9]Other camera-shy people cross the street to avoid you, as if they are afraid of being recognized on TV. [10]If there is one thing I have learned during my internship, it is that the sight of a TV crew and cameras make some people behave strangely.

1. _____
2. _____
3. _____
4. _____
5. _____

6. _____
7. _____
8. _____
9. _____
10. _____

Editing Exercise 5　Subject-Verb Agreement, Pronoun Agreement, Comma Splices, Fragments, End Punctuation, Semicolons

Find and correct the ten sentence errors in the paragraph below. In the blanks provided, write the number of each sentence in which you find an error, followed by your correction. Two of the sentences are correct.

4 subject-verb agreement errors
1 pronoun agreement error
1 comma splice
2 sentence fragments
1 error in punctuation at the end of a sentence
1 semicolon error

[1]Reality television programming may be popular, it is anything but realistic. [2]One unrealistic version of reality TV involve a family living in a situation from the past. [3]Members of a family is placed in a Victorian mansion, a cabin in the

woods, or a mud hut and expected to live as their ancestors did hundreds of years ago. [4]In the age of computers and microwaveable dinners, what is realistic about foraging for berries or pounding out laundry on a rock or an old-fashioned washboard. [5]Still another version of reality programming show the lives of celebrities. [6]On an episode of one show, a former model and her decorator, who is redoing the star's bedroom in pink and leopard, has a conference. [7]Then the celebrity and her entourage take off in a limo to Las Vegas. [8]Where she and her entourage stay in a huge hotel suite and visit casinos, bars, and strip clubs. [9]For most people; however, reality does not involve limos, decorators, or a lavish lifestyle. [10]True reality TV would follow a commuter through heavy traffic or show a parent rushing to get their children off to school. [11]Strangely enough, a true reality program might also feature people sitting in front of the TV. [12]And watching silly shows.

_____

_____

_____

_____

_____

_____

_____

_____

_____

_____

_____

_____

Editing Exercise 6   Pronoun Case, Pronoun Reference, Irregular Verbs, Verb Tense, Quotation Marks, Comma Splices

Find and correct the ten sentence errors in the paragraph below. Each sentence contains an error.

1 pronoun case error
2 pronoun reference errors
4 errors in irregular verb form
1 shift in verb tense from past to present
1 error in quotation marks
1 comma splice

[1]Walking around the block in my tree-lined neighborhood, I seen a white kitten sitting in the shade of an oak. [2]The kitten took one look at me, mewed piteously, and begun to follow me. [3]By the time I reached the end of the block, she is snuggling against my shoulder as I carefully carried her along. [4]I knew my husband did not want another cat, but by the time I reached my front door, I had figured out a way around this. [5]I sat the kitten on the porch and opened the door, saying to my husband, "Look what followed me home." [6]The kitten, later to be called Prudence, stretched her neck, taken a peek inside the living room, and bleated a cry for help. [7]My husband asked Did she really follow you all that way? [8]"I'll bet someone dumped her on the side of the road, and then they just drove off," I said, not answering his question. [9]My husband and me fed Prudence on the front porch for the next several days, just in case a neighbor knocked on our door to reclaim the kitten. [10]The knock on the door never came, Prudence entered the living room on the fourth day and never looked back.

1. _____

2. _____

3. _____

4. _____

5. _____

6. _____

7. _____

8. _____

9. _____

10. _____

Editing Exercise 7   Capitalization, Verb Shifts, Subject-Verb Agreement, Words Commonly Confused, Adjectives and Adverbs, Comma Splices, Run-ons, Fragments

Find and correct the ten sentence errors in the paragraph below. Each sentence contains one error.

1 capitalization error
1 verb shift from past to present
1 subject-verb agreement error
2 errors in words commonly confused
1 confusion of adjective and adverb
1 comma splice
1 run-on sentence
2 sentence fragments

[1]Greek mythology shows that ancient greek gods took terrible revenge on those who opposed or displeased them. [2]When Tantalus, son of Zeus, displeased the gods, he was condemned to float for eternity in a beautifully lake. [3]If he bent to drink from the clear, sparkling water, it recedes from him. [4]If he reached for the luscious grapes hanging overhead. [5]They stayed just out of reach. Sisyphus displeased the gods by telling their secrets he was taught the meaning of frustration. [6]His task for all the years of eternity were to roll a huge, heavy rock up a steep hill. [7]When he had almost reached the top, the rock would invariably break loose and roll to the bottom, poor Sisyphus

had to start again. [8]Arachne bragged that she could weave more skillfully than the gods theirselves. [9]She was sentenced to spend eternity spinning beautiful webs as a eight-legged spider. [10]With gods so cruel and imaginative. [11]It is a wonder that even mythological characters dared to oppose them.

1. _____

2. _____

3. _____

4. _____

5. _____

6. _____

7. _____

8. _____

9. _____

10. _____

Editing Exercise 8   Fragments, Comma Splices, Words Commonly Confused, Run-ons, Apostrophes, Verb Shifts, and Irregular Verb Forms

Find and correct the twenty sentence errors in the essay below. In the blanks provided, write the number of each sentence in which you find an error, followed by your correction.

6 sentence fragments
2 comma splices
3 words commonly confused
3 run-on sentences
1 apostrophe error
2 unnecessary shifts from past to present
3 irregular verb form errors

[1]When my wife and I were first married. [2]I tried to interest her in fishing. [3]I enthusiastically planned a Saturday trip to Waller Mill Pond, my

favorite fishing spot. [4]On the pond, only small electric motors were permitted large, noisy motors might frighten the fish and keep them from biting. [5]Quiet, I explained to Maria, was essential for fishing, once we were on the pond, we would speak only in whispers. [6]Maria did not seem very eager, I was sure that once we were out on the pond, she would enjoy fishing as much as I did. [7]Little did I know that our first fishing trip together would also be our last.

[8]Saturday morning was perfect for fishing. [9]Maria had seemed a little grumpy when I woke her at 5:00 A.M., but she smiled as I silently pointed to a group of ducks gliding across the ponds glass-like surface and a beaver gnawing a thick sapling near the banks of the pond. [10]Tall pines lined the steep walls of the hills surrounding the pond, and the piece was broken only by the occasional "ker-plop" of a fish jumping. [11]When I showed Maria the fat worms that I would use to bait the hook, she wrinkled her nose and turns away with a small exclamation of disgust. [12]I put a finger across my lips to remind her to be quiet she shot me an annoyed look. [13]Then reached for the paperback she had brought with her.

[14]I could hardly wait to get my line in the water. [15]I chosen a particularly fat and lively worm and baited the hook for my first cast. [16]I brought the fishing rod high above my head and flipped the rod to cast the hook the line never hit the water. [17]I felt resistance on the line and simultaneously heard a ear-shattering scream. [18]I had hooked Maria. [19]At the sound of her scream, the ducks spread there wings, lifting themselves above the noise. [20]The plump beaver looks up in alarm and waddled hurriedly into the water. [21]Maria was looking at her arm in horror, and I thought the hook had sank deeply into her flesh. [22]Luckily, the hook had only caught on her wristwatch. [23]Her horror was caused by the fat, slimy, and entirely harmless worm squirming on her arm. [24]After removing the hook from Maria's wristwatch and

the worm from her arm. [25]I cast my line again.
[26]However, at the sound of the scream. [27]The fish
had undoubtedly fled to the shelter of the rocks
and reeds below the surface of the pond. [28]Since
the fish had swam off and Maria was still in an
unusually grumpy mood, I decided it was time to
head for home.

[29]On Saturdays, I still head to my special
fishing spot, but I go without Maria. [30]Whenever I
invite her to fish with me, she seems to have a
shopping trip she can't put off. [31]Or an urgent
need to visit her sister. [32]When I leave the house
at 5:30 A.M. on a Saturday. [33]I am sad to think
that Maria is wasting her morning snuggled under
the covers. [34]She does not know what she is
missing.

_____   _____

_____   _____

_____   _____

_____   _____

_____   _____

_____   _____

_____   _____

_____   _____

_____   _____

Part 3
Readings

Action Hero

Rulon Openshaw

Everyone treated him like a hero. It was easy to get used to . . . maybe a little too easy.

A few years ago, I stopped at a neighborhood market for some late-night ice cream. As I got out of my car, a young man hailed me from across the street. He was college-aged and dressed to the nines: expensive pullover, dress shirt and slacks so sharply creased they could have cut frozen fish. I thought he wanted directions; he had that urgent late-for-a-party look. When he reached me, he pulled up his sweater and smoothly drew a pistol from inside his waistband. "Get in the car," he ordered.

My brain went into hyperspeed. I remembered watching a personal-security expert on a talk show advise victims not to stare at an assailant's face. His reasoning was that if a robber thinks you cannot identify him, he's less likely to kill you. No one asked how much less likely. Given its importance to my future, I focused instead on his weapon—a .38 Smith & Wesson revolver, blued steel, short barrel. I'd fired others like it at pistol ranges. This was no mouse gun. Nervously, I directed my gaze lower. His shoes were highly polished. Strange as it sounds, I admired his sense of style.

The click of the revolver's hammer being cocked snapped my head up eye to eye with his. So much for not looking at his face. Contrary to the belief that when death appears imminent, a person's entire life passes before him, I was completely focused on the moment. Instinct told me that a car trip with this guy would turn out to be a one-way journey for me. I held out my keys. "Take my car," I said in a tone I prayed would inspire calmness and reason. "I'm not getting in."

He hesitated, then ignoring my proffered keys, thrust out a hand and yanked off my shoulder bag. In it were my wallet and a couple of rented videos. He took a step back, his gun still aimed at me. Neither of us spoke.

Laughter broke the silence, making us both turn. Several couples were leaving a Chinese restaurant on the opposite corner. The gunman gave them a fast scan, then lowered his revolver. Holding it against his thigh to conceal it, he began to stride quickly across the almost-trafficless street, my bag clutched under his arm.

Incredibly, I took off after him. "Hey," I shouted to the people in front of the restaurant. "This guy just robbed me." I was halfway across the street when I realized my would-be posse was not mounting up. The gunman, now aware of my proximity, pivoted in my direction. As I watched him raise his gun, every-thing went into slow motion. A tongue of flame flashed from the snub-nosed barrel, followed by a loud crack.

I lost my balance. I felt no pain, but when I looked down, I saw my left leg flopped out sideways at my shin. A half-dollar-sized spot of blood stained my jeans. When I looked up, my assailant was sprinting down a dark side street.   7

Later that night at a nearby hospital, I was told that the bullet had frac-tured my tibia and fibula, the two bones connecting the knee and ankle. Doc-tors inserted a steel rod secured by four screws into my leg. They also gave me a "prosthesis alert" card to show security personnel if the rod set off a metal detector.   8

But a remarkable thing began to happen—my popularity soared. When friends introduced me as "the guy who got shot," women who a moment be-fore had no interest in me came after me like groupies. Men wanted to buy me drinks—they considered me "brave" for running after the gunman. I'm re-minded of war movies in which the green infantrymen behave reverentially around the grizzled vets who have seen action.   9

I found it difficult to forgive myself for what I considered an act of colossal folly. Sometimes, I thought I had chased the kid out of anger at being victim-ized; other times, I attributed my actions to an adrenaline rush that needed a physical outlet. Whatever the reason, I knew it had nothing to do with bravery.   10

Clearly, I was being given credit for something I didn't deserve, yet I was re-luctant to give up my newly acquired status. After all, it wasn't as if I were tak-ing an active part in any deception, I was merely allowing people to come to whatever conclusions they wished. I finally rationalized my decision to maintain the status quo: I considered any misperception to be my compensation for hav-ing gone through a horrible situation.   11

Things went well until the day I was approached by a panhandler. On a whim, I told him I had no money because I'd been unable to work since being shot in a robbery. His eyes grew large, and it was obvious that the information impressed him. "That's heavy," he said, then leaned closer, conspiratorially. "Did you get caught?"   12

■ **Building Vocabulary**

For each question, choose the meaning that most closely defines the un-derlined word or phrase as it is used in the essay.

   1. The phrase dressed to the nines most nearly means
      a. well dressed.
      b. carelessly dressed.
      c. oddly dressed.
      d. shabbily dressed.

2. The word <u>hyperspeed</u> most nearly means
    a. slow motion.
    b. top speed.
    c. full stop.
    d. normal speed.

3. The word <u>reverentially</u> most nearly means
    a. boastfully.
    b. quietly.
    c. bravely.
    d. worshipfully.

4. The word <u>folly</u> most nearly means
    a. bravery.
    b. wisdom.
    c. foolishness.
    d. anger.

5. The phrase <u>the status quo</u> most nearly means
    a. the way things used to be.
    b. the rationalization.
    c. the plan for the future.
    d. the current situation.

■ Understanding the Essay

1. The person who robbed the author at gunpoint
    a. looked like a desperate criminal.
    b. was a homeless person.
    c. looked like a well-dressed college student.
    d. had a police record.

2. The robber was distracted and ran away when
    a. a police car slowly drove by.
    b. the author refused to get into the car with him and instead offered his keys.
    c. some people came out of a nearby restaurant.
    d. Bruno, the author's rottweiler, lunged for the robber's throat.

3. The pattern of development in this essay is mainly
   a. definition.
   b. cause-effect.
   c. narrative.
   d. description.

4. The author implies that the main reason he accepted being treated as a hero was that
   a. he enjoyed the attention he received from women.
   b. his popularity soared and he always had a funny story to tell at parties.
   c. he had been through so much that he felt he deserved the attention.
   d. he knew that chasing the robber was a heroic action.

5. Which of the following familiar sayings is best supported by the essay?
   a. Clothes make the man.
   b. Honesty is the best policy.
   c. Crime does not pay.
   d. You can't judge a book by its cover.

■ Writing in the Margins

These questions encourage you to think not just about the essay but about the issues it raises. Your instructor may ask you to write down your answers, to discuss them in groups, or simply to think about them for class discussion.

1. This essay revolves around misperception. How many instances do you see in the essay where people see things as they are not? How do you account for these misperceptions?

2. It has been said that "perception is everything." What do you think the statement means? Is it true?

3. If this story were a fable or a folktale, it would have a moral. If there is a moral to this story, what is it?

4. To what extent do we rely on appearance when we judge people? What are the benefits and dangers of using appearance to judge others?

5. Is society more dangerous or less dangerous than it was when your parents or grandparents were growing up? How do you know?

Topics for Writing

Assignment 1: Facing Danger

Paragraph or Journal Entry

Have you ever faced a dangerous or potentially dangerous situation? How did you react? Did your reaction surprise you? Write a narrative journal entry or paragraph describing the situation and your reaction to it.

Assignment 2: Judgments and Misjudgments

Paragraph

Has someone ever given you more credit than you deserved or suspected you of something you did not do? Write a narrative paragraph describing the incident. Alternatively, have you ever misjudged another person? Write a narrative paragraph describing that incident.

Assignment 3: Types of Stereotypes

Paragraph

Sometimes, entire groups of people are routinely misjudged. This kind of misjudgment is called stereotyping—attributing positive or negative characteristics to people simply because they are of a particular age, gender, religion, race, or socioeconomic group. Write a classification paragraph in which you discuss three common stereotypes about one particular group. Give specific examples of each stereotype you discuss.

Assignment 4: Protection against Crime

Paragraph or Essay

What steps can people take to protect themselves against crime? Explain in a process paragraph or essay.

Setting Boundaries

Cara DiMarco

Setting boundaries is an act of self-esteem and a way to protect yourself and your emotions. In this essay, Cara DiMarco tells why and how to set boundaries.

What exactly is a boundary? Boundaries can be physically or psychologically   1
based. A physical boundary is determined by how much you want to allow or limit access to your physical self. A mental or emotional boundary is the psychological line you draw around yourself that says this is where you end and other people begin. How sturdy and definite your boundaries are depends on many factors. It largely depends on how much you were taught as a child that you had a right to your own separateness and distinctness, or how much you were expected to allow others access to your mental and emotional inner life. Some families allow each member a great deal of psychological privacy and separateness. Other families function in an enmeshed environment, where individuals aren't allowed private thoughts and feelings, and everything is considered open. This can make functioning in the world a confusing and frightening process if you aren't certain how to set clear boundaries that others understand and respect.

Creating firm, clear boundaries is important because it helps you stay safe   2
in the world and allows you to decide how much you want to let someone into your emotional space. I encountered a good description of boundary setting in a counselor training class, where an instructor represented boundary setting as the difference between having an internal versus an external zipper. Picture that you have a zipper running from beneath your chin down to your belly button. The zipper allows or denies access to your emotions. An external zipper has the pull tab on the outside of your body, while an internal zipper has the pull tab on the inside. With an external zipper, anyone you meet can potentially grab the pull tab and open it as far as they want, allowing themselves access to whatever amount of your private emotional life or personal details that they want. An internal zipper, on the other hand, allows you to control how much emotional access a person has to your feelings and thoughts. When you meet someone, you can decide how safe and trusting you feel and determine how far you want to lower your zipper and whether you want to let that individual in.

Many people have a preset level to which they automatically lower their zip-   3
per when they meet new people. It is their way of assuming that people are trustworthy until they prove otherwise, and also of making certain that they allow people access to only some of their emotional lives until they determine if they want to become more emotionally intimate.

Setting boundaries with people requires <u>assertiveness</u> skills. . . . Part of 4 what makes boundary setting so challenging is that no one likes to have limits placed on them or hear "No, you can't have access to that part of me." If you experience difficulties saying "no," continue to practice in small ways, remembering that you get good at what you practice.

Some relationships allow you to set boundaries in a relatively comfortable, 5 easy way because that person's sense of boundaries will naturally mesh with your own. Others will have very different ideas about what is appropriate, and you may need to agree to disagree on your <u>respective</u> viewpoints. Despite someone's reaction, you never need to apologize for wanting to keep parts of your life private.

Maintaining boundaries is often even more difficult because many people 6 want to test the limits, thinking that if you make an exception for them, it indicates their special status and importance. Let's say you told a friend not to call you between 5:00 and 7:00 P.M. because you are busy with the kids and dinner. You've set that boundary clearly; your friend adheres to it for a time, but eventually she starts calling during those hours. This is where you make a decision about what is the most important thing: Is your friend going through a difficult time and needing extra support from you, or do you need to reassert your boundaries?

To maintain a boundary, <u>reiterate</u> your stand. If your boundary continues 7 to be violated, state the consequences to the other person. Either the boundary is honored or you will spend less time with that person. Sometimes it may not be possible to continue even an important relationship with someone who refuses to respect your boundaries.

By not allowing others more access to your sense of self than you want, you 8 also honor your own preferences and desires, which in itself is an act of self-esteem. People with low self-esteem have a difficult time believing that they are worthy enough to say no to other people. They believe that others are more important than they are, so how dare they say, "This part of me is important, and I'm keeping it private." Setting and maintaining boundaries states that what you want, feel, and are comfortable with is important, you choose to honor that, and you expect others to do the same. And if you'd like, you can visualize boundaries as the fence around the garden of your self-esteem, with your boundaries protecting all of the precious aspects that you've been cultivating and nurturing in your developing self-esteem.

■ Building Vocabulary

For each question, choose the meaning that most closely defines the underlined word or phrase as it is used in the essay.

1. The word <u>sturdy</u> most nearly means
    a. special.
    b. indefinite.
    c. intellectual.
    d. strong.

2. The phrase <u>enmeshed environment</u> most nearly means
   a. an environment in which people are free to do as they please.
   b. an environment in which people are closely emotionally linked.
   c. an environment in which people keep emotions hidden.
   d. an environment in which everyone has strong boundaries.

3. The word <u>assertiveness</u> most nearly means
   a. certainty.
   b. straightforwardness.
   c. shyness.
   d. bullying.

4. The word <u>respective</u> most nearly means
   a. shared.
   b. respectful.
   c. individual.
   d. steady

5. The word <u>reiterate</u> most nearly means
   a. assess.
   b. show interest in.
   c. abandon.
   d. repeat.

■ Understanding the Essay

1. The main idea of this essay is that
   a. setting boundaries requires assertiveness skills.
   b. how strong a person's boundaries are can depend on factors established in childhood.
   c. a friend who repeatedly calls during a time when she has been asked not to call is violating boundaries.
   d. setting firm boundaries is necessary for self-protection and self-esteem.

2. Families that are most likely to foster the setting of strong boundaries are those that
   a. allow the most privacy and individuality.
   b. are the most honest and open about emotional issues.

      c. are the happiest.

      d. provide an enmeshed environment.

3. Is it better to have a boundary that works like an internal zipper or one that works like an external zipper?

      a. External, because it shows that you are open and have no secrets.

      b. Internal, because it allows you to be completely cut off emotionally.

      c. External, because it lets people decide how intimately they want to know you.

      d. Internal, because it allows you to control how much emotional access others have.

4. Paragraph 5 implies that boundaries

      a. will automatically be respected by friends and family members.

      b. are flexible and can be temporarily changed in special situations.

      c. should be maintained no matter what the circumstances.

      d. are too much trouble to maintain.

5. People with low self esteem may have trouble maintaining boundaries because

      a. they don't mind revealing their emotional life.

      b. they have trouble telling people no.

      c. they are eager for people to find out who they really are.

      d. they feel flattered when others want to know their intimate secrets.

▪ Writing in the Margins

These questions encourage you to think not just about the essay but about the issues it raises. Your instructor may ask you to write down your answers, to discuss them in groups, or simply to think about them for class discussion.

1. DiMarco discusses more than one kind of boundary. She talks about emotional boundaries that help people to keep parts of themselves private. She discusses boundaries of time, for example, the family time a person might set aside as a time for no outside intrusion. What other kinds of boundaries do people set? Are they generally helpful or harmful?

2. Do modern conveniences such as cell phones, e-mail, instant messaging, and answering machines make it easier or harder to set boundaries? Can you think of examples?

TOPICS FOR WRITING

Assignment 1: Your Childhood Boundaries

Paragraph or Journal Entry

As a child, were you allowed or encouraged to set boundaries? How has your upbringing affected your ability to set boundaries as an adult?

Assignment 2: Encouraging Children to Set Boundaries

Paragraph

Should parents encourage children to set boundaries? If so, what kinds of boundaries should be encouraged and how should parents encourage the setting of these boundaries?

Assignment 3: On Call

Paragraph or Essay

Write a paragraph or essay explaining how modern technological conveniences such as cell phones, e-mail, instant messaging, and answering machines affect your ability to set boundaries.

Assignment 4: Types of Boundaries

Paragraph or Essay

Write a paragraph or essay describing different kinds of boundaries that people set to protect their time, their emotions, or some other important aspect of themselves.

Against the Wall

Knight-Ridder/Tribune Information Services

It's a black slash of marble embedded in the ground, a memorial that was so controversial when it was first proposed that a more traditional statue was erected to pacify the many who protested. Yet the Vietnam Veterans Memorial, engraved with the names of the dead and missing, has perhaps meant more to Americans than any other war memorial.

1 They come every day, years, even decades after their loved ones were lost.

2 They leave the kinds of things that people have been leaving ever since the wall was built—poems, letters, medals, black lace panties, teddy bears, cans of sardines, six-packs of Bud, toilet paper, wedding rings.

3 Years pass. People get older. But the emotions evoked by the Vietnam Veterans Memorial wall never seem to change.

4 At night, park ranger Pete Prentner walks along the wall with his flashlight, picking up the tangible pieces of lives broken by grief. In the 15 years since the wall was dedicated, nearly 54,000 items have been left here.

5 "No one ever expected this to happen," he said. "It's so personal. It caught everyone by surprise."

6 It now takes almost an hour a night to collect everything left at the wall and even longer on holidays like Memorial Day.

7 Through the years, people have left dollar bills, rosaries, locks of hair, an empty bottle of Chandon champagne and two goblets, a golf trophy with this note, "It's a beautiful day. We'd be playing golf. I'd be beating you by two strokes, sucker."

8 Many remembrances are for people unknown, but loved anyway. There's the gold-framed sonogram images for Sgt. Eddie E. Chervony, with a letter that says "Happy Father's Day, Dad! Here are the first two images of your first grandchild. . . . Dad, this child will know you, just how I have grown to know and love you even though the last time I saw you I was only four months old. Your daughter, Jeanette."

9 The National Park Service collects, catalogs and stores the items in a gigantic, climate-controlled warehouse in suburban Maryland.

10 A few things are exhibited at the Smithsonian Institution and four other museums. Next month, the story of the mementos left at the Wall will be told on a web site. The collectors plan to take some items to schools around the country to teach another generation about the war most know little about.

11 This collection is different from all others, which typically reflect a curator's conscious selections. In this case, the public is the curator.

"It is the public saying this is important," said Duery Felton, Jr., the park 12 service curator and himself a Vietnam vet. "Only the donor and maybe the recipient understand the meaning of the items."

Many artifacts are left anonymously, such as blue diaper pins, a pacifier, 13 Mickey Mouse ears. Others are directly personal, such as this letter to Sgt. Andres Massa: "My sister, Carmen, misses you very much and so do I. P. S. I'm looking out for her. Coco."

Even though Washington is a town full of imposing monuments, no other 14 has provoked such an emotional torrent of tokens and trinkets as the Wall, which draws some three million visitors a year.

The first artifact actually arrived when the wall's foundation was being 15 poured. A man wanted to leave a Purple Heart medal awarded posthumously to his brother in the concrete.

For the first two years, the items were gathered nightly by maintenance 16 people and stored in cardboard boxes in sheds. When the flood didn't stop, they realized they had quite a phenomenon on their hands. Each item collected gets a bar code, is placed in a plastic Zip-Loc bag, and is carted to the warehouse, known as the Museum Resource Center. There, items are handled by technicians in white cotton gloves.

Some items have shocked the rangers, such as cremated ashes dumped on 17 the concrete. "The first time, we didn't know what to do," Prentner recalled. "We called the police. We wondered: Is this like disposing of a body? Luckily, it rained that night, and that's probably what the guy wanted."

There was the flesh-toned double-leg prosthesis, complete with running 18 shoes and black socks, that once belonged to Stephen E. Belville. He was wounded in a foxhole in 1968 and died April 15, 1994.

There was the cardboard covered with cigars and this message for Francis 19 Eugene Sanders: "For 28 Christmas mornings, I've thought of you and our last cigar together. Now for your birthday, it's time for you to catch up to me." It was from his buddy, Sgt. J. Kornsey.

The item that haunted all who saw it: A wrinkled photo of a young North 20 Vietnamese soldier and a little girl with braided pigtails. The accompanying letter said:

"Dear Sir, For twenty-two years, I have carried your picture in my wallet. I 21 was only eighteen years old that day we faced one another on that trail in Chu Lai, Vietnam. Why you didn't take my life I'll never know. You stared at me for so long, armed with your AK-47, and yet you did not fire. Forgive me for taking your life, I was reacting the way I was trained, to kill V. C.* . . . So many times over the years I have stared at your picture and your daughter, I suspect. Each time my heart and guts would burn with the pain of guilt."

At times, it is hard for the rangers and the museum workers to even look at 22 the mementos. "You learn to read, but not read," said Felton, the curator.

*Viet Cong, members of the South Vietnamese National Liberation Front. [Ed.]

In the darkness, with tourists still milling around the wall, Prentner stum- 23
bled upon a letter addressed to Fred: "I always looked up to you without you
even really knowing it. Man, you looked so good in your uniform, jump wings,
spit-shined boots. . . . Love, Frank."

The 35-year-old ranger, who served four years in the Army himself, cannot 24
help being moved.

"I try to distance myself," he said. "Some of these guys disappeared more 25
than 25 years ago, but it is obviously still so emotional. Each one had a name.
Each one had a family and friends. You never know all the people and what
they could have been."

■ Building Vocabulary

For each question, choose the meaning that most closely defines the underlined word or phrase as it is used in the essay.

1. The word mementos most nearly means
   a. moments.
   b. laments.
   c. souvenirs.
   d. flowers.

2. The word curator most nearly means
   a. one who selects items at random.
   b. a caretaker of important artifacts.
   c. a visitor to a museum.
   d. a healer.

3. The word artifacts most nearly means
   a. something artificial.
   b. articles.
   c. items of historical interest.
   d. facts about art.

4. The word imposing most nearly means
   a. insignificant.
   b. granite.
   c. posed.
   d. impressive.

5. The word posthumously most nearly means
   a. humorously.
   b. recently.

  c. after death.

  d. posthaste.

■   **Understanding the Essay**

1. The author's purpose in writing the essay is

  a. to give a brief history of the Vietnam War.

  b. to discuss the problem caused by discarded items at the Vietnam Veterans Memorial.

  c. to show the emotional response to the Vietnam Veterans Memorial.

  d. to profile the park rangers at the Vietnam Veterans Memorial.

2. In fifteen years, how many items were left at the Wall?

  a. over a million.

  b. an average of 172 per day.

  c. 54,000.

  d. No records have been kept.

3. The most likely reason that rangers called the police when they found cremated ashes was that

  a. they knew it was a crime to dispose of cremated ashes in that fashion.

  b. they wanted the perpetrator arrested.

  c. they did not know what else to do.

  d. they were afraid a murder had been committed.

4. The "Dear Sir" letter was left at the Wall

  a. by a former Viet Cong soldier.

  b. to honor a vet who had been killed by the Viet Cong.

  c. by a vet who felt guilty about killing an enemy soldier.

  d. to honor the vet who had killed the Viet Cong soldier in the photograph.

5. Which statement best describes the attitude of the rangers who are assigned to the Wall?

  a. Too young to remember the war, they are unemotional about the Wall and the mementoes left there.

  b. Each day, they are deeply moved by the trinkets and letters left at the Wall.

  c. They deliberately try to detach themselves from the emotional aspects of their job.

  d. They are just waiting for quitting time.

■ **Writing in the Margins**

These questions encourage you to think not just about the essay but about the issues it raises. Your instructor may ask you to write down your answers, to discuss them in groups, or simply to think about them for class discussion.

1. What kind of relationship do you think the man who wrote, "I'd be beating you by two strokes, sucker," had with the man he wrote to? Why?

2. What are the reasons that the Vietnam Veterans Memorial wall evokes such a personal response?

3. The Vietnam War spawned a large antiwar movement in the United States. Is war ever justifiable? Under what circumstances?

4. Which items or notes mentioned in the essay did you find most amusing? Most touching? What prompts people to leave tributes in a public place such as a memorial wall?

TOPICS FOR WRITING

Assignment 1: I Protest!

Paragraph or Journal Entry

During the Vietnam War, the United States was deeply divided over whether the country should be at war. Many young people attended rallies and even burned their draft cards in protest—an illegal act. If you could attend a protest rally today, what social condition, law, or custom would you want to protest? Why? Write a paragraph or journal entry discussing the issue you would protest and your reasons for doing so.

As a prewriting exercise, think of the following questions:

What would you protest?

Who else would be at the rally?

Where would it be held?

What would you wear?

What songs would be sung?

What signs would be carried?

Is there something that you would symbolically burn at this protest rally?

What changes would you hope to see as a result of your protest?

Assignment 2: Letter to a Vietnam Vet

Letter

Choose an item listed in the essay and write a letter to go with it. Pretend you are the person leaving it. Imagine your age, your gender, and the nature of your relationship with the deceased, and let your letter reflect all of these things. Based on your (imagined) relationship with the deceased, decide whether your note should be sad, playful, funny, sexy, sarcastic, or even angry. Be sure to make some mention of the item you are leaving and include a hint about why you chose that item. Does it remind you of an experience you shared with the person? Does it reveal something about what you have done or become since the person died? Let your creativity loose with this assignment.

Assignment 3: Letter to an Ancestor or Loved One

Letter

This assignment is similar to Assignment 2, with a different twist. Imagine that you have a chance to leave a letter and a memento at a memorial wall for loved ones and ancestors. Choose an item and write a letter to a loved one who has died or to one of your ancestors that you have heard about but not known. Be sure to mention the item you have chosen and to hint at what it symbolizes to you. You may reflect on your past with your loved one, or you may tell the person something you would want him or her to know about you now. Be prepared: if you are writing to someone you have lost, the experience can be emotional.

Assignment 4: Honoring the Dead

Paragraph or Essay

Write a paragraph or essay describing the customs followed by your family or your culture for honoring the dead. What are these customs? How and when are they carried out? What purpose do they serve for the living?

Older and Wiser— or Just Older?

William Raspberry

Do the elderly have anything to teach us in our technological society?

A few years ago, a friend of mine was contemplating a major career change. He weighed the options, ran the numbers, talked it over with his wife, and then called his father—in Egypt. 1

My friend holds advanced degrees; his father, through not exactly a peasant, has no professional training. My friend, a longtime resident of the United States, is fairly sophisticated about the way business is done here. His father knows little of such matters. Still, as my friend explained later, it simply never occurred to him to make such an important decision without consulting the old man. Tradition, you know. 2

My friend said his father listened to the options he outlined, asked questions about them and then recommended the path the son had pretty much settled upon. The transoceanic consultation, as I would learn, was partly in recognition of the wisdom the father had accumulated over the years, partly in deference to his age. But that dichotomy exists only in translation. In my friend's tradition, wisdom and age are taken to be virtually synonymous. 3

Nor is this some peculiarly Egyptian artifact. Cultures around the globe have accorded at least symbolic obeisance to the wisdom of age. 4

It used to be a tradition in America, too, until a number of trends conspired to kill it. For instance, fewer Americans are living and working in their hometowns, a trend that separates us physically from our familial elders. One result is that as our parents age, we find ourselves thinking about them less as resources than as problems. What are we going to do about Mother? 5

In addition, our need increasingly is for wisdom that is beyond the ability of our parents to supply. When we needed to know when to plant, how to fix something, or how to convince an employer of our loyalty, the wisdom of the old folk was a wonderful resource. The hard questions nowadays are likely to involve technology or contracts, or worries about such issues as how to manage our careers when even the boss has no loyalty—either to us or to the company we both work for—or how to plan for our financial future. 6

What do the old folk know about financial planning? To them, "mutual fund" may evoke the petty cash jar in the cupboard, "401(k)" an apartment 7 number. That's exaggeration, of course, but it is true that much of what we need to know is beyond the ken of our elders, whose experience-based advice (avoid debt and pay off your mortgage as soon as you can) may be financially unsound.

But it isn't only in families that the wisdom of the aging has undergone de- 8 valuation. Just the other day, the *Wall Street Journal* had a front-page piece on the job difficulties of "middle-aged managers." A few years ago, these moderately successful workers might have been viewed as valuable assets, representing the accumulated wisdom of their companies. Now many of them are struggling to learn new skills, master new technologies and keep fit enough to work ridiculous hours, lest they lose their jobs to younger and more energetic challengers.

Chris Total, the 54-year-old manager featured in the *Journal*'s report, put it 9 more poignantly: "You'd think that with gray hair and wisdom there came some kind of respect."

Sometimes it does. Walter Cronkite, Lloyd Bentsen, Helen Thomas, Pat 10 Moynihan, Ben Bradley, Lloyd Cutler, and C. Deloris Tucker come to mind. Maybe you can think of dozens of others.

But it seems to me that their numbers are shrinking, giving way to upstarts 11 and the hotshots, the streaking meteors who light up the sky and then are gone. Who consults Grandpa before buying a new computer, a new sound system or a new global fund? Who need the folk?

As Total put it: "Things are not what any of us anticipated—that with nat- 12 ural talent, hard work and good moral values, there would come some sense of stability. There is no security and no stability."

Maybe the nameless wit said it better: "Tradition isn't what it used to be." 13

■ Building Vocabulary

For each question, choose the meaning that most closely defines the underlined word or phrase as it is used in the essay.

1. The phrase in deference to most nearly means
   a. out of respect for.
   b. in reference to.
   c. in an attempt to postpone.
   d. to make up for deficiencies in.
2. The word dichotomy most nearly means
   a. language.
   b. division.
   c. surgical procedure.
   d. union.
3. The word obeisance most nearly means
   a. disrespect.
   b. ignorance.

    c. disregard.

    d. honor.

4. The word <u>devaluation</u> most nearly means

    a. evaluation.

    b. reduction in value.

    c. increase in value.

    d. lack of change.

5. The word <u>stability</u> most nearly means

    a. morality.

    b. change.

    c. security.

    d. impermanence.

■ Understanding the Essay

1. Which statement best expresses the main idea of the essay?

    a. In other cultures, the wisdom of age is respected.

    b. In the United States, older people are out of touch with the modern world.

    c. For a variety of reasons, our culture no longer holds the wisdom of the elderly in high esteem.

    d. Unlike people in other countries, citizens of the United States realize that in an increasingly technological world, the elderly have little to contribute to society.

2. The author's friend called his father in Egypt because

    a. he wanted to borrow money.

    b. he needed advice about his career and was afraid he could not make the right decision without help.

    c. it was part of his cultural tradition to seek wisdom from his father.

    d. his father was in the same field as he and was thus a good adviser.

3. Which of the following is *not* mentioned in the essay as a reason people in the United States no longer seek wisdom from parents, grandparents, and other older people?

    a. American society is more mobile today.

    b. Our increasingly youth-oriented society is more likely to embrace the new than the old.

    c. Technology has advanced beyond the grasp of many elderly people.

    d. The financial rules that the elderly lived by may no longer apply.

4. From the example of the middle-aged managers (paragraph 8), you could infer that

    a. the *Wall Street Journal* is exaggerating and reporting irresponsibly.

    b. the worker featured in the *Journal*'s report had probably not kept his skills up to date.

    c. once they reach middle age, most managers can no longer do their jobs properly.

    d. corporate culture is becoming increasingly youth-oriented.

5. Chris Total, the middle-aged manager, believes that over time natural talent, hard work, and good moral values

    a. bring stability.

    b. will lead to a high-paying job.

    c. will bring a sense of personal satisfaction.

    d. are worth nothing in the workplace.

■ Writing in the Margins

These questions encourage you to think not just about the essay but about the issues it raises. Your instructor may ask you to write down your answers, to discuss them in groups, or simply to think about them for class discussion.

1. Is Raspberry's attitude toward "the old folk" sympathetic or unsympathetic? What specific words or phrases in the essay support your answer?

2. From your own observations, is Raspberry right that the old are no longer valued? What specific examples can you find? Can you think of causes that Raspberry has not mentioned? What are the solutions?

3. Many elderly people enter a nursing or retirement home while others live with their children. What are some of the pros and cons of nursing or retirement homes? What are some of the pros and cons of an "extended family" where more than two generations live together?

Group Exercise 1   **Confident? Go solo!**

As the population ages, some foresee "generation wars" in which the elderly and the young fight for limited resources—medical care for the elderly, new schools and day care for the young. In groups, brainstorm to make a list of reasons that the needs of the young should come first. Then make another list of reasons why the needs of the elderly should come first. Which list seems more compelling? How is a choice to be made? Are there any reasonable compromises?

TOPICS FOR WRITING

Assignment 1: R-E-S-P-E-C-T!

Paragraph or Journal Entry

When you are old, how will you go about getting the respect that your wisdom and experience deserve? Explain in a paragraph or journal entry.

Assignment 2: Generation Wars

Paragraph

Write a paragraph based on your responses to the group discussion assignment above. You may argue that the elderly deserve the lion's share of society's resources, that the young deserve most of society's resources, or you may propose a compromise. Make your case convincingly and reasonably.

Assignment 3: An Old Friend

Paragraph

Write a paragraph about an elderly friend or relative whom you believe to be wise. Give specific examples of things that make you believe in the person's wisdom—perhaps advice the person has given or decisions he or she has made about how to live life.

Assignment 4: The Wisdom of Age: Is It Real?

Paragraph or Essay

Interview a person who is at least ten years older than you. The person may be a professor, a relative, a coworker, or a nontraditional student. Ask the person how well-equipped she (or he) feels to handle life and its problems, as opposed to when she was eighteen. Does she feel wiser now? Is she a better, more productive, more motivated worker? What differences has age brought? Would she like to be eighteen again? Report your findings in a paragraph or essay. Before you turn in your final draft, review the chapter on quotation marks, and look at Raspberry's essay to see how he works quotations into his text.

Barbie Madness

Cynthia Tucker

Since the 1950s, Barbie has been a part of the American culture. But critics say that Barbie is just one of the cultural influences that encourages young girls to pursue an impossible standard of physical beauty. Should parents worry? Cynthia Tucker explores the issue.

1   When I was 9 or 10, I was steeped in Barbie madness. So much so that I joined the Barbie fan club. My mother still has the membership document displaying my careful cursive writing alongside the scrawled block letters of a younger sister.

2   Too old to play with baby dolls, I was developing a vicarious interest in high fashion—a world to which Barbie allowed me access. Her overpriced collection of clothes included everything from bridal gowns to swimsuits, all accented by stiletto heels. In fact, her feet were permanently arched so that she could not wear sensible shoes.

3   She wore sheath dresses, capri pants, long gowns. She never got dirty; she never burst a seam (she never bent, of course); she never tripped over those heels.

4   Nor did she ever cause me to believe I would see many real women in the real world who looked or dressed like that. I had never seen a grown woman on the beach in high heels, and if I had—even at 10—I would have thought her nuts. Barbie was fantasy, one of the joyous escapes offered by childhood. My Barbie, white and brunette, never symbolized what I thought anyone ought to look like.

5   After nearly four decades of building a doll with a figure that, by one estimate, gives her measurements of 38-18-34, Mattel is preparing to release a new Barbie of less fantastic proportions. Many parents are breathing a sigh of relief that their daughters will no longer be subjected to such an unrealistic—and possibly damaging—cultural icon. Well, I have good news and bad news for those parents.

6   The bad news is, there will always be damaging cultural icons, plenty of unrealistic representations of women that emphasize youth and a weird voluptuousness/thinness, the combination of which defies physiology. If you think Barbie is the last of them, check out the *Sports Illustrated* swimsuit issue. Check out *Baywatch*. (The syndicated show sells well around the world. Sexism needs little translation.)

7   Now, for the good news: Parents will always have more influence over their children than any doll, any model, any magazine, any movie. Perhaps even

more than their children's peers. Don't take my word for it—scientific research has confirmed it.

A recent study found that no matter a teenager's economic background, a 8 close-knit family helps prevent risky behavior and encourages educational excellence. Might not attentive parents also provide protection against the sexist influences that permeate the culture?

Children learn not just from their parents' rhetoric, but also from their behavior. When a father leaves his family for a younger and more glamorous trophy wife, he gives his children a much more profound lesson about the value of women than Barbie ever could. So does the mother who constantly applauds her adolescent daughter's popularity with boys.

Years ago, Barbie's wardrobe evolved beyond *haute couture* to include professional attire. She also became more ethnically diverse. Now, the doll will get a little nip-and-tuck that widens her waist and de-emphasizes her chest (a bit).

But no matter what she looks like, Barbie will never be as important a role 11 model as Mom and Dad are. When Dad coaches his daughter's soccer team or helps her build a treehouse, he gives her a measure of her worth that overshadows even Barbie's bustline.

■ Building Vocabulary

For each question, choose the meaning that most closely defines the underlined word or phrase as it is used in the essay.

1. The word steeped most nearly means
   a. drenched.
   b. made vertical.
   c. forced.
   d. indifferent.

2. The phrase a vicarious interest most nearly means
   a. an obsession that excludes everything else.
   b. a lukewarm interest.
   c. something that is enjoyed indirectly, through another person or thing.
   d. a dangerous interest.

3. The word fantastic most nearly means
   a. unreal.
   b. wonderful.
   c. damaging.
   d. beautiful.

4. The word icon most nearly means
   a. ambassador.
   b. god.
   c. symbol.
   d. destroyer.

5. The word rhetoric most nearly means
   a. words.
   b. actions.
   c. parents.
   d. behavior.

■ Understanding the Essay

1. The main idea of "Barbie Madness" is that
   a. Barbie is damaging to the self-image of young girls and should be banned.
   b. toys are just toys and nothing more.
   c. the influence of Barbie and other cultural icons is outweighed by the influence of parents on a child's self image.
   d. there is nothing unrealistic about Barbie.

2. When she had a Barbie of her own, the author
   a. considered herself too young to play with dolls.
   b. realized that Barbie was a toy, not a role model.
   c. wanted to be just like Barbie when she grew up.
   d. joined a fan club only because her little sister did.

3. If the author wanted to subscribe to the magazine least likely to show unrealistic images of women, which of the following would she choose?
   a. *Sports Illustrated*
   b. *Business Week*
   c. *Vogue*
   d. *Cosmopolitan*

4. How does Tucker support her statement that parents have more influence than the surrounding culture?
   a. She provides examples from her own life.
   b. She provides no support because her statement is obviously true.
   c. She cites scientific research and gives examples.
   d. She includes interviews with child psychologists.

5. The author would probably agree that a mother who wanted her daughter to be successful and well-rounded would

   a. forbid the child to play with dolls.

   b. teach her to use feminine wiles to get along in a man's world.

   c. insist that she go into a traditionally "male" field such as engineering.

   d. praise her daughter for her achievements and not for her looks.

■ Writing in the Margins

These questions encourage you to think not just about the essay but about the issues it raises. Your instructor may ask you to write down your answers, to discuss them in groups, or simply to think about them for class discussion.

1. In what ways does Barbie present an unrealistic image of women? Are there also toys that present an unrealistic image of men? Do you think these toys can harm the self-image of young girls or boys?

2. Tucker says that the messages that parents send with their own words and behavior overshadow any messages a toy could send. What example does Tucker give of a positive parental message? Which of her examples shows a negative parental message? Can you think of your own examples, both positive and negative?

3. In paragraph 9, Tucker uses the term *trophy wife*. Think about the meaning of the term *trophy*, and then write a sentence defining the term *trophy wife*. What does the term imply about a man's reasons for choosing the woman he marries?

4. Who are some of our cultural icons? What does each say about the things we value as a society?

TOPICS FOR WRITING

Assignment 1: A Favorite Toy

Paragraph or Journal Entry

What was your favorite toy when you were a child? Write a paragraph or journal entry explaining what made it so special. This task will involve not just a description of the toy, but a description of how it made you feel. Did it capture your imagination, encourage one of your special talents, or take you to a fantasy world? Discuss.

Assignment 2: A Child's Self-Worth

Paragraph

What specific steps would you take as a parent to ensure that your child grew up with a healthy sense of self-worth? Write a paragraph outlining and explaining each step.

Assignment 3: Making Barbie Realistic

Paragraph

If Barbie's beauty, her fashionable wardrobe, and her dream house and car present an unrealistic image, then what would a reality-based Barbie be like? In a paragraph, describe what her appearance, clothing, and accessories would be like if she were truly realistic.

Assignment 4: Stereotypes

Paragraph or Essay

A *stereotype* is a kind of misjudgment that attributes negative (and occasionally, positive) characteristics to a people simply because they are of a particular age, gender, religion, race, or socioeconomic group. Can you think of a television show, toy, video game, music video, or advertisement that presents a certain group of people (women, men, teenagers, members of a particular ethnic group, members of a particular profession) in a way that is narrow, stereotypical, or damaging? Write a paragraph or essay describing three of these stereotyped shows, toys, or advertisements.

Living at Warp Speed

Michael Ashcraft

With all of the labor-saving devices we have, why is it that we still don't get any rest? Michael Ashcraft explores the issue.

It's a given these days that practically everyone on the planet is way too busy 1
for his or her own good. We set up unreal expectations of what we can accomplish in any twenty-four-hour period, then beat ourselves up and stress out about not getting it all done.

It's become almost a badge of honor to be busier than is humanly possible. 2
To express a desire to slow down is blasphemy—like the ravings of some sort of sluggard, obviously an underachiever.

Is this the fruit of our success? I thought the whole idea of the technologi- 3
cal revolution was for machines to work faster and more efficiently so that we could work less, or at least less frantically. And then we'd use this extra time for leisure and life enrichment.

But just the opposite seems to have happened. We've worked our ethics 4
into a frenzy. Whenever machines buy us time, we don't save the time for living. Instead, we spend it trying to get more work out of it, leaving us even less room to live than before.

And somehow, this overachieving mindset is seen as socially acceptable. In 5
fact, some companies now offer employees the alleged "benefit" of services that will buy greeting cards, gifts and other personally thoughtful items for alleged "loved" ones, so that employees can keep right on working—free from the distractions of spouses and kids.

Granted, many secretaries have been doing this sort of thing for years for 6
male executives who couldn't pick their kids out of a lineup. But now the busy-busy mindset is not limited by gender.

You don't even have to be employed. People outside the paid workforce 7
also are feeling the pressure to overbook their daily flights.

You see it in stay-at-home mothers racing to find the right size of plastic 8
foam for the school project on the way to soccer practice in between church meetings, all the while working out, making supper and remodeling the kitchen.

We're not only doing this to our adult selves, mind you. By perpetually 9
screaming "GET IN THE CAR WE'RE LATE FOR . . . ," we're also programming this warp speed into our children.

Here's perhaps the most alarming sign of just how far the infection has 10
spread: Some of the busiest, most over-booked people I know are "retired."

And the sad thing is, I don't think most people are happy about the break- 11
neck pace at which we live. You can see it in a subtle shift in what was once an
innocuous social exchange.

Go ahead. Ask someone, "How are you today?"   12

It used to be, people would say something like, "I'm fine, thank you," even   13
if that wasn't exactly true. But now, at best, the answer you often get is a hesitant, "Well, I'm keeping up."

And too many times what you get is someone going on and on about how   14
busy he or she is—as though anyone really wants to hear all the stuff someone
else has to do.

And even if you did want to hear about someone else's impossibly hectic
schedule, who on earth would have the time to listen?

■   **Building Vocabulary**

For each question, choose the meaning that most closely defines the underlined word or phrase as it is used in the essay.

1. The word blasphemy most nearly means
   a. irreverence.
   b. natural.
   c. honorable.
   d. an everyday occurrence.

2. The word sluggard most nearly means
   a. a lazy person.
   b. a crazy person.
   c. an energetic person.
   d. an argumentative person.

3. The word alleged most nearly means
   a. social.
   b. useful.
   c. recalled.
   d. so-called.

4. The word innocuous most nearly means
   a. formal.
   b. harmless.
   c. meaningful.
   d. impressive.

5. The word <u>hectic</u> most nearly means
   a. impossible.
   b. rigid.
   c. busy.
   d. serene.

■ **Understanding the Essay**

1. A good alternate title for the essay would be
   a. "The Modern Search for Serenity."
   b. "The Hectic Pace of Modern Life."
   c. "How to Live a More Balanced Life."
   d. "The Effects of Technology on Modern Life."

2. According to Ashcraft, the technological revolution
   a. has been beneficial because it has increased productivity.
   b. has freed Americans with labor-saving devices and allowed them more leisure.
   c. has enabled Americans to use their minds instead of their hands.
   d. has led to less leisure instead of more.

3. From the statement "some companies now offer employees the alleged 'benefit' of services that will buy greeting cards, gifts, and other personally thoughtful items for alleged 'loved' ones" (paragraph 5), you can infer that the author believes
   a. companies have come a long way from the oppressive working conditions that existed during the early Industrial Revolution.
   b. buying services for employees is an example of corporate generosity toward employees.
   c. the service benefits the company more than it does the employee, and besides, loved ones deserve a personally selected gift.
   d. the modern world is changing, and employees may as well change with it.

4. According to the essay, the symptoms of the modern time crunch affect
   a. those who are employed.
   b. retired people, stay-at-home-mothers, and children.
   c. senior citizens and parents.
   d. all of the above.

5. According to the author, how do people feel about the hectic pace of life?

   a. Most people are unhappy about it.

   b. Most people view it as a necessary evil and try not to let it bother them.

   c. People who are motivated view it as a challenge to be met.

   d. A fast pace is so much a part of modern life that no one notices it anymore.

■ Writing in the Margins

These questions encourage you to think not just about the essay but about the issues it raises. Your instructor may ask you to write down your answers, to discuss them in groups, or simply to think about them for class discussion.

1. Are full-time college students more pressured or less pressured than people who hold full-time jobs? Why?

2. List some factors that make modern life hectic. What changes would need to occur in the workplace and in society to slow down the pace?

3. Discuss some of the "labor-saving devices" that modern Americans take for granted. What kind of labor, specifically, does each device save us?

4. Ashcraft suggests that labor-saving devices cause feelings of guilt. Do you believe that most Americans share a work ethic that drives them to more work and longer hours? Can you think of specific examples?

TOPICS FOR WRITING

Assignment 1: Handling Stress

Paragraph or Journal Entry

Write a paragraph or journal entry discussing the ways that you handle stress. Alternatively, write a paper giving your reader advice on how to handle stress.

Assignment 2: Out of the Rat Race?

Paragraph

Some people long for the simple life. They envision themselves and their families living on a small plot of land, growing their own vegetables, and living free of the rat race. Is the simple life a part of your dream, or do you prefer the rat race? Write a paragraph giving reasons for your preference.

Assignment 3: Technology Rationing

Paragraph

The twentieth century put within the reach of most Americans many labor-saving devices and other technologies that we now take for granted: telephones, computers, coffee makers, washing machines, televisions, CD players, and automobiles, to name a few. If you could keep only one of your modern conveniences, which would it be? Write a paragraph giving your reasons.

Assignment 4: A Day in the Life . . .

Paragraph or Essay

Does your typical day unfold in a leisurely manner, or are you on an endless treadmill of activity? Write a narrative paragraph or essay describing a typical day in your life.

Spanglish Spoken Here

Janice Castro, with Dan Cook and Cristina Garcia

It's not English; it's not Spanish. It's Spanglish—a little bit of both.

In Manhattan a first-grader greets her visiting grandparents, happily exclaiming, "Come here, *sientate!*" Her bemused grandfather, who does not speak Spanish, nevertheless knows she is asking him to sit down. A Miami personnel officer understands what a job applicant means when he says, "*Quiero un* part time." Nor do drivers miss a beat reading a billboard alongside a Los Angeles street advertising CERVEZA—SIX-PACK!   1

This free-form blend of Spanish and English, known as Spanglish, is common linguistic currency wherever concentrations of Hispanic Americans are found in the U.S. In Los Angeles, where 55% of the city's 3 million inhabitants speak Spanish, Spanglish is as much a part of daily life as sunglasses. Unlike the broken-English efforts of earlier immigrants from Europe, Asia, and other regions, Spanglish has become a widely accepted conversational mode used casually—even playfully—by Spanish-speaking immigrants and native-born Americans alike.   2

Consisting of one part Hispanicized English, one part Americanized Spanish and more than a little fractured syntax, Spanglish is a bit like a Robin Williams comedy routine: a crackling line of cross-cultural patter straight from the melting pot. Often it enters Anglo homes and families through the children, who pick it up at school or at play with their young Hispanic contemporaries. In other cases, it comes from watching TV; many an Anglo child watching *Sesame Street* has learned *uno dos tres* almost as quickly as one two three.   3

Spanglish takes a variety of forms, from the Southern California Anglos who bid farewell with the utterly silly "*hasta la* bye-bye" to the Cuban American drivers in Miami who *parquean their carros*. Some Spanglish sentences are mostly Spanish, with a quick detour for an English word or two. A Latino friend may cut short a conversation by glancing at his watch and excusing himself with the explanation that he must "*ir al supermarket.*"   4

Many of the English words transplanted in this way are simply handier than their Spanish counterparts. No matter how distasteful the subject, for example, it is still easier to say "income tax" than *impuesto sobre la renta*. At the same time, many Spanish-speaking immigrants have adopted such terms as VCR, microwave and dishwasher for what they view as largely American phenomena. Still other English words convey a cultural context that is not implicit in the Spanish. A friend who invites you to *lonche* most likely has in mind the brisk American custom of "doing lunch" rather than the languorous afternoon break traditionally implied by *almuerzo*.   5

Mainstream Americans exposed to similar hybrids of German, Chinese or 6
Hindi might be mystified. But even Anglos who speak little or no Spanish are
somewhat familiar with Spanglish. Living among them, for one thing, are 19
million Hispanics. In addition, more American high school and university students sign up for Spanish than for any other foreign language.

Only in the past ten years, though, has Spanglish begun to turn into a na- 7
tional slang. Its popularity has grown with the explosive increases in U.S. immi-
gration from Latin American countries. English has increasingly collided with
Spanish in retail stores, offices and classrooms, in pop music and on street cor-
ners. Anglos whose ancestors picked up such Spanish words as *rancho, bronco,*
tornado, and *incommunicado,* for instance, now freely use such Spanish words as
gracias, bueno, amigo, and *por favor.*

Among Latinos, Spanglish conversations often flow easily from Spanish 8
into several sentences of English and back.

Spanglish is a sort of code for Latinos: the speakers know Spanish, but 9
their hybrid language reflects the American culture in which they live. Many
lean to shorter, clipped phrases in place of the longer, more graceful expressions their parents used. Says Leonel de la Cuesta, an assistant professor of
modern languages at Florida International University in Miami: "In the U.S.,
time is money, and that is showing up in Spanglish as an economy of language." Conversational examples: *taipiar* (type) and *winshi-wiper* (windshield
wiper) replace *escribir a maquina* and *limpiaparabrisas.*

Major advertisers, eager to tap the estimated $134 billion in spending 10
power wielded by Spanish-speaking Americans, have ventured into Spanglish to
promote their products. In some cases, attempts to sprinkle Spanish through
commercials have produced embarrassing gaffes. A Braniff airlines ad that
sought to tell Spanish-speaking audiences they could settle back *en* (in) luxuri-
ant *cuero* (leather) seats, for example, inadvertently said they could fly without
clothes (*encuero*). A fractured translation of the Miller Lite slogan told readers
the beer was "Filling, and less delicious." Similar blunders are often made by
Anglos trying to impress Spanish-speaking pals. But if Latinos are amused by
mangled Spanglish, they also recognize these goofs as a sort of friendly acceptance. As they might put it, *no problema.*

■ Building Vocabulary

For each question, choose the meaning that most closely defines the underlined word or phrase as it is used in the essay.

1. The word bemused most nearly means
   a. unhappy.
   b. puzzled.
   c. crotchety.
   d. sitting.

2. The phrase <u>linguistic currency</u> most nearly means
   a. words used as money.
   b. modern language.
   c. words used to exchange ideas.
   d. misunderstood words.

3. The word <u>languorous</u> most nearly means
   a. leisurely.
   b. short.
   c. language-based.
   d. noisy.

4. The word <u>hybrid</u> most nearly means
   a. plant.
   b. foreign.
   c. native.
   d. blended.

5. The word <u>gaffes</u> most nearly means
   a. blunders.
   b. cases.
   c. hooks.
   d. tricks.

■ Understanding the Essay

1. The authors' purpose in writing the essay is
   a. to define the term *Spanglish.*
   b. to compare English and Spanish
   c. to argue that communication is difficult enough without hybrid languages further confusing the process.
   d. to describe the process of language acquisition.

2. Which of the following phrases does not accurately describe Spanglish?
   a. considered playful and casual.
   b. used as an advertising tool.
   c. frowned on outside Los Angeles.
   d. takes several different forms.

3. According to the passage, acceptance of Spanglish
   a. is wider than acceptance of the language used by immigrants of an earlier era.
   b. has given it the status of a national slang.
   c. is in part due to its use by children.
   d. all of the above
4. According to the essay, Latinos may use Spanglish because
   a. they are trying to break free of the language of their parents.
   b. they are not comfortable with English.
   c. the direct, concise English phrases more accurately reflect the American culture in which they live.
   d. their ancestors contributed words such as *rancho, bronco,* and *incommunicado* to the English language.
5. In response to mangled Spanish phrasing used by advertisers and Anglos, Latinos are most likely to say
   a. *"Hasta la* bye-bye."
   b. *"No problema."*
   c. *"Yo quiero una cerveza."*
   d. "Give me a break, *por favor."*

■ **Writing in the Margins**

These questions encourage you to think not just about the essay but about the issues it raises. Your instructor may ask you to write down your answers, to discuss them in groups, or simply to think about them for class discussion.

1. Some countries guard their language zealously against encroachment by other languages. The French government, for instance, has taken measures discouraging the incorporation of English into the French language. But some people would argue that borrowing from other languages is one of the primary agents of growth and change in language. What is your view?
2. The essay says that Spanglish is becoming a national slang. In spite of attempts by language purists to suppress or discourage slang, it thrives in many different forms. Does slang have purpose and value? What is its place in the English language?

Group Exercise 2

Form groups of five. Your mission is to find five words widely used in English that come directly from other languages, unaltered in form or spelling. Find words from at least three different languages. Examples include *banana* (from the Wolof language of Africa), *scenario* (Italian), *bureau* (French), *pretzel* (German), *hibachi* (Japanese), and *parka* (Inuit).

Here are some steps you can take in your search:

1. Brainstorm with your group to think of words that you believe may come from other languages. When your list is complete, check the words in a hardback dictionary that includes information on word origins.

2. Try an Internet search. First, search for narrow phrases such as "words from other languages," "word origins," or "foreign words." Enclosing the terms in quotation marks as you type them into the search engine will ensure that the exact term is queried rather than each separate word. If the terms don't work, try them on a different search engine. If you still get no results, try broader terms such as "words" or "vocabulary."

3. Search for the information in books on language and vocabulary in the reference section of your library.

TOPICS FOR WRITING

Assignment 1: Becoming Bilingual

Paragraph or Journal Entry

If you could design the American educational system, would every child learn a second language? Write a paragraph or journal entry explaining why or why not.

Assignment 2: Levels of Language

Paragraph

Everyone has different levels of language—different ways of speaking in different situations. Write a paragraph categorizing the levels of language you regularly use and describe situations where you would be likely to use each level. For example, you might use slang when you are with friends, informal language with teachers and parents, and formal language in interviews or on the job. Describe each level in detail. Consider the following questions as you do your prewriting for this topic: What specific words might you use on one level but not another? Are there words that might be acceptable on one level but forbidden on another? Are there levels where you tend to speak more quickly? To pronounce words more carefully? To speak more softly or more loudly? To use incomplete sentences?

Assignment 3: Advantages of Hybrid Languages

Paragraph

In a community where speakers of different languages coexist, what are some of the advantages or disadvantages of a hybrid language like Spanglish? Write a paragraph explaining advantages, disadvantages, or both.

Assignment 4: Speaking Your Language

Paragraph or Essay

"I just can't get along with my father. We don't even speak the same language anymore."

"I knew right away I would like Thea. We just seemed to speak the same language."

Sometimes, the word *language* is used as a metaphor for a deeper kind of understanding. If someone "speaks your language," that means you have common interests or shared values. If someone "does not speak your language," there may be such a difference in the activities and beliefs that you find important that it's hard to find common ground.

Think of someone who "speaks your language" or someone who does not. After prewriting on that person and the communication between the two of you, write a paragraph or essay analyzing the reasons that you and the other person communicate so well or so poorly.

Recipe for a Sick Society

Donna Britt

How can we foil those pesky do-gooders and make kids violent in the process? Donna Britt has some answers.

1   Just for laughs, let's pretend. Say we wanted to create, in a relatively peaceful society, a nation of youthful killers or just millions of aggressive young jerks. How could we do it?

2   We'd have to start young. Analyzing infants, we'd realize their desperate need for love and intimacy. We would also note that a baby's only real job is to study, digest and mimic everything he or she encounters.

3   Then we'd go to work.

4   We'd create an economy where in most families, both parents needed to work outside the home to survive. Soon after birth, babies would be placed with caregivers who would tend to their basic needs.

5   Working moms and dads would remain on the job for ever-increasing hours. Their "free" time at home would be eaten up by paying bills, cooking, cleaning, helping with homework and finishing work uncompleted at the job. Relaxed time with kids? Rare to nonexistent.

6   Even so, many children would still receive considerable love and attention, especially at home. To minimize that, we could design, say, an electronic box that beamed seductive, violent images—fistfights, beatings, rapes and murders into every dwelling.

7   A few troublesome kids would realize such images are fiction. So we would invent "news shows" highlighting real-life mayhem from local, national and even international sources. The box could also provide "talk shows" on which real people aired their problems before slapping, kicking and otherwise attacking one another as audiences cheered.

8   But this might fail to make enough kids violent. So what if we invented strikingly realistic visual "games" for use on the box? Using the games, children could shoot, impale or beat to death lifelike images of people and monsters.

9   Some pesky parents would, of course, limit their kids' exposure to the box and the games. To deal with that, we could create public living rooms. Here, kids could share with strangers the thrill of experiencing—on gigantic screens complete with sophisticated sound systems—vivid moving images of stabbings, garrotings, explosions and dismemberments. No one killed would be mourned for more than a minute; every death would be as choreographed as a ballet. Killjoys might try to keep small children from seeing these images, but we'd get around that by making versions of the images available to be seen later on the box.

In certain parts of the country, rural and urban, we could glorify guns, 10
make folks think they can't live without firearms. Then we could make it relatively easy for anyone, even kids, to get them.

Still not enough? What if we did something with music? We could some- 11
how attach violent, materialistic or overtly sexualized images to music. We
could persuade certain music-makers to celebrate guns, greed and irresponsible sex in their songs! They, too, could provide images for the box—of threatening-looking men and barely dressed women, all singing about the glories of
instant, consequence-free gratification of every urge.

In schools, we could avoid offering any classes in conflict resolution, rela- 12
tionship building or tolerance. We could stage "sporting events" in which
young athletes' viciousness is accepted, even encouraged.

To be sure kids got the pro-violence message, we adults could pretend to 13
abhor brutishness. We could bemoan violence ceaselessly in the media, and
feign astonishment each time a youngster assaulted or killed someone. "How
could this happen?" we'd wail after each brutality.

With straight faces, we could present shows on the box about "Children 14
Who Kill," write shocked editorials, swear to "get to the bottom" of the problem. Then, *we wouldn't change a thing.*

So. If a society actually did those crazy things, would kids—not every kid, 15
but way too many of them—behave in frighteningly aggressive ways?

Maybe. But what intelligent, caring culture could be that stupid?   16

■ Building Vocabulary

For each question, choose the meaning that most closely defines the underlined word or phrase as it is used in the essay.

1. The word seductive most nearly means
   a. alluring.
   b. repellent.
   c. simple.
   d. sexual.

2. The word mayhem most nearly means
   a. maybe.
   b. violence.
   c. politics.
   d. news.

3. The word choreographed most nearly means
   a. gruesome.
   b. peaceful.
   c. spontaneous.
   d. planned.

4. The word <u>materialistic</u> most nearly means
   a. dealing with the things money can buy.
   b. having to do with matters of the heart.
   c. spiritual.
   d. realistic.

5. The word <u>gratification</u> most nearly means
   a. satisfaction.
   b. denial.
   c. punishment.
   d. longing.

■ Understanding the Essay

1. Britt's *stated* purpose (not her implied purpose) is
   a. to prevent violence.
   b. to tell the reader how to create a nation of aggressive youth.
   c. to show how the media corrupt youth.
   d. to describe a peaceful society.

2. Which statement best expresses the *implied* main idea of the essay?
   a. Our society is relatively peaceful and is likely to remain that way.
   b. By following a few simple steps, we can create a society of violent youth.
   c. Inadequate parental attention and violence on television, in movies, and in video games is fostering violence in young people.
   d. Serious problems in the economic structure of the United States are leading to the breakdown of the family.

3. The economy that Britt describes in paragraphs 4 and 5 is
   a. an entirely fictional example.
   b. the economy of the United States in the 1950s.
   c. the economy of the United States today.
   d. the economy of a country less prosperous than the United States.

4. According to the essay, "troublesome kids" are the ones who
   a. can tell the difference between television and real life.
   b. perform violent acts and sometimes even kill.
   c. do not take school seriously enough.
   d. play violent video games.

5. In paragraph 14, the author implies that those who write editorials and swear to get to the bottom of the problem of youth violence are

a. misguided, because violence is natural.

b. sincere and well-meaning.

c. effective, because they make people think.

d. hypocritical, because no action is taken.

■ Writing in the Margins

These questions encourage you to think not just about the essay but about the issues it raises. Your instructor may ask you to write down your answers, to discuss them in groups, or simply to think about them for class discussion.

1. Britt's essay is a form of *satire*. Satire is a type of writing that seeks to change society by holding its practices and customs up to ridicule. Notice, too, how Britt poses as an outsider to society, pretending to come up with ideas that are already an ingrained part of our culture. What customs does Britt invite her readers to see as ridiculous? What changes do you think she would like to see in society?

2. Do you believe that violence on television, in video games, and in music videos can encourage violent behavior in young people?

3. How big a problem is violence in American society? What can be done to stop it?

TOPICS FOR WRITING

Assignment 1: Close to Home

Paragraph or Journal Entry

Write a paragraph or journal entry telling how violence has touched your life or the life of someone you know.

Assignment 2: Violence Czar

Paragraph

You have just been appointed violence czar. Your budget is unlimited, and you have complete freedom to devise a plan and try it out for a year. You may call on any advisers and use any resources you wish, and you may try anything as long as it is within the law and does not violate the Constitution of the United States. Whom would you consult? What would you do? How would you reduce violence in the United States? Write a paragraph describing the steps you would take if you were the violence czar.

Assignment 3: Seeds of Violence

Paragraph

In a paragraph, discuss some of the causes of violence in American society.

Assignment 4: A Satire

Paragraph or Essay

Write a satire modeled after Britt's. Take the position of outsider and write a paragraph or essay about a problem that exists in your school, in your workplace, in your city, or in society in general. If you wish, use Britt's method and give a recipe for homelessness, racism, apathy, or whatever problem you choose to discuss.

Don't Blame Me! The New "Culture of Victimization"

John J. Macionis

Is America becoming a nation of people who refuse to take responsibility? Sociologist John J. Macionis weighs the evidence.

A New York man recently leaped in front of a moving subway train; lucky enough to survive, he sued the city, claiming the train failed to stop in time to prevent his serious injuries. (A court awarded him $650,000.) In Washington, D.C., after realizing that he had been videotaped smoking crack cocaine in a hotel room, the city's mayor blamed his woman companion for "setting him up" and charged that the police were racially motivated in arresting him. After more than a dozen women accused former Senator Bob Packwood of sexual harassment, he tried to defuse the scandal by checking into an alcohol treatment center. In the most celebrated case of its kind, Dan White, who gunned down the mayor of San Francisco and a city council member, blamed this violent episode on insanity caused by having eaten too much junk food (the so-called Twinkie defense). In each of these cases, someone denies personal responsibility for an action, claiming to be a victim. Rather than taking the blame for our mishaps and misdeeds, in other words, more and more members of our society are pointing the finger elsewhere. Such behavior has prompted sociologist Irving Horowitz to announce a developing "culture of victimization" in which "everyone is a victim" and "no one accepts responsibility for anything."

One indication of this cultural trend is the proliferation of "addictions," a term that people once associated only with uncontrollable drug use. We now hear about gambling addicts, compulsive overeaters, sex addicts, and even people who excuse mounting credit-card debts as shopping addiction. Bookstores overflow with manuals to help people come to terms with numerous new medical or psychological conditions ranging from "The Cinderella Complex" to "The Casanova Complex" and even "Soap Opera Syndrome." And the U.S. courts are ever more clogged by lawsuits driven by the need to blame someone—and often to collect big money—for the kind of misfortune that we used to accept as part of life.

What's going on here? Is U.S. culture changing? Historically, our way of life has been based on a culture of "rugged individualism," the notion that people are responsible for whatever triumph or tragedy befalls them. But this value has been eroded by a number of factors. First, everyone is more aware (partly through the work of sociologists) of how society shapes our lives. This knowledge has expanded the categories of people claiming to be victims well beyond those who have suffered historical disadvantages (such as African Americans and women) to include even well-off people. On college campuses, moreover, a sense that "everybody gets special treatment but us" is prompting white males to view themselves as the latest "victims."

Second, since they began advertising their services in 1977, lawyers have   4
encouraged a sense of injustice among clients they hope to shepherd into court. The number of million-dollar lawsuit awards has risen more than twenty-five-fold in the last twenty-five years.

Third, there has been a proliferation of "rights groups" that promote what   5
Amitai Etzioni calls "rights inflation." Beyond the traditional constitutional liberties are many newly claimed rights, including those of hunters (as well as those of animals), the rights of smokers (and nonsmokers), the right of women to control their bodies (and the rights of the unborn), the right to own a gun (and the right to be safe from violence). Expanding and competing claims for unmet rights, then, generate victims (and victimizers) on all sides.

Does this shift signal a fundamental realignment in our culture? Perhaps,   6
but the new popularity of being a victim also springs from some well-established cultural forces. For example, the claim to victimization depends on a long-standing belief that everyone has the right to life, liberty, and the pursuit of happiness. Yet this new explosion of "rights" does more than alert us to clear cases of injustice; it threatens to erode our sense of responsibility as members of a larger society.

■ **Building Vocabulary**

For each question, choose the meaning that most closely defines the underlined word or phrase as it is used in the essay.

1. The word defuse most nearly means
   a. inflame.
   b. detonate.
   c. worsen.
   d. ease.

2. The word celebrated most nearly means
   a. condemned.
   b. publicized.
   c. suppressed.
   d. cheered.

3. The word shepherd most nearly means
   a. graze.
   b. farm.
   c. guide.
   d. fleece.

4. The phrase more than twenty-five-fold most nearly means
   a. twenty-five.
   b. more than twenty-five.
   c. more than the original number times twenty-five.
   d. less than twenty-five.

5. The word proliferation most nearly means
   a. rapid growth.
   b. profit.
   c. decrease.
   d. fantasy.

■ Understanding the Essay

1. Which statement most nearly expresses the main idea of the essay?
   a. People in our society no longer allow their rights to be trampled on by others.
   b. People often claim to be addicts or victims of disease rather than blaming themselves for their troubles.
   c. Increasingly, people are avoiding responsibility by blaming their woes on outside factors.
   d. People who eat junk food are apt to commit violent crimes.

2. The "culture of victimization" is characterized by
   a. refusal to accept responsibility.
   b. a prevalence of "addictions."
   c. lawsuits.
   d. all of the above.

3. The author implies that African Americans and women
   a. are among the most vocal in claiming their rights.
   b. have more reason to call themselves victims than some other groups.
   c. are the only groups that have any right to claim they are victims.
   d. are less likely to think of themselves as victims than other groups.

4. A driver runs a red light while talking on a cell phone and hits a pedestrian. If the driver were a "rugged individualist," what would he say to the pedestrian?

   a. "Get up, Pilgrim; it's only a scratch."

   b. "I will take full responsibility for your hospital bills as soon as I sue my cell phone company."

   c. "What are *you* whining about? As a color-blind male, I am discriminated against by the red light/green light traffic signal system. Good thing I have this cell phone to call my lawyer."

   d. "I'm sorry. It was my fault."

5. The author believes that the "rights explosion"

   a. signals a shift in our cultural ideals.

   b. has roots that stretch back as far as the Declaration of Independence.

   c. is a threat to our sense of responsibility.

   d. all of the above.

■ Writing in the Margins

These questions encourage you to think not just about the essay but about the issues it raises. Your instructor may ask you to write down your answers, to discuss them in groups, or simply to think about them for class discussion.

1. Do you see evidence of the "rights explosion" that the author discusses? What are some of the advantages and disadvantages of the focus on individual rights?

2. Many people criticize the explosion of frivolous lawsuits and astronomical monetary awards in our society. Do you agree that this kind of problem has increased? To what do you attribute the problem?

3. When applied to behavior, are the words *addiction, complex,* and *syndrome* likely to increase or decrease an individual's sense of responsibility? Why?

TOPICS FOR WRITING

Assignment 1: Rabbit or Coyote?

Paragraph or Journal Entry

What are the advantages and/or disadvantages of seeing oneself as a victim? As a "rugged individualist"? Explain in a paragraph or journal entry.

Assignment 2: The Rights Explosion

Paragraph

Do you believe the "rights explosion" has gotten out of hand? Write a paragraph giving specific examples to support your answer.

Assignment 3: Rights and Responsibilities

Paragraph

It has been said that every right we gain brings with it a corresponding responsibility. Below are listed some rights that citizens of the United States take for granted. In a paragraph, discuss one of these rights and the corresponding responsibilities that go along with it.

having children	attending school
driving	expressing an opinion
choosing a career	choosing where to live
voting	choosing a mate

Assignment 4: "Certain Unalienable Rights"

Paragraph or Essay

In the Declaration of Independence, Thomas Jefferson wrote that, simply by virtue of being born, everyone has "certain unalienable rights"—that is, rights that cannot simply be taken away at the whim of government. Jefferson listed "life, liberty, and the pursuit of happiness" among those rights. What right or rights do you believe every human being should have? Write a paragraph or essay explaining your choice(s).

Assignment 5: Judgment Day

Paragraph, Journal Entry, or Essay

Macionis points out that lawsuits are common in our society. Imagine that you are a judge appointed to decide one of the following lawsuits. As a judge, you must approach each objectively, without assuming they are "frivolous lawsuits" of the kind Macionis discusses. Like any collection of lawsuits, some of the examples will have more merit than others. Pick any of the four cases and write a paragraph, journal entry, or essay giving your decision as a judge and your reasons for the decision.

Lawsuit A: The Case of the Nonsinging Server

A woman takes a job as a server in a restaurant. After she accepts the job, she finds that if a customer is celebrating a birthday, all servers are required to gather around the table and sing. She explains to her manager that her religion does not celebrate holidays or birthdays, and she does not feel right about singing to celebrate a customer's birthday. The manager understands and excuses her from the requirement, but when a new shift manager is hired six months later, the employee is told she will be fired if she does not join in the songs. She refuses to sing and is fired. She sues, claiming she has been discriminated against on the basis of her religion. The restaurant's lawyers argue that like any other employee, she is subject to firing if she cannot perform all the duties of the job.

Lawsuit B: The Case of the Harassed Designer

Shortly after earning his degree in graphic arts design, Dan is hired by an advertising agency. His boss takes him under her wing, giving him plum projects, a corner office, and special attention. But one evening, as they are working late, the attention becomes a bit *too* special. When Dan tells his boss he is not interested in a sexual relationship, she immediately apologizes for stepping over the line. Though his boss never again approaches him sexually, one year later, Dan's office is a converted janitor's closet, and he is working on routine jobs usually assigned to administrative assistants rather than graphic designers. In a year when average raises are 7 percent, Dan's raise is 1 percent. Dan files a sexual harassment lawsuit for one million dollars. The company's lawyers say that since the boss apologized and since Dan still has his job, his complaint is not valid.

Lawsuit C: The Case of the Bungled Burglary

A family goes on vacation, and Tom, burglar, attempts to break in. Sturdy burglar bars cover the window, and the house is wired with an alarm system. But Tom goes up on the roof, intending to let himself in through a skylight. Instead, he falls off the roof and breaks several bones. Tom later files a lawsuit for $500,000 for medical expenses and pain and suffering. The lawyer for the vacationing homeowner argues that since the injuries were sustained during an attempted felony, the burglar is entitled to nothing.

Lawsuit D: The Case of the Overweight Achiever

Sally, president of the Math Club and a member of the Debate Team at the small college she attends, has finished all of her academic course work with a 4.0 average and has passed two physical education classes: Bowling and First Aid, with a C and an A. However, she has failed a third required course, Jogging and Fitness, three times. No matter how hard she tries, her weight will not allow her to do enough pushups and situps or jog a mile quickly enough to pass the "basic physical requirement" section of the course. After unsuccessful appeals to the head of the Physical Education Department and the college's administration to allow her to fulfill the course requirements in some other way, Sally sues the college for five million dollars. Her lawyer argues that the college's rigid physical education policies discriminate against people who have a genetic tendency toward obesity. However, Sally says that she is not really interested in the money. She is willing to settle for the right to fulfill the requirements of the course in another way so that she can complete her degree. The college's lawyers argue that Sally is simply being asked to fulfill the same requirements as all other students, and that if she cannot complete those requirements, she should not be awarded a degree.

How 'bout Us?

Leonard Pitts

When the divorce rate climbs higher with every passing year and friends' relationships crumble with increasing frequency, it's easy to wonder, "How 'bout us?"

"Them, too?" That's the disbelieving question I asked when Marilyn told me about some friends of ours whose marriage is falling apart. I don't know why I'm surprised; lately it seems like every couple we know is splitting up. 1

My wife seems to take it in stride, better able than I to accept that these things happen. I guess I'm naive. Guess I've listened to too many love songs. Not that I can still hear them as I did when I was young. There is an edge of lamentation now that I didn't catch back then, a scrim of bitter sharpening the sweet. It makes Al Green sound keening and sad as he sings, "Let's stay together." 2

And then there's the old Champaign song that says, "Some people can love one another for life. How 'bout us?" 3

Indeed. This month, it'll be 16 years since my wife and I married. Sixteen years of children, challenges and change. Sixteen years of a far-from-perfect man and a less-than-flawless woman, holding on. Sixteen years. How 'bout us? 4

The question pokes me in the ribs sometimes as I watch her cooking dinner or sleeping. After all, we walk the same path our friends do, face the same turns on the same rough road. How 'bout us? Why couldn't what happened in their homes happen in ours? 5

Change comes, after all. I'm not the man who married her; she's not the woman who promised herself to me. And here another song imposes itself. The melody is simple, the orchestration unadorned, but Bruce Springsteen's voice lifts and carries the words. "If as we're walking, a hand should slip free, I'll wait for you. And should I fall behind, wait for me." 6

It takes years to reach the stage where you can sing that promise and know what it means, children. I sure didn't know 16 years ago. I don't think my young friend Darrin does now. If tomorrow troubles him, he gives no sign. All I've seen are expectation and hope as he prepares to be married. Seems like just yesterday he and Mary Ann were on the way to their prom, posing in the flash of instant cameras and looking for all the world like they had escaped from the top of a wedding cake. Now they're doing it for real, and you wonder whether they understand what they're getting into. Do they know how things can change? 7

Not that it matters. When they take their vows, I will be <u>unconditionally</u>   8
happy for them even knowing the things they don't yet know, even understanding that change has sharp edges, even feeling the ground shake. Even then.

Because it's worth it, isn't it? Worth the risk and the fear just to reach with-   9
out looking and feel another hand clasp yours. To get lost and know that
somewhere ahead, she waits without being asked.

I am saddened to see friends going separate ways, sobered by how many   10
times I've asked that question lately: "Them too?" But I am also reminded that
there's a difference between promises and guarantees.

A guarantee requires no <u>exertion</u>, but you have to work at a promise. A   11
guarantee can't fail, but a promise is guarded from failure only by vigilance and
will. A guarantee comes from Sears or Circuit City. A promise from us.

Few things are less secure or require a greater investment of faith. But that's   12
what a marriage comes down to in the end, isn't it? Promises, promises. Some
days, you fear that it's not enough. Some days you hear "How 'bout us?" and
you're standing there with your promises hanging out and you think you must
be crazy. Some days you feel like the emperor parading around in his wonderful
new clothes. Some days.

Then you stumble from the darkness and there she is like she always was,   13
and you wonder why you ever doubted. The fear <u>recedes</u> like night sweats and
thunderstorms, leaving a calm in its wake.

The promise is kept. I know few feelings better than that, few truths sweeter   14
than this: If I fall behind, she waits for me.

■ Building Vocabulary

For each question, choose the meaning that most closely defines the underlined word or phrase as it is used in the essay.

1. The word <u>keening</u> most nearly means
   a. nifty.
   b. joyous.
   c. wailing.
   d. melodic.

2. The word <u>unadorned</u> most nearly means
   a. simple.
   b. complex.
   c. unpleasant.
   d. strident.

3. The word <u>unconditionally</u> most nearly means
   a. somewhat.
   b. cautiously.

    c. partially.

    d. completely.

4. The word <u>exertion</u> most nearly means

    a. work.

    b. fulfillment.

    c. achievement.

    d. expectation.

5. The word <u>recedes</u> most nearly means

    a. increases.

    b. sneaks up.

    c. decreases.

    d. drips.

■ Understanding the Essay

1. Which statement best expresses the writer's purpose?

    a. to lament the increasing divorce rate in the United States.

    b. to persuade young people to wait before marrying.

    c. to discuss love songs.

    d. to reflect on the uncertainties of love.

2. Pitts says that he has been married

    a. longer than any of his friends.

    b. for sixteen years.

    c. since he was sixteen.

    d. too long.

3. For Pitts, the sweetest truth of his marriage is expressed in

    a. a Champaign song.

    b. an Al Green song.

    c. a Bruce Springsteen song.

    d. the traditional wedding song, "O Promise Me."

4. The tone of the essay can best be characterized as

    a. cynical.

    b. sentimental.

    c. objective.

    d. melancholy.

5. Based on the essay, if Pitts had a television show, it might be called
   a. *Bachelor Party.*
   b. *This Old Spouse.*
   c. *Living Single.*
   d. *Divorce Court.*

■ **Writing in the Margins**

These questions encourage you to think not just about the essay but about the issues it raises. Your instructor may ask you to write down your answers, to discuss them in groups, or simply to think about them for class discussion.

1. What do you think are some of the reasons for the high divorce rate and general instability of relationships today?
2. What does Pitts say the difference is between a promise and a guarantee? What does he mean?
3. Do you believe that states should enact laws making divorces more difficult to obtain?
4. Fifty years ago, people grew up with the expectation that marriage would be in their future. Today, many young people have no expectation or desire to marry. What changes have taken place in society that might encourage people to remain single?

TOPICS FOR WRITING

Assignment 1: Losing Love

Paragraph or Journal Entry

Alfred, Lord Tennyson wrote, "'Tis better to have loved and lost/Than never to have loved at all." Do you agree? Write a paragraph or journal entry explaining why.

Assignment 2: D-I-V-O-R-C-E

Paragraph

Write a paragraph discussing factors in society or factors within a marriage that contribute to divorce.

Assignment 3: How to Have a Successful Marriage

Paragraph

Imagine that a friend or relative who is about to marry comes to you and asks for advice for a successful marriage. Write a process paragraph giving that person advice.

Assignment 4: Reality Check

Paragraph or Essay

If you are now or have ever been married, write a paragraph or essay comparing or contrasting your expectations about marriage with the realities of marriage. Did it turn out the way you thought it would? If so, what specific expectations were met? If not, what specific areas of marriage were different than you imagined that they would be?

Mixed Blessings

Jim Auchmutey

There's a fine line between grace and disgrace when it comes to giving thanks at Thanksgiving.

If there's one time you want to unhinge a really good blessing, it's Thanksgiving. After all, giving thanks is the whole reason for the holiday—not turkey or the Macy's parade or that football game from Detroit that used to look better when they didn't play it in a dome and you could watch huge men slide helplessly in the snow. Thanksgiving is to blessings what the Super Bowl is to football. Maybe that's why one of my most vivid memories of the day is the time my family dropped the ball.   1

We were sitting around the table clowning about something one of the nephews did when suddenly, without warning, my father decided to have a conversation with his maker. "Dear Lord," he began, and the rest of us looked around puzzled, then closed our eyes hard and tried to follow his turn-on-a-dime shift from the scatological to the theological. We didn't make it. I heard a muffled snicker and noticed my sister Suzy biting her lip and turning pink. Next to her, my mother's bowed head bounced like one of those bobbing dolls. The sillies swept the table like a wave, and we all burst into laughter.   2

All of us, that is, but my father. He stopped praying and looked at us balefully like a kicked puppy. "I don't imagine that one made it to the ceiling," he said.   3

Thanksgiving is the least Southern of our major holidays when you consider that New Englanders invented it and that Abraham Lincoln made it a national observance during the Civil War. In another way, though, Thanksgiving seems very Southern. It's the one day when the great majority of Americans say grace—a custom that persists in this region like no other.

This Thanksgiving, for the first time in my 42 years, I will not be at my family's table listening to my father bless the meal. I will be away. In considering what sort of grace I should say on this landmark occasion, I have categorized some of the major types of blessings: 4

The Hallmark Homily

A homespun appreciation for loved ones safely returned to hearth. Think of the Waltons holding hands around the table while Grandpa waxes folksy.   5

Rim Shot!

There's a whole genre of blessings meant to amuse rather than give thanks. 6
Who can forget the eloquent Archie Bunker praying, "Bless the meat and damn
the skin, open your kisser and cram it in"? Or the subversive Bart Simpson?
"Dear God, we paid for all this stuff ourselves, so thanks for nothing."

God's a Busy Deity, Get to the Point

My father was amazed at the interim pastor who opened a family night supper 7
with "Lord, bless this meal. Amen"—and nothing else. I can beat that brevity by
four words; when they asked me to say grace in vacation Bible school, I re-
sponded like countless smart asses before and since by saying just that:
"Grace." Don't imagine that one made it to the ceiling either.

The Stemwinder

Awed by a bounty of food, some beseechers serve up a bounty of words. An 8
uncle of mine is notorious for this. Asked to say grace, he inhales deeply and
grips the back of his chair with a white-knuckled intensity that suggests we'll be
filibustered before being filled. No one so far has had the nerve to do what a
woman did at the soup kitchen where my parents volunteer. Impatient with the
prayer, she announced, "I'm HAWN-gry!"

The Roundelay

It doesn't seem fair that women usually cook the feast but men usually get to 9
carve the bird and pronounce the incantation. Bill Coady, a minister friend of
mine, gets around this by asking everyone at the table to say a line of thanks in
a sort of chain blessing. There were sixteen people at his and Deb's table last
year, and somehow the turkey didn't get cold.

Something Borrowed, Something True

Almost everyone remembers a blessing from childhood. Sometimes they're still 10
the best. Julia Pitkin of Nashville coauthored a cookbook of menus and table
graces called *Bless This Food*. Of all the elegant verse gathered in the volume, her
favorite is the one her young sons recite at home, the old Johnny Appleseed
ditty: "The Lord is good to me, and so I thank the Lord, for giving me the things
I need, the sun, the rain, and the appleseed. The Lord is good to me."

That's probably what I'll do Thursday: Replay one from the hit parade. It 11
worked for my colleague Celestine Sibley.

In *The Celestine Sibley Sampler,* there's a 1951 gem about a woman who took 12
her daughter to a café for breakfast. Everyone seemed glum and silent as the
radio played Korean War news. Then the little girl said a blessing out loud—

"God is great, God is good, Let us thank Him for our food . . ."—and the place came to life with smiles and conversation.

As the preacher said, prayer works.   13

■ Building Vocabulary

For each question, choose the meaning that most closely defines the underlined word or phrase as it is used in the essay.

1. The phrase from the scatological to the theological most likely means
   a. from spiritual discussion to prayer.
   b. from prayer to crude jokes.
   c. from crude jokes to prayer.
   d. from logical to illogical.

2. The word balefully most nearly means
   a. reproachfully.
   b. conspiratorially.
   c. laughingly.
   d. approvingly.

3. The word beseechers most nearly means
   a. those who cook.
   b. those who eat.
   c. those who pray.
   d. those who interrupt.

4. The word filibustered most nearly means
   a. force fed.
   b. being forced to listen.
   c. ignored.
   d. silenced.

5. The word glum most nearly means
   a. unhappy.
   b. cheerful.
   c. talkative.
   d. hungry.

■ Understanding the Essay

1. Which of the following would be the best alternate title for this essay?
   a. "Why I Am Thankful"
   b. "Ways We Give Thanks"

      c. "Prayer Works"

      d. "A Thanksgiving Alone"

2. When the writer's father said, "I don't imagine that one made it to the ceiling," he meant

      a. that the prayer was not loud enough.

      b. that God did not hear the prayer.

      c. that his family had been wrong to distract him while he was saying grace.

      d. that the proper attitude for prayer was missing.

3. The primary method of development for this essay is

      a. classification.

      b. comparison-contrast.

      c. argument.

      d. process.

4. The author states that the custom of saying grace is most common in

      a. the South.

      b. the Northeast.

      c. the Midwest.

      d. the United States.

5. Look at the last line, "As the preacher said, prayer works." In the context of the rest of the passage, this sentence is the author's way of saying

      a. everyone should pray.

      b. people who give thanks before a meal are less likely to suffer the ill effects of indigestion or food poisoning.

      c. the little girl's prayer had a positive effect on the people in the diner.

      d. people are likely to get what they pray for.

■ Writing in the Margins

These questions encourage you to think not just about the essay but about the issues it raises. Your instructor may ask you to write down your answers, to discuss them in groups, or simply to think about them for class discussion.

1. Rituals and customs are often connected with the cooking, serving, and eating of meals. There are rituals concerning seating, proper behavior, and proper topics of conversation at meals. Some cultures even have dietary prohibitions against certain kinds of food, such as pork or beef. Discuss some of the food customs or rituals you know about. Do you know anything about their origins?

2. Every religion practices some sort of prayer or meditation. Meditation or contemplation is also common outside of a religious context. What purposes do prayer and meditation serve?

3. Is the custom of families gathering around the table disappearing in modern culture? Discuss.

TOPICS FOR WRITING

Assignment 1: Food for Thought

Paragraph or Journal Entry

Write a paragraph or journal entry describing your favorite food. Be sure to include all of the five senses: sight, hearing, taste, touch, and smell. Make your description so realistic that your reader's mouth waters. Alternatively, describe the worst meal you ever ate.

Assignment 2: "Grace"ful Examples

Paragraph

Write a paragraph giving examples of your experiences with the custom of saying grace. You might describe how your relationship to the custom has changed since childhood, or you might discuss how your experiences vary according to place or situation.

Assignment 3: Real Meals

Paragraph

Not every meal is an elaborate Thanksgiving feast, with sparkling glassware on the table and the tantalizing aroma of roast turkey in the air. Sometimes meals are quick: Slim-Fast at the desk or Healthy Choice from the microwave. Sometimes they are "meals on wheels": Kentucky Fried Chicken or Burger King from the drive-through. Those are just two of many possibilities. Write a paragraph classifying the kinds of meals that you eat. Use three different categories of classification. Make sure that you have a single basis for classification: price, speed, quality, ease of preparation, number or kind of dinner companions, and so on.

Assignment 4: Your Favorite Holiday

Paragraph or Essay

The essay "Mixed Blessings" centers around the Thanksgiving holiday. What is your favorite holiday? Write a paragraph or essay telling why. Note: Holidays with special traditions—the Fourth of July with its barbecues and fireworks, Halloween with its jack-o'-lanterns, costumes, and treats—provide ample opportunity for description.

One for the Books

Rheta Grimsley Johnson

Some predict that as computers become more prevalent, books will gradually disappear. Rheta Grimsley Johnson weighs the issue.

1   In 1875 the folks at Remington asked Mark Twain to write a testimonial for their new typewriter. Here's how he answered:

2   "Please do not use my name in any way. Please do not even divulge the fact that I own a machine. I have entirely stopped using the Type Writer for the reason that I never could write a letter with it to anybody without receiving a request by return mail that I would not only describe the machine but state what progress I had made in the use of it. . . . I don't like to write letters, and so I don't want people to know that I own this curiosity breeding little joker."

3   Twain's main complaint was that the typewriter's novelty caused people to ignore the content of his letters. Technology overshadowed genius. The "curiosity breeding little joker" had become more important than the dictation of one of the great brains of last century.

4   I found that anecdote in a paperback called *The Typewriter Legend,* on sale for a pittance at my local library.

5   It was an ink smudge of a February day, dark and messy, and so I trotted on down to the book sale. Cheap books call out to me like "Night Train" to a wino. I love the feel of used volumes, the esoteric titles that inevitably end up in cardboard boxes labeled "SALE BOOKS."

6   In all, I bought about one thousand pages of words for ten dollars. That's a lot of pages, a lot of words. I got Robert Penn Warren's long poem, "Chief Joseph of the Nez Perce," and a book of Herblock cartoons and a stack of children's books for my niece and nephews. All the way home I congratulated myself for enterprise and frugality.

7   If you believe the shibboleths of today's high-tech boosters, the screen has replaced the book as the symbol, the literal repository, the ultimate source of most knowledge. After centuries of use, the book's spine and pages have been replaced with electronic scrolls.

8   But you cannot do with a screen what I've been doing the past few days with Jacki Lyden's memoir, *Daughter of the Queen of Sheba.* At least not without a lot of trouble and miles of extension cord.

9   *Sheba* has gone to bed with me, and to Pollard's Drive-In, where I sat at the raggedy lunch counter and alternated turning pages and eating turnip greens. I read a few pages while soaking in a hot tub.

10

The typewriter—this according to my new, old book on the machine—became truly important only after becoming so ubiquitous that it was invisible. That will have to happen to computers, too. Otherwise, novelty will continue to overwhelm content. We'll all be doing things on computers not because we need to, but because we can.

11

I studied my fellow booklovers at the library sale. We didn't look special, or endangered. There were noisy children, out of school for Presidents Day. There was a retired man, searching for books on the Civil War. There was a skinny teenager, checking out the hobby section. A tough-looking woman in jeans picked up a book called *Filing for Divorce in Georgia* and said to her son, "I wish I'd had this a few years ago."

12

All of us could have gone into the next room and surfed the Net for free, I suppose, but we wouldn't have left with a satisfying sack, a collection of coverless volumes branded with other owners' names and stamped at the back with ink from the pad of some efficient librarian. "DISCARD," they say.

13

Not yet. Not quite yet.

■ Building Vocabulary

For each question, choose the meaning that most closely defines the word or phrase as it is used in the essay.

1. The word testimonial most nearly means
   a. recommendation.
   b. description.
   c. book.
   d. last will and testament.

2. The word anecdote most nearly means
   a. antidote.
   b. story that makes a point.
   c. story that rambles.
   d. page.

3. The word shibboleths most nearly means
   a. expensive computers.
   b. widely held ideas.
   c. books.
   d. symbols.

4. The word ubiquitous most nearly means
   a. widespread.
   b. transparent.

   c. scarce.

   d. cheap.

5. The word <u>novelty</u> most nearly means

   a. thoughtfulness.

   b. anything relating to a book.

   c. computer programming.

   d. the attraction of something new.

■ Understanding the Essay

1. Which statement best expresses the main idea of the essay?

   a. According to computer experts, computers are becoming a replacement for books.

   b. Inexpensive books can often be found at library book sales.

   c. Computers are useful tools, but—at least so far—they cannot replace books.

   d. Mark Twain was one of the first to use a typewriter, but he did not want to give a testimonial for it.

2. Johnson includes the story about Mark Twain because

   a. Twain is a much-beloved American author.

   b. Twain was one of the first well-known people to use a typewriter.

   c. she sees similarities in people's reactions to typewriters in Twain's day and to computers today.

   d. she knows that typewriters and computers serve similar functions in writing.

3. When Johnson writes "cheap books call out to me like 'Night Train' to a wino" (paragraph 5), she means that

   a. winos are often well-read individuals.

   b. she enjoys feeding her addiction to books without spending much money.

   c. Night Train is her beverage of choice when she reads books.

   d. she does not have enough money to pay full price for books.

4. Which of the following is *not* mentioned as something the author could do with a book but not with a computer?

   a. take it to bed.

   b. turn down the pages to mark her place.

   c. visit a restaurant.

   d. relax in a hot tub.

5. The people at the book sale Johnson went to were
   a. all ages and of diverse interests.
   b. mostly older people on limited incomes.
   c. children out of school for Presidents Day.
   d. people who were not likely to be computer literate.

■ **Writing in the Margins**

These questions encourage you to think not just about the essay but about the issues it raises. Your instructor may ask you to write down your answers, to discuss them in groups, or simply to think about them for class discussion.

1. Do you see any evidence that computers are taking the place of books, magazines, and newspapers? If so, what is the evidence? On the other hand, is there evidence that books, magazines, and newspapers are flourishing despite computers?
2. What are some of the ways that computers have changed libraries?
3. Is there a place in education (and in the lives of most Americans) for both books and computers? How are their functions separate? How do they overlap?

TOPICS FOR WRITING

Assignment 1: Autobiography of a Reader

Paragraph or Journal Entry

Write a paragraph or journal entry detailing your lifelong experience with books and reading. Since you can't do justice to your entire reading life in a paragraph, try describing a typical memory about reading, an incident that involved reading, or a reading habit from three different stages of your life.

Assignment 2: Computers for Research

Paragraph

Write a paragraph discussing the advantages and/or disadvantages of using a computer for research instead of relying on traditional printed matter.

Assignment 3: Bargain Basement

Paragraph or Essay

For the author of "One for the Books," part of the thrill of the library sale was getting a bargain. Do you enjoy shopping at flea markets, secondhand stores, or yard sales? Write a paragraph or essay telling why or why not.

Assignment 4: "Paging" Yourself

Paragraph or Essay

What kinds of reading material do you prefer? Why? Answer in a paragraph or essay.

American Space, Chinese Place

Yi-Fu Tuan

Is it important to you to look out of your living-room window and see wide open spaces, or would you prefer cozy, walled surroundings? Yi-Fu Tuan sees distinct differences between Chinese and American culture.

Americans have a sense of space, not of place. Go to an American home in exurbia, and almost the first thing you do is drift toward the picture window. How curious that the first compliment you pay your host inside his house is to say how lovely it is outside his house! He is pleased that you should admire his vistas. The distant horizon is not merely a line separating earth from sky, it is a symbol of the future. The American is not rooted in his place, however lovely: his eyes are drawn by the expanding space to a point on the horizon, which is his future. By contrast, consider the traditional Chinese home. Blank walls enclose it.

Step behind the spirit wall and you are in a courtyard with perhaps a miniature garden around the corner. Once inside the private compound you are wrapped in an ambiance of calm beauty, an ordered world of buildings, pavement, rock, and decorative vegetation. But you have no distant view: nowhere does space open out before you. Raw nature in such a home is experienced only as weather, and the only open space is the sky above. The Chinese is rooted in his place. When he has to leave, it is not for the promised land on the terrestrial horizon, but for another world altogether along the vertical, religious axis of his imagination.

The Chinese tie to place is deeply felt. Wanderlust is an alien sentiment. The Taoist classic *Tao Te Ching* captures the ideal of rootedness in place with these words: "Though there may be another country in the neighborhood so close that they are within sight of each other and the crowing of cocks and barking of dogs in one place can be heard in the other, yet there is no traffic between them; and throughout their lives the two peoples have nothing to do with each other." In theory if not in practice, farmers have ranked high in Chinese society. The reason is not only that they are engaged in the "root" industry of producing food but that, unlike pecuniary merchants, they are tied to the land and do not abandon their country when it is in danger.

Nostalgia is a recurrent theme in Chinese poetry. An American reader of translated Chinese poems well be taken aback—even put off—by the frequency

1

2

3

4

as well as the sentimentality of the lament for home. To understand the strength of this sentiment, we need to know that the Chinese desire for stability and rootedness in place is prompted by the constant threat of war, exile, and the natural disasters of flood and drought. Forcible removal makes the Chinese keenly aware of their loss. By contrast, Americans move, for the most part, voluntarily. Their nostalgia for home town is really longing for childhood to which they cannot return: in the meantime the future beckons and the future is "out there," in open space. When we criticize American rootlessness we tend to forget that it is a result of ideals we admire, namely, social mobility and optimism about the future. When we admire Chinese rootedness, we forget that the word "place" means both location in space and position in society: to be tied to place is also to be bound to one's station in life, with little hope of betterment. Space symbolizes hope; place, achievement and stability.

■ Building Vocabulary

For each question, choose the meaning that most closely defines the underlined word or phrase as it is used in the essay.

1. The word vistas most nearly means
   a. visitors.
   b. vegetation.
   c. views.
   d. interior decoration.

2. The word ambiance most nearly means
   a. expensively elegant surroundings.
   b. ceremonial Chinese robe.
   c. vehicle for transporting the sick.
   d. atmosphere.

3. The word terrestrial most nearly means
   a. earthly.
   b. celestial.
   c. attractive.
   d. otherworldly.

4. The word wanderlust most nearly means
   a. thirst for knowledge.
   b. attraction to the opposite sex.
   c. urge to travel.
   d. search for extraterrestrials.

5. The word <u>pecuniary</u> most nearly means
   a. farming.
   b. monetary.
   c. listless.
   d. simple.

■ Understanding the Essay

1. Which of the following statements best expresses the main idea of the essay?
   a. The American and Chinese cultures are vastly different.
   b. While the Chinese are attached to the land, Americans enjoy closeting themselves in luxurious homes.
   c. While Americans love travel and open spaces, the Chinese are rooted in their homes.
   d. Home is where the heart is, no matter whether one is American or Chinese.

2. Which of the following is *not* mentioned as a reflection of the Chinese feeling for home?
   a. high regard for farmers
   b. traditional poetry
   c. colors chosen for interior spaces
   d. lack of a view

3. The pattern of development in this essay is mainly
   a. definition.
   b. cause-effect.
   c. narrative.
   d. comparison-contrast.

4. According to the essay, an American who longs for home is really longing for
   a. a return to the land.
   b. childhood.
   c. the future.
   d. travel.

5. Which of the following possible reasons for the difference between Chinese and American sentiments toward home is most strongly supported by the essay?

a. American culture is more unsettled and less stable.

b. Americans, unlike the Chinese, have always moved voluntarily.

c. The Chinese have an older and thus more conservative culture.

d. Nostalgia is more prevalent in the Chinese culture than in the American culture.

■ **Writing in the Margins**

These questions encourage you to think not just about the essay but about the issues it raises. Your instructor may ask you to write down your answers, to discuss them in groups, or simply to think about them for class discussion.

1. Can you name some reasons not mentioned in the essay that might account for travel and frequent moves being a part of the American culture?

2. Given the Chinese attitude toward home, how would you expect the Chinese to treat their elderly? (William Raspberry's essay "Older and Wiser—or Just Older?" on page 455 might help to provide insight for discussion of this question.)

3. What can the design, color and furniture choice, upkeep, and landscaping of a house say about its occupants?

4. Why do you believe that home ownership is such a big part of the American Dream?

TOPICS FOR WRITING

Assignment 1: It's Not Wired for Cable, but It's Home

Paragraph or Journal Entry

The cruise ship you were on has sunk, but you are safely adrift in a lifeboat. The boat you are in becomes caught in a swift current, and soon the other lifeboats are just specks bobbing on the green water near where the boat sank. You and your companions drift to a large, uninhabited island. There is no telling how long you will be here, so you decide to make a home of sorts. You notice a tall sturdy grass and a stand of bamboo-like trees growing near the sandy beach. Set in a hill toward the middle of the island are several caves. Trees of all types abound. Where will you live? Would you choose to live alone or with one or more of your companions from the lifeboat? Assume that you are capable of the labor involved, perhaps with a bit of help from your companions, and make a home to suit your basic needs. For each decision you make (grass hut versus cave, hill versus beach) explain why you made the choice you did. The paragraph or journal entry you write will exercise your imagination and may reveal something about your preferred living conditions.

Assignment 2: Stay or Go?

Paragraph

Write a paragraph discussing the advantages and/or disadvantages of living in the same area all one's life.

Assignment 3: Home Is . . .

Paragraph

Write a definition paragraph defining the word *home*. Make the definition a personal one—tell your reader what *home* means to you.

Assignment 4: Yours and Mine

Paragraph or Essay

Write a paragraph or essay comparing or contrasting your home with the home of a friend or relative.

Disorders R Us

Michael Skube

In the old days, says Michael Skube, people had character flaws. Today, they have disorders.

I have certain compulsions. One is to clean the coffee grinder every morning like a man shining shoes. I wipe the cartridge that holds the grounds until it's spotless. Then I clean the grinders, picking away at every exposed ground of coffee. I'd take the thing out and scrub them with steel wool, but I'm afraid I'd never get it back together again. 1

The whole operation takes ten minutes, sometimes more. My wife wonders about this, but it's time well spent. I don't want coffee the next day tainted by stale grounds. 2

When I was a child, it was my job to wash the dinner dishes while my older sister dried. It quickly became evident that I take an extremely long time to wash and rinse a dish. I still do. I'm the master of the triple rinse. While I washed, she stood by, rapping her fingers on the counter. One night she summarily ripped the rag out of my hand, saying, "If you want to be here all night, I'm going to wash and let you dry. I know you'll do a good job." 3

I wish you could see how dry I got those dishes. I know this is a disorder of some sort. I just don't know which one. 4

There are so many. 5

Of all the countries on earth, we are the leader in disorders. The one most hung up on pathology. If we don't have attention deficit disorder, we have one or another kind of personality disorder. Or anxiety disorder. Or mood disorder. Other cultures just don't seem to have the problems we do. 6

Or maybe they just don't have the psychiatrists and psychologists we do. 7

There is a tome called the *Diagnostic and Statistical Manual of Mental Disorders,* and it's thicker than the repair manuals mechanics use. A recent edition doesn't list just anxiety disorder; it lists eleven separate kinds. It lists seventeen kinds of mood disorder. And eleven kinds of personality disorder. It lists disorders by the hundreds. 8

The entire premise of therapeutic culture that pervades American life is summed up in that one word—disorder. There is something wrong with us. We need to be diagnosed and treated. 9

The corollary of this is that our problems—to the extent that they're actually problems—aren't part of our character, they're medical. Once it's put that way, we're off the hook. 10

Nothing we can do about it, except see the doctor and take our pills. 11

The epidemic of ADD cases is only the most visible example of the impulse   12
to pathologize more or less ordinary behavior. There are classrooms in which
half the students are on Ritalin. Kids are diagnosed and labeled if they're not
"on-task," teacher-talk for behaving like little soldiers, and they're diagnosed if
they concentrate too well. I know of a twelve-year-old girl who will read contentedly for hours. The teacher thinks something's wrong and told the parents
she thinks their daughter has ADD.

We should at least be honest and call these children patients.   13

By one recent study, fully one-fourth of the students in the nation's public   14
schools have a "learning disability." As you might expect, federal money plays a
part. When the Individuals with Disabilities Education Act went into effect in
1976, most schoolchildren it covered were physically impaired in some way.
Less than one-quarter had learning disabilities. By 1992, those with learning
disabilities represented fifty-two percent—2,369,385 disabled children—with
more than one billion dollars in federal money going to schools for programs
to teach them.

And their numbers are growing. We're identifying more disorders every day.   15
It doesn't require a perverse imagination to foresee a time when most people
will be disabled, with a minority of odd birds who don't have a label (a disability in itself?).

People swallow this hooey uncritically. "Well, the psychiatrist (or psycholo-   16
gist or guidance counselor or whoever) diagnosed him, so it must be true." You
want to throttle these nincompoops as much as you do the charlatans who've
duped them.

Be grateful for skeptics like G. E. Zuriff, a clinical psychologist at the Mass-   17
achusetts Institute of Technology. In an article titled "Medicalizing Character"
in the Spring 1996 issue of *The Public Interest,* Zuriff wrote:

> Unlike physical disease, most psychological problems cannot be attributed to any
> known physiological pathology. Although we can safely assume that psychological
> problems are related to the central nervous system, the fact is that we know very lit-
> tle about the biological basis for schizophrenia, even less about anxiety and depres-
> sion, and virtually nothing about the physiological causes of personality disorders.

All too often, a diagnosis is little more than an educated guess, and some-   18
times it's not that educated. I can make guesses as well as the next person. For
myself, I'm counting forty-two actual disorders, including No. 301.4 ("obsessive-
compulsive personality disorder"), all kinds of syndromes and quite a few com-
plexes. Is there a label for people who can't take psycho-babble seriously? I
want to label a few people, hard. If somebody can work "disorder" into it for
me, so much the better. It would give it a scientific touch. But it comes out to
the same thing: They're frauds.

■ Building Vocabulary

For each question, choose the meaning that most closely defines the underlined word or phrase as it is used in the essay.

1. The word pathology most likely means
   a. cultures.
   b. personality.
   c. disease.
   d. knowledge.

2. The word premise most nearly means
   a. theory.
   b. promise.
   c. property.
   d. problem.

3. The underlined word corollary most nearly means
   a. opposite.
   b. therapy.
   c. diagnosis.
   d. result.

4. The word perverse most nearly means
   a. healthy.
   b. twisted.
   c. limited.
   d. required.

5. The word skeptics most nearly means
   a. academics.
   b. believers.
   c. doubters.
   d. experts in disorders.

■ Understanding the Essay

1. A good alternate title for this essay would be
   a. "Helping Kids with Learning Disabilities."
   b. "The ADD Epidemic."
   c. "Learning Disabilities: The Great Hoax."
   d. "What is 'Normal'? A Layperson's Guide to Diagnosing Common Disorders."

2. The opening example is intended to illustrate
   a. the author's obsessive-compulsive disorder.
   b. the kind of relatively normal behavior that is often labeled a disorder.

      c. how the author's childhood behavior has carried over into adulthood.

      d. the author's lack of tolerance for mess and dirt.

3. Which of the following is *not* true according to the essay?

      a. The *Diagnostic and Statistical Manual of Mental Disorders* lists eleven kinds of anxiety disorder.

      b. People in the United States have fewer disorders than those in other countries.

      c. In some classrooms, over 50 percent of the children are taking medication for ADD.

      d. Relatively little is known about the physical basis for psychological problems.

4. The essay implies that labeling behavior a "disorder"

      a. makes the behavior easier to treat and control.

      b. can foster a lack of self-esteem in those who are labeled.

      c. is less common in our culture than it used to be.

      d. encourages people not to take responsibility for what they do.

5. The example of the twelve-year-old who reads contentedly for hours while her teacher worries that she has ADD illustrates

      a. how well Ritalin works.

      b. the ridiculous lengths to which labeling can be carried.

      c. how all children should behave.

      d. the effectiveness of American schools.

■ Writing in the Margins

These questions encourage you to think not just about the essay but about the issues it raises. Your instructor may ask you to write down your answers, to discuss them in groups, or simply to think about them for class discussion.

1. The author asserts in paragraph 12 that there are some "classrooms in which half the students are on Ritalin." Based on your observations, is the statement true?

2. While the author clearly believes that we are too willing to label all kinds of behavior "disorders," others regard ADD and other disorders as real problems that can be treated medically. What kind of evidence would it take to conclusively prove that one view or the other is correct? Does any such evidence exist, as far as you know?

3. Do you believe, as the author does, that diagnosis of disorders has been carried too far? Why or why not?

4. Discuss the author's statement in paragraph 10 that labeling problems as "medical" lets us "off the hook." What does the author mean? Do you agree or disagree?

TOPICS FOR WRITING

Assignment 1: All in Your Head

Paragraph or Journal Entry

Have you ever had a disability or problem that was not taken seriously? Write a paragraph or journal entry about how the experience made you feel and how you resolved the problem.

Assignment 2: Close to Home

Paragraph

Have you ever been diagnosed with a learning disability? How did you react? Do you now accept or reject the idea that you have a disability? How has the diagnosis affected your academic life? (If the topic does not apply to you, feel free to write your paragraph about a close friend or relative who has been through the experience.)

Assignment 3: Faking It

Paragraph

If Skube is right that even normal behavior is labeled as a disorder and that such labeling allows people to avoid responsibility, imagine the possibilities. If you are habitually late getting up in the morning, perhaps you have "alarm clock resistance disorder." If you fail a test, perhaps it's due to "study avoidance syndrome" or maybe "success phobia." Think about your own self-defeating behaviors (or those of a friend) and invent disorders, syndromes, and phobias to explain or excuse those behaviors. Then write a paragraph explaining one or more of the "disorders" and how they affect your life.

Assignment 4: Coping with College

Paragraph or Essay

Learning disorders aside, most people find it difficult to cope with the demands of college. If a friend asked you for advice on meeting the demands of college successfully, what would you say? Write a paragraph or essay giving advice. You may confine your advice to academic life or you may broaden the topic to include balancing the demands of family and work against the demands of school.

Civil Rites

Caroline Miller

Are good manners dead in the modern world, or will the next generation chart a new course for etiquette? Maybe there's hope, says Caroline Miller.

1   I was taking my kids to school not long ago when I had one of those experiences particular to parents—a moment that nobody else notices, but that we replay over and over because in it we see something new about our children.

2   On this morning the bus was standing-room-only as we squeezed on at our regular stop. Several blocks later my son, Nick, found a free seat halfway back on one side of the bus and his little sister, Elizabeth, and I took seats on the other.

3   I was listening to Lizzie chatter on about something when I was surprised to see Nick get up. I watched as he said something quietly to an older, not quite grandmotherly woman who didn't look familiar to me. Suddenly I understood: He was offering her his seat.

4   A little thing, but still I was flooded with gratitude. For all the times we have talked about what to do and what not to do on the bus—say "Excuse me," cover your mouth when you cough, don't point, don't stare at people who are unusual looking—this wasn't something I had trained him to do. It was a small act of gallantry, and it was entirely his idea.

5   For all we try to show our kids and tell them how we believe people should act, how we hope *they* will act, it still comes as a shock and a pleasure—a relief, frankly—when they do something that suggests they understand. All the more so because in the world in which Nick is growing up, the rules that govern social interaction are so much more ambiguous than they were when we were his age. Kids are exposed to a free-for-all of competing signals about what's acceptable, let alone what's admirable. It's a world, after all, in which *in your face* is the style of the moment. Civility has become a more or less elusive proposition.

6   I was reminded of this incident on the train the other day, on another crowded morning, as I watched a young man in an expensive suit slip into an open seat without so much as losing his place in the *New York Times,* smoothly beating out a silver-haired gentleman and a gaggle of young women in spike heels.

7   My first thought was that his mother would be ashamed of him. And then I thought, with some amusement, that I am hopelessly behind the times. For all I know, the older man would've been insulted to be offered a seat by someone two or three decades his junior. And the women, I suppose, might consider chivalry a sexist custom. Besides, our young executive or investment banker probably had to compete with women for the job that's keeping him in Italian loafers; why would he want to offer a potential competitor a seat?

Of course, this sort of confusion is about much more than etiquette on public transportation. It's about what we should do for each other, and expect of each other, now that our roles are no longer closely dictated by whether we are male or female, young or old.   8

Not for a minute do I mourn the demise of the social contract that gave men most of the power and opportunity, and women most of the seats on the bus. But operating without a contract can be uncomfortable, too. It's as if nobody quite knows how to behave anymore; the lack of predictability on all fronts has left all our nerve endings exposed. And the confusion extends to everything from deciding who goes through the door first to who initiates sex.   9

Under the circumstances, civility requires a good deal more imagination than it once did, if only because it's so much harder to know what the person sitting across from you—whether stranger or spouse—expects, needs, wants from you. When you don't have an official rulebook, you have to listen harder, be more sensitive, be ready to improvise.   10

But of course improvising is just what Americans do best. And unlike the European model, our particular form of civility here in the former colonies aims to be democratic, to bridge our diverse histories with empathy and respect. At a moment when so many people are clamoring for attention, and so many others are nursing their wounds, the need for empathy and respect is rather acute.   11

And so, as we encourage our children to define themselves actively, to express themselves with confidence, we hope they will also learn to be generous—with those they don't know, as well as with those they love. And we hope they will care enough, and be observant enough, to be able to tell when someone else needs a seat more than they do.   12

■ Building Vocabulary

For each question, choose the meaning that most closely defines the underlined word or phrase as it is used in the essay.

1. The word gallantry most nearly means
   a. love.
   b. defiance.
   c. courtesy.
   d. pettiness.
2. The word ambiguous most nearly means
   a. certain.
   b. demanding.
   c. unclear.
   d. competitive.

3. The word <u>demise</u> most nearly means
   a. death.
   b. establishment.
   c. understanding.
   d. law.

4. The word <u>improvise</u> most nearly means
   a. progress.
   b. follow a rigid code of conduct.
   c. conform.
   d. invent new solutions.

5. The word <u>acute</u> most nearly means
   a. urgent.
   b. accurate.
   c. charming.
   d. small.

■ **Understanding the Essay**

1. Miller's purpose in writing the essay is
   a. to impress the need for manners on a new generation.
   b. to compare the manners of a former age with those of today.
   c. to show how proud she is of her son.
   d. to point out that etiquette is more complex than it used to be.

2. On the bus, Miller's son Nick
   a. covers his mouth when he coughs.
   b. refuses to sit with Miller and her daughter.
   c. makes her ashamed.
   d. does something Miller had not trained him to do.

3. The author implies in paragraph 7 that the young man in the expensive suit
   a. may have been in tune with modern etiquette.
   b. was inexcusably rude.
   c. needed the seat more than the older man or the young women.
   d. may have had a hidden disability.

4. According to the author, people in the modern world must
   a. look out for themselves and forget about etiquette.
   b. avoid being polite to competitors.

   c. be flexible and consider others' needs.

   d. return to the good manners of an earlier age.

5. Which of the following is *not* mentioned as a factor in the confusion over manners?

   a. Women's roles in society have changed.

   b. Parents do not adequately train their children.

   c. The modern style is "in your face."

   d. People find it harder to know what others want.

■ Writing in the Margins

These questions encourage you to think not just about the essay but about the issues it raises. Your instructor may ask you to write down your answers, to discuss them in groups, or simply to think about them for class discussion.

1. Are manners still important in the modern world?

2. Miller suggests that some older forms of etiquette might actually be offensive. Can you think of examples of etiquette you would find offensive, that would make you uncomfortable, or that are simply no longer useful?

3. One area of etiquette that is changing is dating etiquette. As recently as the 1960s and 1970s, for instance, asking for a date was usually the male's prerogative, as was paying for it. It would not be unlikely that he would hold the car door for his date, pull out her chair in the restaurant, and perhaps even order for her. Now, customs have changed, and the rules are less clear. Whose job do you believe it is to ask for the date? To pay for it? What is dating etiquette like today?

TOPICS FOR WRITING

Assignment 1: Are Manners Obsolete?

Paragraph or Journal Entry

Are manners still necessary? Write a paragraph or journal entry explaining why or why not.

Assignment 2: Interview Etiquette

Paragraph

Write a paragraph describing the rules of etiquette a job candidate should follow to impress the interviewer.

Assignment 3: The Dating Game

Paragraph

If you could write the rules of etiquette for dating, what would they be, and why? Write a paragraph discussing the most important rules and the reasons behind them.

Assignment 4: Classroom Manners

Paragraph or Essay

Write an example paragraph or essay classifying the types of mannerly or unmannerly behavior you observe in your college classes. (For help in constructing a classification paper, see Chapter 8.)

All the Rage

Dave Barry

You've heard of Road Rage. Humorist Dave Barry also explains Parking Lot Rage, Shopping Cart Rage, and other sources of anger that are all the rage.

1   If you do much driving on our nation's highways, you've probably noticed that, more and more often, bullets are coming through your windshield. This is a common sign of Road Rage, which the opinion-makers in the news media have decided is a serious problem, ranking just behind global warming and ahead of Asia.

2   How widespread is Road Rage? To answer that question, researchers for the National Institute of Traffic Safety recently did a study in which they drove on the interstate highway system in a specially equipped observation van. By the third day, they were deliberately running motorists off the road.

3   "These people are *morons!*" their official report stated.

4   That is the main cause of Road Rage: the realization that many of your fellow motorists have the brain of a cashew. The most common example, of course, is the motorists who feel a need to drive in the lefthand lane even though they are going slower than everybody else.

5   Nobody knows why they do this. Maybe they belong to some kind of religious cult that believes the right lane is sacred and must never come in direct contact with tires. Maybe one time, years ago, these motorists happened to be driving in the left lane when their favorite song came on the radio, so they've driven there ever since.

6   But whatever makes these people drive this way, there's nothing you can do. You can honk at them, but it will have no effect. People have been honking at them for years: It's a normal part of their environment. They've decided, for some mysterious reason, wherever they drive, there is honking.

7   I am familiar with this problem because I live and drive in Miami, which bills itself as the Inappropriate-Lane-Driving Capital of the World, and where the left lane is thought of not so much as a thoroughfare as a public recreational area, where motorists feel free to stop, hold family reunions, barbecue pigs, play volleyball, etc. Compounding this problem is another common type of Miami motorist, the aggressive young male whose car has a sound system so powerful that the driver must go faster than the speed of sound at all times, or else the nuclear bass notes emanating from his rear speakers will catch up to him and cause his head to explode.

So the tiny minority of us Miami drivers who actually qualify as normal find 8
ourselves constantly being trapped behind people drifting along on the interstate at the speed of diseased livestock, while at the same time being tailgated
and occasionally bumped from behind by testosterone-deranged youths who
got their driver training from watching "Star Wars." And of course nobody ever
signals or yields, and people are constantly cutting us off, and *after a while we
start to feel some rage, OK? You got a problem with that,* mister opinion-maker?

In addition to Road Rage, I frequently experience Parking Lot Rage, which 9
occurs when I pull into a crowded supermarket parking lot, and I see people
get into their car, clearly ready to leave, so I stop my car and wait for them to
vacate the spot, and . . . nothing happens. They just stay there! *What the hell are
they doing in there?? Cooking dinner???*

When I finally get into the supermarket, I often experience Shopping Cart 10
Rage. This is caused by the people—and you just know these are the same people who drive slowly in the left-hand lane—who routinely manage, by careful
placement, to block the entire aisle with a shopping cart. If we really want to
keep illegal immigrants from entering the United States, we should employ
Miami residents armed with shopping carts; we'd only need about two dozen
to block the entire Mexican border.

What makes the supermarket congestion even worse is that shoppers are 11
taking longer and longer to decide what to buy, because every product in America now comes in an insane number of styles and sizes. For example, I recently
went to the supermarket to get orange juice. For just one brand, I had to decide between Original, Homestyle, Pulp Plus, Double Vitamin C, Grovestand,
Calcium or Old Fashioned; I also had to decide whether I wanted the 167-ounce,
32-ounce, 64-ounce, 96-ounce or six-pack size. This is *way* too many choices. It
caused me to experience Way Too Many Product Choices Rage. I would have
called the orange juice company and complained, but I probably would have
wound up experiencing Automated Phone Answering System Rage (". . . For
questions about Pulp Plus in the 32-ounce size, press 23. For questions about
Pulp Plus in the 64-ounce size, press 24. For questions about . . .").

My point is that there are many causes of rage in our modern world, and if 12
we're going to avoid unnecessary violence, we all need to "keep our cool." So
let's try to be more considerate, OK? Otherwise I will kill you.

■ Building Vocabulary

For each question, choose the meaning that most closely defines the underlined word or phrase as it is used in the essay.

1. The word bills most nearly means
   a. currency.
   b. labels.
   c. charges.
   d. appropriates.

2. The word emanating most nearly means
   a. murmuring.
   b. coming.
   c. trickling.
   d. tinkling.

3. The word vacate most nearly means
   a. leave.
   b. remain in.
   c. enter.
   d. locate.

4. The word routinely most nearly means
   a. boringly.
   b. kindly.
   c. deliberately.
   d. habitually.

5. The word congestion most nearly means
   a. crowding.
   b. shopping.
   c. food.
   d. stuffiness.

■ Understanding the Essay

1. Barry's purpose in writing the essay is
   a. to analyze the modern phenomenon of Road Rage and to suggest solutions.
   b. to document recent research by the National Institute of Traffic Safety.
   c. to discuss several different causes of rage.
   d. to amuse the reader by poking fun at a serious subject.

2. In the essay, Barry does all of the following *except*
   a. sympathize with those who feel Road Rage.
   b. side with the victims of drivers with Road Rage.
   c. blame people who drive slowly in the left-hand lane.
   d. imply that drivers who feel Road Rage are the normal ones.

3. The tone of the essay is
    a. objective.
    b. angry.
    c. humorous.
    d. biased.

4. One type of rage *not* mentioned in the essay is
    a. Way Too Many Product Choices Rage.
    b. Car Dealership Ripoff Rage.
    c. Shopping Cart Rage.
    d. Automated Phone Answering System Rage.

5. Barry's persona in the essay is that of a person who
    a. is barely in control himself.
    b. has too often been a victim of enraged drivers.
    c. is trying to take a reasoned, logical approach to an illogical topic.
    d. does not care about the subject he is writing about.

■ Writing in the Margins

These questions encourage you to think not just about the essay but about the issues it raises. Your instructor may ask you to write down your answers, to discuss them in groups, or simply to think about them for class discussion.

1. Exaggeration of the truth is one tool of the humorist. What instances of exaggeration can you point out in Barry's essay?
2. Barry's humorous essay reflects a modern phenomenon that has become fairly serious. What are some of the ways that people lose control on the road and in other public places, and what are some of the reasons behind the phenomenon?
3. What driving behaviors strike you as most dangerous and/or annoying?

TOPICS FOR WRITING

Assignment 1: Rage On!

Paragraph or Journal Entry

Do you have a pet peeve that drives you into a frenzy? It could be the woman who gets into the "fifteen items or less" line with twenty-five items, a fistful of coupons, and an expired debit card. Or perhaps it's the driver who tailgates you on the highway with his high-beams shining into your rearview mirror. What makes *you* angry? Rage on—in a controlled way—in a paragraph or journal entry.

Assignment 2: You-Name-It Rage

Paragraph

Write a paragraph describing a kind of rage that affects you. Use one of Barry's categories or, if you wish, make up your own.

Assignment 3: Driving You Crazy

Paragraph

Write a paragraph describing the kinds of drivers likely to incite road rage.

Assignment 4: Shop Till You Drop

Paragraph or Essay

These days, grocery stores are often cavernous places that sell not just groceries, but books, prescription drugs, housewares, and prepared foods. At some grocery stores, people can do their banking, pick up their dry cleaning, rent a video, and even work out. Malls, too, are becoming larger and more elaborate. On the opposite end of the scale, shopping from home through catalogs or computers is becoming more popular. A customer can order clothing, books, housewares, CDs, and computer equipment through mail-order catalogs or online sites. Even groceries can be purchased online. If given a choice, would you prefer shopping at huge malls and mega-stores or doing your shopping from home? Write a paragraph or essay telling why.

Conversational Ballgames

Nancy Masterton Sakamoto

For the author, conversing in English was easy, but Japanese conversation was a whole different ballgame.

After I was married and had lived in Japan for a while, my Japanese gradually   1
improved to the point where I could take part in simple conversations with my
husband and his friends and family. And I began to notice that often, when I
joined in, the others would look startled, and the conversational topic would
come to a halt. After this happened several times, it became clear to me that I
was doing something wrong. But for a long time, I didn't know what it was.

Finally, after listening carefully to many Japanese conversations, I discov-   2
ered what my problem was. Even though I was speaking Japanese, I was handling the conversation in a Western way.

Japanese-style conversations develop quite differently from Western-style   3
conversations. And the difference isn't only in the languages. I realized that just
as I kept trying to hold Western-style conversations even when I was speaking
Japanese, so my English students kept trying to hold Japanese-style conversations even when they were speaking English. We were unconsciously playing entirely different conversational ballgames.

A Western-style conversation between two people is like a game of tennis. If   4
I introduce a topic, a conversational ball, I expect you to hit it back. If you
agree with me, I don't expect you simply to agree and do nothing more. I expect you to add something—a reason for agreeing, another example, or an
elaboration to carry the idea further. But I don't expect you always to agree. I
am just as happy if you question me, or challenge me, or completely disagree
with me. Whether you agree or disagree, your response will return the ball
to me.

And then it is my turn again. I don't serve a new ball from my original start-   5
ing line. I hit your ball back again from where it has bounced. I carry your idea
further, or answer your questions or objections, or challenge or question you.
And so the ball goes back and forth, with each of us doing our best to give it a
new twist, an original spin, or a powerful smash.

And the more vigorous the action, the more interesting and exciting the   6
game. Of course, if one of us gets angry, it spoils the conversation, just as it
spoils a tennis game. But getting excited is not at all the same as getting angry.
After all, we are not trying to hit each other. We are trying to hit the ball. So
long as we attack only each other's opinions, and do not attack each other

personally, we don't expect anyone to get hurt. A good conversation is supposed to be interesting and exciting.

If there are more than two people in the conversation, then it is like doubles in tennis or like volleyball. There's no waiting in line. Whoever is nearest and quickest hits the ball, and if you step back, someone else will hit it. No one stops the game to give you a turn. You're responsible for taking your own turn. 7

But whether it's two players or a group, everyone does his best to keep the ball going, and no one person has the ball for very long. 8

A Japanese-style conversation, however, is not at all like tennis or volleyball. It's like bowling. You wait for your turn. And you always know your place in line. It depends on such things as whether you are older or younger, a close friend or a relative stranger to the previous speaker, in a senior or junior position, and so on. 9

When your turn comes, you step up to the starting line with your bowling ball, and carefully bowl it. Everyone else stands back and watches politely, murmuring encouragement. Everyone waits until the ball has reached the end of the alley, and watches to see if it knocks down all the pins, or only some of them, or none of them. There is a pause, while everyone registers your score. 10

Then, after everyone is sure that you have completely finished your turn, the next person in line steps up to the same starting line, with a different ball. He doesn't return your ball, and he does not begin from where your ball stopped. There is no back and forth at all. All the balls run parallel. And there is always a suitable pause between turns. There is no rush, no excitement, no scramble for the ball. 11

No wonder everyone looked startled when I took part in Japanese conversations. I paid no attention to whose turn it was, and kept snatching the ball halfway down the alley and throwing it back at the bowler. Of course the conversation died. I was playing the wrong game. 12

This explains why it is almost impossible to get a Western-style conversation or discussion going with English students in Japan. I used to think that the problem was their lack of English language ability. But I finally came to realize that the biggest problem is that they, too, are playing the wrong game. 13

Whenever I serve a volleyball, everyone just stands back and watches it fall, with occasional murmurs of encouragement. No one hits it back. Everyone waits until I call on someone to take a turn. And when that person speaks, he doesn't hit my ball back. He serves a new ball. Again, everyone just watches it fall. 14

So I call on someone else. This person does not refer to what the previous speaker has said. He also serves a new ball. Nobody seems to have paid any attention to what anyone else has said. Everyone begins again from the same starting line, and all the balls run parallel. There is never any back and forth. Everyone is trying to bowl with a volleyball. 15

And if I try a simpler conversation, with only two of us, then the other person tries to bowl with my tennis ball. No wonder foreign English teachers in Japan get discouraged. 16

Now that you know about the difference in the conversational ballgames, you may think that all your troubles are over. But if you have been trained all your life to play one game, it is no simple matter to switch to another, even if you know the rules. Knowing the rules is not at all the same thing as playing the game. 17

Even now, during a conversation in Japanese I will notice a startled reaction, and belatedly realize that once again I have rudely interrupted by instinctively trying to hit back the other person's bowling ball. It is no easier for me to "just listen" during a conversation, than it is for my Japanese students to "just relax" when speaking with foreigners. Now I can truly sympathize with how hard they must find it to try to carry on a Western-style conversation. If I have not yet learned to do conversational bowling in Japanese, at least I have figured out one thing that puzzled me for a long time. After his first trip to America, my husband complained that Americans asked him so many questions and made him talk so much at the dinner table that he never had a chance to eat. When I asked him why he couldn't talk and eat at the same time, he said that Japanese do not customarily think that dinner, especially on fairly formal occasions, is a suitable time for extended conversation. 18

Since Westerners think that conversation is an indispensable part of dining, and indeed would consider it impolite not to converse with one's dinner partner, I found this Japanese custom rather strange. Still, I could accept it as a cultural difference even though I didn't really understand it. But when my husband added, in explanation, that Japanese consider it extremely rude to talk with one's mouth full, I got confused. Talking with one's mouth full is certainly not an American custom. We think it very rude, too. Yet we still manage to talk a lot and eat at the same time. How do we do it? 19

For a long time, I couldn't explain it, and it bothered me. But after I discovered the conversational ballgames, I finally found the answer. Of course! In a Western-style conversation, you hit the ball, and while someone else is hitting it back, you take a bite, chew, and swallow. Then you hit the ball again, and then eat some more. The more people there are in the conversation, the more chances you have to eat. 20

But even with only two of you talking, you still have plenty of chances to eat. 21

Maybe that's why polite conversation at the dinner table has never been a traditional part of Japanese etiquette. Your turn to talk would last so long without interruption that you'd never get a chance to eat. 22

■ Building Vocabulary

For each question, choose the meaning that most closely defines the underlined word or phrase as it is used in the essay.

1. The word elaboration most nearly means
   a. explanation.
   b. challenge.

   c. refusal to comment.

   d. simple agreement.

2. The word previous most nearly means

   a. later.

   b. earlier.

   c. effective.

   d. relative.

3. The word registers most nearly means

   a. specifies.

   b. votes on.

   c. writes down.

   d. takes in.

4. The word instinctively most nearly means

   a. automatically.

   b. rudely.

   c. deliberately.

   d. belatedly.

5. The word indispensable most nearly means

   a. needless.

   b. unpleasant.

   c. impolite.

   d. necessary.

■ Understanding the Essay

1. A good alternate title for this essay would be

   a. "Take Me Out to the Ballgame."

   b. "Japanese Conversational Style."

   c. "Two Cultures, Two Conversational Styles."

   d. "American Talk."

2. Which of the following statements best describes Sakamoto's occupation?

   a. She taught English to Japanese students.

   b. She was the athletic director at a Japanese school.

   c. She taught Japanese to English-speaking students.

   d. She was a student taking courses in Japan.

3. The primary pattern of development in this essay is
   a. cause-effect.
   b. definition.
   c. narration.
   d. comparison-contrast.

4. If Western conversation is like a tennis game, Japanese conversation is like
   a. volleyball.
   b. mixed doubles.
   c. bowling.
   d. baseball.

5. The author implies all of the following *except*
   a. her Japanese friends and in-laws were startled by her conversational style.
   b. knowing a language may not be enough to ensure good communication.
   c. rudeness may unintentionally result if one violates a culture's conversational style.
   d. American conversational style is superior because it is more lively.

■ **Writing in the Margins**

These questions encourage you to think not just about the essay but about the issues it raises. Your instructor may ask you to write down your answers, to discuss them in groups, or simply to think about them for class discussion.

1. In looking at the Japanese and American conversational styles, what do you see as the advantages and disadvantages of each?

2. From time to time, someone proposes a "universal language" that would enable people from different cultures to communicate more effectively. For example, Esperanto, a made-up language that is a blend of several languages, including Spanish and English, has been proposed as a language that would bridge all cultures if everyone would only learn it. What are the barriers that stand in the way of successfully carrying out such a proposal? If those barriers could be overcome, is a "universal second language" a good idea? What are some of its advantages and disadvantages?

Group Exercise 3

Form groups of three, four, or five and discuss the rules of a Japanese-style conversation as you understand them from the essay. Then, with the members of your group, try to hold a Japanese-style conversation. Then discuss the following questions as a class: Was it easy or difficult? Did anyone break the rules? What was difficult? What was fun? What seemed strange to you?

A possible alternative activity is to have four or five volunteers from the class sit in a semicircle in front of the class and converse, Japanese-style, while the rest of the class observes. Be sure to outline the rules that the group will go by before the conversation starts.

TOPICS FOR WRITING

Assignment 1: Communicating Across Cultures

Paragraph or Journal Entry

Have you ever needed to communicate with someone whose language you could not speak or someone whose language you could speak only in a limited way? Write a paragraph or journal entry describing the barriers to communication and telling how you overcame (or tried to overcome) those barriers.

Assignment 2: Your Conversational Style

Paragraph

Conversational styles differ among individuals as well as cultures. Write a paragraph discussing the characteristics of your personal conversational style. Give specific supporting examples.

Assignment 3: Classifying Conversationalists

Paragraph

Write a paragraph classifying people's conversational styles. Think of your own terms of classification or use some of the terms below. Be sure to explain or give examples of each particular style.

the steamroller	the egotist
the butterfly	the comedian
the echo	the snoop
the naysayer	the whiner

Assignment 4: Shocked by Your Style

Paragraph or Essay

Sakamoto describes the startled way her Japanese friends would look at her when she interrupted a conversation. Have you ever met someone whose style—the way they spoke, looked, or acted—originally shocked you or put you off, but whom you later came to like and understand? Write a paragraph or essay about that person. Be sure to include an account of your first meeting; then tell what happened to change your mind about the person.

Alternatively, was one of your friends put off by your style at first? Describe your friend's initial reaction as well as the reasons for his or her change of heart.

I Wonder: Was It Me or Was It My Sari?

Shoba Narayan

The author had always tried to fit in to the American way of life. Now, it was America's turn to adjust to her.

1   A sari for a month. It shouldn't have been a big deal but it was. After all, I had grown up around sari-clad women in India. My mother even slept in one.

2   In India, saris are adult attire. After I turned 18, I occasionally wore a sari for weddings and holidays and to the temple. But wearing a sequined silk sari to an Indian party was one thing. Deciding to wear a sari every day while living in New York, especially after 10 years in Western clothes, sounded outrageous, even to me.

3   The sari is six yards of fabric folded into a graceful yet cumbersome garment. Like a souffle, it is fragile and can fall apart at any moment. When worn right, it is supremely elegant and unabashedly feminine. However, it requires sacrifices.

4   No longer could I sprint across the street just before the light changed. The sari forced me to shorten my strides. I couldn't squeeze into a crowded subway car for fear that someone would accidentally pull and unravel my sari. I couldn't balance four grocery bags in one hand and pull out my house keys from a convenient pocket with the other. By the end of the first week, I was lumbering around my apartment, feeling clumsy and angry with myself. What was I trying to prove?

5   The notion of wearing a sari every day was relatively new for me. During my college years—the age when most girls in India begin wearing saris regularly—I was studying in America. As an art student at Mount Holyoke, I hung out with purple-haired painters and rabble-rousing feminists wearing ink-stained khakis and cut-off T shirts. During a languid post-graduation summer in Boston, when I sailed a boat and volunteered for an environmental organization, I wore politically correct, recycled Salvation Army clothes. After getting married, I became a Connecticut housewife experimenting with clothes from Jones New York and Ann Taylor. Through it all, I tried to pick up the accent, learn the jargon and affect the posture of the Americans around me.

6   Then I moved to New York and became a mother. I wanted to teach my 3-year-old daughter Indian values and traditions because I knew she would be

profoundly different from her preschool classmates in religion (we are Hindus), eating habits (we are vegetarians) and the festivals we celebrated. Wearing a sari every day was my way of showing her that she could melt into the pot while retaining her individual flavor.

It wasn't just for my daughter's sake that I decided to wear a sari. I was 7 tired of trying to fit in. Natalie Cole had never spoken to me as eloquently as M.S., a venerable Indian singer. I couldn't sing the lyrics of Ricky Martin as easily as I could sing my favorite Hindi or Tamil songs. Much as I enjoyed American cuisine, I couldn't last four days without Indian food. It was time to flaunt my ethnicity with a sari and a bright red bindi on my forehead. I was going to be an immigrant, but on my own terms. It was America's turn to adjust to me.

Slowly, I eased into wearing the garment. Strangers stared at me as I 8 sashayed across a crowded bookstore. Some of them caught my eye and smiled. At first, I resented being an exhibit. Then I wondered: perhaps I reminded them of a wonderful holiday in India or a favorite Indian cookbook. Grocery clerks enunciated their words when they spoke to me. Everywhere, I was stopped with questions about India as if wearing a sari had made me an authority. One Japanese lady near Columbus Circle asked to have her picture taken with me. A tourist had thought that I was one, too, just steps from my home.

But there were unexpected advantages. Indian cabdrivers raced across 9 lanes and screeched to a halt in front of me when I stepped into the street to hail a taxi. When my daughter climbed high up the Jungle-Gym in Central Park, I gathered my sari and prepared to follow, hoping it wouldn't balloon out like Marilyn Monroe's dress. One of the dads standing nearby watched my plight and volunteered to climb after her. Chivalry in New York? Was it me or was it my sari?

Best of all, my family approved. My husband complimented me, my par- 10 ents were proud of me. My daughter oohed and aahed when I pulled out my colorful saris. When I cuddled her in my arms, scents from the vetiver sachets that I used to freshen my sari at night escaped from the folds of cloth and soothed her to sleep. I felt part of a long line of Indian mothers who had rocked their babies this way.

Soon, the month was over. My self-imposed regimen was coming to an 11 end. Instead of feeling liberated, I felt a twinge of unease. I had started enjoying my sari.

Saris were impractical for America, I told myself. I would continue to wear 12 them, but not every day. It was time to revert to my sensible khakis. It was time to become American again.

■ Building Vocabulary

For each question, choose the meaning that most closely defines the underlined word or phrase as it is used in the essay.

1. The word <u>outrageous</u> most nearly means
   a. angry.
   b. wild and crazy.
   c. sensible.
   d. out of style.

2. The word <u>cumbersome</u> most nearly means
   a. hard to manage.
   b. easy to wear.
   c. beautiful.
   d. charming.

3. The word <u>lumbering</u> most nearly means
   a. hauling wood.
   b. dancing.
   c. moving gracefully.
   d. moving clumsily.

4. The word <u>affect</u> most nearly means
   a. influence.
   b. imitate.
   c. infect.
   d. reject.

5. The word <u>profoundly</u> most nearly means
   a. thoroughly.
   b. superficially.
   c. partly.
   d. slightly.

■ Understanding the Essay

1. As stated in the essay, one of the main reasons the author decides to wear a sari for a month is
   a. to get back in touch with her cultural identity.
   b. to enjoy the comfort and freedom of movement that a sari provides.
   c. to add variety and cultural flair to her wardrobe.
   d. to show her daughter that it's possible to be different and still fit in.

2. In India, what is the custom for wearing a sari?
   a. Saris are worn on special occasions such as weddings, parties, and visits to the temple.
   b. Women and female children wear saris for everyday events such as school, work, and play.
   c. Adult females may wear saris for everyday events, special occasions, and even sleeping.
   d. Men and women wear saris on special occasions.

3. Which of the following is *not* mentioned as a disadvantage of wearing a sari in New York?
   a. Strangers stare at her.
   b. She is unable to sprint across the street.
   c. She finds it difficult to hail a cab.
   d. She can't ride in a crowded subway.

4. In the years before she decided to wear a sari for a month, the author tended to
   a. not worry at all about what she wore.
   b. dress conservatively so that no one would notice her.
   c. wear expensive designer clothing.
   d. dress to fit in with the people she associated with.

5. The advantages of wearing the sari include all but which of the following?
   a. Receiving unexpected courtesies from strangers.
   b. Feeling connected to her heritage.
   c. Being able to run, jump, and move freely.
   d. Enjoying her family's approval.

■ **Writing in the Margins**

These questions encourage you to think not only about the essay but about the issues it raises. Your instructor may ask you to write down your answers, to discuss them in groups, or simply to think about them for class discussion.

1. The author writes at the end of Paragraph 7, "It was America's turn to adjust to me." What is the background of this statement? How do you imagine the author feels about her decision to let America adjust to her?

2. What message does clothing send to others? Give at least one example of specific attire and the message it sends. What message do you think Shoba Narayan's sari sent to the people around her?

TOPICS FOR WRITING

Assignment 1: Someone Else's Turn to Adjust

Paragraph or Journal Entry

The author writes, "It was America's turn to adjust to me." After trying to fit in to American life, she is ready to stand out, and let other people adjust to her. Have you ever been in a situation where you were no longer willing to fit in with someone else's views about how you should be? Although you may not have put it in exactly the same words, it was time for that person (or group) to adjust to you. Write a paragraph or journal entry about your experience of deciding to let someone else adjust to you.

Assignment 2: You Are What You Wear

Paragraph

The old saying, "Clothes make the man," implies that people will take a person for what he or she appears to be. Can you describe a time when people treated you differently because of your attire? Write a paragraph describing such an incident and the effect that it had on you.

Assignment 3: Your Cultural Heritage

Paragraph

In the United States, most families originally came from somewhere else. Some, like the author of the essay you just read, try to stay in close touch with their heritage. As generations pass, however, many families grow away from their original culture and become "just Americans." What is your family's cultural heritage? Do you and your family celebrate that culture in any way? Answer in a paragraph.

Assignment 4: The Fabric of Your Life

Paragraph or Essay

Many people undergo similar metamorphoses as their lives change, as they change, as their circumstances change. Think of the various ways you have dressed and the various images you have projected over the past several years (or however long a period of time you wish to include). Then, in a paragraph or essay, write a brief history of the changes in the way you dress. Include a description of the clothing you typically wore, the image you believe it projected, and your reason for choosing the styles you did.

Music: A Universal Language

Candace Dyer

Music is something everyone understands. It may even provide a glimpse of paradise.

1   On the final, wrenching trills of "When a Man Loves a Woman," Percy Sledge waded into the adoring crowd, which surged ecstatically toward him.

2   The dewy 20-year-old standing next to me shook his head in amazement, not at the music but at its effect. "Look at that! I've gotta become a musician," he said in the heady throes of revelation. "Look at the way everybody absolutely worships those guys. The women especially. That's it! I'm getting a guitar tomorrow!"

3   I could almost see a cartoon light bulb bobbing over his head. He was on to something. In that instant, the young man understood what Shakespeare meant with the words, "If music be the food of love, play on."

4   What is the appeal of musicians? Why did young women collapse like feverish rag dolls before The Beatles, and why did Odysseus' sailors need to be tied down when passing the sirens? What is the narcotic magnetism that makes us want to rush the stage, to throw our arms around the band members' shoulders and tell them we understand their pain, that, in fact, they are singing about us?

5   While it doesn't necessarily have to be shared, music is the most communal of the arts. And it arguably carries the most sensory impact. It reverberates in the bones, insinuates its rhythms into the blood, like nothing else.

6   Dubbed "the universal language," and "the brandy of the damned," music can incite an orgy, lull a baby to sleep, deepen a trance, inspire a couch potato to dance, and prompt an invalid in a nursing home to clap to a beat. Some research on the subconscious holds that musical instruments are the symbols of sex organs in dreams.

7   But the tunes are more than physical. Several belief systems present music as a way of elevating animalistic impulses and emotions into a spiritual experience. Music becomes a means of redemption. Orpheus, the musician of Greek mythology, used his lyre to charm the rulers of Hades into releasing his wife. And preachers use "Amazing Grace" to pull their flocks to the altar.

8   Shakespeare's contemporaries touted the "music of the spheres." In the beginning, goes the theory, the harmony of the universe was heralded by angels who stood on surrounding planets and filled the heavens with song. After tasting the forbidden fruit and getting the bum's rush from paradise, we no longer

could hear the angels. We could, however, detect them in fragments when we made music—our own little riffs of divine harmony.

That idea explains my guitar-strumming friend's sweeping observation that 9 "really, there's no bad music." The chops of those world-weary jazz cats and the gravelly voice of the blues singer and the purr of a slinky chanteuse may actually be glimmers of our better days in Eden.

No wonder musicians—whether using a tribal drum or a Stratacaster—wield 10 catnip-like powers on their listeners. They're a conduit for a dream of paradise lost. Musicians take the "fallen" raw materials of our living and transform them into something beautiful with a symmetry of its own. Something that calls on us to dance, love, think, and cry.

When I was walking to my car after the Percy Sledge performance, one of 11 the band members invited me to have a drink with the group in an RV. They wore colorful tuxedo-like suits, and one sported a wide-brimmed, cobalt-blue hat. I leaned back and inhaled the "cool" in the air while they talked shop.

Sweaty, energized from the gig and chugging a bottle of Crown Royal, Percy 12 entered the cabin and scanned the faces. He stopped on mine. I was beaming at him like the newest, brainwashed initiate in a cult.

"Look at that, what a smile!" he said. "That's the smile of an entertainer. 13 You gotta be an entertainer with a smile like that. You a singer, girl?" he asked.

"No, but your music puts a smile on my face," I said.   14

The others told him I write. Then Percy and I spoke briefly of the similarities 15 between words and music, that they both are ways to reach other people.

"I know you know what I'm talking about," he said.   16

I winked, and he raised his bottle as if in toast.   17

Call me naive, but I don't think he was just jive-talking a groupie.   18

■ Building Vocabulary

For each question, choose the meaning that most closely defines the underlined word or phrase as it is used in the essay.

1. The word ecstatically most nearly means
   a. joyously.
   b. mindlessly.
   c. threateningly.
   d. sadly.

2. The phrase the heady throes of revelation most nearly means
   a. a moment of analysis.
   b. a painful moment of understanding.
   c. a powerful moment of understanding.
   d. a calm moment.

3. The word <u>communal</u> most nearly means
   a. musical.
   b. artful.
   c. expressive.
   d. shared.

4. The word <u>insinuates</u> most nearly means
   a. implies.
   b. works.
   c. walks.
   d. immunizes.

5. The word <u>contemporaries</u> most nearly means
   a. modern people.
   b. thinking people.
   c. those who live during the same time.
   d. theatergoers.

6. The word <u>touted</u> most nearly means
   a. praised.
   b. disliked.
   c. pouted.
   d. ignored.

7. The word <u>chanteuse</u> most nearly means
   a. male singer.
   b. cat.
   c. snake.
   d. female singer.

8. The word <u>conduit</u> most nearly means
   a. transmitter.
   b. water pipe.
   c. barrier.
   d. paradise.

9. The word <u>initiate</u> most nearly means
   a. new member.
   b. singer.
   c. hypnotist.
   d. undercover spy.

10. The word <u>naive</u> most nearly means
    a. inspired.
    b. well-informed.
    c. unsophisticated.
    d. lost.

■ **Understanding the Essay**

1. The author's friend wanted to become a musician
    a. because music, the universal language, speaks to everyone.
    b. because guitar music touched his soul.
    c. because he wants to be more attractive to women.
    d. because he wants to emulate his hero, Percy Sledge.

2. Pick the best statement of the main idea from the choices below.
    a. Musicians have it made because they find it easy to attract the opposite sex.
    b. Shakespeare and his contemporaries believed that a celestial music allowed people to hear faint echoes of paradise in the music they played.
    c. Music is a way of communicating.
    d. Music is powerful and affects almost everyone.

3. Based on the information in the passage, which of the following would be most likely to bring people together in shared enjoyment?
    a. Watching a performance of Shakespeare's play, *Twelfth Night*.
    b. Sitting in while prominent "jazz cats" discuss musical technique.
    c. Listening to a symphony orchestra perform Bach's Cantata No. 208, "Sheep May Safely Graze."
    d. Standing with a tour group in the Sistine Chapel and looking up at the ceiling painted by Michelangelo.

4. Which of the following does the author mention as a possible reason for music's universal popularity?
    a. Society thrusts it on us from the cradle on.
    b. People get easily bored and need some background noise.
    c. Peer pressure makes each generation favor a particular type of music.
    d. It suggests an earlier, better time in paradise.

5. It is implied that for the author, the meeting with Percy Sledge
   a. was simply a case of groupie meeting singer.
   b. made her decide to be a singer, too.
   c. revealed a common bond.
   d. was a thrilling moment only because of her long-standing admiration for the singer.

■ Writing in the Margins

These questions encourage you to think not just about the essay but about the issues it raises. Your instructor may ask you to write down your answers, to discuss them in groups, or simply to think about them for class discussion.

1. In the essay, music is called "the food of love," "the brandy of the damned," and "the universal language." Explain in your own words what you think each of these metaphors means.

2. Music can bring people together, but in the United States, it often separates the generations. Why does each generation need its own music? What does the music of your generation say about you and your contemporaries?

TOPICS FOR WRITING

Assignment 1: Your Theme Song

Paragraph or Journal Entry

If you had to choose a theme song for your life, what would it be? Write a paragraph or journal entry explaining your choice.

Assignment 2: Mood Music

Paragraph

Most people fit music to their mood. A sad country ballad might fit in times of love lost, a dance rhythm might fit an upbeat, energetic mood, and classical music might suit a quiet, thoughtful mood. Write a paragraph describing the different kinds of music you enjoy listening to when you are in different moods. Be specific about the type of music, and feel free to mention specific song titles, singers, or musicians.

Assignment 3: Groupies

Paragraph

What is a *groupie*? Write a paragraph defining the term. Be sure to give specific examples of typical groupie behavior.

Assignment 4: On the Road Again

Paragraph or Essay

In the essay, Dyer described her friend's instant decision to buy a guitar when he saw the crowd's reaction to Percy Sledge. While being a musician has its perks, there is also a downside: endless hours of travel, time away from home and family, and the insecurity of knowing that one's livelihood depends solely on the preferences of a fickle public. Would the life of a musician appeal to you? Write a paragraph or essay telling why or why not.

Assignment 5: Music of a Generation

Paragraph or Essay

From big band to Motown to disco to rap, people seem to retain a special affection for the music they heard as they entered adulthood. In a paragraph or essay, compare and/or contrast the music of your generation with the music of a generation that came before or after. You might want to explore the clothing, attitudes, or activities that came along with the music of the two generations you discuss. (For the generation that matured in the late 1950s, for example, it was rock 'n' roll, poodle skirts, and dancing to the jukebox at the local ice cream parlor. The disco generation of the 1970s wore polyester and danced on lighted disco floors to Donna Summer.)

What If My Friends Hadn't Run?

Bill Pippin

What does it take to make an ordinary person pick up a gun and point it at another person? In this essay, a law-abiding family man recalls the day he picked up a gun in anger.

When I was a boy, I loved watching Gene Autry and Roy Rogers movies and then acting out my fantasies, galloping around the yard on a stick horse and shooting at bad men with my cap gun. On my 9th birthday, when Dad asked, "What'll it be—a bike or a .22 rifle?" naturally I chose the rifle. On the high plains at the edge of our little oilfield town of Lamont, Wyo., Dad showed me how to load my Remington single-shot and shoot at tin cans. In less time than it takes to eject a spent cartridge, that rifle was as familiar to me as a cap gun.   1

That summer of 1947, while my parents were away, I was hanging out near the house with my friends Donald and J.W., along with Donald's 4-year-old brother, Danny, looking for something to do. "I know," said J.W. "Let's play jujitsu."   2

"Yeah," I agreed, because it sounded like fun. That was before the two older boys started practicing the Japanese martial art on me, throwing me back and forth, trying different holds they'd seen in World War II movies or news-reels. Finally, I lost my temper and yelled, "Knock it off!"   3

They only laughed. By the time they got tired, I was dirty, bruised, outraged and crazy mad. "I'll show you guys," I said, gritting back tears. Stumbling into the house, I snatched my .22 out of the closet, then stood on a chair to reach the top shelf of the kitchen cabinet, where we kept the box of long-rifle shells. As I went back outside I slid one into the chamber.   4

When the two older boys heard the rifle bolt snap home, their faces paled. Donald grabbed Danny's hand and headed south, crow-hopping along as fast as his little brother's short legs would allow. J.W. took a threatening step my way but scampered off when I pointed the rifle at him and snapped, "Get outta here!"   5

The sight of those three fleeing in terror infused me with volcanic power. I couldn't resist firing a shot over their heads. The sharp crack sent J.W. rocket-ing past Donald, who then ran so hard little Danny skipped over the sagebrush like a rag doll. My laughter quickly sucked the fire out of my anger. A day or two later, my former tormentors and I were friends again, and the incident was forgotten.   6

My family moved away from Wyoming in 1951, but I returned with my wife, Zona, a few years ago, when I took a new job in Cheyenne. This spring I was surprised by a call from Donald, asking, "Are you the Billy Pippin I knew in Lamont fifty years ago?" I was ecstatic to hear from my childhood buddy. Like me, he'd moved around a lot, and he now lives in Douglas, only a couple of hours away. Soon after that, my now bald chum and his wife, Gwen, drove down to Cheyenne to have lunch with Zona and me.

Sharing warm memories over iced tea and sandwiches was a blast: the tar-paper shanties we lived in that lacked even electricity; our two-room school that stood so close to an oil derrick you could hit it with a rock; the hot summer's day we biked nearly 20 miles to Muddy Gap to skinny-dip for a brief hour in a shallow pond.

When I reminded Donald of the time I chased him with my rifle, he laughed. But Zona and Gwen didn't laugh. They didn't even smile. In the awkward silence that followed, Donald reached for a pickle, shrugging as if to say, "We were only kids."

That's true. But I've been thinking about it, and I don't honestly know what I would have done that day in 1947 if my friends hadn't run. It troubles me. I guess my saving grace is that I wasn't planning to hurt anyone; I just wanted them to stop messing with me and chose the most effective deterrent I had at my disposal—a gun. But I do know that what happened never would have if an adult had been present, if my gun had been locked away or if my friends hadn't made me madder than hell. I also know that "only kids" may serve as an excuse for childish misconduct, but not for what I did. Certainly not for the kind of coldblooded carnage we've seen recently.

And on that sunny spring day, as Donald and I looked across the table at each other, the seriousness of what happened more than 50 years ago hit me like a slap in the face. I took a deep breath, overwhelmed by a rush of pure gratitude so powerful that for a moment I couldn't swallow. I was thankful that my role models had been Roy Rogers and Gene Autry, not Sylvester Stallone and Arnold Schwarzenegger. Thankful that my rifle had been a .22 single-shot, not an assault weapon. Thankful that after all this time Donald and I were still friends. Thankful that the memories we now shared brought laughter instead of tears.

When Donald and Gwen left, I gave them both a huge bearhug. More than anything else, I was thankful that I could.

■ Building Vocabulary

For each question, choose the meaning that most closely defines the underlined word or phrase as it is used in the essay.

1. The word spent most nearly means
   a. used.
   b. new.

    c. faulty.

    d. fresh.

2. The word <u>tormentors</u> most nearly means

    a. followers.

    b. friends.

    c. admirers.

    d. abusers.

3. The word <u>ecstatic</u> most nearly means

    a. understandable.

    b. joyous.

    c. resentful.

    d. reluctant.

4. The word <u>carnage</u> most nearly means

    a. childishness.

    b. pranks.

    c. bloodshed.

    d. innocence.

5. The word <u>overwhelmed</u> most nearly means

    a. unaffected.

    b. angered.

    c. overpowered.

    d. inactive.

■ Understanding the Essay

1. Which statement best expresses the essay in one sentence?

    a. When his friends torment him, an angry boy seeks a dangerous way of stopping them.

    b. A young man is forced to defend himself with a gun.

    c. A grown man finally confronts the horrible consequences that could have resulted from a childhood act of anger.

    d. A young man loses a friend when he points a gun at him, but is reunited with the friend in adulthood.

2. The author implies that the older boys who practiced jujitsu on him

    a. were violent bullies rather than true friends.

    b. were trying to teach him about the martial arts.

    c. were not really hurting him.

    d. were friends who were playing a little more roughly than usual.

3. What effect did the sight of his friends running in terror have on the author?
   a. He realized that pointing a gun at them was foolish and dangerous.
   b. He felt ashamed.
   c. He felt powerful.
   d. He never touched a gun again.

4. At the dinner table with his old friend, the author feels
   a. overwhelming gratitude.
   b. deep guilt.
   c. hidden resentment.
   d. slight boredom.

5. When he thinks of the incident, the author blames
   a. the fact that the gun was not locked away and no adults were present.
   b. his friends.
   c. himself.
   d. all of the above.

■ Writing in the Margins

These questions encourage you to think not just about the essay but about the issues it raises. Your instructor may ask you to write down your answers, to discuss them in groups, or simply to think about them for class discussion.

1. The essay suggests that the author, Bill Pippin, is now a responsible adult. If the childhood episode had turned out differently, how might his life have changed?

2. How often do you suppose acts of violence occur because an ordinary person, pushed to the limit, becomes angry and grabs a weapon? What is the solution?

TOPICS FOR WRITING

Assignment 1: What If . . .

Paragraph or Journal Entry

Bill Pippin, the author of this essay, asks, "What if my friends hadn't run?" Most people have a "what if" story about a time when their actions brought them a heartbeat away from disaster. What's your "what if" story? Tell it in a journal entry or a paragraph.

Assignment 2: Should Guns Be Regulated?

Paragraph

Discussion of gun violence always brings up the question of regulation of firearms. Many other countries ban private ownership of handguns. Write a paragraph discussing whether the United States should make stricter laws regulating the ownership of firearms.

Assignment 3: Violence and the Media

Paragraph or Essay

The author mentions being "thankful that [his] role models had been Roy Rogers and Gene Autry, not Sylvester Stallone and Arnold Schwarzenegger." Do you believe that violence in entertainment media such as movies, television, video games, and music videos can influence young people to become violent? Answer in a paragraph.

Assignment 4: Reunions

Paragraph or Essay

If you could be reunited with one of your friends from elementary school, who would it be and why? Write a paragraph that describes your relationship with the person and your reasons for wanting to see him or her again.

Acknowledgments

Rulon Openshaw, "Action Hero" from *The New York Times Magazine* (January 5, 1997). Copyright © 1997 by Rulon Openshaw. Reprinted with the permission of the author.

Cara DiMarco, "Setting Boundaries" from *Moving Through Life Transitions with Power and Purpose,* Second Edition, by Cara DiMarco. Copyright © 2000 by Cara DiMarco. Reprinted by permission of Pearson Education, Inc., Upper Saddle River, NJ.

"Against the Wall: National Park Service Collects, Stores Items Left Along the Vietnam Veterans' Memorial" from *The Macon Telegraph* (May 24, 1997). Copyright © 1997 by Knight-Ridder Newspapers.

William Raspberry, "Older and Wiser—or Just Older?" (editor's title, originally titled "Age No Longer Revered in American Society") from *The Macon Telegraph* (May 9, 1997). Copyright © 1997 The Washington Post Writers Group. Reprinted with permission.

Cynthia Tucker, "Barbie Madness" (editor's title, originally titled "For Kids, Parents' Warmth Beats Barbie's Cool") from *The Atlanta Journal/Constitution* (November 23, 1997). Reprinted with permission from *The Atlanta Journal* and *The Atlanta Constitution.*

Michael Ashcraft, "Living at Warp Speed." Originally published in *The Dispatch,* Moline, Illinois, March 27, 1996 under the headline "How Are We Today? Too Busy!" Reprinted by permission of Michael Ashcraft.

Janice Castro, with Dan Cook and Cristina Garcia, "Spanglish Spoken Here" from *Time* (July 11, 1988). Copyright © 1988 TIME Inc., reprinted by permission.

Donna Britt, "Recipe for a Sick Society" (editor's title, originally titled "Dying Young: America's Fatal Flaws") from *The Atlanta Constitution* (March 31,

1998). Copyright © 1997 The Washington Post Writers Group. Reprinted with permission.

John J. Macionis, "Don't Blame Me! The New 'Culture of Victimization'" from *Sociology*, Sixth Edition, by John J. Macionis. Copyright © 1997 by John J. Macionis. Reprinted by permission of Pearson Education, Inc., Upper Saddle River, NJ.

Leonard Pitts, "How 'bout Us?" (editor's title, originally titled "Holding on to Love for Dear Life") from *The Atlanta Constitution* (June 5, 1997). Syndicated by *The Miami Herald*. Reprinted by permission from *The Miami Herald* via The Copyright Clearance Center.

Jim Auchmutey, "Mixed Blessings" from *The Atlanta Journal/Constitution* (November 23, 1997). Reprinted with permission from *The Atlanta Journal* and *The Atlanta Constitution*.

Rheta Grimsley Johnson, "One for the Books" (editor's title, originally titled "Printer's Ink Not Yet Erased by Computers") from *The Atlanta Constitution* (February 18, 1998). Reprinted with permission from *The Atlanta Journal* and *The Atlanta Constitution*.

Yi-Fu Tuan, "American Space, Chinese Place" from *Harper's* magazine (July 1974). Copyright © 1974 by *Harper's* Magazine. Reprinted with the permission of *Harper's*.

Michael Skube, "Disorders R Us" (editor's title, originally titled "'Disorders R Us' Becomes Our Motto") from *The Atlanta Constitution* (March 24, 1998). Reprinted with permission from *The Atlanta Journal* and *The Atlanta Constitution*.

Caroline Miller, "Civil Rites" from *Lear's* (August 1993). Reprinted by permission of Caroline Miller.

Dave Barry, "All the Rage" (editor's title, originally titled "Responding to Bad Drivers Is All the Rage") from *The Atlanta Journal/Constitution* (February 8, 1998). Copyright © 1998 by Dave Barry. Reprinted with the permission of the author.

Nancy Masterton Sakamoto, "Conversational Ballgames" from *Polite Fictions: Why Japanese and Americans Seem Rude to Each Other* by Nancy Sakamoto and Reiko Naotsuka. Reprinted with permission of Kinseido Limited, Publishers.

Shoba Narayan, "I Wonder: Was It Me or Was It My Sari?" from *Newsweek* (March 13, 2000). All rights reserved. Reprinted by permission.

Candace Dyer, "Music: A Universal Language" (editor's title, originally titled "A Groupie for Musicians Explains") from *The Macon Telegraph* (March 10, 1997). Copyright © 1997 by Knight-Ridder Newspapers.

Bill Pippin, "What If My Friends Hadn't Run?" from *Newsweek* (January 10, 2000). All rights reserved. Reprinted by permission.

Index

Texas Academic Skills Program Objectives

Florida Exit Test Competencies